Y0-BEB-539

OUR BISHOPS SPEAK

Our Bishops Speak

NATIONAL PASTORALS AND ANNUAL
STATEMENTS OF THE HIERARCHY OF
THE UNITED STATES

RESOLUTIONS OF EPISCOPAL COM-
MITTEES AND COMMUNICATIONS OF
THE ADMINISTRATIVE BOARD OF
THE NATIONAL CATHOLIC WELFARE
CONFERENCE

1919-1951

WITH A FOREWORD, NOTES, AND INDEX

By the Very Rev. Raphael M. Huber, S.T.D., O.F.M.Conv.

ASSOCIATE PROFESSOR, CATHOLIC UNIVERSITY

THE BRUCE PUBLISHING COMPANY
MILWAUKEE

PREFACE

With the publication of this volume, the Catholic Church in America completes a retrospect of some thirty eventful years — a retrospect which is, at once, rewarding and inspiring. No serious student of the Church's role in American society since World War I will wish to ignore the rich source material contained in the documents herein published; but this is not only a book for serious students of Church affairs. It is, as well, an inspiring record of Catholic thinking, writing, and leadership during a dramatic and challenging period of American history. Within these pages, even the most careful reader will find ample cause to be grateful for the insights they afford, for the wise and penetrating observations they contain.

There surely is no need here to speak of the importance and significance of the years covered by this volume. They are years which have spoken for themselves; years marked by profound social shocks; years of striking and bewildering change; years in which old errors returned under new and beguiling guises; tense years in which devastating blows were struck at the roots of society — blows which have left the American home and family with crippling effects.

Looking back over these years now, we can see clearly what damage and havoc they wrought, what pain, confusion, and disillusionment they ushered into our society. However, no particular merit attaches itself to hindsight. It takes merit of a special kind, though, to see clearly the shape of things to come and to make effective warnings against impending harm. As we read this volume, we are struck by the foresight it shows, by the incisive and realistic analysis of contemporary society it offers; and there is an added poignancy to our reading when we look about and see how little heeded have been the warnings and wisdom of these pronouncements.

A perusal of this volume indicates how completely the thought of the United States bishops has ranged over the period between 1919 and 1951. No force or idea having effect upon our society during that period has been neglected. Within that thirty-year phase, America had to face and recover from two world wars; international problems arose

v

in which the Catholic Church at large, and the Church in the United States in particular, had a vital interest; social reconstruction after World Wars I and II demanded sound direction, encouragement, and action; intense persecution of the Church in Mexico, Spain, Poland, and elsewhere, had to be stigmatized; the amazing development of the motion picture, with its great threat to moral standards, had to be acknowledged, and out of that acknowledgment there would come the Legion of Decency; educational problems, the sanctity of the marriage bond, and the welfare of the child and the family — all these had to be faced, and not only faced, but dealt with.

This book is an eloquent witness to the manner in which these problems were dealt with and it should serve as a profitable source of study to American Catholics. Divided into four categories, it contains (1) the pastorals of the archbishops and bishops of the United States, published on the occasion of their annual meetings in Washington, D. C., (2) letters sent in the name of the archbishops and bishops of the United States to individuals, (3) resolutions of episcopal committees, and (4) statements of the Administrative Board of the National Catholic Welfare Conference.

It will serve as a fitting companion to the volume entitled *The National Pastorals of the American Hierarchy: 1791–1919,* published in 1923 by the National Catholic Welfare Council, under the editorship of the late Monsignor Peter Guilday. This earlier volume embraced Bishop Carroll's Pastoral Letter of 1792; the Pastoral Letter to the laity and to the clergy after the First Provincial Council of 1829; the National Pastorals issued after each of the six succeeding Provincial Councils; the National Pastorals of the Plenary Councils of 1852, 1866, 1884; and, finally, the Pastoral Letter of the American Bishops of 1919 — thirteen documents in all. Since its publication, however, no similar work had been attempted.

That this second volume now appears, is largely due to the initiative of the late Archbishop John T. McNicholas, O.P., of Cincinnati, who long entertained the hope that such a volume would be published. During the latter years of his life, while Chairman of the Administrative Board, N.C.W.C., he began to collect copies of every National Pastoral of the Bishops of the United States, as well as the official pronouncements of archbishops and bishops of the Administrative Board, and of episcopal committees, which were issued since the beginning of the National Catholic Welfare Conference and its predecessor organization, the National Catholic Welfare Council. When it was apparent that he could not complete this work so dear to his heart, because of the heavy inroads of sickness, he turned the material he had so painstakingly gathered together over to Monsignor Howard J. Carroll, General Secretary of N.C.W.C. The Very Reverend Dr. Raphael Huber, O.F.M.Conv., Professor of American Church History, Theology Department, Catholic University of America, graciously undertook the task of arranging the documents in chronological order, of annotating and indexing them. A special word of gratitude is now due him for the splendid service he has performed in fulfilling this assignment.

Death claimed Archbishop McNicholas on April 22, 1950, before he could see the publication of this work. Its appearance now is in the nature of a literary monument to one whose zeal, wisdom, and continuing inspiration figured so largely in the statements and pronouncements herein collected. The Catholic Church in America drew heavily upon the mind, counsel, and pen of Archbishop McNicholas; but no matter how heavily it drew, his reserve of talent and generosity was always large enough to make allowance for each new claim. A resourceful and prudent leader, he was blessed with a great sense of the Church's role in society. His gifted pen contributed many of the cogent and searching observations contained in this volume. To him it is of little moment that any words of praise are written here in his behalf. It is to him of greater moment that this volume of statements and documents of the Church he loved so deeply and served so ably has now been published and made available to a large and wide audience.

✠ FRANCIS P. KEOUGH
Archbishop of Baltimore
Chairman, Administrative Board
National Catholic Welfare Conference

FOREWORD

For several years before his death April 22, 1950, the Most Reverend John T. McNicholas, O.P.,[1] Archbishop of Cincinnati and at the time of his demise Chairman of the Administrative Board of the National Catholic Welfare Conference, fostered the idea of collecting into one volume the statements of the hierarchy of the United States of America issued either at the close of their annual meetings in Wash-

---

[1] Most Rev. John Timothy McNicholas, D.D. (1877–1950), was born December 15, 1877, Kiltmaugh, County Mayo, Ireland. Educated: St. Joseph's College, Philadelphia, Pa.; St. Rose's Convent, Springfield, Ky.; St. Joseph's Convent, Somerset, Ohio; The Minerva University, Rome, Italy. Received the Dominican habit, October 10, 1894; professed as a Dominican, October 10, 1895. Ordained October 10, 1901, Somerset, by Archbishop Henry Moeller of Cincinnati. Member of the faculty and master of students in the Dominican House of Studies, Washington, D. C., 1905–1907. Appointed National Director of the Holy Name Society, 1908. Engaged in pastoral work in the archdiocese of New York, 1913–1917. Socius to the Dominican Master General, Rome, 1917–1918. Elected to the see of Duluth, July 18, 1918. Consecrated, September 8, 1918, Rome, by Thomas Pius Cardinal Boggiani, O.P., Bishop of Porto and Santa Rufina. Made an assistant to the pontifical throne, February 18, 1923. Translated to the see of Indianapolis, May 18, 1925, but never took possession of his see. Promoted to the metropolitan see of Cincinnati, July 8, 1925.

Besides his episcopal duties Archbishop McNicholas founded the *Holy Name Journal* (1908); established and maintained the *Institutum Divi Thomae*, a postgraduate school of science (1935), one of the units of the Athenaeum of Ohio, founded by the Archbishop in 1928; promoted the "Home Missions of America," a society of priests dedicated to the evangelization of rural districts, etc. The Archbishop was long active in the work of the National Catholic Welfare Conference. From 1929 to 1935, and again from November, 1941, to November, 1944, he was a member of the N.C.W.C. Administrative Board and Episcopal Chairman of the N.C.W.C. Education Department. Re-elected to the Board in 1946, 1947, and 1948, he was called upon by the archbishops and bishops elected with him to serve as their chairman. Only two weeks before his death (April 22, 1950), he was re-elected president of the National Catholic Educational Association.

For ten years, from 1933 to 1943, he was chairman of the Episcopal Committee on Motion Pictures, which founded and sponsored the National Legion of Decency. Since 1934 he was chairman of the Pontifical Commission for the Sacred Sciences of the Catholic University of America. He was long a member of the board of trustees of the university.

See Rev. Joseph Bernard Code, D.Sc. Hist., *Dictionary of the American Hierarchy* [New York-Toronto: Longmans, Green & Co., 1940], p. 232; *The Register,* National Edition, Denver, April 30, 1950; *The Catholic Review,* Washington, D. C., April 28, 1950. N.C.W.C. "News Release," April 24, 1950; *Catholic Action,* May, 1950, pp. 10–12. *The Official Catholic Directory, Anno Domini,* 1949 [New York: Kenedy, 1949], p. 46.

ington, D. C., or otherwise; and the acts of the Administrative Board of the same N.C.W.C. published either on the occasion of its annual spring sessions or through its episcopal chairman as times and occasions dictated. When Archbishop McNicholas became incapacitated through illness, feeling undoubtedly the approach of death, he consigned his collection of documents to Monsignor Howard J. Carroll, General Secretary, and Monsignor Paul F. Tanner, Assistant General Secretary of the N.C.W.C., for the eventual publication. It has been my privilege to co-operate with them in this work.

In 1923 the late Monsignor Dr. Peter Guilday, Ph.D., published in one volume, through the N.C.W.C., *The National Pastorals of the American Hierarchy: 1791-1919*. These included not only Bishop John Carroll's[2] "Pastoral Letter" begun shortly after the close of the First National Synod of Baltimore (November 7-10, 1791) and published on May 28, 1792; but also the Pastoral Letters to the Laity and to the Clergy of 1829; the Pastorals of the six succeeding Provincial Councils of Baltimore (1883, 1837, 1840, 1843, 1846, and 1849); and of the three Plenary Councils of Baltimore (1852, 1866, and 1884).[3] Included like-

---

[2] Most Reverend John Carroll (1735–1815), the first bishop of the United States of America, was born January 8, 1735, Upper Marlboro, Prince George County, Maryland, the son of Daniel and Eleanor (Darnall) Carroll. Educated, Bohemia Manor School, Bohemia Manor, Md.; St. Omer's College, St. Omer, French Flanders; the Jesuit novitiate (Watten, France); the Jesuit novitiate, Liége, The Lowlands. Ordained February 14, 1761, Liége, by Bishop Peter Jacquet, Titular-Bishop of Hippo and Auxiliary Bishop of Liége. Joined the Society of Jesus in 1753; before the suppression of the Society in 1773, engaged in teaching in Europe; did missionary work in Maryland, 1773–1776. Invited by Congress in 1776 to be one of a commission to go to Canada to secure that country's neutrality in the American War of Independence. Named superior of the missions in the thirteen United States of America with the power to administer the Sacrament of Confirmation, June 6, 1784. Accepted the post of Prefect Apostolic, February 27, 1785. Took up his residence in Baltimore, Md.; appealed to Congress to protect and maintain religious liberty; and became one of the three trustees of St. John's College, Annapolis, Md., 1786. Elected to the newly erected see of Baltimore, November 6, 1789. Consecrated, August 15, 1790, Ludworth Castle, Dorset, England, by Bishop Charles Walmesly, O.S.B., Titular Bishop of Pamatha and Vicar Apostolic of the Western District of England. Convened the first synod for the priests of the diocese of Baltimore, November 7, 1791; founded St. Mary's Seminary, Baltimore, Md., and Georgetown College, Georgetown, Md., 1791; founded St. Mary's College, Baltimore, 1803. Promoted to the newly erected metropolitan see of Baltimore, April 8, 1808; appointed administrator of the diocese of Louisiana and the Two Floridas, August 18, 1811. Died December 3, 1815, Baltimore; buried, Baltimore.

Cf. J. G. Shea, *Life and Times of the Most Rev. John Carroll* (1888); Peter Guilday, *The Life and Times of John Carroll, Archbishop of Baltimore: 1735–1815* (1922); Joseph B. Code, *Dictionary of the American Hierarchy, op. cit.*, pp. 41–42; *The Official Catholic Directory*, A.D. 1949, *op. cit.*, p. 10.

[3] Cf. Msgr. Peter Guilday, *The Councils of Baltimore* (New York: Macmillan, 1922).

wise in the collection was the first "Pastoral Letter" published outside
of a National Synod, Provincial or Plenary Council, namely that of
1919 formulated and published by wish of the entire hierarchy of the
United States of America in the annual meeting of September, 1919,
under the name of James Cardinal Gibbons,[4] Archbishop of Baltimore,
September 26, 1922. Since that time none of the subsequent "National
Pastorals," corporate statements of the hierarchy of the United States,
or publications of the Administrative Board of the N.C.W.C. issued
either prior to 1922 or thereafter have been published in a single
volume. To fill this gap the present volume was contemplated.

Some of the documents contained herein are taken from the archives
of the N.C.W.C. and published for the first time; others were culled
from *Catholic Action,* the national monthly of the N.C.W.C.; others
finally were excerpted from already published statements issued by

---

[4] James Cardinal Gibbons (1834–1921) was born July 23, 1834, Baltimore, Md.,
the son of Thomas and Bridget (Walsh) Gibbons. Educated: St. Charles College,
Ellicott City, Md.; St. Mary's Seminary, Baltimore. Ordained, June 30, 1861, Baltimore, by Archbishop Francis Patrick Kenrick, of Baltimore. Engaged in pastoral
work in the archdiocese of Baltimore (St. Bridget's Church), 1861–1865; became
secretary to Archbishop Martin John Spalding of Baltimore, 1865; acted as assistant
chancellor of the Second Plenary Council of Baltimore, 1866. Elected to the titular
see of Adramyttium, March 3, 1866, and named first Vicar Apostolic of North
Carolina. Consecrated, August 16, 1868, Baltimore, by Archbishop Martin J. Spalding.
Was the youngest among 767 prelates in attendance at the Vatican Council, 1869–1870.
Promoted to the see of Richmond, July 30, 1872. Named Titular Bishop of Jonopolis
and Bishop Coadjutor of Baltimore, with the right of succession, May 25, 1877.
Succeeded to the metropolitan see of Baltimore, October 3, 1877. Presided over the
Third Plenary Council of Baltimore as Apostolic Delegate, 1884. Took an active
part in national life. Active in the foundation of the Catholic University of America,
Washington, D. C. Created a Cardinal Priest of the Holy Roman Church with the
title of Santa Maria in Trastevere, June 7, 1886. Received the cardinalatial biretta
from Archbishop Peter Richard Kenrick of St. Louis, June 30, 1886, in Baltimore;
received the red hat from Pope Leo XIII, in Rome, March 17, 1887. Obtained
ecclesiastical support of the Knights of Labor; presided over the celebrations in
1889 of the centennial of the American Hierarchy; was opposed to Cahenslyism, i.e.,
the appointment of Catholic bishops in the United States on the basis of national
groups; first American cardinal to take part in a papal election, 1903; active in the
pacification of the Philippines following the War with Spain; became president of
the recently organized National Catholic War Council, 1917. Died, March 24, 1921,
Baltimore; buried, Baltimore.

Author of: *The Faith of Our Fathers* (1877); *Our Christian Heritage* (1889); *The
Ambassador of Christ* (1896); *Discourses and Sermons* (1906); *Retrospect of Fifty
Years* (1916).

Cf. J. T. Reilly, *Collections in the Life and Times of Cardinal Gibbons* (1890–1903);
A. E. Smith and V. de Paul Fitzpatrick, *Cardinal Gibbons, Churchman and Citizen*
(1921); A. S. Will, *Life of Cardinal Gibbons, Archbishop of Baltimore* (1922); James
J. Walsh, *Our American Cardinals* (1926); Brendan A. Finn, *Twenty-four American
Cardinals* (Boston, 1948), 45–75; Jos. B. Code, *Dictionary of the American Hierarchy
op. cit.,* pp. 131–132; *Catholic Directory* (1949), *op. cit.,* p. 10.

the N.C.W.C. Press Department. The source of each statement is given in a corresponding footnote.

The original "National Catholic War Council" was founded during the hectic days of World War I (1914–1918). When the United States became involved in that great struggle the Catholic bishops of the nation, assembled at their annual meeting (April, 1917), addressed to President Wilson a pledge of loyalty of the Catholic hierarchy, of the clergy, and of the Catholic people of this country (Document No. 14). The first act of this united front was the creation of a "Bishop Ordinary of the U. S. Army and Navy Chaplains" in the person of the late Archbishop of New York, Patrick Cardinal Hayes,[5] at that time Auxiliary Bishop of New York. The project was approved by the Holy See on November 24, 1917. With extraordinary zeal and ability Bishop Hayes organized overnight his Army Vicariates. Eventually he enlisted and directed almost one thousand priests as chaplains. Every diocese co-operated. The result was a revelation of Catholic strength, responsibility, and opportunity.

But not only on the battlefields and on the high seas were our soldiers, sailors, and marines under the spiritual care of our chaplains to redeem the pledge of loyalty our bishops had given to the Commander in Chief of the American forces; also at home the Catholic body of the country under the guidance of these same bishops were determined to dedicate their full concerted resources to the

---

[5] Patrick Cardinal Hayes (1867–1938) was born November 20, 1867, New York, New York, the son of Daniel and Mary (Gleason) Hayes. Educated: Manhattan College, New York; St. Joseph's Seminary, Troy, New York; Catholic University of America, Washington, D. C. Ordained, September 8, 1892, Troy, by Archbishop Michael S. Corrigan of New York. Engaged in pastoral work in the archdiocese of New York, 1894–1903, 1915–1919. President of Cathedral College, New York, and chancellor of the archdiocese of New York, 1903–1914. Made a Domestic Prelate of the papal household, 1907. Elected to the titular see of Tagaste, July 3, 1914, and named Auxiliary Bishop of New York. Consecrated October 28, 1914, New York, by John Murphy Cardinal Farley, Archbishop of New York. Appointed Ordinary of the Chaplains of the United States Army and Navy, November 29, 1917. Promoted to the metropolitan see of New York, March 10, 1919. Created Cardinal Priest of the Holy Roman Church with the title of Santa Maria in Via, March 24, 1924. Appointed a member of the Sacred Congregation "Pro Ecclesia Orientali," 1931. Named *legatus a latere* to the National Eucharistic Congress in Cleveland, Ohio, August 20, 1935. Named an officer of the Legion of Honor of France, October, 1919; given the Grand Cross of Devotion of the Knights of Malta, November, 1927; appointed Cardinal Protector of the American branch of the Knights of Malta, March, 1928. Died, September 4, 1938, St. Joseph's Villa, Sullivan County, New York; buried, New York.

Cf. James J. Walsh, *Our American Cardinals* (1926); Joseph P. Code, *Dictionary of the American Hierarchy, op. cit.*, pp. 148–149; *Catholic Directory* (1949), *op. cit.*, p. 121; Finn, *Twenty-four American Cardinals, op. cit.*, pp. 169–190.

country's welfare. It was at this juncture that the bishops of the country organized the "National Catholic War Council" authorized to supervise and unify the Catholic lay activities of the United States in war and postwar service. The fairly innumerable Catholic agencies, most prominent of which was the national and international work of the Knights of Columbus, were unified under the "Administrative Committee of the National Catholic War Council." In a letter of President Wilson authorizing the nationwide common "War Drive," this organization was officially recognized by the government of the United States as the channel of Catholic activity. The Knights of Columbus, thus organized, were specifically mentioned as one of the seven great welfare organizations of the United States of America. Through the united efforts of all the Catholic agencies, however, the Catholic body, clerical as well as lay, shared in the fruits of the great "drive" on the home front. Credit must be given, and was given, to the late Most Reverend Peter J. Muldoon,[6] Bishop of Rockford (died October 8, 1927), at that time chairman of the "National Catholic War Council," for his extraordinary leadership in a position never before tried and in a work that put to the fullest test, before the eyes of all fellow citizens, the worth of Catholic faith and Catholic services in the well-being of our country.

Bishop Muldoon was ably assisted in his strenuous task by the late Monsignor John Burke, C.S.P.[7] From 1917 to 1922 he served as

---

[6] Most Rev. Peter Muldoon (1863–1927) was born October 10, 1863, Columbia, California. Educated: St. Mary's College, Marian Co., Ky.; St. Mary's Seminary, Baltimore, Md. Ordained, December 18, 1886, Brooklyn, New York, by Bishop John Loughlin of Brooklyn. Engaged in pastoral work in the archdiocese of Chicago, 1886–1888. Elected to the titular see of Tamasus, July 10, 1901, and appointed Auxiliary Bishop of Chicago. Consecrated July 25, 1901, Chicago, by Sebastian Cardinal Martinelli, O.S.A. Appointed first Bishop of Rockford, September 28, 1908. Made an assistant at the pontifical throne, June 8, 1921. First chairman of the National Catholic War Council. Died October 8, 1927, Rockford, Ill.; buried, Rockford. At the entrance to the assembly chamber of the Administrative Board of the National Catholic Welfare Conference, Washington, D. C., the following bronze plaque has been erected to his memory: "To RIGHT REVEREND PETER J. MULDOON, D.D. Bishop of Rockford. One of the Founders of the National Catholic War Council, 1917. Member and Vice-Chairman of the Administrative Committee, Chairman, Social Action Department; National Catholic Welfare Conference 1919–1927, Priest: Bishop: Patriot: — This Tablet is Erected by His Fellow Bishops of the Administrative Committee that His memory may be held in Respect, Reverence and Affection. 1862–1927." Cf. Joseph B. Code, *Dictionary of the American Hierarchy, op. cit.,* p. 248; *Catholic Directory* (1949), *op. cit.,* p. 496.

[7] Cf. *Catholic Action* (N.C.W.C., Washington, D. C.), 18: 12A (December 15, 1936). The whole number is dedicated to the memory of Monsignor John Burke, C.S.P.

chairman of the "Committee of Six," an advisory committee of the
Secretary of War on religious and moral questions. Its membership
was made up of one Catholic, four Protestants, and one Jew. In 1918
Father Burke also became the chairman of the committee on "Special
War Activities." In 1919 the Administrative Board of the "National
Catholic Welfare Council" appointed him to the office of general secretary, a position to which it reappointed him each succeeding year
until his death, October 30, 1936. In recognition of his outstanding
achievements the War Department conferred on Father Burke in 1919
the Distinguished Service Medal. The names of Bishop Muldoon and
Monsignor Burke will ever loom high on the horizon of the N.C.W.C.

Among other such pioneers of Catholic Action, under hierarchical
supervision and direction, should also be honorably mentioned the
names of such distinguished laymen and laywomen as Mr. Charles
McMahon and Miss Agnes Regan, in whose memory Cardinal Mooney,
on April 20, 1950, dedicated the Agnes Regan Hall of Social Services
at the Catholic University of America at Washington, D. C.

When the titanic struggle of World War I had ended, what was to
become of the efficient Catholic war organization that had achieved
such great material, spiritual, and charitable good? Was it to disband
and thus overlook the important facts brought out by its long years
of fruitful operations, particularly its possibilities for concerted Catholic Action also in times of peace?

On February 20, 1919, seventy-seven bishops of the United States
met in Washington to celebrate the golden episcopal jubilee of James
Cardinal Gibbons, the illustrious Archbishop of Baltimore. In answer
to the joint letter sent on this occasion to Pope Benedict XV his
Holiness, under date of April 10, 1919, deigned to address a letter[8]
to the American Episcopate which had an important bearing upon the
reorganization of the "National Catholic War Council" to meet new
peacetime emergencies. But from here on we will let the afore-
mentioned Archbishop John T. McNicholas, who was to publish and
to write the preface to this present work, tell the story. Thus in death
his lips still speak to us.

It was on the occasion of a luncheon rendered the clergy following
the enthronization of the newly consecrated Most Reverend Patrick A.
O'Boyle, D.D.,[9] as Archbishop of Washington, January 21, 1948, that

---

[8] Cf. *Acta Apostolicae Sedis,* 11:6 (May, 1919), 169–174.

[9] Most Rev. Archbishop Patrick Aloysius O'Boyle, born July 18, 1896, attended St.
Paul's parochial and high school, St. Theresa's preparatory school, and St. Thomas
College, all in Scranton, prior to entering, in 1916, St. Joseph's Seminary, Yonkers,

Archbishop McNicholas then chairman of the Administrative Board of the N.C.W.C. uttered these memorable words:[10]

Thirty years ago the eminent Ordinary of the Archdiocese of Baltimore, Cardinal Gibbons, was preparing to observe quietly, as he had hoped, the fiftieth anniversary of his consecration as a Bishop. Seven years previously, there had been an unprecedented observance of the Silver Jubilee of His Eminence in the Sacred College of Cardinals. President Taft, ex-President Theodore Roosevelt, the Supreme Justice of the United States, members of the President's Cabinet and of the United States Senate and House of Representatives bore eloquent testimony to the patriotic work of Cardinal Gibbons as an American citizen. The day of the Golden Jubilee of the episcopacy of Cardinal Gibbons was passed in silence and in prayer.

Pope Benedict XV, however, realizing that few Bishops in the history of the Church celebrate the fiftieth anniversary of their episcopal consecration, and taking into consideration the life of the illustrious Prelate and the vast influence that he exercised as a Prince of the Church and as a simple, humble and patriotic American citizen, deemed it fitting that the Jubilee be observed at a later date. Our Holy Father sent a Papal envoy to the United States to convey the personal congratulations of His Holiness, to express his paternal solicitude for the Church of America, and to encourage a stronger bond of unity among the Bishops of the United States.

His Holiness appreciated the patriotic work of the Bishops through the National Catholic War Council. The Papal Representative sent by the Pope, Archbishop (later Cardinal) Cerretti; His Eminence, Cardinal O'Connell;[11]

New York. He was ordained May 21, 1921, in St. Patrick's Cathedral, New York, by the late Cardinal Hayes and served for five years as curate at St. Columba's parish in New York's lower west side. In 1926, he was made Executive Secretary of the Catholic Guardian Society. After a two-year course at the New York School of Social Work he became Assistant Director of the child care department of Catholic Charities of the New York archdiocese (1933–1936). In 1936, he became Executive Director of the Mission of the Immaculate Virgin at Mount Loretto, Staten Island, a home caring for more than 1000 dependent children. He headed this institution for seven years, and during this time, 1941, he was named a Papal Chamberlain. In 1943 he was appointed Executive Director of War Relief Services-N.C.W.C. On June 21, 1944, Pius XII created him a Domestic Prelate. Shortly thereafter (1946) he was named Consultor of the archdiocese of New York and Executive Director of Catholic Charities. On December 3, 1947, he was appointed Archbishop of Washington. Under his jurisdiction fall the District of Columbia and the five counties of Montgomery, Prince Georges, Charles, Calvert, and St. Mary's in the state of Maryland, formerly attached to the archdiocese of Baltimore.

Cf. *Catholic Directory* (1949), *op. cit.*, p. 212: N.C.W.C. "News Release," December 2, 1947; January 5, 1948-F.

10 *Catholic Action*, March, 1948, pp. 10–11.

11 His Eminence, William Henry Cardinal O'Connell (1859–1944) was born December 8, 1859, Lowell, Massachusetts, the son of John and Bridget (Farley) O'Connell. Educated at St. Charles College, Ellicott City, Md.; Boston College, Boston, Mass.; North American College, Rome, Italy. Ordained June 8, 1884, Rome, by Lucido Maria Cardinal Parrochi, Vicar-General to His Holiness, Pope Leo XIII. Engaged in pastoral work in the archdiocese of Boston, 1885–1895. Rector of the North Amer-

the Apostolic Delegate, now His Eminence, Cardinal Fumasoni-Biondi, and seventy-seven Bishops were present at the Pontifical Jubilee Mass celebrated by Cardinal Gibbons at Mount Saint Sepulchre, Washington, at which Archbishop (later Cardinal) Mundelein preached.[12] After the Pontifical Mass, when the Bishops convened to hear the message of Archbishop Cerretti, they were told that Our Holy Father deeply appreciated the war work of the American hierarchy, a work united to that of the Vicar of Christ in order to mitigate as much as possible the horrors of war.

It is more than probable that some form of organization would have suc-

---

ican College, Rome, 1895–1901. Made a Domestic Prelate of the papal household, June 9, 1897. Elected to the see of Portland, Maine, February 8, 1901. Consecrated May 19, 1901, Rome, by Francesco Cardinal Satolli. Acted as special envoy to Japan, 1905. Made an assistant to the pontifical throne, January 4, 1905. Named Titular Bishop of Constantia and appointed Coadjutor Archbishop of Boston with the right of succession, February 21, 1906. Succeeded to the metropolitan see of Boston, August 31, 1907. Received the Sacred Pallium, January 29, 1908. Created a Cardinal Priest of the Holy Roman Church with the title of San Clemente, November 27, 1911; took possession of his church, December 8, 1911. Repaired San Clemente. Convened the fifth and sixth synods for the priests of the archdiocese of Boston, in 1909 and 1919, respectively. Made *The Pilot* the official organ of the archdiocese of Boston, 1908. Acted as Papal Legate to the National Convention of the Holy Name Society, Washington, D. C., September, 1924. Frequently presided over the annual meetings of the archbishops and bishops at Washington, D. C. Decorated by the Japanese, Italian, and French governments. Died April 22, 1944; buried at Boston.

Author of: *Letters of Cardinal O'Connell: 1876–1901* (1915); *Recollections of Seventy Years* (Boston, 1934).

Cf. James J. Walsh, *Our American Cardinals* (1926); Finn, *Twenty-four American Cardinals*, pp. 95–122; Joseph B. Code, *Dictionary of the American Hierarchy, op. cit.*, pp. 259–260; *Catholic Directory* (1949), *op. cit.*, p. 17; Morgan, *Speaking of Cardinals* (New York, 1946), pp. 16–31, 263.

[12] His Eminence, George William Cardinal Mundelein (1872–1909), was born July 2, 1872, New York, New York, the son of Francis and Mary (Goetz) Mundelein. Educated: Manhattan College, New York; St. Vincent's Seminary, Beatty, Pa.; Urban College of the Propaganda, Rome, Italy. Ordained June 8, 1895, Rome, by Bishop Charles Edward McDonnell of Brooklyn. Engaged in pastoral work in the diocese of Brooklyn, assistant secretary, and the secretary to Bishop McDonnell of Brooklyn, 1895–1897. Chancellor of the diocese of Brooklyn, 1897–1909. Made a Domestic Prelate of the papal household, November 26, 1906. Elected to the titular see of Loryma, June 30, 1909, and appointed Auxiliary Bishop of Brooklyn. Consecrated, Brooklyn, New York, September 21, 1909, by Bishop Charles Edward McDonnell of Brooklyn. Promoted to the metropolitan see of Chicago, December 9, 1915. Received the Sacred Pallium, January 27, 1916. Founded Quigley Preparatory College, Chicago, Ill., 1918, and the Seminary of St. Mary of the Lake, Mundelein, Ill., 1921. Created a Cardinal Priest of the Holy Roman Church with the title of Santa Maria del Popolo, March 26, 1924. Host to the Twenty-Eighth International Eucharistic Congress, June, 1926. Died, October 2, 1939, Mundelein; buried, Mundelein.

Author: *Two Crowded Years* (1918) and *Letters of a Bishop to His Flock* (1927).

Cf. Paul R. Martin, *The First Cardinal of the West* (1934); James J. Walsh, *Our American Cardinals* (1926); Finn, *Twenty-Four American Cardinals, op. cit.*, pp. 149–168; Joseph B. Code, *Dictionary of the American Hierarchy, op. cit.*, pp. 249–250; *Catholic Directory* (1949), *op. cit.*, p. 29. Morgan, *Speaking of Cardinals, op. cit.*, pp. 80, 93, 263.

ceeded the National Catholic War Council (which meant the Bishops of the United States). But when the many Prelates present heard Archbishop Cerretti say that His Holiness looked to them to initiate and to plan courageously in order to counteract the evils of the times following a World War, and also to build constructively for the future of the Church, it was evident to the Bishops present that the Holy Father wished them to continue a post-war organization.

I was present on that occasion. His Eminence, Cardinal Gibbons, presided at the morning meeting. Cardinal O'Connell called the Bishops together for the afternoon session. Cardinal Begin of Canada attended the afternoon meeting. That memorable day, February 20, 1919, is really the birthday of the National Catholic Welfare Council. Characteristic enthusiasm and energy were displayed, especially by the Bishops who had been active in the War Council.

Less than two months after the return of Archbishop Cerretti to Rome, the Hierarchy of the United States received an epochal letter from Pope Benedict XV.[13] His Holiness cordially approved the resolve of the Bishops to meet annually to discuss matters of the highest import for the welfare of both Church and Country. His Holiness commended especially the two commissions on education and the social question. That same letter told the Bishops explicitly that, "Greater efforts are demanded of you than of all others, owing to the vast influence which you exercise among your people. Retaining, as they do, a most firm hold on the principles of reasonable liberty and of Christian civilization, they are destined to have the chief role in the restoration of peace and order, and in the reconstruction of human society on the basis of these same principles, when the violence of these tempestuous days shall have passed."

How farseeing was the Pontiff in the Watchtower of Peter and how applicable his words are today! How eager our Bishops are at this moment to work with our Country for the peace of the world! The success of America's world mission of peace would be assured were it not for the subversive forces of atheistic Communism.

On September 24, 1919, ninety-two Bishops took part in the first meeting of the National Catholic Welfare Council.[14]

---

[13] Archbishop McNicholas refers here to the Brief *Communes* of April 10, 1919, mentioned in Note 8.

[14] On that occasion Archbishop Edward J. Hanna of San Francisco was elected first chairman of the Administrative Board, Bishop Peter Muldoon of Rockford, vice-chairman (cf. footnote 6); and Archbishop Austin Dowling of St. Paul, treasurer (cf. footnote 15).

Archbishop Edward J. Hanna (1860–1944) was born July 21, 1860 at Rochester, New York, the son of Edward and Anna (Clarke) Hanna. Educated: Urban College of the Propaganda, Rome, Italy; University of Munich, Germany; University of Cambridge, England. Ordained May 30, 1885, Rome, by Julius Lenti, Patriarch of Constantinople. Took his S.T.D. degree, together with the late Rt. Rev. Msgr. Pace, before Pope Leo XIII. Member of the faculty of the Urban College of the Propaganda, Rome, Italy, 1886–1887; member of the faculty of St. Andrew's Seminary, Rochester, 1887–1893; member of the faculty of St. Bernard's Seminary, Rochester, 1893–1912; elected to the titular see of Titiopolis, October 22, 1912, and named Auxiliary Bishop of San Francisco. Consecrated December 4, 1912, Rochester, by

It may not be out of place to say that many and varied difficulties presented themselves in forming this organization. Archbishop Dowling,[15] one of the most farsighted members of the Hierarchy and a Prelate who to a great extent influenced the thought and decisions of the first years of the Welfare Council, did not come to the first meeting. He said to me in his usual frank manner: "I think we have an organization that cannot function." The absolute voluntary element of the Council, which was and is necessary to safeguard every Bishop in his jurisdiction, and which neither imposed nor could impose any obligation on its members, was necessarily regarded as an obstacle. On the other hand, there was the desire for united action, for corporate expression and decisions; there was urgent need of information for the Bishops, especially for prelates of poor dioceses, distant from the great centers of population. The period called for constructive movements in which Bishops would unite and carry out the recommendations of the commissions or committees, including especially those of the Administrative Committee, as it was called for many years.

Some of us who were the younger Bishops of those days clearly saw the difficulties. We knew the obstacles. We appreciated the hesitancy of the older and wiser Bishops, whose long experience and service caused them to give a word of caution. Not daunted, however, many Bishops worked indefatigably for the continuance of the National Catholic Welfare Council, in order to give it permanency or to prove to the satisfaction of the general body of Bishops that the Welfare Council could not function. I must acknowledge that I had doubts at times about the ultimate success of the Council. I never wavered, however, in urging that we give the Welfare Council twenty years of experiment before deciding ultimately against it.

It is now a matter of history that difficulties multiplied, that some Bishops were positively opposed to the Welfare Council and others were dubious about the service that it could render. The impression gained headway that the Bishops wished the Holy See to suppress the Welfare Council. The opposition of some Bishops and the hesitancy of others gave us a clearly defined issue. I read carefully the memorial presented to the Holy See in 1922.

Today I realize more clearly than ever that the Bishops who courageously

---

Archbishop John V. Bonzano, Apostolic Delegate to the United States. Promoted to the metropolitan see of San Francisco, June 1, 1915. Appointed first chairman of the Executive Department of the N.C.W.C., 1919. Resigned his see and translated to the titular archepiscopal see of Gortyna, March 2, 1935. Died at Rome, Italy, July 10, 1944. Remains later transferred to San Francisco.

Cf. Joseph B. Code, *Dictionary of the American Hierarchy, op. cit.,* pp. 145–146; *Catholic Directory* (1949), *op. cit.,* p. 197.

[15] Archbishop Austin Dowling (1868–1930) was born April 6, 1868, New York, New York, the son of Daniel and Mary (Santry) Dowling. Educated: Manhattan College, New York; St. John's Seminary, Brighton, Mass.; Catholic University, Washington, D. C. Ordained, June 24, 1891, Providence, Rhode Island. Elected to the newly erected see of Des Moines, January 31, 1912. Consecrated April 25, 1912, by Bishop Matthew Harkins of Providence. Promoted to the metropolitan see of St. Paul, March 10, 1919. Died, November 29, 1930, St. Paul, Minn.; buried at St. Paul. For many years chairman of the Executive Board of the N.C.W.C. Cf. Document No. 15; Joseph B. Code, *Dictionary of the American Hierarchy, op. cit.,* pp. 83–84; *Catholic Directory* (1949), *op. cit.,* p. 185.

faced the difficulties and trials of the first years of the Welfare Council found the formula to do two things which seemed incompatible: first, to safeguard completely the voluntary element of the Bishops' Meeting, which enabled each Ordinary to continue entirely free in his decisions; and, secondly, to recommend matters so prudently to the Welfare Council that the Bishops welcomed corporate action.

As we look back on those years, we can only thank God for the great courageous Pope that sat in the Chair of Peter, Pius XI, who received the whole question of the Welfare Council, and who, in a spirit of magnificent triumph, restored, commended, and blessed the National Catholic Welfare Council to be known henceforth not as a Council, but as a Conference. In expressing thanks to Almighty God, we must not fail to mention the name of Archbishop Schrembs,[16] who worked indefatigably in Rome for its reorganization, and of his secretary on that Mission, the late Archbishop Ryan of Omaha.[17] More than ninety Bishops declared humbly their con-

---

[16] Archbishop Joseph Schrembs (1866–1945), Bishop of Cleveland, was born March 12, 1866, at Wuzelhofen, near Ratisbon, Bavaria, Germany, the son of George and Mary (Gess) Schrembs. Educated: St. Vincent's College, Beatty, Pa.; Grand Seminary, Montreal, Canada; Laval University, Montreal. Ordained, June 29, 1889, at Grand Rapids, Mich. Engaged in pastoral work in the diocese of Grand Rapids, 1889–1911. Appointed Vicar-General of the diocese of Grand Rapids, January 15, 1903. Made a Domestic Prelate of the papal household, 1906. Elected to the titular see of Sophene, January 8, 1911, and appointed Auxiliary Bishop of Grand Rapids. Consecrated February 22, 1911, Grand Rapids, by Bishop Henry J. Richter of Grand Rapids. Translated to the newly erected see of Toledo, August 11, 1911. Appointed an assistant to the pontifical throne, December 18, 1926. Translated to the see of Cleveland, January 16, 1921. Decorated by the Italian, Polish, Hungarian, and Czechoslovakian governments. Host to the Seventh National Eucharistic Congress, Cleveland, September, 1935. Member of the National Catholic War Council, of the Administrative Committee and of the Board of Trustees of the Catholic University of America, Washington, D. C. President and Protector of the Priests' Eucharistic League in the United States. Raised to the archepiscopal dignity, *pro persona*, March 25, 1939; received the Sacred Pallium, *pro persona*, December 10, 1939. Died November 2, 1945; buried in Cleveland.

Cf. Code, *Dictionary of the American Hierarchy, op. cit.*, pp. 316–317; *Catholic Directory* (1949), *op. cit.*, p. 282.

[17] Archbishop James Hugh Ryan (1886–1947) was born December 15, 1886, Indianapolis, Ind., the son of John Marshall and Bridget (Rogers) Ryan. Educated, Dusquesne University, Pittsburgh, Pa.; Seminary of Mt. St. Mary of the West, Cincinnati, Ohio; North American College, Rome, Italy; Urban College of the Propaganda, Rome. Ordained, June 5, 1909, Rome, Italy, by Pietro Cardinal Respighi, Vicar-General to His Holiness, Pope Pius X. Member of the faculty of St. Mary-of-the-Woods College, St. Mary-of-the-Woods, Ind., 1911–1921. Member of the faculty of the Catholic University of America, Washington, D. C., 1922–1928. Executive Secretary of the National Catholic Welfare Conference, 1920–1928. Rector of the Catholic University of America, Washington, D. C., 1928–1935. Elected to the titular see of Modra, August 15, 1933. Consecrated, October 25, 1933, Indianapolis, by Bishop Joseph Chartrand of Indianapolis. Translated to the see of Omaha, August 6, 1935. Elected to the archepiscopal dignity, August 7, 1949. Decorated by the governments of Italy, Jugoslavia, France, and Poland. Made a Knight of Malta, 1935; died November 23, 1947.

Author: *Directory of Catholic Colleges and Schools* (1921); *A Catechism of*

victions regarding the annual meeting of the Bishops. Pope Pius XI subsequently declared the Conference, "Not only useful, but also necessary for you."

Our present Pontiff, gloriously reigning, has ever been the sympathetic friend, the kind counsellor, and, now, the Common Father of the Christian world, who looks upon the Welfare Conference as the strong support of Catholic action and the generous promoter of Christian charity. In his Encyclical Letter, *Sertum Laetitiae*,[18] His Holiness generously praises the works of the Conference. The many encouraging cablegrams of Our Holy Father, Pope Pius XII, have been an inspiration to our Bishops, and an incentive to do more for the Kingdom of God, united in the closest bonds with the Vicar of Christ.

The second World War gave further opportunities to the National Catholic Welfare Conference to extend its work and to organize a world apostolate of charity. This undertaking won the quick approval and support of the Bishops. The Archbishop of New York was asked to allow a priest of his jurisdiction to undertake the tremendous task of assembling forces, of uniting and coordinating them. The priest happily chosen by Archbishop (now Cardinal) Spellman,[19] was His Excellency, Archbishop O'Boyle of Washington. His work is monumental and will ever live in the annals of the history of charity of our Country and of the world. It continues according to the formulas that he laid down. I can testify that it has been a great privilege to work with him. His quiet manner, his generous spirit, his genius for organization, his calm and wise decisions, and his spirit of counsel endeared him to all of us who worked with him.

I venture to think that the Bishops of the United States unanimously

---

Catholic Education (1922); *An Introduction to Philosophy* (1924); and the *Encyclicals of Pius XI* (1927).

Cf. Code, *Dictionary of the American Hierarchy*, pp. 300–310; *Catholic Directory* (1949), *op. cit.*

[18] *Sertum Laetitiae*, November 1, 1939; *Acta Apostolicae Sedis*, 31:15 (November 25, 1939), 635–656. English translation by the N.C.W.C., Washington 5, D. C.

[19] Francis Cardinal Spellman (1889—) was born May 4, 1889, at Whitman, Mass., the son of William and Ellen (Conway) Spellman. Educated: Fordham College, New York, N. Y.; North American College, Rome, Italy. Ordained, May 14, 1916, Rome, Italy, by Guiseppe Ceppetelli, Patriarch of Constantinople and Vicegerent of Rome. Engaged in pastoral work in the diocese of Boston, 1916–1918, 1932–1939. Vice-Chancellor of the archdiocese of Boston, 1918–1922; editor of the *Boston Pilot*, 1924–1925. An attaché in the Secretariate of State, the Vatican, 1925–1932. Elected to the titular see of Sila, July 30, 1932, and appointed Auxiliary Bishop of Boston. Consecrated, September 8, 1932, Rome, by Eugenio Cardinal Pacelli, Papal Secretary of State, now His Holiness Pope Pius XII. Decorated by the government of Italy. Given the Grand Cross of the Knights of Malta, 1932. Promoted to the metropolitan see of New York, April 15, 1939. Appointed Bishop Ordinary for the Army and Navy of the United States, December 10, 1930; Created Cardinal, February 18, 1946; titular church SS. John and Paul, Rome.

Author: *The Word of God* (1920); *In the Footsteps of the Master* (1924).

Cf. Code, *Dictionary of the American Hierarchy*, pp. 331–332; *Catholic Directory* (1949), p. 121; Thomas B. Morgan, *Speaking of Cardinals, op. cit.*, pp. 124–151; Brendan A. Finn, *Twenty-four American Cardinals, op. cit.*, pp. 449–465.

rejoice that Archbishop O'Boyle now presides over the Diocese which is the center of activity for the Departments, Commissions, and Committees of the National Catholic Welfare Conference. This organization has proved not only its usefulness, but its necessity. It has proved that the voluntary element — by which each Bishop is left absolutely free in his diocese, under the direction of the Vicar of Christ — is not an impediment but rather a help in our conferences, which have developed, first of all, a common mind, and this in turn has led to united episcopal action. The recommendations of the Administrative Board and of the general body of Bishops are so disinterestedly weighed and so delicately presented that they are unanimously adopted.

We face today the difficulties of obstruction and of the chaos and want and poverty and starvation and disease that subversive forces are promoting as a means of gaining world control. These days will pass, and they will pass swiftly when an Omnipotent God terminates Divine patience in dealing with those persons and governments that directly and blasphemously attack His powers, His supremacy, His government of the world, denying His very existence and satanitically instilling that denial into the minds and hearts of the youth of our day. Let us hope that peaceful days of the world will enable our Conference to do constructive things for Church and Country.

In conclusion, may I say that a large section of the history of the Church in the United States has been written during the past thirty years, and that history is chiefly concerned with the achievements of the N.C.W.C.

When World War I was over the name of the "National Catholic War Council" was at first changed to that of "National Catholic Welfare Council" but when later (July 4, 1922)[20] opposition was voiced by the Holy See to the term "Council" because "open to some misunderstandings, and in fact has not been acceptable to all" because of its canonical connotation embodying conciliar legislation, the word "Council" was changed to that of "Conference"[21] so that henceforth the official name of the organization was to be "National Catholic Welfare Conference" (N.C.W.C.).

The change of name from "Council" to "Conference," however, had more than a passing significance. As indicated, the organization of the bishops of the United States was to be looked upon as having advisory powers only, not jurisdictional. It could recommend, but not enjoin.[22]

---

[20] Cf. Instructions of the Sacred Consistorial Congregation, July 4, 1922 (in the Archives of the N.C.W.C.).

[21] The Sacred Consistorial Congregation had submitted, for the approval of the Bishops, the name "The National Catholic Welfare Committee," ibid.

[22] "As the decisions of the Bishops at these meetings have nothing in common with conciliar legislation which is governed by a precept of the Sacred Canons (Cod. Can., 281, ff) they will not have force of law, since, as from the beginning, it has been closely understood the meetings are held for friendly conference about measures of a common public interest for the safeguarding of the Church's work in the United States" (ibid.).

It could publicize the joint statements as expressing the common view-points of all the bishops assembled, but it could not enforce its deliberations or resolutions on other bishops not present, nor on the dioceses of the absentee bishops, who in fact "are not bound to attend these meetings either in person or by a representative."[23] It was for this reason that the term "National Pastorals" used in the first seven Provincial Councils of Baltimore, in the three Plenary Councils, and in the first four joint communications of the bishops of the N.C.W.C., was dropped in later communications to the Catholics of the United States and the general word "statements" or "resolutions" adopted. The bishops in councils assembled, once approved by the Holy See and presided over by its delegate (in case of a Plenary Council) could issue "National Pastorals" with jurisdictional force (e.g., that of burial in a Catholic cemetery, erection of parochial schools, etc.) much the same as any Ordinary could and can do for the flock of his own diocese; but not otherwise. When not in formal council, the bishops merely deliberate, suggest, and recommend to *all* the bishops, present and absent, their resolutions for universal adoption. If this had been properly understood by all the bishops of the United States in the early years of the N.C.W.C. much misunderstanding, which at one time threatened its very existence, would have been avoided.

Collectively speaking, nevertheless, the statements of the bishops in "friendly conference" assembled do enjoy the dignity of a collective magisterium of the Church in the United States and as such deserve serious consideration. Our bishops are the mouthpiece of all Catholic Americans subject to their individual jurisdiction. Hence the title of this work: OUR BISHOPS SPEAK. They voice their sentiments either on the occasion of their annual meetings, usually held at the Catholic University in the nation's capital in the fall of the year, or through the episcopal Administrative Board of the Conference. At times the bishops publish their statements under their own names; at times under the names of the Administrative Board. Whenever the statements were issued at the end of a regular meeting of bishops, they are included in the first category of this book.

Frequently, however, the bishops prefer to leave important matters that develop during the year to the Administrative Board to handle. (At first it bore the name of "Administrative Committee.") The Administrative Board usually meets at Washington in the spring of the

---

[23] *Ibid.*

year. It is headed by a chairman, elected by the Board for a term of one year. He is assisted by a vice-chairman. The episcopal members of the Board are selected by the assembled bishops. Where the work entailed warrants it, one or two other bishops are selected to assist the episcopal heads of the departments. These are known as assistant bishops. At present the Administrative Board is composed of the following members: the chairman, the vice-chairman, secretary, and treasurer. The Administrative Board through the heads of each department supervises the work of the following approved departments based on the Brief *Communes* of Pope Benedict XV, April 10, 1919:[24]

a) The Executive Department
b) The Department of Education
c) The Legal Department
d) The Press Department
e) The Department of Catholic Action Study
f) The Department of Lay Organization
g) The Department of Social Action (Social Work and Hospitals)
h) The Department of Youth

Besides these standing departments there are also the following episcopal committees:

American Board of Catholic Missions
Committee on the Propagation of the Faith
Committee on the Confraternity of Christian Doctrine
Committee on Seminaries
Catholic Committee for Refugees
Committee to Complete the Shrine of Immaculate Conception
Bishops' Committee for Polish Relief
Bishops' Committee for the Spanish Speaking
Bishops' War Emergency and Relief Committee
Bishops' Committee for Montezuma Seminary
Committee on Motion Pictures
Committee on the National Organization for Decent Literature
Committee on the Mexican Seminary (subcommittee of the
  Relief Committee)
Standing Committee on Military Service Legislation
Pontifical Committee for the North American College at Rome
Special Committee to Promote the Pope's Peace Plan

---

[24] Cf. *Acta Apostolicae Sedis,* 11:6 (May, 1919), 169–174.

Each of the episcopal committees may (and does) issue statements from time to time but these are not included (excepting by way of note or appendix) in the publications of this book.[25]

Besides their annual "Pastorals" or collective statements issued at the end of each meeting (Section A) the hierarchy as such has addressed, as times or circumstances dictated, letters to individuals (Section B) or voiced their sentiments on various topics through the regularly constituted heads of the departments or of the episcopal committees (Section C).

In the Appendix certain other relevant matters pertaining to Catholic life have been inserted.

As a rule, though, the documents herewith published are restricted to the joint pronouncements of the bishops in conference assembled, or otherwise issued in their name; or to the resolutions and statements of the Administrative Board. A mere glance at the contents of the 82 documents included in this work will bear testimony to the importance of the collection. It is a font of Catholic information, knowledge, and direction — an abbreviated encyclopedia of Catholic Action. Every effort has been made to compile a good and workable index. A "thumbnail" bibliography of each bishop mentioned is also included.

In his sermon at the consecration of the Most Reverend Michael J. Ready, D.D., as Bishop of Columbus, His Excellency, Archbishop Edward Mooney of Detroit (now His Eminence, Cardinal of St. Susanna's Church in Rome) uttered these memorable words:

> The consecration of the Bishop on whom hands have been laid this morning strikingly brings to mind a significant effort of the Church in our own country to render more effective the spiritual dynamic of doctrinal and structural unity with which Christ endowed His Church. This effort is embodied in the work of the National Catholic Welfare Conference with which Bishop Ready has, for thirteen years, been so prominently identified. The Bishops, who, with the encouragement and blessing of the Holy Father, established the Conference twenty-five years ago, had indeed a broad vision and a high hope of the great good which could come from this cooperative dedication of the spiritual power of Catholic unity to the cause of morality and social welfare. But even the most sanguine could hardly have foreseen the wide sweep and the beneficent results of the activities which have stemmed from that providential initiative. Through the Conference the Bishops of

---

[25] Many of these statements will be found in *Catholic Action,* published by the N.C.W.C., or in the N.C.W.C. news releases. The N.C.W.C. publication was called N.C.W.C. *Bulletin* from June, 1919, to December, 1929; N.C.W.C. *Review* from January, 1930, to December, 1931; N.C.W.C. *Catholic Action* from January, 1932, up to the present time.

the United States have, in these years, stood united as never before in the promotion of the religious and social apostolate which is their God-given responsibility. They have used the various departments of the Conference in fostering the development of Catholic education, in defending the Catholic school against open attacks on its constitutional freedom, in strengthening the Catholic press for its vital tasks in American life, in disseminating the social teachings of the Church and applying them to present-day problems, in working constructively to thwart subversive activities and to promote industrial peace through cooperation between capital and labor, in protecting the interests of religion in proposed legislation without descending into the arena of partisan politics, in coordinating lay effort for spiritual aims in the wide field of Catholic action.

Agencies that grew out of the Conference have earned our gratitude by what they have done to uphold at least a minimum of moral standards on the screen, the stage and the corner news stands. These agencies have served us all by constructive planning for the religious instruction of Catholic children who are not in Catholic schools, for the preservation of Christian ideals in family life and for the development of a special interest in the religious welfare of scattered rural communities.

When war came, the existence of the Conference made it possible for the Catholic Bishops of America quickly to muster the spiritual forces at their command in support of our Country's total effort to meet the challenge of ruthless aggressors. The Conference is the ever-ready instrument for the practical expression of American Catholic sympathy with nations ground down under the heel of brutal oppressors and for the insistent voicing of American Catholic concern for the fate of religion in many lands where our own Country, in view of its position of power among the United Nations, is charged with a heavy responsibility. The Conference has been the medium for an impressive demonstration of American Catholic charity dispensed either directly or through the Common Father of Catholic Christendom whose merciful hands could often reach where our own were barred. It provides, as well, a means for corporate Catholic participation in wide programs of relief under national or international auspices. It has facilitated the meeting of minds in common counsel which has enabled the Catholic Bishops of the United States to speak with a united voice on the grave moral issues of world peace and world order and to sound a timely warning of the disaster that impends if preoccupation with merely political or commercial interests to the disregard of moral principles, blinds the victorious nations to the dangers that lie ahead.[26]

How much the Holy See appreciates the work of the N.C.W.C. can readily be seen not only from the previously quoted Brief of Benedict XV (*Communes*) but also from the letter of Pope Pius XI to the National Catholic Welfare Council under date of August 10, 1927;[27] and from the cablegram of our present Holy Father, Pope

---

[26] Cf. *Catholic Action,* 27:1 (January, 1945), pp. 4–5.
[27] On file in the Archives of the N.C.W.C.

Pius XII, happily reigning, under date of November 9, 1941.[28] Said the Holy Father on another occasion:

> Over a manifold activity of the laity, carried on in various localities according to the need of the times is placed the National Catholic Welfare Conference, an organization which supplies a ready and well-adopted instrument for your episcopal ministry.[29]

His Excellency, the Most Reverend Amleto Cicognani, D.D., Apostolic Delegate to the United States, voiced in his own name the sentiments of the Supreme Pontiffs when on the occasion of the consecration of the above-named Bishop Michael J. Ready, the former Secretary General of the N.C.W.C., he said:

> The N.C.W.C., inspired by the principles of the Gospel and by the teachings of the Holy See, treats practical questions and problems in the fields of religion, family, beneficence, social service, education, rural life, journalism, administrative and legal matters and at the present time deals with many difficult problems that have arisen due to the war and its effects. Its beneficial results reach every diocese and parish throughout the nation and are even seen in plentiful assistance rendered in many foreign lands.
>
> At all times the work of the N.C.W.C. has received the utmost encouragement from the Holy See. It suffices to point out that only since last October until today in no less than three splendid documents, a letter to the Press Department and two personal telegrams, His Holiness, Pope Pius XII, has again expressed his heartfelt gratitude and his complete satisfaction to the Conference.
>
> It is easily understandable that a work of the Bishops, although restricted to what we call Catholic Action, is directed to and aims at the purpose of the Church itself. The ultimate end of the Church is the sanctification of souls and their salvation, just as the ultimate end of every living person is to save his soul. There is, however, this difference, that the means of sanctification has been entrusted to the Church and not to individuals, and the custody and administration of these means have been committed to the Supreme Pontiff and to the Bishops who govern the Church. There is an obligation of vigilance and provision that all the faithful may find that spiritual sustenance which is their right. To better fulfill the duties of their Apostolate, especially in the vast field of Catholic Action, the Bishops of the United States organized the N.C.W.C.[30]

In conclusion the editor wishes to express his gratitude to the Rt. Rev. Msgr. Howard J. Carroll, General Secretary, to the Very Rev. Monsignor Paul Tanner, Assistant General Secretary of the

---

[28] On file in the Archives of the N.C.W.C.
[29] Cf. *Catholic Action,* 30:3 (March, 1940), p. 2
[30] Cf. N.C.W.C. "News Release" of December 18, 1944.

N.C.W.C., at whose suggestion and under whose kind direction this compilation was begun and finished; likewise to their efficient corps of secretaries for their generous co-operation.

RAPHAEL M. HUBER, O.F.M.CONV. .

Associate Professor of Church History

Washington, D. C.   *Catholic University*

CONTENTS

PART I

ANNUAL STATEMENTS AND OTHER COMMUNICATIONS OF THE HIERARCHY OF THE UNITED STATES

SECTION A

ANNUAL STATEMENTS OF THE BISHOPS

SECTION B

RESOLUTIONS AND LETTERS OF THE HIERARCHY SENT TO INDIVIDUALS

SECTION C

RESOLUTIONS AND STATEMENTS OF THE HIERARCHY OF THE UNITED STATES ON EPISCOPAL COMMITTEES ON VARIOUS TOPICS

PART II

STATEMENTS OF THE ADMINISTRATIVE BOARD OF THE N.C.W.C.

APPENDIX

RELEVANT MATTERS OF
N.C.W.C. DEPARTMENTS

PART I

ANNUAL STATEMENTS AND OTHER COMMUNICATIONS OF THE HIERARCHY OF THE UNITED STATES

SECTION A

ANNUAL STATEMENTS OF THE BISHOPS

1. THE HIERARCHY OF THE UNITED STATES

PASTORAL LETTER OF 1919*

September 26, 1919

The archbishops and bishops of the United States in conference assembled, to their clergy and faithful people — Grace unto you and peace from God our Father and from the Lord Jesus Christ.

VENERABLE BRETHREN OF THE CLERGY,

BELOVED CHILDREN OF THE LAITY:

Thirty-five years have elapsed since the Fathers of the Third Plenary Council of Baltimore addressed their pastoral letter to the faithful of their charge. In it they expressed their deliberate thought upon the state of religion at the time, upon its needs and its abundant resources. Surveying the growth of the Church during a century, they saw with thankfulness the evident design of God in behalf of our country; and turning to the future, they beheld the promise of a still more fruitful development. With wise enactment and admonition they imparted new vigor to our Catholic life. With a foresight which we can now appreciate, they prepared the Church in America to meet, on the solid ground of faith and discipline, the changing conditions of our earthly existence. As Pope Leo XIII of happy memory declared: "the event has proven, and still does prove, that the decrees of Baltimore were wholesome and timely. Experience has demonstrated their value for the maintenance of discipline, for stimulating the intelligence and zeal of the clergy, for protecting and developing the Catholic education of youth" (Encyc., *Longinqua oceani spatia,* January 6, 1895).

The framers of the legislation were men of power, shewing forth in their wisdom the dignity of prophets and instructing the people with holy words. They are gone, nearly all, to their rest and reward; but their godly deeds have not failed. They have left us a sacred

---

* May be had in pamphlet form at the N.C.W.C. Headquarters, Washington 5, D. C.

inheritance; their labors are held in remembrance and their names in benediction forever.

Following the example of our predecessors, and like them trusting in the guidance of the Holy Spirit, we lately took counsel together for the welfare of the Church and of our country. The whole hierarchy of the United States assembled in Washington to consider the problems, the needs, and the possibilities for good which invite us to new undertakings. In the record of the last three decades, we found much to console and inspire us. We also knew well that you with whom and for whom we have labored would rejoice in considering how abundantly God has blessed our endeavors. And we therefore determined, for His glory and for your comfort, to point out the significant phases in our progress, and to set forth the truths which contain the solution of the world's great problems.

This course we adopted the more hopefully because of the approval and encouragement given us by our Holy Father, Pope Benedict XV, in the letter which he sent us last April. Knowing how deeply the Sovereign Pontiff is concerned for the restoration of all things in Christ, and how confidently he looks at this time to the Church in America, we felt that by uniting our thought and our effort we should co-operate, in the measure of our opportunity, toward his beneficent purpose. In his name, and in our own, we greet you, dear brethren, as children of the Holy Catholic Church and as citizens of the Republic on whose preservation the future of humanity so largely depends. We exhort you, as of one mind and heart, to ponder well the significance of recent events, so that each of you, as circumstance requires, may rightly fulfill his share of our common obligation.

First of all, it is our bounden duty to offer up praise and thanksgiving to almighty God who, in His gracious Providence, has restored the nations to peace. He has shown us His mercy, and the light of His countenance is shining upon us, that we may know His way upon earth, which is the way of salvation for all the peoples. Now that the storm is subsiding, we can see the true meaning of its causes. We can review more calmly the changes and movements which brought it about; and we can discern more surely their import for our various human interests.

In the spiritual order, there has been a steady advance. The issue between truth and error, with regard to all that religion implies, is now quite clearly drawn. As human devices, intended to replace the Gospel, have gradually broken down, Christianity, by contrast, appears distinct and firm in its true position. The Church indeed has suffered because it would not sanction the vagaries of thought and policy which were leading the world to disaster. And yet the very opposition which it encountered, an opposition which would have destroyed the work of man, has given the Church occasion for new manifestations of life. With larger freedom from external inter- ference, it has developed more fully the power from on high with which the Holy Spirit endued it. Far from being weakened by the failure of outward support, its activity is seen as the expression of its inner vitality. Its vigor is shown in its ready adaptation to the varying conditions of the world, an adaptation which means no supine yielding and no surrender of principle, but rather the exertion of power in supplying as they arise, the needs of humanity. Because it maintains inviolate the deposit of Christian faith and the law of Christian morality, the Church can profit by every item of truth and every means for the betterment of man which genuine progress affords. It thrives wherever freedom really lives, and it furnishes the only basis on which freedom can be secure.

The inner vitality of the Church has been shown and enhanced by the action of the Holy See in giving fresh impetus to the minds and hearts of the faithful; in stimulating philosophical, historical, and biblical studies; in creating institutions of learning; in revising the forms of liturgical prayer; in quickening devotion; and in re- ducing to a compact body of law the manifold enactments of canonical legislation. At the same time, the Sovereign Pontiffs have promoted the welfare of all mankind by insisting on the principles which should govern our social, industrial and political relations, by deepening respect for civil authority; by enjoining upon Catholics everywhere the duty of allegiance to the State and the discharge of patriotic obligation. They have condemned the errors which planned to betray humanity and to undermine our civilization. Again and again, the charity of Christ constraining them, they have sought out the peoples which sat in darkness and the shadow of death; and they have urged all Christians who are yet "as children tossed to and fro and carried about with every wind of doctrine," to enter the haven of the Church and anchor upon the confession of "one Lord, one faith, one baptism" (Eph. 4:14, 5).

THE HOLY SEE AND THE CHURCH IN AMERICA

From these salutary measures the Church in America has derived in full its share of benefit. But it has also received, to its great advantage, especial marks of pontifical favor. To Pope Leo XIII we are indebted for the establishment of the Apostolic Delegation, whereby we are brought into closer union with the Holy See. The presence in our midst of the representative of the Holy Father has invigorated our ecclesiastical life, and facilitated to a marked degree the administration of our spiritual affairs, in keeping with our rapid development.

Though its organization had extended to every part of the United States, the Church, until 1908, was still on a missionary basis, as it had been from the beginning. By the action of Pope Pius X, it was advanced to full canonical status and ranked with the older Churches of Europe. It now observes the same laws and enjoys the same relations with the Apostolic See.

From the beginning of his pontificate, Pope Benedict XV, though burdened with sorrow and trial, has given his children in America continual proof of his fatherly care. He has guided us with his counsel, encouraged us with his approbation, and rejoiced in our prosperity. Recognizing the importance of America for the world's restoration, he sees from his exalted position the broader range of opportunity which now is given the Church in our country. By word, and yet more by example, he shows how effectually the Catholic spirit can renew the face of the earth.

NEEDS OF THE HOLY SEE

It is a source of happiness for us that the Catholics of America have appreciated the evidences of paternal affection bestowed on them by the Vicar of Christ. For we can truly say that no people is more loyal to the Holy See, none more diligent in providing for its needs. Our assistance at the present time will give the Holy Father special consolation, owing to the fact that the faithful in so many countries are no longer able to share with him their scanty means. It is to the Pope, on the contrary, that they, in their destitution, are looking for aid. And it is in their behalf that he has more than once appealed. Touching, indeed, are the words with which he implores all Christians throughout the world, and "all who have a sense of humanity," for the love of the Infant Saviour, to help him in rescuing from hunger and death the children of Europe. In the same encyclical letter (*Paterno iam diu*, November 24, 1919), he commends most highly the bishops and the faithful of the United States for their prompt and generous response to his earlier appeal, and he offers their action as an example to all other Catholics. Let us continue to deserve his approval.

It is sufficient for us to know that the Holy Father, with numberless demands upon him, is in need.

THE GROWTH OF THE CHURCH IN OUR COUNTRY

The growth of the Church in America was fittingly brought to view at the celebration, in 1889, of the first centenary of the hierarchy. Within a hundred years, the number of dioceses had risen from one to seventy-five. During the last three decades the same rate of progress has been maintained, with the result that at present one sixth of the citizens of the United States are members of the Catholic Church, in a hundred flourishing dioceses.

But what we regard as far more important is the growth and manifestation of an active religious spirit in every diocese and parish. "We are bound to give thanks always to God for you, brethren, as it is fitting, because your faith groweth exceedingly, and the charity of every one of you toward each other aboundeth" (2 Thess. 1:3). You have not contented yourselves with bearing the Catholic name or professing your faith in words: you have shown your faith by your works; by the performance of your religious duties, by obedience to the laws of the Church, and by co-operation in furthering the kingdom of God. For thus "the whole body, being compacted and fitly joined together, by what every joint supplieth, according to the operation in the measure of every part, maketh increase of the body unto the edifying of itself in charity" (Eph. 4:16).

With you, dear brethren of the clergy, we rejoice in the fruits of your zeal, your loyalty, and your concern for the welfare of the souls entrusted to your care. You have learned by a happy experience how much can be accomplished through your daily ministration, your immediate contact with the people, your words of advice and instruction, above all, through your priestly example. To you we gladly attribute the provision of the material means which are needed for the worship of God and for the countless forms of charity. You "have loved the beauty of his house and the place where his glory dwelleth" (Ps. 25:8). What is yet more essential, you have builded in the souls of your people, and especially in the little ones of Christ, the temple of the living God. In the work of our Catholic schools, you have both the honor and the responsibility of laying the first foundation. We know that you have laid it with care, and that the whole structure of Catholic education is securely based upon Jesus Christ, the chief cornerstone: "in whom all the building being fitted together, groweth up into an holy temple in the Lord . . . an habitation of God in the Spirit" (Eph. 2:21).

You, likewise, beloved children of the laity, we heartily commend for your willingness, your correspondence with the intent of your pastors, your support so cheerfully given to the cause of religion. When we consider that every church and school, every convent, asylum and hospital represents the voluntary offering brought by you, out of your plenty and more often out of your want, we cannot but marvel and glorify God who has made you "worthy of his vocation and fulfilled in you all the good pleasure of his goodness and the work of faith in power" (2 Thess. 1:11). For as faith is expressed in deeds, so, conversely, is it strengthened by doing: "by works faith is made perfect" (James 2:22). And since the bond of perfection is charity, we look upon your generosity both as an evidence of your good will toward the whole of God's Church and as a token of His heavenly favor. "Wherefore, brethren, labor the more that by good works you may make sure your calling and election" (2 Peter 1:10).

FAITH

We would have you bear always in mind that your faith is your most precious possession and the foundation of your spiritual life, since "without faith, it is impossible to please God" (Heb. 11:6). Without faith, the outward forms of worship avail us nothing, the sacraments are beyond our reach, the whole plan and effect of redemption is made void. It behooves us, then, to guard with jealous care the treasure of faith by thankfulness to God for so great a gift and by loyalty to "the Church of the living God, the pillar and ground of the truth" (1 Tim. 3:15). The fact that unbelief is so common, that firm and definite teaching of Christian truth is so often replaced by vague uncertain statements, and that even these are left to individual preference for acceptance or rejection — the fact, in a word, that by many faith is no longer regarded as of vital consequence in religion, should the more determine us to "watch, stand fast in the faith, do manfully and be strengthened" (1 Cor. 16:13). While we must needs look with sorrow upon the decay of positive belief, let us recognize, with gratitude, the wisdom of Him who, being the "author and finisher of our faith," established in His Church a living authority to "teach all nations, teaching them to observe all things whatsoever I have commanded you" (Matt. 28:20). Let us also consider the splendid courage with which that mission has been accomplished through the centuries, by the witness of martyrs, the constancy of faithful peoples, the zeal of preachers and pastors, the firmness of pontiffs who, amid the storms of error and the assaults of worldly power, stood fast in the faith upon the assurance given them by Christ: "the gates of hell shall not prevail" (Matt. 16:18).

The Catholic who appreciates the blessing of faith and the sacrifices which generous men and women in all ages have made to preserve it, will take heed to himself and beware of the things whereby some "have made shipwreck concerning the faith" (1 Tim. 1:19). For this disaster is usually the end and culmination of other evils, of sinful habits, of neglect of prayer and the sacraments, of cowardice in the face of hostility to one's belief, of weakness in yielding to the wishes of kindred or friends, of social ambition and the hope of advantage in business or public career. More subtle are the dangers arising from an atmosphere in which unbelief is mingled with culture and gentle refinement, or in which the fallacy spreads that faith is hopelessly at variance with scientific truth. To counteract these influences, it is necessary that they who love the truth of God, should "the more and more abound in knowledge and in all understanding" (Phil. 1:9). As they advance in years, they should lay firmer hold upon the teachings of religion and be prepared to explain and defend it. They will thus "Continue in faith, grounded and settled and immovable from the hope of the Gospel" (Col. 1:23), ready always to give "a reason of that hope that is in them" (1 Peter 3:15), and, if needs be, to "contend earnestly for the faith once delivered to the saints" (Jude 3).

THE SCRIPTURES

To the Church which is taught all truth by the Holy Spirit, Christ entrusted the whole deposit of divine revelation. To the watchful care of the Church we owe the preservation of that Book from which Christians in every age have derived instruction and strength. How needful was the warning of the Apostle that "no prophecy of Scripture is made by private interpretation" (2 Peter 1:20), appears in the history of those movements which began by leaving each individual to take his own meaning from the sacred text and now, after four centuries, have ended in rejecting its divine authority. The Church, on the contrary, with true reverence for the Bible and solicitude for the spiritual welfare of its readers, has guarded both it and them against the dangers of false interpretation. In the same spirit, dear brethren, we exhort you to acquire a loving familiarity with the written word: "for what things soever were written, were written for our learning; that through patience and the comfort of the Scriptures we might

have hope" (Rom. 15:4). This intimate knowledge of Holy Writ will
bring you close to the person and life of our Saviour and to the labors
of His Apostles. It will renew in your hearts the joy with which the
first Christians received the tidings of salvation. And it will deepen in
you the conviction that the Scriptures are indeed the word of God,
"which can instruct you unto salvation by the faith which is in Christ
Jesus" (2 Tim. 3:15) — a conviction which cannot be shaken either
by the disputations of the learned who "stumble at the word," or by
the errors of the unlearned and unstable who wrest the Scriptures
"to their own destruction" (2 Peter 3:16).

THE CATHOLIC SPIRIT

The knowledge of our holy religion will enkindle in you a love of
the Church, which Christ so loved that He gave Himself for it, purchasing it with His blood. It is the Church not of one race or of one
nation, but of all those who truly believe in His name. The more you
dwell upon its teaching, its practice, and its history, the stronger will
be your sense of unity with the multitude of believers throughout the
world. You will clearly understand that the true interests of each part,
of each diocese and parish, are the interests of the Church Universal.
"You are the body of Christ and members of member. And if one
member suffer anything, all the members suffer with it; or, if one
member glory, all the members rejoice with it" (1 Cor. 12:26–27).
This is the practical meaning of Catholicity and its saving strength
as opposed to the weakness of localism. The really Catholic mind is
careful not only for the needs which affect its immediate surroundings,
but for those also which press upon the Church in less prosperous
sections, or which, in far countries, hinder the spread of religion.
Such was the mind of those Christians to whom St. Paul appealed in
behalf of their distant brethren: "In this present time, let your
abundance supply their want; that their abundance may also supply
your want, that there may be an equality" (2 Cor. 8:14).

Your Catholic sense will also enable you to see how tireless the
Church has been in providing both for the souls of men and for their
temporal needs: how much of what is best in modern civilization,
how much that we value in the way of liberty and law, of art and
industry, of science, education, and charity, is due to the Catholic
spirit. Like its Founder, the Church has gone about the world doing
good to all men; and with Him the Church can say: "the works that
I do in the name of my Father, they give testimony of me. . . . though
you will not believe me, believe the works" (John 10:25, 38). And this

ministry of love the Church will continue. It will adopt all agencies and means that may render its service of better effect; it will quicken them all with the fervor of charity lest they harden to mechanical form; and it will take utmost care that they be employed to draw men nearer to Christ.

The spirit that made Vincent de Paul a saint and a hero of charity lives on in his followers. According to the pattern which he gave, they minister to those who are in any distress, quietly and effectually. Of late they have notably increased their power for good. Through the Conference of Catholic Charities, a "great door and evident" is opened upon a wider range of usefulness. To all who are joined together in this holy undertaking we say with the Apostle: "May the Lord multiply you and make you abound in charity one toward another and toward all men; as we do also toward you" (1 Thess. 3:12).

PRAYER

Be instant, therefore, dear brethren, in helping those who suffer or want; but take heed also to your own spiritual life, that in thought and purpose and motive, as well as in outward deed, you may be acceptable in the sight of God. From the teaching of the Church and from your own experience, you know that without the divine assistance you cannot walk in the footsteps of Christ. And you need not be reminded that the principal means of grace are prayer and the sacraments.

Through prayer we lift up our hearts to God, and He in turn enlightens our minds, kindles our affections, gives power to our wills. For whether we adore His majesty or praise Him for His wonderful works, whether we render Him thanks for His goodness or beseech Him for pardon or beg Him to help and defend us, our prayer is pleasing to Him: it goes up as incense before Him, as the voice of His children to the Father who loves them, who pursues them with mercy and offers them speedy forgiveness. Wherefore, in joy and in sorrow, in adversity and in prosperity, "in everything by prayer and supplication with thanksgiving, let your petitions be made known to God" (Phil. 4:6).

We are certain that amid the trials of the last few years, you have prayed without ceasing — for those who had gone from you to the post of duty and danger, for your country, for the untold millions who fell in the struggle. Many of you surely have found that it is "a holy and wholesome thought to pray for the dead that they may be loosed from sins" (2 Mach. 12:46). This doctrine and practice, so fully according with the impulse of human affection, appeals to us now with singular force. For those who mourn, it is a source of comfort; for all, it is the exercise of pure charity. And no petition could be more pleasing to the Father of mercies than that which implores Him to grant to our departed brethren everlasting rest in a place of refreshment, light, and peace. The remembrance of those who are gone before us with the token of faith will raise up our hearts above worldly desires; and whereas we are saddened by the certain prospect of death, yet we shall be comforted with the promise of immortal life, knowing that "if our earthly house of this habitation be dissolved, we have a building of God, a house not made with hands, eternal in heaven" (2 Cor. 5:1).

We heartily commend the beautiful practice of family prayer. "Where there are two or three gathered in my name, there am I in the midst of them" (Matt. 18:20). If this is true of the faithful in general, it applies with particular meaning to those who are members of the same household. The presence of Jesus will surely be a source of blessing to the home where parents and children unite to offer up prayer in common. The spirit of piety which this custom develops, will sanctify the bonds of family love and ward off the dangers which so often bring sorrow and shame. We appeal in this matter with special earnestness to young fathers and mothers, who have it in their power to mold the hearts of their children and train them betimes in the habit of prayer.

THE SACRIFICE AND THE SACRAMENTS

This will also inspire them with love for the public services of the Church and, above all, for the central act of Catholic worship, the Holy Sacrifice of the Mass. For the truly Catholic heart, there can be no need of insisting on the duty which the Church enjoins of hearing Mass on Sundays and festivals of obligation. We have only to stir up the faith that is in us, and consider that on the altar is offered the same clean oblation whereby the world was redeemed on the Cross; and as today no Christian can stand unmoved on Calvary, or pass with indifference along the road which Jesus trod, so is it inconceivable that any who believe in the word of Christ and His Church, should allow household cares or business pursuits or the love of pleasure and ease to keep them away from Mass. Negligence in respect of this duty may often result from lack of proper instruction; and we therefore desire to impress upon parents, teachers, and pastors the importance and the necessity of explaining to those in their charge, the origin, nature, and value of the Holy Sacrifice, the meaning of the sacred rites with which it is offered, and the order of the liturgy as it advances from season to season. There is so much beauty in the worship of the Church, so much power to fill the mind with great thoughts and lift up the heart to heavenly things, that one who hears Mass with intelligent devotion cannot but feel in his soul an impulse to holier living. Such is the experience of those especially who begin each day by attending at Mass, and we rejoice to know that their number is increasing. They will grow in faith and fervor, and their piety will be for all a source of edification.

It is likewise consoling to see in our time a revival of the spirit which, in primitive ages, led the Christian to receive each day "the Bread that came down from heaven." In the Holy Eucharist, the love of Jesus Christ for men passes all understanding. "He that eateth my flesh and drinketh my blood abideth in me and I in him" (John 6:57). A worthy communion unites us with our Saviour, and even transforms our spiritual being, so that we may say with the Apostle: "I live, now not I; but Christ liveth in me" (Gal. 2:20). As by His continual abiding within it, the Church is holy and without blemish, so does the presence of Christ in each soul purify it even as He is pure, and give it power to do all things in Him who strengthens it.

The sense of our unworthiness may incline us to draw back from the holy table; but, as St. Paul tells us: "Let a man prove himself and so let him eat of that bread and drink of the chalice" (1 Cor. 11:28). Only sin can separate us from the love of God which is in Christ Jesus our Lord, and for sin He has provided a remedy in the sacrament of His mercy. "If we confess our sins, he is faithful and just to forgive us our sins and to cleanse us from all iniquity" (1 John 1:9). Through these two sacraments, the one given for the healing of our souls, the other for their nourishment, we are established in the life of grace and are "filled unto all the fullness of God" (Eph. 3:19).

Mary the Mother of Christ

What grace can accomplish in His creatures, God has shown in the person of her whom He chose to be His mother, preserving her from all stain and endowing her with such pureness of heart that she is truly "full of grace" and "blessed among women." The unique privilege of Mary as co-operating in the Incarnation, entitles her to reverence and honor; but in the Catholic mind it is love that prompts veneration for the Mother of Christ. It is indeed beyond comprehension that any who sincerely love Jesus, should be cold or indifferent in regard to His Mother. No honor that we may pay her can ever equal that which

God Himself has conferred, and much less can it detract from the honor that is due to Him.

In keeping with her singular dignity is the power of Mary's intercession. If the prayers of holy men avail to obtain the divine assistance, the petitions of Mary in our behalf must be far more efficacious. With good reason, then, does the Church encourage the faithful to cultivate a tender devotion for the Blessed Virgin. But if all generations should call her blessed, and if the peoples of earth should glory in her protection, we in the United States have a particular duty to honor Mary Immaculate as the heavenly Patroness of our country. Let her blessed influence preserve our Catholic homes from all contagion of evil, and keep our children in pureness of heart. Let us also pay her the tribute of public honor in a way that will lead all our people to a fuller appreciation of Mary, the perfect woman and the surpassing model of motherhood. As Pope Benedict has declared, it is eminently fitting that the devotion of American Catholics to the Mother of God should find expression in a temple worthy of our celestial Patroness. May the day soon dawn when we shall rejoice at the completion of so grand an undertaking; for, as the Holy Father says in commending the project of the National Shrine of the Immaculate Conception, "our human society has reached that stage in which it stands in most urgent need of the aid of Mary Immaculate, no less than of the joint endeavors of all mankind" (*Letter to the Hierarchy,* April 10, 1919).

CATHOLIC EDUCATION

The nursery of Christian life is the Catholic home; its stronghold, the Catholic school. "In the great coming combat between truth and error, between Faith and Agnosticism, an important part of the fray must be borne by the laity. . . . And if, in the olden days of vassalage and serfdom, the Church honored every individual, no matter how humble his position, and labored to give him the enlightenment that would qualify him for higher responsibilities, much more now, in the era of popular rights and liberties, when every individual is an active and influential factor in the body politic, does she desire that all should be fitted by suitable training for an intelligent and conscientious discharge of the important duties that may devolve upon them."

The timely warning contained in these words from the Pastoral Letter of 1884 shows how clearly our predecessors discerned the need, both present and future, of Christian education. Their forecast has been verified. The combat which they predicted has swept around all the sources of thought, and has centered upon the school. There, especially, the interests of morality and religion are at stake; and there, more than anywhere else, the future of the nation is determined. For that reason, we give most hearty thanks to the Father of Lights who has blessed our Catholic schools and made them to prosper. We invoke His benediction upon the men and women who have consecrated their lives to the service of Christian education. They are wholesome examples of the self-forgetfulness which is necessary in time of peace no less than in crisis and danger. Through their singleness of purpose and their sacrifice, the Church expresses the truth that education is indeed a holy work, not merely a service to the individual and society, but a furtherance of God's design for man's salvation. With them we realize, more fully than ever before, the necessity of adhering to the principles on which our schools are established. If our present situation is beset with new problems, it is also rich in opportunity; and we are confident that our teachers will exert themselves to the utmost in perfecting their work. Their united counsel in the Catholic Educational Association has already produced many excellent results, and it justifies the hope that our schools may be organized into a system that will combine the utilities of free initiative with the power of unified action. With a common purpose so great and so holy to guide them, and with a growing sense of solidarity, our educators will recognize the advantage which concerted effort implies both for the Catholic system as a whole and for each of the allied institutions.

We deem it necessary at this time to emphasize the value for our people of higher education, and the importance of providing and receiving it under Catholic auspices. "Would that even now, as we trust will surely come to pass in the future, the work of education were so ordered and established that Catholic youth might proceed from our Catholic elementary schools to Catholic schools of higher grade and in these attain the object of their desires" (*Third Plenary Council: Acts and Decrees,* 208). This wish and ideal of our predecessors, in a gratifying measure, has been realized through the establishment of Catholic high schools and the development of our Catholic colleges. These have more than doubled in number; they have enlarged their facilities and adjusted their courses to modern requirements. We congratulate their directors and teachers, and with them we see, in the present condition of their institutions, the possibility and the promise of further achievement in accordance with their own aspirations.

In educational progress, the teacher's qualification is the vital element. This is manifestly true of the Catholic school, in which the teacher's personality contributes so much toward the building of character and the preservation of faith along with the pupil's instruction in knowledge. If, therefore, the aim of our system is to have Catholic youth receive its education in its completeness from Catholic sources, it is equally important, and even more urgently necessary, that our teachers should be trained under those influences and by those agencies which place the Catholic religion at the heart of instruction, as the vitalizing principle of all knowledge and, in particular, of educational theory and practice. We note with satisfaction that our teachers are eager for such training, and that measures have been taken to provide it through institutes, summer schools, and collegiate courses under university direction. We are convinced that this movement will invigorate our education and encourage our people, since the work of teachers who are thoroughly prepared is the best recommendation of the school.

We cannot too highly approve the zeal and liberality of those who, with large amount or small, have aided us in building up our schools. For what we value as significant in their action is not alone the material help which it renders, essential as this has become; but rather and chiefly the evidence which it affords of their spiritual sense and perception. It shows that they appreciate both the necessity of Catholic education and the unselfish devotion of our teachers. At a time, especially, when vast fortunes are so freely lavished upon education in other lines, it is edifying to see our people either dedicating their individual wealth to the cause of religious instruction or, as members of Catholic associations, combining their means for the same noble purpose. They, assuredly, have given an object lesson, teaching all by their example, "to do good, to be rich in good works, to give easily, to communicate to others, to lay up in store for themselves a good foundation against the time to come, that they may lay hold on the true life" (1 Tim. 6:18–19).

THE CATHOLIC UNIVERSITY

It was the progress of our academies, colleges, and seminaries from colonial days onward, that made the university possible; and it was the demand, created by them, for larger opportunities that made it a necessity. Established, at the instance of the bishops, by Pope Leo XIII, it represents the joint action of the Holy See and the American Hierarchy in behalf of higher education. Like the first universities of Europe, it was designed to be the home of all the sciences and the common base of all our educational forces. This twofold purpose has guided its development. As in the Ages of Faith and Enlightenment, the various religious orders gathered at the centers of learning which the Holy See had established, so in our own day, the orders have grouped their houses of study about the university, in accordance with the express desire of its founders. "We exhort you all," said the Pontiff, "to affiliate your seminaries, colleges and other Catholic institutions of learning with your University on the terms which its statutes suggest" (Apostolic Letter, *Magni Nobis gaudii,* March 7, 1889). As the process of affiliation is extended to our high schools, it benefits them and also provides a better class of students for our colleges. In keeping, then, with the aims of its founders, the university exists for the good and the service of all our schools. Through them and through their teachers, it returns with interest the generous support of our clergy and laity.

"By no means surprising or unexpected," said Pope Pius X, "is the steady and vigorous growth of the Catholic University which, located at Washington, the Capital City of the American Republic, built up by the offerings of the Catholic people and invested by the Apostolic See with full academic authority, is now become the fruitful parent of knowledge in all the sciences both human and divine. . . . We are fully determined on developing the Catholic University. For we clearly understand how much a Catholic university of high repute and influence can do toward spreading and upholding Catholic doctrine and furthering the cause of civilization. To protect it, therefore, and to quicken its growth is, in our judgment, equivalent to rendering most valuable service to religion and to country alike" (*Letter to the Cardinal Chancellor,* January 5, 1912).

To the same intent, Pope Benedict XV writes: "We have followed with joy its marvellous progress so closely related to the highest hope of your Churches . . . well knowing that you have all hitherto contributed in no small measure to the development of this seat of higher studies, both ecclesiastical and secular. Nor have we any doubt but that henceforth you will continue even more actively to support an institution of such great usefulness and promise as is the University" (*Letter to the Hierarchy,* April 10, 1919).

It is our earnest desire that the university should attain fully the scope of its founders, and thereby become an educational center worthy of the Church in America, worthy also of the zeal which our clergy and laity have shown in behalf of education. Its progress and prosperity will make it, as the Holy Father trusts, "the attractive center about which all will gather who love the teachings of our Catholic Faith."

CATHOLIC SOCIETIES

Considering the great good accomplished by our Catholic societies, the Fathers of the Third Plenary Council expressed the desire "to see their number multiplied and their organization perfected." That desire has been fulfilled. The rapid development of our country provides ample occasion, even under normal conditions, for those activities which attain success through organization. Continually, new problems appear and opportunities arise to spread the Faith, to foster piety, to counteract tendencies which bode evil, either openly or under attractive disguise. In response to these demands, our Catholic associations have increased their usefulness by selecting special lines of activity, and by following these out wherever the cause of religion was in need or in peril. Through the hearty co-operation of clergy and laity, these agencies have wrought "good to all men, especially to those who are of the household of the faith" (Gal. 6:10). They have enlisted our Catholic youth in the interests of faith and charity, provided in numberless ways for the helpless and poor, shielded the weak against temptation, spread sound ideals of social and industrial reform and furthered the public welfare by their patriotic spirit and action. We rejoice in the fruits of their fellowship, and we desire of them that they strive together for the highest and best, "considering one another to provoke unto charity and to good works" (Heb. 10:24).

The tendency on the part of our societies to coalesce in larger organizations is encouraging. It arises from their consciousness of the Catholic purpose for which each and all are striving; and it holds out the promise of better results, both for the attainment of their several objects and for the promotion of their common cause, the welfare of the Church. The aim which inspired the Federation of our Catholic Societies, and which more recently has led to the Federation of Catholic Alumnae, is worthy of the highest commendation. It manifests a truly Catholic spirit, and it suggests wider possibilities for good which a more thorough organization will enable us to realize.

We regard as specially useful the work of associations like the Church Extension Society and the Missionary Unions, in securing the blessings of religion and the means of worship for those who suffer from poverty or isolation. The sections of our country in which Catholics are few offer, no less than the populous centers, a field for zealous activity; and we heartily encourage all projects for assisting those who, in spite of adverse circumstances, have preserved the faith, for reclaiming many others who have lost it, and for bringing to our non-Catholic brethren the knowledge of our holy religion.

HOME MISSIONS

As we thus survey the progress of the Church in our country and throughout the world, we cannot but think of the greater good which might result if men of worthy disposition were all united in faith. For we gladly recognize the upright will and generosity of many who are not yet "come to the city of the living God" and "to the Church of the first-born" (Heb. 12:22). We know that among them are men of judgment, who with spiritual insight are looking to the Catholic Church for the sure way of salvation; and that not a few, with exceptional talent for historical research, have set forth in their scholarly writings the unbroken succession of the Church of Rome from the Apostles, the integrity of its doctrine, and the steadfast power of its discipline. To all such earnest inquirers we repeat the invitation given them by Pope Leo XIII: "Let our fervent desire toward you, even more than our words, prevail. To you we appeal, our brethren who for over three centuries have differed from us regarding our Christian faith; and to all of you likewise who in later times, for any reason whatsoever, have turned away from us. Let us all 'meet together in the unity of faith and of the knowledge of the Son of God' (Eph. 4:13). Suffer that we invite you to the unity which has always existed in the Catholic Church and which never can fail. Lovingly we stretch forth our hands to you; the Church, our mother and yours, calls upon you to return; the Catholics of the whole world await you with brotherly longing, that you together with us may worship God in holiness, with hearts united in perfect charity by the profession of one Gospel, one faith and one hope" (Apostolic Letter, *Praeclara gratulationis,* June 20, 1894).

We give thanks to our Lord Jesus Christ, for His mercy upon so many who were scattered abroad and in distress even as sheep that have no shepherd. Year by year, "the multitude of men and women who believe in the Lord is more increased" (Acts 5:14). But though conversions are numerous, much remains to be done. "Other sheep I have that are not of this fold: them also I must bring, and they shall hear my voice, and there shall be one fold and one shepherd" (John 10:16).

Pray fervently, therefore, that light may be given to those who yet are seeking the way, that they may understand the nature of that union and concord so clearly set forth by Christ Himself, when He prayed to the Father, not only for His Apostles, "but for them also who through their word shall believe in me: that they all may be one,

as thou, Father, in me and I in thee; that they also may be one in us,
that the world may believe that thou hast sent me" (John 17:20, 21).
Now Christ and the Father are one, not by any outward bond of the
least possible agreement but by perfect identity in all things.

NEGRO AND INDIAN MISSIONS

In our own country there are fields of missionary labor that call in
a special manner for assiduous cultivation. There are races less fortunate in a worldly sense and, for that very reason, more fully dependent on Christian zeal. The lot of the Negro and Indian, though latterly
much improved, is far from being what the Church would desire. Both
have been hampered by adverse conditions, yet both are responsive to
religious ministration. In the eyes of the Church there is no distinction of race or of nation; there are human souls, and these have all
alike been purchased at the same great price, the blood of Jesus Christ.

This is the truth that inspires our Catholic missionaries and enables
them to make such constant efforts in behalf of those needy races.
We commend their work to the faithful in every part of our country. In the name of justice and charity, we deprecate most earnestly
all attempts at stirring up racial hatred; for this, while it hinders the
progress of all our people, and especially of the Negro, in the sphere
of temporal welfare, places serious obstacles to the advance of religion
among them. We concur in the belief that education is the practical
means of bettering their condition; and we emphasize the need of
combining moral and religious training with the instruction that is
given them in other branches of knowledge. Let them learn from the
example and word of their teachers the lesson of Christian virtue: it
will help them more effectually than any skill in the arts of industry,
to solve their problems and to take their part in furthering the
general good.

FOREIGN MISSIONS

"The mission which our Lord Jesus Christ, on the eve of His return
to the Father, entrusted to His disciples, bidding them 'go into the
whole world and preach the Gospel to every creature' (Mark 16:15) —
that office most high and most holy — was certainly not to end with
the life of the Apostles: it was to be continued by their successors even
to the consummation of the world, as long, namely, as there should
live upon earth men to be freed by the truth" (Apostolic Letter,
Maximum Illud, November 30, 1919).

These words of the Holy Father, addressed, with his characteristic love of souls, to all the bishops of the Church, have for us in America a peculiar force and significance. The care of our Catholic population, which is constantly increased by the influx of immigrants from other countries, hitherto has fully occupied the energies of our clergy and of our missionary organizations. Until quite recently, the Church in the United States was regarded as a missionary field. As such it has drawn upon Europe for recruits to the priesthood and the religious orders, and for financial assistance, which it owes so largely to the Society for the Propagation of the Faith.

The time now has come to show our grateful appreciation: "freely have you received, freely give" (Matt. 10:8). Wherever we turn in this whole land, the memory of the pioneers of our Faith confronts us. Let it not appeal in vain. Let it not be said, to our reproach, that American commerce has outstripped American Catholic zeal, or that others have entered in to reap where Catholic hands had planted, perchance where Catholic blood had watered the soil.

"Lift up your eyes, and see the countries, for they are white already to harvest" (John 4:35). Consider the nations that lie to the south of our own, and in them the manifold needs of religion. Look to the farther east where of old a Francis Xavier spread the light of the Gospel. Think of the peoples in Asia, so long estranged from the Faith which their forefathers received from the Apostles. In some of these lands, entire populations grow up and pass away without hearing the name of Christ. In others, the seed of God's word has been planted and there is promise of vigorous growth; but there is none to gather the fruit. "The harvest indeed is great, but the laborers are few" (Matt. 9:37).

"Pray ye therefore the Lord of the harvest that he send forth laborers into his harvest" (*ibid.*, 38). This, as the Holy Father reminds us, is our first obligation in regard to the missions. However eager the missionaries, they will labor in vain, unless God give the increase. This is also the appropriate object of the Apostleship of Prayer, whose members, to our great joy, are steadily becoming more numerous. Let all the faithful associate themselves with it and thus contribute, by their prayers at least, to the success of the missions.

In the next place, measures must be taken to increase the supply of laborers. They were few before the war; and now they are fewer. Unite with us, therefore, in praying that the special grace and vocation, which this holy enterprise demands, may be granted more abundantly. We gladly encourage young men who feel in their souls the prompting and desire for the missionary career. And we bless with cordial approval the efforts of those who, in our colleges and seminaries, develop this apostolic spirit and train up workers for the distant parts of the vineyard.

We appeal, finally, to the generosity of the faithful in behalf of the devoted men who already are bearing the heat of the day and the burden. They have given all. Let us help them at least to overcome the difficulties which the war has occasioned, and to develop the work which they are doing, with inadequate means, in their schools, orphanages, and other institutions. So shall we have some part in their labors, and likewise in their reward. For "he that reapeth receiveth wages, and gathereth fruit unto life everlasting; that both he that soweth and he that reapeth, may rejoice together" (John 4:36).

VOCATIONS

As the departments of Catholic activity multiply, and as each expands to meet an urgent need, the problem of securing competent leaders and workers becomes day by day more serious. The success of a religious enterprise depends to some extent upon the natural ability and character of those who have it in charge. But if it be truly the work of God, it must be carried on by those whom He selects. To His Apostles the Master said: "You have not chosen me: but I have chosen you, and have appointed you, that you should go and should bring forth fruit; and your fruit should remain" (John 15:16). Of the priesthood St. Paul declares: "Neither doth any man take the honor to himself, but he that is called of God" (Heb. 5:4). The same applies, in due proportion, to all who would enter the Master's service in any form of the religious state. And since our educational, charitable, and missionary undertakings are for the most part conducted by the priest, the Brother, and the Sister, the number of vocations must increase to supply the larger demand.

God, assuredly, in His unfailing providence, has marked for the grace of vocation those who are to serve Him as His chosen instruments. It lies with us to recognize these vessels of election and to set them apart, that they may be duly fashioned and tempered for the uses of their calling. To this end, we charge all those who have care of souls to note the signs of vocation, to encourage young men and women who manifest the requisite dispositions, and to guide them with prudent advice. Let parents esteem it a privilege surpassing all worldly advantage, that God should call their sons or daughters to His service. Let teachers also remember that, after the home, the school is the garden in which vocations are fostered. To discern them in time, to hedge them about with careful direction, to strengthen and protect them against worldly allurement, should be our constant aim.

In our concern and desire for the increase of vocations, we are greatly encouraged as we reflect upon the blessings which the Church has enjoyed in this respect. The generosity of so many parents, the sacrifices which they willingly make that their children may follow the calling of God, and the support so freely given to institutions for the training of priests and religious, are edifying and consoling. For such proofs of zeal, we return most hearty thanks to Him who is pleased to accept from His faithful servants the offerings of the gifts which He bestows.

The training of those who are called to the priesthood is at once a privilege and a grave responsibility. This holiest of all educational duties we entrust to the directors and teachers of our seminaries. Because they perform it faithfully, we look with confidence to the future, in the assurance that our clergy will be fully prepared for the tasks which await them. "That the man of God may be perfect, furnished to every good work" (2 Tim. 3:17) is the end for which the seminary exists. The model which it holds up is no other than Jesus Christ. Its course of instructions begin with St. Paul's exhortation: "holy brethren, partakers of the heavenly vocation, consider the apostle and high priest of our confession, Jesus" (Heb. 3:1); and it ends with the promise: "thou shalt be a good minister of Christ Jesus, nourished up in the words of faith and of the good doctrine which thou hast attained unto" (1 Tim. 4:6).

THE CATHOLIC PRESS

The functions of the Catholic Press are of special value to the Church in our country. To widen the interest of our people by acquainting them with the progress of religion throughout the world, to correct false or misleading statements regarding our belief and practice, and, as occasion offers, to present our doctrine in popular form — these are among the excellent aims of Catholic journalism. As a means of forming sound public opinion, it is indispensable. The vital issues affecting the nation's welfare usually turn upon moral principles. Sooner or later, discussion brings forward the question of right and wrong. The treatment of such subjects from the Catholic point of view is helpful to all our people. It enables them to look at current events and problems in the light of the experience which the Church has gathered through centuries, and it points the surest way to a solution that will advance our common interests.

The unselfish zeal displayed by Catholic journalists entitles them to a more active support than hitherto has been given. By its very nature the scope of their work is specialized; and, within the limitations thus imposed, they are doing what no other agency could accomplish or attempt, in behalf of our homes, societies, and schools.

In order to obtain the larger results and the wider appreciation which their efforts must deserve and which we most earnestly desire, steps must be taken to co-ordinate the various lines of publicity and secure for each a higher degree of usefulness. Each will then offer to those who are properly trained, a better opportunity for service in this important field.

At all times helpful to the cause of religion, a distinctively Catholic literature is the more urgently needed now that, owing to the development in our country and the progress of education, there has grown up a taste for reading and, among many of our people, a desire for accurate knowledge of the Church. In recent times, and notably during the past three decades, there has been a gratifying increase in the number of Catholic authors, and their activity has been prolific of good results. By the simple process of telling the truth about our faith and its practices, they have removed, to a considerable extent, those prejudices and erroneous views which so often hinder even fair-minded thinkers from understanding our position. As so much had been accomplished by individual writers in this and other countries, it was wisely thought that even greater benefit would accrue from their co-operation. The realization of this idea in the *Catholic Encyclopedia* has given us a monumental work, and opened to all inquirers a storehouse of information regarding the Church, its history, constitution, and doctrine. It has furthermore shown the value and power for good of united effort in behalf of a high common purpose; and we therefore trust that while serving as a means of instruction to our clergy and people, it will give inspiration to other endeavors with similar aim and effect, in every field of Catholic action.

THE OBVIOUS OUTCOME

The progress of the Church, which we have reviewed, has been no easy achievement. There have been trials and difficulties; and, as Christ predicted, there have been frequent attempts to hamper the Church just where and when it was doing the greatest good for our common humanity.

In the net result, however, the Church has been strengthened, to its own profit and to that of the world at large. In an age that is given to material pursuits, it upholds the ideals of the spiritual life. To minds that see only intellectual values, it teaches the lesson of moral obligation. Amid widespread social confusion, it presents in concrete form the principle of authority as the basis of social order. And it appears as the visible embodiment of faith and hope and charity, at the very time when the need of these is intensified by conditions in the temporal order.

SECULAR CONDITIONS

The temporal order, in the last thirty-five years, has undergone radical changes. It has been affected by movements which, though checked for a time or reversed, have steadily gathered momentum. Their direction and goal are no longer matters of surmise or suspicion. Their outcome is plainly before us.

During the first three decades of this period, the advance of civilization was more rapid and more general than in any earlier period of equal length. The sound of progress, echoing beyond its traditional limits, aroused all the nations to a sense of their possibilities, and stirred each with an ambition to win its share in the forward movement of the world. At the same time, the idea of a human weal for whose promotion all should strive and by whose attainment all should profit, seemed to be gaining universal acceptance. If rivalry here and there gave occasion for friction or conflict, it was treated as incidental: the general desire for harmony, apparently, was nearing fulfillment.

Toward this end the highest tendencies in the secular order were steadily converging. A wider diffusion of knowledge provided the basis for a mutual understanding of rights and obligations. Science, while attaining more completely to the mastery of nature, placed itself more effectually at the service of man. Through its practical applications, it hastened material progress, facilitated the intercourse of nation with nation, and thus lowered the natural barriers of distance and time. But it also made possible a fuller exchange of ideas, and thereby revealed to the various peoples of the earth that, in respect of need, aspiration, and purpose, they had more in common than generally was supposed. It helped them to see that however they differed in race, tradition, and language, in national temper and political organization, they were humanly one in the demand for freedom with equal right and opportunity.

As this consciousness developed in mankind at large, the example of our own country grew in meaning and influence. For a century and more, it had taught the world that men could live and prosper under free institutions. During the period in question, it has continued to receive the multitudes who came not, as in the early days, from a few countries only, but from every foreign land, to enjoy the blessings of liberty and to better their worldly condition. In making them its own, America has shown a power of assimilation that is without precedent in the temporal order. With their aid it has undertaken and achieved industrial tasks on a scale unknown to former generations. The wealth thus produced has been used in generous measure to build up institutions of public utility. Education, in particular, has flourished; its importance has been more fully recognized, its problems more widely discussed, the means of giving and obtaining it more freely supplied. While its aim has been to raise the intellectual level and thereby enhance the worth of the individual, experience has shown the advantage of organized effort for the accomplishment of any purpose in which the people as a whole, or any considerable portion, has an interest. Hence the remarkable development of associations which, though invested with no authority, have become powerful enough to shape public opinion and even to affect the making of laws. If, in some instances, the power of association has been directed toward ends that were at variance with the general good and by methods which created disturbance, there has been, on the whole, a willingness to respect authority and to abide by its decisions.

Thus, as it appears, the whole trend of human affairs was securing the world in peace. The idea of war was farthest from the minds of the peoples. The possibility of war had ceased to be a subject for serious discussion. To adjust their disputes, the nations had set up a tribunal. The volume of seeming prosperity swelled.

CATHOLIC WAR ACTIVITIES

Once it had been decided that our country should enter the war, no words of exhortation were needed to arouse the Catholic spirit. This had been shown in every national crisis. It had stirred to eloquent expression the Fathers of the Third Plenary Council.

"We consider the establishment of our country's independence, the shaping of its liberties and laws, as a work of special Providence, its framers 'building better than they knew,' the Almighty's hand guiding them. . . . We believe that our country's heroes were the instruments of the God of nations in establishing this home of freedom; to both the Almighty and to His instruments in the work we look with grateful reverence; and to maintain the inheritance of freedom which they have left us, should it ever — which God forbid — be imperilled, our Catholic citizens will be found to stand forward as one man, ready to pledge anew 'their lives, their fortunes and their sacred honor.' "

The prediction has been fulfilled. The traditional patriotism of our Catholic people has been amply demonstrated in the day of their country's trial. And we look with pride upon the record which proves, as no mere protestation could prove, the devotion of American Catholics to the cause of American freedom.

To safeguard the moral and physical welfare of our Catholic soldiers and sailors, organized action was needed. The excellent work already accomplished by the Knights of Columbus, pointed the way to further undertaking. The unselfish patriotism with which our various societies combined their forces in the Catholic Young Men's Association, the enthusiasm manifested by the organizations of Catholic women, and the eagerness of our clergy to support the cause of the nation, made it imperative to unify the energies of the whole Catholic body and direct them toward the American purpose. With this end in view, the National Catholic War Council was formed by the hierarchy. Through the Committee on Special War Activities and the Knights of Columbus Committee on War Activities, the efforts of our people in various lines were co-ordinated and rendered more effective, both in providing for the spiritual needs of all Catholics under arms and in winning our country's success. This unified action was worthy of the Catholic name. It was in keeping with the pledge which the hierarchy had given our Government: "Our people, now as ever, will rise as one man to serve the nation. Our priests and consecrated women will once again, as in every former trial of our country, win by their bravery, their heroism and their service new admiration and approval" (*Letter to the President*, April 18, 1917).

To our chaplains especially we give the credit that is their due for the faithful performance of their obligations. In the midst of danger and difficulty, under the new and trying circumstances which war inevitably brings, they acted as priests.

The account of our men in the service adds a new page to the record of Catholic loyalty. It is what we expected and what they took for granted. But it has a significance that will be fairly appreciated when normal conditions return. To many assertions it answers with one plain fact.

THE NATIONAL CATHOLIC WELFARE COUNCIL

In view of the results obtained through the merging of our activities for the time and purpose of war, we determined to maintain, for the ends of peace, the spirit of union and the co-ordination of our forces. We have accordingly grouped together, under the National Catholic Welfare Council, the various agencies by which the cause of religion is furthered. Each of these, continuing its own special work in its chosen field, will now derive additional support through general co-operation. And all will be brought into closer contact with the hierarchy, which bears the burden alike of authority and of responsibility for the interests of the Catholic Church.

Under the direction of the Council and, immediately, of the Administrative Committee, several departments have been established, each with a specific function, as follows:

The Department of Education, to study the problems and conditions which affect the work and development of our Catholic schools;

The Department of Social Welfare, to co-ordinate those activities which aim at improving social conditions in accordance with the spirit of the Church;

The Department of Press and Literature, to systematize the work of publication;

The Department of Societies and Lay Activities, to secure a more thoroughly unified action among our Catholic organizations.

For the development and guidance of missionary activity, provision has been made through The American Board of Catholic Missions, which will have in charge both the Home and the Foreign Missions.

The organization of these departments is now in progress. To complete it, time and earnest co-operation will be required. The task assigned to each is so laborious and yet so promising of results, that we may surely expect, with the divine assistance and the loyal support of our clergy and people, to promote more effectually the glory of God, the interests of His Church, and the welfare of our country.

LESSONS OF THE WAR

In order that our undertakings may be wisely selected and prudently carried on, we should consider seriously the lessons of the War, the nature of our present situation, and the principles which must guide the adjustment of all our relations.

Our estimate of the war begins, naturally, with the obvious facts: with the number of peoples involved, the vastness and effectiveness of their armaments, the outlay in treasure and toil, the destruction of life and the consequent desolation which still lies heavy on the nations of Europe. Besides these visible aspects, we know somewhat of the spiritual suffering — of the sorrow and hopelessness which have stricken the souls of men. And deeper than these, beyond our power of estimation, is the moral evil, the wrong whose magnitude only the Searcher of hearts can determine.

For we may not forget that in all this strife of the peoples, in the loosening of passion and the seething of hate, sin abounded. Not the rights of man alone but the law of God was openly disregarded. And if we come before Him now in thankfulness, we must come with contrite hearts, in all humility beseeching Him that He continue His mercies toward us, and enable us so to order our human relations that we may both atone for our past transgressions and strengthen the bond of peace with a deeper charity for our fellow men and purer devotion to His service.

We owe it to His goodness that our country has been spared the suffering and desolation which war has spread so widely. Our homes, our natural resources, our means of intercourse and the institutions which uphold the life of our nation have all been preserved. We are free, without let or hindrance, to go forward in the paths of industry, of culture, of social improvement and moral reform. The sense of opportunity has quickened us, and we turn with eagerness to a future that offers us boundless advantage.

Let us not turn hastily. Our recent experience has taught us innumerable lessons, too full and profound to be mastered at once. Their ultimate meaning a later generation will ponder and comprehend. But even now we can recognize the import of this conspicuous fact: a great nation, conscious of power yet wholly given to peace and unskilled in the making of war, gathered its might and put forth its strength in behalf of freedom and right as the inalienable endowment of all mankind. When its aims were accomplished, it laid down its arms, without gain or acquisition, save in the clearer understanding of its own ideals and the fuller appreciation of the blessings which freedom alone can bestow.

The achievement was costly. It meant interruption of peaceful pursuits, hardship at home, and danger abroad. Not one class or state or section, but the people as a whole had to take up the burden. This spirit of union and sacrifice for the commonweal found its highest expression in the men and women who went to service in distant lands. To them, and especially those who died that America might live, we are forever indebted. Their triumph over self is the real victory, their loyalty the real honor of our nation, their fidelity to duty the bulwark of our freedom.

To such men and their memory, eulogy is at best a poor tribute. We shall not render them their due nor show ourselves worthy to name them as our own, unless we inherit the spirit and make it the soul of our national life. The very monuments we raise in their honor will become a reproach to us, if we fail in those things of which they have left us such splendid example.

THE PRESENT SITUATION

We entered the war with the highest of objects, proclaiming at every step that we battled for the right and pointing to our country as a model for the world's imitation. We accepted therewith the responsibility of leadership in accomplishing the task that lies before mankind. The world awaits our fulfillment. Pope Benedict himself has declared that our people, "retaining a most firm hold on the principles of reasonable liberty and of Christian civilization, are destined to have the chief role in the restoration of peace and order on the basis of those same principles, when the violence of these tempestuous days shall have passed" (*Letter to the Hierarchy,* April 10, 1919).

This beyond doubt is a glorious destiny, far more in keeping with the aims of our people than the triumph of armies or the conquest of wider domain. Nor is it an impossible destiny, provided we exemplify in our own national life "the principles of reasonable liberty and of Christian civilization."

At present, however, we are confronted with problems at home that give us the gravest concern. Intent as we were on restoring the order of Europe, we did not sufficiently heed the symptoms of unrest in our country, nor did we reckon with movements which, in their final result, would undo both our recent achievement and all that America has so far accomplished.

These are due, partly, to the disturbance which war invariably causes, by turning men away from their usual occupations, by reducing production, increasing taxation and adding to the number of those who are dependent and helpless. The majority of the people do not realize to what an extent the necessities of war diverted industrial and other activities from their ordinary course. There naturally results irritation and impatience at the slowness with which reconstruction proceeds.

Deeper and more ominous is the ferment in the souls of men, that issues in agitation not simply against defects in the operation of the existing order, but also against that order itself, its framework and very foundation. In such a temper men see only the facts — the unequal distribution of wealth, power, and worldly advantage — and against the facts they rebel. But they do not discern the real causes that produce those effects, and much less the adequate means by which both causes and effects can be removed. Hence, in the attempt at remedy, methods are employed which result in failure, and beget a more hopeless confusion.

To men of clearer vision and calmer judgment, there comes the realization that the things on which they relied for the world's security have broken under the strain. The advance of civilization, the diffusion of knowledge, the unlimited freedom of thought, the growing relaxation of moral restraint — all these, it was believed, had given such ample scope to individual aims and desires that conflict, if it arose at all, could be readily and thoroughly adjusted.

The assumption is not borne out by the facts. On the contrary, as in the war, destruction was swifter and wider because of the progress of science, so our present situation is complicated by increased ability to plan, to organize, and to execute in any direction that may lead to any success. Education provided at the public expense can now be used as the strongest means of attacking the public weal; and to this end it will surely be used unless thinking and doing be guided by upright motives. The consciousness of power, quickened by our achievement in war but no longer checked by discipline nor directed to one common purpose, has aroused parties, organizations, and even individuals to a boldness of undertaking hitherto unknown. The result is an effort to press onward in the pursuit of self-appointed ends, with little regard for principles and still less for the altruism which we professed on entering the war.

On the other hand, it is true, intelligence, initiative, and energy have been exerted to accomplish higher and worthier aims. It was thought that the enthusiasm and eagerness for service which war had called forth, might easily be directed toward useful and needed reforms. With this persuasion for their impulse and guidance, various movements have been inaugurated either to uproot some evil or to further some promising cause.

Now it is obvious that neither the pursuit of lofty ideals nor earnest devotion to the general welfare, can do away with the fact that we are facing grave peril. Much less can we hide that fact from view by increasing the means and following the inclination to pleasure. No sadder contrast indeed can be found than that which appears between careless enjoyment in countless forms, and the grim struggle that is shaking the foundations of social existence. Craving for excitement and its reckless gratification may blind us to danger; but the danger is nonetheless real.

The practical conclusion which the present situation forces upon us is this: to bring order out of confusion, we must first secure a sound basis and then build up consistently. Mere expedients no longer suffice. To cover up evil with a varnish of respectability or to rear a grand structure on the quicksand of error, is downright folly. In spite of great earnestness on the part of their leaders, reforms without number have failed, because they moved along the surface of life, smoothing indeed its outward defects, yet leaving the source of corruption within.

CHRIST AND THE CHURCH

One true reform the world has known. It was effected, not by force, agitation, or theory, but by a Life in which the perfect ideal was visibly realized, becoming the "light of men." That light has not grown dim with the passing of time. Men have turned their eyes away from it; even His followers have strayed from its pathway; but the truth and the life of Jesus Christ are real and clear today — for all who are willing to see. There is no other name under heaven whereby the world can be saved.

Through the Gospel of Jesus and His living example, mankind learned the meaning, and received the blessing, of liberty. In His person was shown the excellence and true dignity of human nature, wherein human rights have their center. In His dealings with men, justice and mercy, sympathy and courage, pity for weakness and rebuke for hollow pretense were perfectly blended. Having fulfilled the law, He gave to His followers a new commandment. Having loved His own who were in the world, He loved them to the end. And since He came that they might have life and have it more abundantly, He gave it to them through His death.

The Church which Christ established has continued His work, upholding the dignity of man, defending the rights of the people, relieving distress, consecrating sacrifice, and binding all classes together in the love of their Saviour. The combination of authority and reasonable freedom which is the principal element in the organization of the Church, is also indispensable in our social relations. Without it, there can be neither order nor law nor genuine freedom.

But the Church itself would have been powerless save for the abiding presence of Christ and His Spirit. "Without me, you can do nothing"; but again, "Behold I am with you all days." Both these sayings are as true today as when they were spoken by the Master. There may be philosophies and ideals and schemes of reform; the wise may deliberate and the powerful exert their might; but when the souls of men have to be reached and transformed to a better sense, that justice may reign and charity abound, then more than ever is it true that without Christ our efforts are vain.

THE SOURCES OF EVIL

Instructed by His example, the Church deals with men as they really are, recognizing both the capacities for good and the inclinations to evil that are in every human being. Exaggeration in either direction is an error. That the world has progressed in many respects is obviously true; but it is equally plain that the nature of man is what it was twenty centuries ago. Those who overlooked this fact were amazed at the outbreak of war among nations that were foremost in progress. But now it is evident that beneath the surface of civilization lay smoldering the passions and jealousies that in all time past had driven the nations to conflict. Pope Benedict expressed this truth when he pointed to the causes of war; lack of mutual good will, contempt for authority, conflict of class with class, and absorption in the pursuit of the perishable goods of this world, with utter disregard of things that are nobler and worthier of human endeavor (encyclical, *Ad beatissimi*, November 1, 1914).

These are the seed and prolific sources of evil. As tendencies perhaps, they cannot be wholly extirpated; but to justify them as principles of action, to train them into systems of philosophy and let them, through education, become the thought of the people, would be fatal to all our true interests. As long as the teaching of false theory continues, we cannot expect that men will act in accordance with truth. It is a mistake to suppose that philosophy has a meaning for only the chosen few who enjoy the advantage of higher education and leisurely thinking; and it is worse than a mistake to punish men for acting out pernicious ideas, while the development and diffusion of those same ideas is rewarded as advancement of knowledge. We surely need no further proof of the dangers of materialism, of atheism, and of other doctrines that banish God from His world, degrade man to the level of the brute, and reduce the moral order to a struggle for existence. Argument against such doctrines, or theoretical testing of their value, is superfluous, now that we see the result of their practical application. And while, with every legitimate means we strive, as we must, to uphold the rights of the public by the maintenance of order, let us be fully convinced that we are dealing with the final and logical outcome of false doctrine. Here again the source lies farther back. If we find that the fruit is evil, we should know what to do with the root.

THE FUNDAMENTAL ERROR

It cannot be denied that the growth of knowledge and its application to practical needs have made the earth a better habitation for man; many appear to consider it as his first and only abode. As the means of enjoyment are multiplied, there is an increasing tendency to become absorbed in worldly pursuits and to neglect those which belong to our eternal welfare. The trend of speculative thought is in the same direction; for while the development of science continually affords us evidence of law and order and purpose in the world about us, many refuse to acknowledge in creation the work of an intelligent author. They profess to see in the universe only the manifestation of a Power, whose effects are absolutely determined through the operation of mechanical forces; and they extend this conception to life and all its relations. But once this view is accepted, it is easy to draw the conclusion that the really decisive factor in human affairs is force. Whether by cunning or by violence, the stronger is sure to prevail. It is a law unto itself and it is accountable to none other, since the idea of a Supreme Lawgiver has vanished.

This indeed is the root evil whence spring the immediate causes of our present condition. God, from whom all things are and on whom all things depend, the Creator and Ruler of men, the source and sanction of righteousness, the only Judge who with perfect justice can weigh the deeds and read the hearts of men, has, practically at least, disappeared from the whole conception of life so far as this is dominated by a certain type of modern thought. Wherever this sort of thinking is taken as truth, there is set up a scheme of life, individual, social, and political, which seeks, not in the eternal but in the human and transitory, its ultimate foundation. The law of morals is regarded as a mere convention arranged by men to secure and enjoy the goods of this present time; and conscience itself as simply a higher form of the instinct whereby the animal is guided. And yet withal it lies in the very nature of man that something must be supreme, something must take the place of the divine when this has been excluded; and this substitute for God, according to a predominant philosophy, is the State. Possessed of unlimited power to establish rights and impose obligations, the State becomes the sovereign ruler in human affairs; its will is the last word of justice, its welfare the determinant of moral values, its service the final aim of man's existence and action.

God the Supreme Ruler

When such an estimate of life and its purpose is accepted, it is idle to speak of the supreme value of righteousness, the sacredness of justice, or the sanctity of conscience. Nevertheless, these are things that must be retained, in name and in reality: the only alternative is that supremacy of force against which humanity protests. To make the protest effectual, it is imperative that we recognize in God the source of justice and right; in His law, the sovereign rule of life; in the destiny which He has appointed for us, the ultimate standard by which all values are fixed and determined. Reverent acknowledgment of our dependence on Him and our responsibility to Him, acknowledgment not in word alone but in the conduct of our lives, is at once our highest duty and our strongest title to the enjoyment of our rights. This acknowledgment we express in part by our service of prayer and worship. But prayer and worship will not avail, unless we also render the broader service of good will which, in conformity with His will, follows the path of duty in every sphere of life.

As we are not the authors of our own being, so we are not, in an absolute sense, masters of ourselves and of our powers. We may not determine for ourselves the ultimate aim of our existence or the means of its attainment. God has established, by the very consti- tution of our nature, the end for which He created us, giving us life as a sacred trust to be administered in accordance with His design. Thereby He has also established the norm of our individual worth, and the basis of our real independence. Obedience to His law, making our wills identical with His, invests us with a personal dignity which neither self-assertion nor the approval of others can ever bestow. The man who bows in obedience to the law of his Maker rises above himself and above the world to an independence that has no bounds save the Infinite. To do as God commands, whatever the world may think or say, is to be free, not by human allowance but under the approval of Him whose service is perfect freedom.

In the light of this central truth, we can understand and appreciate the principle on which our American liberties are founded — "that all men are endowed by their Creator with certain inalienable rights." These are conferred by God with equal bounty upon every human being, and, therefore, in respect of life, liberty, and the pursuit of happiness, the same rights belong to all men and for the same reason. Not by mutual concession or covenant, not by warrant or grant from the State, are these rights established; they are the gift and bestowal of God. In consequence of this endowment, and therefore in obedience to the Creator's will, each of us is bound to respect the rights of his fellow men. This is the essential meaning of justice, the great law antecedent to all human enactment and contrivance, the only foundation on which may rest securely the fabric of society and the structure of our political, legal, and economic systems.

JUSTICE

The obligation to give every man his due is binding at all times and under all conditions. It permits no man to say, I will be just only when justice falls in with my aims, or furthers my interests; and I will refrain from injustice when this would expose me to failure, to loss of reputation, or to penalty enacted by law. The obligation is binding in conscience, that representative of God which He has established in our innermost selves, which requires our obedience not merely out of self-respect or as a matter of our preference, but as speaking in His name and expressing His mandate.

Let this spirit of justice and conscientious observance prevail in the dealings of man with man: it will soon determine what practices are honest, what methods are justified by the necessities of competition, by economic law, by opportunity of profit, by the silence of the civil law or the laxity of its administration. It will weigh in the same even balance the deeds of every man, whatever his station or power; and it will appraise at their true moral value all schemes and transactions, whether large or small, whether conducted by individuals or groups or complex organizations.

The same spirit of justice that condemns dishonesty in private dealings, must condemn even more emphatically any and every attempt on the part of individuals to further their interests at the expense of the public welfare. The upright citizen refuses as a matter of conscience to defraud his neighbor, to violate his pledges, or to take unfair advantage. Likewise, in his business relations with the community as a whole, whatever the character of his service, he is careful to observe the prescriptions of justice. He feels that if it is wrong to overreach or circumvent his brother in any matter, the wrong is not less but far more grievous when inflicted on the commonwealth.

ORIGIN OF AUTHORITY

The true remedy for many of the disorders with which we are troubled is to be found in a clearer understanding of civil authority. Rulers and people alike must be guided by the truth that the State is not merely an invention of human forethought, that its power is not created by human agreement or even by nature's device. Destined as we are by our Maker to live together in social intercourse and mutual co-operation for the fulfillment of our duties, the proper development of our faculties, and the adequate satisfaction of our wants, our association can be orderly and prosperous only when the wills of the many are directed by that moral power which we call authority. This is the unifying and co-ordinating principle of the social structure. It has its origin in God alone. In whom it shall be vested and by whom exercised is determined in various ways, sometimes by the outcome of circumstances and providential events, sometimes by the express will of the people. But the right which it possesses to legislate, to execute and administer is derived from God Himself. "There is no power but from God; and those that are, are ordained of God" (Rom. 13:1). Consequently, "he that resisteth the power, resisteth the ordinance of God" (*ibid.*, 2).

POWERS OF THE STATE

The State, then, has a sacred claim upon our respect and loyalty. It may justly impose obligations and demand sacrifices for the sake of the common welfare which it is established to promote. It is the means to an end, not an end in itself; and because it receives its power from God, it cannot rightfully exert that power through any act or measure that would be at variance with the divine law, or with the divine economy for man's salvation. As long as the State remains within its proper limits and really furthers the common good, it has a right to our obedience. And this obedience we are bound to render, not merely on grounds of expediency but as a conscientious duty. "Be subject of necessity, not only for wrath but also for conscience sake" (*ibid.*, 5).

The end for which the State exists and for which authority is given it, determines the limit of its powers. It must respect and protect the divinely established rights of the individual and of the family. It must safeguard the liberty of all, so that none shall encroach upon the rights of others. But it may not rightfully hinder the citizen in the discharge of his conscientious obligation, and much less in the performance of duties which he owes to God. To all commands that would prevent him from worshiping the Creator in spirit and truth, the citizen will uphold his right by saying with the Apostles: "We ought to obey God rather than men" (Acts 5:29).

Where the State protects all in the reasonable exercise of their rights, there liberty exists. "The nature of human liberty," says Leo XIII, "however it be considered, whether in the individual or in society, whether in those who are governed or in those who govern, supposes the necessity of obedience to a supreme and eternal law, which is no other than the authority of God, commanding good and forbidding evil; and so far from destroying or even diminishing their liberty, the just authority of God over men protects it and makes it perfect" (encyclical, *Libertas praestantissimum*, June 20, 1888).

The State itself should be the first to appreciate the importance of religion for the preservation of the commonweal. It can ill afford at any time, and least of all in the present condition of the world, to reject the assistance which Christianity offers for the maintenance of peace and order. "Let princes and rulers of the people," says Pope Benedict XV, "bear this in mind and bethink themselves whether it be wise and salutary, either for public authority or for the nations themselves, to set aside the holy religion of Jesus Christ, in which that very authority may find such powerful support and defense. Let them seriously consider whether it be the part of political wisdom to exclude from the ordinance of the State and from public instruction, the teaching of the Gospel and of the Church. Only too well does experience show that when religion is banished, human authority totters to its fall. That which happened to the first of our race when he failed in his duty to God, usually happens to nations as well. Scarcely had the will in him rebelled against God when the passions arose in rebellion against the will; and likewise, when the rulers of the people disdain the authority of God, the people in turn despise the authority of men. There remains, it is true, the usual expedient of suppressing rebellion by force; but to what effect? Force subdues the bodies of men, not their souls" (encyclical, *Ad beatissimi*, November 1, 1914).

CHARITY

The spiritual endowment of man, his rights, and his liberties have their source in the goodness of God. Infinitely just as Ruler of the world, He is infinitely good as Father of mankind. He uses His supreme authority to lay upon men the commandment of love. "Thou shalt love the Lord thy God with thy whole heart, and with thy whole soul, and with thy whole mind. This is the greatest and the first commandment. And the second is like to this: thou shalt love thy neighbor as thyself" (Matt. 22:37–39).

Let us not persuade ourselves that we have fully complied with the divine law in regard to our relations with our fellow men, when we have carefully discharged all the obligations of justice. For its safeguard and completion, the stern law of justice looks to the gentler but nonetheless obligatory law of charity. Justice presents our fellow man as an exacting creditor, who rightly demands the satisfaction of his rightful claims. Charity calls on us as children of the one universal family whose Father is God, to cherish for one another active brotherly love second only to the love which we owe to Him. "It is not enough," says St. Thomas, "that peace and concord reign among the citizens: love also must prevail. Justice prevents them from injuring one another; it does not require them to help one another. Yet it often happens that some need aid which falls under no obligation of justice. Here charity steps in and summons us to further service in the name of the love we owe to God" (*Contra Gentes,* III, 129). Though different in kind from justice, the precept of charity imposes duties which we may not disregard. To love the neighbor is not simply a matter of option or a counsel which they may follow who aim at moral perfection: it is a divine command that is equally binding on all. It extends beyond kindred and friends to include all men, and it obligates us in thought and will no less than in outward action.

As commonly understood, charity is manifested in deeds that tend to the relief of suffering in any of its various forms, or that provide opportunities of advancement for those who have none, or that add somewhat to the scant pleasure of many laborious lives. And these beyond question are deeds that deserve all praise. But it is in the source whence they come, in the good will which prompts them, that the essence of charity consists. We may love others from a sense of our common humanity, from sympathy, from natural pity for pain and distress. Yet this benevolence is securely based and immeasurably ennobled, when it is quickened with the higher motive of love for God, the heavenly Father. Then the pale form of altruism or humanitarianism is replaced by the divine presence of charity.

By its very nature, charity is a social virtue. Wherever a social group is formed — in the home, the community, the civic association

— good will is a necessity. It is charity rather than justice that overcomes selfishness, casts out rancor, forbids hatred, clears away misunderstanding, leads to reconciliation. After justice has rendered impartial decision, it is charity that brings men back to fellowship. And if at times it be fitting that mercy should season justice, the quality of mercy itself is but charity touched to compassion.

THE LAW OF THE GOSPEL

The law of charity is essentially the law of the Gospel, the "new commandment" which Jesus gave His disciples. It is the distinctive badge of the Christian: "By this shall all men know that you are my disciples, if you have love one for another" (John 13:35). And more than this: the Incarnation itself was evidence of the divine good will toward men: "By this hath the charity of God appeared toward us, because God hath sent his only begotten Son into the world that we may live by him" (1 John 4:9).

It is therefore significant that, as the world moves farther away from Christ and loses the spirit of His teaching, there should be less and less of the charity which He would have His disciples to practice. On the other hand, we, as Christians, must ask ourselves whether we have so fully observed the "new commandment" of love as to leave the world without excuse for its unbelief. There are countless forms of charity which seek no publicity and ask no earthly reward: these the world could hardly be expected to know. But it cannot help seeing such evidences of love as appear in the ordinary conduct of genuine Christians, in their daily intercourse, their speech and habits of thought. That men in exceptional conditions should rise to great heights of self-sacrifice is proof indeed of a natural disposition, which may remain latent until it is stirred into action by sudden disaster or national peril; then it becomes heroic. Charity, however, does not wait for such occasions; it finds its opportunity in season, and out of season, and it makes heroes of men in peace no less than in war. This, then, should be our concern, this constant exercise of good will toward all men, that they may see in us the disciples of Christ and be led to Him through the power of love.

SOCIAL RELATIONS

The security of the nation and the efficiency of government for the general weal depend largely upon the standards which are adopted, and the practices which are admitted, in social relations.

This is characteristic of a democracy, where the makers of law are commissioned to do the will of the people. In matters pertaining to morality, legislation will not rise above the level established by the general tone and tenor of society. It is necessary, then, for the preservation of national life, that social morality, in its usage and sanction, be sound and steadfast and pure.

MARRIAGE

This aim can be accomplished only by reaching the sources in which life has its origin, and from which the individual character receives its initial direction. As the family is the first social group, it is also the center whose influence permeates the entire social body. And since family life takes its rise from the union of husband and wife, the sanctity of marriage and of marital relations is of prime importance for the purity of social relations.

The esteem in which marriage is held furnishes an index of a people's morality. If honor and respect be due an institution in proportion to its sacredness, its significance for human happiness and the measure of responsibility which it implies, marriage must claim the reverence of every mind that is capable of paying tribute to anything good. A lowering of the general estimate is a symptom of moral decline.

That such a lowering has taken place is due, in part, to the disregard of those requirements which even the prospect of marriage imposes. While emphasis is laid, and rightly, upon physical qualifications, not sufficient importance is attached to moral fitness, the real basis of marital happiness.

It is essential, in the first place, that clean living before marriage be equally obligatory on men and women. The toleration of vicious courses in one party while the other is strictly held to the practice of virtue, may rest on convention or custom; but it is ethically false, and it is plainly at variance with the law of God, which enjoins personal purity upon each and all.

Those who contemplate marriage should further make sure that their motives are upright. Where the dominant aim is selfish, where choice is controlled by ambition or greed, and where superficial qualities are preferred to character, genuine love is out of the question: such marriages are bargains rather than unions, and their only result is discord.

The same consequence may be expected from one-sided views of the marital relation. It is a vain idealism that anticipates joy in perfection, but takes no thought of the mutual forbearance which is constantly needed, or of the courage which trial demands, or of the serious obligations which family life implies. Illusion in such matters is the worst kind of ignorance.

On the other hand, it is idealism of the truest and most practical sort that sees in marriage the divinely appointed plan for co-operating with the Creator in perpetuating the race, and that accepts the responsibility of bringing children into the world, who may prove either a blessing or a curse to society at large.

Where such ideals prevail, the fulfillment of marital duties occasions no hardship. Neither is there any consideration for the fraudulent prudence that would improve upon nature by defeating its obvious purpose, and would purify life by defiling its source. The selfishness which leads to race suicide, with or without the pretext of bettering the species, is, in God's sight, "a detestable thing" (Gen. 38:10). It is the crime of individuals for which, eventually, the nation must suffer. The harm which it does cannot be repaired by social service, nor offset by pretended economic or domestic advantage. On the contrary, there is joy in the hope of offspring, for "the inheritance of the Lord are children; and his reward, the fruit of the womb" (Ps. 126). The bond of love is strengthened, fresh stimulus is given to thrift and industrious effort, and the very sacrifices which are called for become sources of blessing.

For the Christian the performance of these duties is lightened by the fact that marriage is not a mere contract: it is a sacrament and therefore, in the truest sense, a holy estate. It sanctifies the union of husband and wife, and supplies them with graces that enable them to fulfill their obligations. Hence it is that the Church invests the celebration of marriage with a solemnity becoming its sacramental importance, performs the sacred rite at the foot of the altar, and unites it in the nuptial Mass with the sublimest of religious functions.

Originating in such solemn circumstances, the family life receives, at its very inception, a blessing and a consecration. The "sacredness of home" has a definite meaning, deeper than its natural privacy, its intimacy and inviolability: the home is sacred because it is established with God's benediction to carry out His purpose in regard to mankind.

Public authority and social sanction unite to safeguard the home, to protect its rights and condemn their violation. But its strongest defense is in the keeping of those who make it, in their mutual fidelity and careful observance of their respective duties. These alone can ward off temptation and forestall the intrusion from without of influences which, through treachery, bring about ruin.

There is need of greater vigilance in protecting the home at this time, owing to conditions which tend to weaken its influence. The demands of industry, of business, and of social intercourse subject the family tie to a strain that becomes more severe as civilization advances. Parents who are sensible of their obligations, will exert themselves to meet external pressure by making the home more attractive. They will set their children the example of giving home their first consideration. And while they contribute their share of service and enjoyment as their social position requires, they will not neglect their children for the sake of amusement or pleasure.

In this matter we appeal with special earnestness to Catholic mothers, whose position in the home gives them constant opportunity to realize its needs and provide for its safety. Let them take to heart the words of Holy Scripture in praise of the virtuous woman: "Strength and beauty are her clothing. . . . She hath opened her mouth in wisdom and the law of clemency is on her tongue. She hath looked well to the paths of her house and hath not eaten her bread in idleness. Her children rose up and called her blessed; her husband, and he praised her" (Prov. 31:25–28). The home that is ruled by such a woman has nothing to fear in the way of domestic trouble.

DIVORCE

Of itself and under normal conditions, marital love endures through life, growing in strength as time passes and renewing its tenderness in the children that are its pledges. The thought of separation even by death is repugnant, and nothing less than death can weaken the bond. No sane man or woman regards divorce as a good thing; the most that can be said in its favor is that, under given circumstances, it affords relief from intolerable evil.

Reluctantly, the Church permits limited divorce: the parties are allowed for certain cause to separate, though the bond continues in force and neither may contract a new marriage while the other is living. But absolute divorce which severs the bond, the Church does not and will not permit.

We consider the growth of the divorce evil an evidence of moral decay and a present danger to the best elements in our American life. In its causes and their revelation by process of law, in its

results for those who are immediately concerned and its suggestion
to the minds of the entire community, divorce is our national scandal.
It not only disrupts the home of the separated parties, but it also
leads others who are not yet married, to look upon the bond as a
trivial circumstance. Thus, through the ease and frequency with
which it is granted, divorce increases with an evil momentum until
it passes the limits of decency and reduces the sexual relation to
the level of animal instinct.

This degradation of marriage, once considered the holiest of human
relations, naturally tends to the injury of other things whose efficacy
ought to be secured, not by coercion, but by the freely given respect
of a free people. Public authority, individual rights and even the
institutions on which liberty depends, must inevitably weaken. Hence
the importance of measures and movements which aim at checking
the spread of divorce. It is to be hoped that they will succeed;
but an effectual remedy cannot be found or applied, unless we aim
at purity in all matters of sex, restore the dignity of marriage, and
emphasize its obligations.

Social Intercourse

By divine ordinance, each human being becomes a member of the
larger social group, and in due course enters into social relations.
These are, and should be, a means of promoting good will and
an occasion for the practice of many virtues, notably of justice
and charity.

That social enjoyment is quite compatible with serious occupation and with devotion to the public good is evident from the
services rendered during the war by all classes of people, and
especially by those who gave up their comfort and ease in obedience
to the call of their country. Let this same spirit prevail in time
of peace and set reasonable limits to the pursuit of pleasure. With
the tendency to excess and the craving for excitement, there comes
a willingness to encourage in social intercourse abuses that would
not be tolerated in the privacy of home. For the sake of notoriety,
the prescriptions of plain decency are often set aside, and even the
slight restraints of convention are disregarded. Fondness for display
leads to lavish expenditure, which arouses the envy of the less
fortunate classes, spurs them to a foolish imitation, and eventually
brings about conflict between the rich and the poor.

Though many of these abuses are of short duration, their effect
is nonetheless harmful: they impair the moral fiber of our people

and render them unfit for liberty. The plainest lessons of history show that absorption in pleasure is fatal to free institutions. Nations which had conquered the world were unable to prevent their own ruin, once corruption had sapped their vitality. Our country has triumphed in its struggle beyond the sea; let it beware of the enemy lurking within.

There should be no need of legal enactments to improve our social relations, and there will be none, if only we act on the principle that each of us is in duty bound to set good example. Society, no less than its individual members, is subject to God's law. Neither convention nor fashion can justify sin. And if we are prompt to remove the causes of bodily disease, we must be just as energetic in banishing moral contagion.

"Ye are the salt of the earth: but if the salt lose its savour, wherewith shall it be salted?" (Matt. 5:13.) Let Catholics in particular reflect on this saying, and keep it before their minds under all circumstances, whether at home or abroad. Each in his own social sphere has a mission to perform, sometimes by explaining or defending the faith, sometimes by condemning what is wrong, but always by doing what is right. It is the eloquence of deeds that convinces where words are of no avail. The light is silent. "So let your light shine before men, that they may see your good works and glorify your Father who is in heaven" (Matt. 5:16).

WOMAN'S INFLUENCE

In society, as in the home, the influence of woman is potent. She rules with the power of gentleness, and, where men are chivalrous, her will is the social law. To use this power and fashion this law in suchwise that the world may be better because of her presence is a worthy ambition. But it will not be achieved by devices that arouse the coarser instincts and gratify vanity at the expense of decency. There will be less ground to complain of the wrong inflicted on women, when women themselves maintain their true dignity. "Favor is deceitful and beauty is vain; the woman that feareth the Lord, she shall be praised" (Prov. 31:30).

The present tendency in all civilized countries is to give woman a larger share in pursuits and occupations that formerly were reserved to men. The sphere of her activity is no longer confined to the home or to her social environment; it includes the learned professions, the field of industry and the forum of political life. Her ability to meet the hardest of human conditions has been tested by the experience of war; and the world pays tribute, rightfully, to her patriotic spirit, her courage, and her power of restoring what the havoc of war had well-nigh destroyed.

Those same qualities are now to undergo a different sort of trial; for woman, by engaging in public affairs, accepts, with equal rights, an equal responsibility. So far as she may purify and elevate our political life, her use of the franchise will prove an advantage; and this will be greater if it involve no loss of the qualities in which woman excels. Such a loss would deprive her of the influence which she wields in the home, and eventually defeat the very purpose for which she has entered the public arena. The evils that result from wrong political practice must surely arouse apprehension, but what we have chiefly to fear is the growth of division that tends to breed hatred. The remedy for this lies not in the struggle of parties, but in the diffusion of good will. To reach the hearts of men and take away their bitterness, that they may live henceforth in fellowship one with another — this is woman's vocation in respect of public affairs, and the service which she by nature is best fitted to render.

INDUSTRIAL RELATIONS

In 1891, Pope Leo XIII published his encyclical, *Rerum Novarum,* a document which shows the insight of that great Pontiff into the industrial conditions of the time, and his wisdom in pointing out the principles needed for the solving of economic problems. "That the spirit of revolutionary change which has long been disturbing the nations of the world, should have passed beyond the sphere of politics and made its influence felt in the cognate sphere of practical economics, is not surprising. The elements of the conflict now raging are unmistakable, in the vast expansion of industrial pursuits and the marvelous discoveries of science; in the changed relations between masters and workmen; in the enormous fortunes of some few individuals and the utter poverty of the masses; in the increased self-reliance and closer mutual combination of the working classes; as also, finally, in the prevailing moral degeneracy. The momentous gravity of the state of things now obtaining fills every mind with painful apprehension; wise men are discussing it; practical men are proposing schemes; popular meetings, legislatures and rulers of nations are all busied with it — and actually there is no question that has taken a deeper hold on the public mind."

How fully these statements apply to our present situation, must be clear to all who have noted the course of events during the year just elapsed. The war indeed has sharpened the issues and intensified the conflict that rages in the world of industry; but the elements, the parties, and their respective attitudes are practically unchanged. Unchanged also are the principles which must be applied if order is to be restored and placed on such a permanent basis that our people may continue their peaceful pursuits without dread of further disturbance. So far as men are willing to accept those principles as the common ground on which all parties may meet and adjust their several claims, there is hope of a settlement without the more radical measures which the situation seemed but lately to be forcing on public authority. But in any event, the agitation of the last few months should convince us that something more is needed than temporary arrangements or local readjustments. The atmosphere must be cleared so that, however great the difficulties which presently block the way, men of good will may not, through erroneous preconceptions, go stumbling on from one detail to another, thus adding confusion to darkness of counsel.

NATURE OF THE QUESTION

"It is the opinion of some," says Pope Leo XIII, "and the error is already very common, that the social question is merely an economic one, whereas in point of fact, it is first of all a moral and religious matter, and for that reason its settlement is to be sought mainly in the moral law and the pronouncements of religion" (apostolic letter, *Graves de communi*, January 18, 1901). These words are as pertinent and their teaching as necessary today as they were nineteen years ago. Their meaning, substantially, has been reaffirmed by Pope Benedict XV in his recent statement that "without justice and charity there will be no social progress." The fact that men are striving for what they consider to be their rights puts their dispute on a moral basis; and wherever justice may lie, whichever of the opposing claims may have the better foundation, it is justice that all demand.

In the prosecution of their respective claims, the parties have, apparently, disregarded the fact that the people as a whole have a prior claim. The great number of unnecessary strikes which have occurred within the last few months is evidence that justice has been widely violated as regards the rights and needs of the public. To assume that the only rights involved in an industrial dispute are those of capital and labor is a radical error. It leads, practically, to the conclusion that at any time and for an indefinite period, even the most necessary products can be withheld from general use until the controversy is settled. In fact, while it lasts, millions of persons are compelled to suffer hardship for want of goods and services which they require for reasonable living. The first step, therefore, toward correcting the evil is to insist that the rights of the community shall prevail, and that no individual claim conflicting with those rights shall be valid.

Among those rights is that which entitles the people to order and tranquillity as the necessary condition for social existence. Industrial disturbance invariably spreads beyond the sphere in which it originates, and interferes, more or less seriously, with other occupations. The whole economic system is so compacted together and its parts are so dependent one upon the other, that the failure of a single element, especially if this be of vital importance, must affect all the rest. The disorder which ensues is an injustice inflicted upon the community; and the wrong is the greater because, usually, there is no redress. Those who are responsible for it pursue their own ends without regard for moral consequences and, in some cases, with no concern for the provisions of law. When such a temper asserts itself, indignation is aroused throughout the country and the authorities are urged to take action. This, under given circumstances, may be the only possible course; but, as experience shows, it does not eradicate the evil. A further diagnosis is needed. The causes of industrial trouble are generally known, as are also the various phases through which it develops and the positions which the several parties assume. The more serious problem is to ascertain why, in such conditions, men fail to see their obligations to one another and to the public, or seeing them, refuse to fulfill them except under threat and compulsion.

MUTUAL OBLIGATIONS

"The great mistake in regard to the matter now under consideration is to take up with the notion that class is naturally hostile to class, and that the wealthy and the workingmen are intended by nature to live in mutual conflict" (*Rerum Novarum*). On the contrary, as Pope Leo adds, "Each needs the other: Capital cannot do without Labor, nor Labor without Capital. Religion is a powerful agency in drawing the rich and the bread-winner together, by reminding each class of its duties to the other and especially of the obligation of justice. Religion teaches the laboring man and the artisan to carry out honestly and fairly all equitable agreements freely arranged, to refrain from injuring person or property, from using violence and creating disorder. It teaches the owner and employer that the laborer is not their bondsman, that in every man they must respect his dignity and worth as a man and as a Christian; that labor is not a thing to be ashamed of, if we listen to right reason and to Christian philosophy, but is an honorable calling, enabling a man to sustain his life in a way upright and creditable; and that it is shameful and inhuman to treat men like chattels, as a means for making money, or as machines for grinding out work." The moral value of man and the dignity of human labor are cardinal points in this whole question. Let them be the directive principles in industry, and they will go far toward preventing disputes. By treating the laborer first of all as a man, the employer will make him a better workingman; by respecting his own moral dignity as a man, the laborer will compel the respect of his employer and of the community.

The settlement of our industrial problems would offer less difficulty if, while upholding its rights, each party were disposed to meet the other in a friendly spirit. The strict requirements of justice can be fulfilled without creating animosity; in fact, where this arises, it is apt to obscure the whole issue. On the contrary, a manifest desire to win over, rather than drive, the opponent to the acceptance of equitable terms, would facilitate the recognition of claims which are founded in justice. The evidence of such a disposition would break down the barriers of mistrust and set up in their stead the bond of good will. Not an armistice but a conciliation would result; and this would establish all parties in the exercise of their rights and the cheerful performance of their duties.

Respective Rights

The right of labor to organize, and the great benefit to be derived from workingmen's associations, was plainly set forth by Pope Leo XIII. In this connection, we would call attention to two rights, one of employees and the other of employers, the violation of which contributes largely to the existing unrest and suffering. The first is the right of the workers to form and maintain the kind of organization that is necessary and that will be most effectual in securing their welfare. The second is the right of employers to the faithful observance by the labor unions of all contracts and agreements. The unreasonableness of denying either of these rights is too obvious to require proof or explanation.

A dispute that cannot be adjusted by direct negotiation between the parties concerned should always be submitted to arbitration. Neither employer nor employee may reasonably reject this method on the ground that it does not bring about perfect justice. No human institution is perfect or infallible; even our courts of law are sometimes in error. Like the law court, the tribunal of industrial arbitration provides the nearest approach to justice that is practically attainable; for the only alternative is economic force, and its decisions have no necessary relation to the decrees of justice. They show which party is economically stronger, not which is in the right.

The right of labor to a living wage, authoritatively and eloquently reasserted more than a quarter of a century ago by Pope Leo XIII, is happily no longer denied by any considerable number of persons. What is principally needed now is that its content should be adequately defined, and that it should be made universal in practice, through whatever means will be at once legitimate and effective. In particular, it is to be kept in mind that a living wage includes not merely decent maintenance for the present, but also a reasonable provision for such future needs as sickness, invalidity, and old age. Capital likewise has its rights. Among them is the right to "a fair day's work for a fair day's pay," and the right to returns which will be sufficient to stimulate thrift, saving, initiative, enterprise, and all those directive and productive energies which promote social welfare.

Benefits of Association

In his pronouncement on Labor (*Rerum Novarum*) Pope Leo XIII describes the advantages to be derived by both employer and employee from "associations and organizations which draw the two classes more closely together." Such associations are especially needed at the present time. While the labor union or trade union has been, and still is, necessary in the struggle of the workers for fair wages and fair conditions of employment, we have to recognize that its history, methods, and objects have made it essentially a militant organization. The time seems now to have arrived when it should be, not supplanted, but supplemented by associations or conferences, composed jointly of employers and employees, which will place emphasis upon the common interests rather than the divergent aims of the two parties, upon co-operation rather than conflict. Through such arrangements, all classes would be greatly benefited. The worker would participate in those matters of industrial management which directly concern him and about which he possesses helpful knowledge; he would acquire an increased sense of personal dignity and personal responsibility, take greater interest and pride in his work, and become more efficient and more contented. The employer would have the benefit of willing co-operation from, and harmonious relations with, his employees. The consumer, in common with employer and employee, would share in the advantages of larger and steadier production. In a word, industry would be carried on as a co-operative enterprise for the common good, and not as a contest between two parties for a restricted product.

Deploring the social changes which have divided "society into two widely different castes" of which one "holds power because it holds wealth," while the other is "the needy and powerless multitude," Pope Leo XIII declared that the remedy is "to induce as many as possible of the humbler classes to become owners" (*Rerum Novarum*). This recommendation is in exact accord with the traditional teaching and practice of the Church. When her social influence was greatest, in the Middle Ages, the prevailing economic system was such that the workers were gradually obtaining a larger share in the ownership of the lands upon which, and the tools with which, they labored. Though the economic arrangements of that time cannot be restored, the under-lying principle is of permanent application and is the only one that will give stability to industrial society. It should be applied to our present system as rapidly as conditions will permit.

Whatever may be the industrial and social remedies which will approve themselves to the American people, there is one that, we feel confident, they will never adopt. That is the method of revolution. For it there is neither justification nor excuse under our form of government. Through the ordinary and orderly processes of education, organization, and legislation, all social wrongs can be righted. While these processes may at times seem distressingly slow, they will achieve more in the final result than violence or revolution. The radicalism, and worse than radicalism, of the labor movement in some of the countries of Europe, has no lesson for the workers of the United States, except as an example of methods to be detested and avoided.

Pope Benedict has recently expressed a desire that the people should study the great encyclicals on the social question of his predecessor, Leo XIII. We heartily commend this advice to the faithful and, in-deed, to all the people of the United States. They will find in these documents the practical wisdom which the experience of centuries has stored up in the Holy See and, moreover, that solicitude for the welfare of mankind which fitly characterizes the Head of the Catholic Church.

NATIONAL CONDITIONS

Our country had its origin in a struggle for liberty. Once established as an independent republic, it became the refuge of those who preferred freedom in America to the conditions prevailing in their native lands. Differing widely in culture, belief, and capacity for self-government, they had as their common characteristics the desire for liberty and the pursuit of happiness. Within a century, those diverse elements had been formed together into a nation, powerful, prosperous, and contented. As they advanced in fortune, they broadened in generosity; and today, the children of those early refugees are restoring the breath of life to the peoples of Europe.

These facts naturally inspire us with an honest pride in our country, with loyalty to our free institutions and confidence in our future. They should also inspire us with gratitude to the Giver of all good gifts, who has dealt so favorably with our nation: "He hath not done in like manner to every nation" (Ps. 147). Our forefathers realized this, and accordingly there is evident in the foundation of the Republic and its first institutions a deep religious spirit. It pervades the home, establishes seats of learning, guides the deliberation of lawmaking bodies. Its beneficent results are our inheritance; but to enjoy this and transmit it in its fullness to posterity, we must preserve in the hearts of the people the spirit of reverence for God and His law, which animated the founders of our nation. Without that spirit, there is no true patriotism; for whoever sincerely loves his country, must love it for the things that make it worthy of the blessings it has received and of those for which it may hope through God's dispensation.

We are convinced that our Catholic people and all our citizens will display an equally patriotic spirit in approaching the tasks which now confront us. The tasks of peace, though less spectacular in their accomplishment than those of war, are not less important and surely not less difficult. They call for wise deliberation, for self-restraint, for promptness in that emergency and energy in action. They demand, especially, that our people should rise above all minor considerations and unite their endeavors for the good of the country. At no period in our history, not even at the outbreak of war, has the need of unity been more imperative. There should be neither time nor place for sectional division, for racial hatred, for strife among classes, for purely partisan conflict imperiling the country's welfare. There should be no toleration for movements, agencies, or schemes that aim at fomenting discord on the ground of religious belief. All such attempts, whatever their disguise or pretext, are inimical to the life of our nation. Their ultimate purpose is to bring discredit upon religion, and to eliminate its influence as a factor in shaping the thought or the conduct of our people. We believe that intelligent Americans will understand how foreign to our ideas of freedom and how dangerous to freedom itself are those designs which would not only invade the rights of conscience but would make the breeding of hatred a conscientious duty.

Care for Immigrants

Such movements are the more deplorable because they divert attention from matters of public import that really call for improvement, and from problems whose solution requires the earnest co-operation of all our citizens. There is much to be done in behalf of those who, like our forefathers, come from other countries to find a home in America. They need an education that will enable them to understand our system of government and will prepare them for the duties of citizenship. They need warning against the contagion of influences whose evil results are giving us grave concern. But what they chiefly need is that Christian sympathy which considers in them the possibilities for good rather than the present defects, and, instead of looking upon them with distrust, extends to them the hand of charity. Since many of their failings are the consequence of treatment from which they suffered in their homelands, our attitude and action toward them should, for that reason, be all the more sympathetic and helpful.

Clean Politics

The constant addition of new elements to our population obliges us to greater vigilance with regard to our internal affairs. The power of assimilation is proportioned to the soundness of the organism; and as the most wholesome nutriment may prove injurious in cases of functional disorder, so will the influx from other countries be harmful to our national life, unless this be maintained in full vigor. While, then, we are solicitous that those who seek American citizenship should possess or speedily attain the necessary qualifications, it behooves us to see that our political system is healthy. In its primary meaning, politics has for its aim the administration of government in accordance with the express will of the people and for their best interests. This can be accomplished by the adoption of right principles, the choice of worthy candidates for office, the direction of partisan effort toward the nation's true welfare and the purity of election; but not by dishonesty. The idea that politics is exempt from the requirements of morality, is both false and pernicious: it is practically equivalent to the notion that in government there is neither right nor wrong, and that the will of the people is simply an instrument to be used for private advantage.

The expression or application of such views accounts for the tendency, on the part of many of our citizens, to hold aloof from politics. But their abstention will not effect the needed reform, nor will it arouse from their apathy the still larger number who are so intent upon their own pursuits that they have no inclination for political duties. Each citizen should devote a reasonable amount of time and energy to the maintenance of right government by the exercise of his political rights and privileges. He should understand the issues that are brought before the people, and co-operate with his fellow citizens in securing, by all legitimate means, the wisest possible solution.

PUBLIC OFFICE AND LEGISLATION

In a special degree, the sense and performance of duty is required of those who are entrusted with public office. They are at once the servants of the people and the bearers of an authority whose original source is none other than God. Integrity on their part, shown by their impartial treatment of all persons and questions, by their righteous administration of public funds and by their strict observance of law, is a vital element in the life of the nation. It is the first and most effectual remedy for the countless ills which invade the body politic and, slowly festering, end in sudden collapse. But to apply the remedy with hope of success, those who are charged with the care of public affairs, should think less of the honor conferred upon them than of the great responsibility. For the public official above all others, there is need to remember the day of accounting, here, perhaps, at the bar of human opinion, but surely hereafter at the judgment seat of Him whose sentence is absolute: "Give an account of thy stewardship" (Luke 16:2).

The conduct of one's own life is a serious and often a difficult task. But to establish, by the use of authority, the order of living for the whole people, is a function that demands the clearest perception of right and the utmost fidelity to the principles of justice. If the good of the country is the one real object of all political power, this is preeminently true of the legislative power. Since law, as the means of protecting right and preserving order, is essential to the life of the State, justice must inspire legislation, and concern for the public weal must furnish the single motive for enactment. The passing of an unjust law is the suicide of authority.

The efficacy of legislation depends on the wisdom of laws, not on their number. Fewer enactments, with more prudent consideration of each and more vigorous execution of all, would go far toward bettering our national conditions. But when justice itself is buried under a multiplicity of statutes, it is not surprising that the people grow slack in observance and eventually cease to respect the authority back of the laws. Their tendency then is to assume the function which rightly belongs to public executive power, and this they are more likely to do when aroused by the commission of crimes which, in their opinion, demand swift retribution instead of the slow and uncertain results of legal procedure. The summary punishment visited on certain offenses by those who take the law into their own hands may seem to be what the criminal deserves; in reality, it is a usurpation of power and therefore an attack upon the vital principle of public order. The tardiness of justice is surely an evil, but it will not be removed by added violations of justice, in which passion too often prevails and leads to practices unworthy of a civilized nation.

THE PRESS

For the removal of evil and the furtherance of good in the social and political spheres, an enlightened public opinion is requisite. The verdict rendered by the people must express their own judgment, but this cannot be safely formed without a knowledge of facts and an appreciation of the questions on which they have to decide. As the needed information ordinarily is supplied by the press, it is at once obvious that the publicist has a large measure both of influence and of responsibility. He speaks to the whole public, and often with an authority that carries conviction. In a very real sense he is a teacher, with the largest opportunity to instruct, to criticize, to fashion opinions, and to direct movements. When the use of this great power is guided by loyalty to truth, to moral principle and patriotic duty, the press is an agency for good second only to public authority. When through its influence and example, the people are led to respect law, to observe the precept of charity, to detest scandal and condemn wrongdoing, they may well regard the press as a safeguard of their homes and a source of purity in their social and political relations. From it they will learn whatsoever things are just and pure, whatsoever are lovely and of good report. But no man has a right to scatter germs of moral corruption any more than he has to pollute the water supply of a city. The press, which condemns the one as a criminal deed, cannot lend countenance, much less co-operation, to the other.

INTERNATIONAL RELATIONS

Though men are divided into various nationalities by reason of geographical position or historical vicissitude, the progress of civilization facilitates intercourse and, normally, brings about the exchange of good offices between people and people. War, for a time, suspends these friendly relations; but eventually it serves to focus attention upon them and to emphasize the need of readjustment. Having shared in the recent conflict, our country is now engaged with international problems and with the solution of these on a sound and permanent basis. Such a solution, however, can be reached only through the acceptance and application of moral principles. Without these, no form of agreement will avail to establish and maintain the order of the world.

Since God is the Ruler of nations no less than of individuals, His law is supreme over the external relations of States as well as in the internal affairs of each. The sovereignty that makes a nation independent of other nations does not exempt it from its obligations toward God; nor can any covenant, however shrewdly arranged, guarantee peace and security, if it disregard the divine commands. These require that in their dealings with one another, nations shall observe both justice and charity. By the former, each nation is bound to respect the existence, integrity, and rights of all other nations; by the latter, it is obliged to assist other nations with those acts of beneficence and good will which can be performed without undue inconvenience to itself. From these obligations a nation is not dispensed by reason of its superior civilization, its industrial activity, or its commercial enterprise; least of all, by its military power. On the contrary, a State which possesses these advantages is under a greater responsibility to exert its influence for the maintenance of justice and the diffusion of good will among all peoples. So far as it fulfills its obligation in this respect, a State contributes its share to the peace of the world: it disarms jealousy, removes all ground for suspicion, and replaces intrigue with frank co-operation for the general welfare.

The growth of democracy implies that the people shall have a larger share in determining the form, attributions, and policies of the government to which they look for the preservation of order. It should also imply that the calm deliberate judgment of the people, rather than the aims of the ambitious few, shall decide whether, in case of international disagreement, war be the only solution. Knowing that the burdens of war will fall most heavily on them, the people will be slower in taking aggressive measures, and, with an adequate sense of what charity and justice require, they will refuse to be led or driven into conflict by false report or specious argument. Reluctance of this sort is entirely consistent with firmness for right and zeal for national honor. If it were developed in every people, it would prove a more effectual restraint than any craft of diplomacy or economic prudence. The wisest economy, in fact, would be exercised in making the principles of charity and justice an essential part of education. Instead of planning destruction, intelligence would then discover new methods of binding the nations together; and the good will which is now doing so much to relieve the distress produced by war would be so strengthened and directed as to prevent the recurrence of international strife.

One of the most effectual means by which States can assist one another is the organization of international peace. The need of this is more generally felt at the present time when the meaning of war is so plainly before us. In former ages also, the nations realized the necessity of compacts and agreements whereby the peace of the world would be secured. The success of these organized efforts was due, in large measure, to the influence of the Church. The position of the Holy See and the office of the Sovereign Pontiff as Father of Christendom were recognized by the nations as powerful factors in any understanding that had for its object the welfare of all. A "Truce of God" was not to be thought of without the Vicar of Christ; and no other truce could be of lasting effect. The popes have been the chief exponents, both by word and act, of the principles which must underlie any successful agreement of this nature. Again and again they have united the nations of Europe, and history records the great services which they rendered in the field of international arbitration and in the development of international law.

The unbroken tradition of the Papacy, with respect to international peace, has been worthily continued to the present by Pope Benedict XV. He not only made all possible efforts to bring the recent war to an end, but was also one of the first advocates of an organization for the preservation of peace. In his letter to the American people on the last day of the year, 1918, the Holy Father expressed his fervent hope and desire for an international organization, "which by abolishing conscription will reduce armaments, by establishing international tribunals will eliminate or settle disputes, and by placing peace on a solid foundation will guarantee to all independence and equality of rights." These words reveal the heart of the Father whose children are found in every nation, and who grieves at the sight of their fratricidal struggle. That they were not then heeded or even rightly understood is but another evidence of the degree to which the passions aroused by the conflict had warped the judgment of men. But this did not prevent the Pontiff from intervening in behalf of those who were stricken by the fortunes of war, nor did it lessen his determination to bring about peace. To him and to his humane endeavor, not Catholics alone, but people of all creeds and nationalities, are indebted for the example of magnanimity which he gave the whole world during the most fateful years of its history.

EDUCATION

The interests of order and peace require that our domestic, social, and national relations be established on the solid basis of principle. For the attainment of this end, much can be done by wise legislation and by organized effort on the part of associations. We are confident that such effort and enactment will hasten the desired result. With their practical sense and their love of fairness, the American people understand that our national life cannot develop normally without adequate protection for the rights of all and faithful performance of duty by every citizen. And as they united to secure freedom from other nations, they now will strive together to realize their country's ideals.

Once more, however, we must emphasize the need of laying a sure foundation in the individual mind and conscience. Upon the integrity of each, upon his personal observance of justice and charity, depends the efficacy of legislation and of all endeavor for the common good. Our aim, therefore, should be, not to multiply laws and restrictions, but to develop such a spirit as will enable us to live in harmony under the simplest possible form, and only the necessary amount, of external regulation. Democracy, understood as self-government, implies that the people as a whole shall rule themselves. But if they are to rule wisely, each must begin by governing himself, by performing his duty no less than by maintaining his right.

NEED OF SOUND EDUCATION

Inasmuch as permanent peace on a sound basis is the desire of all our people, it is necessary to provide for the future by shaping the thought and guiding the purpose of our children and youth toward a complete understanding and discharge of their duties. Herein lies the importance of education and the responsibility of those to whom it is entrusted. Serious at all times, the educational problem is now graver and more complex by reason of the manifold demands that are made on the school, the changes in our industrial conditions, and, above all, by reason of the confusion and error which obscure the purpose of life and therefore of true education.

Nevertheless, it is mainly through education that our country will accomplish its task and perpetuate its free institutions. Such is the conviction that inspires much of the activity displayed in this field, whether by individuals or by organizations. Their confidence is naturally strengthened by the interest which is taken in the school, the enlarged facilities for instruction and the increased efficiency of educational work.

But these again are so many reasons for insisting that education shall move in the right direction. The more thorough it becomes, the greater is its power either for good or for evil. A trained intelligence is but a highly tempered instrument, whose use must depend on the character of its possessor. Of itself knowledge gives no guarantee that it will issue in righteous action, and much less that it will redound to the benefit of society. As experience too plainly shows, culture of the highest order, with abundance of knowledge at its command, may be employed for criminal ends and be turned to the ruin of the very institutions which gave it support and protection. While, therefore, it is useful to improve education by organizing the work of the schools, enriching the content of knowledge, and refining the methods of teaching, it is still more necessary to insure that all educational activity shall be guided by sound principles toward the attainment of its true purpose.

PRINCIPLES OF CATHOLIC EDUCATION

The Church in our country is obliged, for the sake of principle, to maintain a system of education distinct and separate from other systems. It is supported by the voluntary contributions of Catholics who, at the same time, contribute as required by law to the maintenance of the public schools. It engages in the service of education a body of teachers who consecrate their lives to this high calling; and it prepares, without expense to the State, a considerable number of Americans to live worthily as citizens of the Republic.

Our system is based on certain convictions that grow stronger as we observe the testing of all education, not simply by calm theoretic discussion, but by the crucial experience of recent events. It should not have required the pitiless searching of war to determine the value of any theory or system, but since that rude test has been so drastically applied and with such unmistakable results, we judge it opportune to restate the principles which serve as the basis of Catholic education.

First: The right of the child to receive education and the correlative duty of providing it are established on the fact that man has a soul created by God and endowed with capacities which need to be developed, for the good of the individual and the good of society. In its highest meaning, therefore, education is a co-operation by human agencies with the Creator for the attainment of His purpose in regard to the individual who is to be educated, and in regard to the social order of which he is a member. Neither self-realization alone nor social service alone is the end of education, but rather these two in accordance with God's design, which gives to each of them its proportionate value. Hence it follows that education is essentially and inevitably a moral activity, in the sense that it undertakes to satisfy certain claims through the fulfillment of certain obligations. This is true independently of the manner and means which constitute the actual process; and it remains true, whether recognized or disregarded in educational practice, whether this practice include the teaching of morality or exclude it or try to maintain a neutral position.

Second: Since the child is endowed with physical, intellectual, and moral capacities, all these must be developed harmoniously. An education that quickens the intelligence and enriches the mind with knowledge, but fails to develop the will and direct it to the practice of virtue, may produce scholars, but it cannot produce good men. The exclusion of moral training from the educative process is more dangerous in proportion to the thoroughness with which the intellectual powers are developed, because it gives the impression that morality is of little importance, and thus sends the pupil into life with a false idea which is not easily corrected.

Third: Since the duties we owe our Creator take precedence of all other duties, moral training must accord the first place to religion, that is, to the knowledge of God and His law, and must cultivate a spirit of obedience to His commands. The performance, sincere and complete, of religious duties, ensures the fulfillment of other obligations.

Fourth: Moral and religious training is most efficacious when it is joined with instructions in other kinds of knowledge. It should so permeate these that its influence will be felt in every circumstance of life, and be strengthened as the mind advances to a fuller acquaintance with nature and a riper experience with the realities of human existence.

Fifth: An education that unites intellectual, moral, and religious elements is the best training for citizenship. It inculcates a sense of responsibility, a respect for authority, and a considerateness for the rights of others which are the necessary foundations of civic virtue — more necessary where, as in a democracy, the citizen, enjoying a larger freedom, has a greater obligation to govern himself. We are convinced that, as religion and morality are essential to right living and to the public welfare, both should be included in the work of education.

There is reason to believe that this conviction is shared by a considerable number of our fellow citizens who are not of the Catholic faith. They realize that the omission of religious instruction is a defect in education and also a detriment to religion. But in their view the home and the Church should give the needed training in morality and religion, leaving the school to provide only secular knowledge. Experience, however, confirms us in the belief that instead of dividing education among these several agencies, each of them should, in its own measure, contribute to the intellectual, moral, and religious development of the child, and by this means become helpful to all the rest.

THE RIGHT TO EDUCATE

In order that the educative agencies may co-operate to the best effect, it is important to understand and safeguard their respective functions and rights. The office of the Church instituted by Christ is to "teach all nations," teaching them to observe whatsoever He commanded. This commission authorizes the Church to teach the truths of salvation to every human being, whether adult or child, rich or poor, private citizen or public official.

In the home with its limited sphere but intimate relations, the parent has both the right and the duty to educate his children; and he has both, not by any concession from an earthly power, but in virtue of a divine ordinance. Parenthood, because it means co-operation with God's design for the perpetuation of humankind, involves responsibility, and therefore implies a corresponding right to prepare for complete living those whom the parent brings into the world.

The school supplements and extends the educational function of the home. With its larger facilities and through the agency of teachers properly trained for the purpose, it accomplishes in a more effectual way the task of education for which the parent, as a rule, has neither the time, the means, nor the requisite qualifications. But the school cannot deprive the parent of his right nor absolve him from his duty, in the matter of educating his children. It may properly supply for certain deficiencies of the home in the way of physical training and cultivation of manners; and it must, by its discipline as well as by explicit instruction, imbue its pupils with habits of virtue. But it should not, through any of its ministrations, lead the parent to believe that having placed his children in school, he is freed from responsibility, nor should it weaken the ties which attach the child to parent and home. On the contrary, the school should strengthen the home influence by developing in the child those traits of character which help to maintain the unity and happiness of family life. By this means it will co-operate effectually with the parent and worthily discharge its function.

Since the child is a member not only of the family, but also of the larger social group, his education must prepare him to fulfill his obligations to society. The community has the right to insist that those who as members share in its benefits shall possess the necessary qualifications. The school, therefore, whether private or public as regards maintenance and control, is an agency for social welfare, and as such it bears responsibility to the whole civic body.

While the social aspect of education is evidently important, it must be remembered that social righteousness depends upon individual morality. There are virtues, such as justice and charity, which are exercised in our relations with others; but there is no such thing as collective virtue which can be practiced by a community whose individual members do not possess it in any manner or degree. For this very reason the attempt to develop the qualities of citizenship without regard for personal virtue, or to make civic utility the one standard of moral excellence, is doomed to failure. Integrity of life in each citizen is the only sure guarantee of worthy citizenship.

FUNCTION OF THE STATE

As the public welfare is largely dependent upon the intelligence of the citizen, the State has a vital concern in education. This is implied in the original purpose of our government which, as set forth in the preamble to the Constitution, is "to form a more perfect union, establish justice, ensure domestic tranquillity, provide for the common defense, promote the general welfare, and secure the blessings of liberty to ourselves and our posterity."

In accordance with these purposes, the State has a right to insist that its citizens shall be educated. It should encourage among the people such a love of learning that they will take the initiative and, without restraint, provide for the education of their children. Should they through negligence or lack of means fail to do so, the State has the right to establish schools and take every other legitimate means to safeguard its vital interests against the dangers that result from ignorance. In particular, it has both the right and the duty to exclude the teaching of doctrines which aim at the subversion of law and order and therefore at the destruction of the State itself.

The State is competent to do these things because its essential function is to promote the general welfare. But on the same principle it is bound to respect and protect the rights of the citizen and especially of the parent. So long as these rights are properly exercised, to encroach upon them is not to further the general welfare, but to put it in peril. If the function of government is to protect the liberty of the citizen, and if the aim of education is to prepare the individual for the rational use of his liberty, the State cannot rightfully or consistently make education a pretext for interfering with rights and liberties which the Creator, not the State, has conferred. Any advantage that might accrue even from a perfect system of State education would be more than offset by the wrong which the violation of parental rights would involve.

In our country, government thus far has wisely refrained from placing any other than absolutely necessary restrictions upon private initiative. The result is seen in the development of our resources, the products of inventive genius, and the magnitude of our enterprises. But our most valuable resources are the minds of our children, and for their development at least the same scope should be allowed to individual effort as is secured to our undertakings in the material order.

The spirit of our people in general is adverse to State monopoly, and this for the obvious reason that such an absorption of control would mean the end of freedom and initiative. The same consequence is sure to follow when the State attempts to monopolize education; and the disaster will be much greater inasmuch as it will affect, not simply the worldly interests of the citizen, but also his spiritual growth and salvation.

With great wisdom our American Constitution provides that every citizen shall be free to follow the dictates of his conscience in the matter of religious belief and observance. While the State gives no preference or advantage to any form of religion, its own best interests require that religion as well as education should flourish and exert its wholesome influence upon the lives of the people. And since education is so powerful an agency for the preservation of religion, equal freedom should be secured to both. This is the more needful where the State refuses religious instruction any place in its schools. To compel the attendance of all children at these schools would be practically equivalent to an invasion of the rights of conscience, in respect of those

parents who believe that religion forms a necessary part of education.
Our Catholic schools are not established and maintained with any
idea of holding our children apart from the general body and spirit
of American citizenship. They are simply the concrete form in which
we exercise our rights as free citizens, in conformity with the dictates
of conscience. Their very existence is a great moral fact in American
life. For while they aim, openly and avowedly, to preserve our Catholic
faith, they offer to all our people an example of the use of freedom
for the advancement of morality and religion.

OUR HIGHER DESTINY

The adjustment of the relations which we have considered is intended to further our welfare on earth. That mankind through freedom
and peace should advance in prosperity is a large and noble aim. But
it is not the ultimate aim of human existence; nor is it the highest
criterion whereby the value of all other ends and the worth of our
striving for any of them can be rightly determined. "For we have not
here a lasting city, but we seek one that is to come" (Heb. 13:14). We
look for "a City that hath foundations; whose builder and maker is
God" (*ibid.,* 11:10).

In the light of our higher destiny, we can judge and surely appraise
the things which men desire, which they hate or despise or fear. We
can see in their true perspective the manifold changes of the world,
and in their right proportion its losses and gains, its achievements
and failures. We can understand the confusion, the dismay, and the
dread of what may come, which have clouded the vision of many. For
these are the final result of the vast experiment whereby the world
would have proven its self-sufficiency. To those who imagine that
humanity has outgrown the need of religion, that result is bewildering.
To the Catholic mind it brings distress, but no perplexity. It repeats,
with an emphasis proportioned to the weight of disaster, the lesson
which history has written again and again as the meaning of such
upheavals.

"They shall perish, but thou shalt continue; and they shall all
grow old as a garment. And as a vesture shalt thou change them, and
they shall be changed; but thou art the self-same, and thy years shall
not fail" (Heb. 1:11, 12; Ps. 101:27, 28). What is declared in these
words, as regards the heavens and the earth, is likewise true of our
human affairs. And the more fully we realize that change is the law
of our existence, the more readily should we turn our thought, with
humble confidence, toward our Creator and His eternal law.

As we look upon the record which the past unfolds, we cannot but note that it is filled with the struggles of mankind, with their building up and tearing down, with searchings for truth which often end in illusion, with strivings after good which lead to disappointment. The very monuments which were reared to celebrate human triumph remain simply to tell of subsequent downfall. Not rarely the greatness of human achievement is learned from the vast extent of its ruins.

But above it all, standing out clearly through the mists of error and the grosser darkness of evil, is One, in raiment white and glistening, who has solved the problem of life, has given to sorrow and pain a new meaning, and, by dying, has overcome death: "Jesus Christ yesterday, and today; and the same forever" (Heb. 13:8).

There are numberless paths, but the Way is one. There are many degrees of knowledge, but only one Truth. There are plans and ideals of living, but in real fulfillment there is only one Life. For none other than He could say: "I am the way and the truth and the life" (John 14:6).

Pray, therefore, dearly beloved, that the spirit of Jesus Christ may abide with us always, that we may walk on His footsteps in justice and charity, and that the blessing of God may descend abundantly upon the Church, our country, and the whole American people.

Given at Washington, in conference, on the 26th day of September, in the year of our Lord, 1919.

In his own name and in the name of the hierarchy,

✝ JAMES CARDINAL GIBBONS,
Archbishop of Baltimore

2. THE HIERARCHY OF THE UNITED STATES

PASTORAL LETTER ON MEXICO*

December 12, 1926

The cardinals, archbishops, and bishops of the Catholic Church in the United States of America to the clergy and faithful — Peace and benediction in our Lord Jesus Christ, Teacher of the truth that makes us free.

Sympathy to those who suffer for conscience' sake has never been refused by the great heart of the American people. They, almost instinctively, sense all oppression to be a destroyer of unity at home, as well as an abundant source of the misunderstandings and hatreds that divide nations and peoples and injure the cause of international amity and world peace. If then we, as American bishops, had no other reason for issuing this pastoral than to show our deep sympathy with the suffering people of Mexico in the persecution now raging against religion in that country, it would be justified; but there are other reasons, carrying even greater weight and urgency, that make of this act a duty. They are found in the fact that Mexico is our neighbor — with all the power that propinquity gives to the force of good or evil example — a republic which it was intended should be modeled on lines similar to ours, and a nation with a Christian population whose devotion to the Catholic Church makes a special call upon the charity of the faithful everywhere, but more especially upon those of the United States.

Even stronger reasons for the issuing of this pastoral arise out of the higher considerations of duty to those principles upon which all just government must be founded, principles which guard rights conferred upon man, not by States, but by God Himself. None, much less bishops of the Church that holds the spiritual allegiance of almost the

---

* May be had in pamphlet form: N.C.W.C. Headquarters, Washington 5, D. C. Cf. also Nos. 22, 29, 31, 34, 58, 63.

entire Mexican population, can be indifferent when these vital principles are attacked as boldly and as cruelly as is being done in Mexico today. This duty of defense and protest, first and most properly, has been recognized by the bishops of Mexico themselves in admirably worded petitions against oppression as well as in timely, edifying, and intimate letters to their flocks. Their action may well be seconded by us, their brothers separated by national frontiers, but nevertheless bound to them in the bonds of a common faith, as well as by ties of fraternal charity made stronger in mutual understanding, esteem, and friendship.

We Speak in the Interests of Both Church and State

All the more do we feel an obligation to speak boldly and publicly on the religious persecution raging in Mexico, because the common Father of Christendom, Pius XI, Vicar of Jesus Christ, has urged the faithful of the whole world to unite with him in sympathy and prayer to God for the afflicted Church. He thus manifests at once his deep sorrow over her trials and his keen perception of the danger that this persecution threatens to "the peace of Christ in the Kingdom of Christ" everywhere. He who has made it plain that his dearest wish, as well as the supreme motive of all his official actions, is nothing less than the reign of the Prince of Peace over all hearts, and who offers a sick and disturbed world the remedy of the Master's teachings and the Master's love, has, by his timely appeal, recognized its gravity and the threat it carries to religion the world over.*

Yet another and still stronger motive urges us to speak. It is that the present conflict, as one part of a war against religion in Mexico which had its inception almost a century ago, to a greater degree than any preceding it comes from an attempt at nothing less than the destruction of the divine constitution of the Church by reducing her to the status of a State-controlled schismatical body, without the right to form, train, and educate her own clergy, to have a sufficient number of them for the care of souls, to find means for her support, to develop works in accord with her mission of charity and enlightenment, and to apply the teachings of the Gospel to the formation of a public conscience. Sad experience, as well as right reason, tells us what would follow the success of such an attempt, and what it would mean to Church as well as to State.

---

* The encyclical of Pius XI referred to by the Bishops is the *Iniquis Afflictisque*, of November 18, 1926. See *Acta Apost. Sedis*, 18 (1926), 465–477.

The Mexican Church thus controlled and bound, as the civil power seeks to control and bind her, nominally might be separated, but really would be a department of the political machinery of the State. Her dignities and offices would be the perquisites of politicians; her voice the changing voice of political action. She would be despised by her faithful and justly mocked by her enemies. Her bond of unity with the Church Universal would first be weakened and then snapped asunder. The Mexican government asks the Church to accept a slavery that could mean nothing today but an infection caught from evil surroundings, and tomorrow a decline into mortal sickness inevitably ending with her passing from the life of the Mexican people.

WE SPEAK AS AMERICANS AS WELL AS CATHOLICS

To the State would come no less evil results. With the check of religious influence gone, history for her also would be repeated. She would forget her dreams of democracy and actually become a despotism. Corruption would increase with power to confer ecclesiastical emoluments upon the unworthy. She would merit and receive the hatred of just men at home and the contempt of just men abroad. A "Holy Synod," doing the unholy work of despotism, would gradually absorb her strength and seize her power as a most convenient machinery of government. Whatever of good is in her ideals would be shattered on one of the oldest rocks that lie hidden in the waters of political life.

The question that we are considering then is vital both to the Church and to the State. However blind may be the advocates of such plans in government to their evils, the Mexican Church prefers, if she must, to perish defending her divine constitution and the religious rights of her people rather than to accept the alternative of a slavery that would mean the disgrace of faithlessness, as well as ultimate ruin to her spiritual mission. In fact, the Church in Mexico has no choice; for merely to continue her public religious functions under these oppressive and unjust conditions would be an open declaration that she had submitted to them, and thus had taken a first step toward divorcing herself from the unity of the Church Universal.

If, then, because of the fact that the persecution in Mexico is directed against all the principles of religion, we should speak as the servants of God; if, because it is unloosed particularly against the religion of the majority of the people of Mexico, we should speak as Catholics; there are grave reasons, too, why we have a duty to speak as Americans attached to the institutions of our country and loving them for the benefits they have conferred upon us all. The government of Mexico has, indeed, by its actions in our very midst, made it necessary that we should no longer guard silence, for it has carried its war on religion beyond its own boundaries through organized propaganda in many countries, but especially in our own.

WE CONSIDER THE MEXICAN GOVERNMENT IN THE LIGHT OF AMERICAN AND CHRISTIAN PRINCIPLES

Through its diplomatic and consular agents in the United States that government appeals to the American people to justify its actions. In consequence we have before us the extraordinary spectacle of a foreign government, not only filling our country with propaganda in favor of its own internal plans and policies, but even attempting to justify and defend, in our nation, laws and conduct at variance with fundamentals set down in imperishable documents by the Fathers of this Republic. Misinterpreting our good-natured tolerance for a neighbor still disturbed by consequences of many military upheavals, the government of Mexico has thus presumed to appeal to our fellow citizens for approval. This actually amounts to the submission of its case for judgment in a court beyond its own boundaries; pleading, not before its own citizens who, according to its Constitution, form the only court competent to pass upon it, but before strangers who claim no jurisdiction over their neighbor's political affairs, and whose only interest in them is a desire for the well-being of the people of Mexico and their own peace in amicable mutual relations. The government of Mexico cannot, therefore, object, under such circumstances, if the case it has thus presented for judgment be considered in the light of American principles, as embodied in our fundamental laws, and in the light of Christian principles, since it appeals for the sympathy of Christians; nor, since it claims great zeal for the advancement of education, if the statements it has presented in support of its pleading be submitted to the test of history. These are the things we purpose to do, so that, not only will our own citizens be fully informed of the interests at stake, but the Mexican people will not be without benefit of advocate before the court to which their rulers have actually but mistakenly appealed.

PART I

LIBERTY IN THE LIGHT OF THE AMERICAN AND MEXICAN CONSTITUTIONS

The government of Mexico bases its case upon repeated assurances that it is merely enforcing the Constitution and fundamental laws of the Mexican nation. It will not be out of place then to compare this Constitution and these laws with our own, at least in so far as they affect the right of conscience. In no better way can the points at issue be made clear.

The difference between the conception of civil and religious freedom upheld by the American Constitution and that of the makers and defenders of the present Constitution of Mexico will be best understood by contrasting the two instruments. This will show that only by slurring over or concealing the actual facts of the case can the Mexican government hope to secure the sympathy of thoughtful and unbiased Americans, whose ideas of civic justice and right are radically different from those expressed in Mexican law. The contrast will prove this without argument. Certainly there is no basis for argument, unless it be in an attempt, not to reconcile our policies with those of the Mexican government, but to prove that ours are wrong. In fact, what the government of Mexico actually asks us to do, in begging our sympathy and approval, is nothing less than to condemn the work of the Fathers of this Republic, register dissatisfaction with the Constitution they gave us, and demand its overthrow; for no American can accept the Mexican theory of government as being in accord with fundamental justice without repudiating his own traditions and ideals. The very audacity and boldness of the Mexican government in thus appealing to us for sympathy in favor of laws and conduct at variance with our most cherished political convictions has been, perhaps, the chief reason why the fact of their opposition to these convictions has been overlooked. Possibly it is for the same reason that some Christian people everywhere have overlooked also the fact that the present government of Mexico is making war on one of the essentials of Christianity, namely, liberty of conscience, on which Leo XIII clearly set forth the Christian position. "Another liberty," he writes, "is widely advocated, namely, liberty of conscience. If by this is meant that everyone may, as he chooses, worship God or not, it is sufficiently refuted by the arguments already adduced. But it may also be taken to mean that every man in the State may follow the will of God, and, from a consciousness of duty and free from every obstacle, obey His commands. This, indeed, is true liberty, a liberty worthy of the sons of God, which nobly maintains the dignity of man, and is stronger than all violence or wrong — a liberty which the Church has always desired and held most dear. This is the kind of liberty the apostles claimed for themselves with intrepid constancy, which the apologists of Christianity confirmed by their writings, and which the martyrs in vast numbers consecrated by their blood. And deservedly so; for this Christian liberty bears witness to the absolute and most just dominion of God over man, and to the chief and supreme duty of man toward God. It has nothing in common with a seditious and rebellious mind; and in no tittle derogates from obedience to public authority; for the right to command and to require obedience exists only so far as it is in accordance with the authority of God, and is within the measures that He has laid down. But when anything is commanded which is plainly at variance with the will of God, there is a wide departure from this divinely constituted order, and at the same time a direct conflict with divine authority; therefore, it is right not to obey."[1]

THE DIVINE MISSION OF THE CHURCH

In a thousand other passages this illustrious Pontiff, his predecessors and successors, have set forth Catholic teaching on this and kindred topics with which we are now concerned. The doctrines of the Church are not secrets. With her Master she can say, "In secret I have spoken nothing."[2] According to that teaching, it is God's will, contained in both His natural and positive law, which is the first law of life, public and private. To discover that will through the searching process of a sincere and enlightened conscience, using the means which God has furnished, and then to follow its lead is every man's native right and duty. "This is my beloved Son: hear ye him,"[3] is the burden or the message of God to the human race. Therefore do we cling to Christ as "the way, the truth and the life."[4] He in turn charges His Apostles and their successors with the task of continuing His mission of teaching and of sanctifying the coming generations. "He that heareth you heareth me and he that despiseth you despiseth me."[5] To them consequently the Catholic looks as to his authoritative guides in the pathway that leads to eternity. To these "dispensers of the mysteries of God"[6] the Catholic owes conscientious obedience in such matters as have been confided to their care by the chief Shepherd of our souls, who is Christ. Only by arbitrary interference outside its own independent proper sphere of action can the State obstruct the due fulfillment of the pastoral ministry; and this the Mexican government seeks to do, denying in effect the final authority of the will of God

---

[1] Encyclical, *Libertas Praestantissimum,* June 20, 1888.
[2] John 17:20.
[3] Matt. 17:5.
[4] John 14:6.
[5] Luke 10:16.
[6] 1 Cor. 4:1.

plainly expressed to man for his spiritual guidance, and by a bold act of arbitrary power invading its rights in favor of the State.

Passing from the consideration of the conception of civil and religious liberty in constitutions to the constitutions themselves, we are met with the plea of the Mexican government that it is doing no more than enforcing its own. Here, however, at the outset, it is confronted with two important facts: first, that, though the antireligious laws of the country date[7] from 1857, yet no government until now has ever attempted to give them full effect: and second, that, though these laws were reaffirmed and made more drastic in the Constitution of 1917, yet President Carranza himself suggested changing the clauses affecting religion,[8] and President Obregon never attempted to enforce all of them during the four years of his administration. These two facts show that it was tacitly recognized how far removed such laws were from justice and from the approval of the Mexican people. The appeal to the Constitution, however, does take our eyes off persons and, for the moment, directs attention to the written instrument by which such persons seek to justify their acts. It is in order, therefore, to inquire into the nature and purpose of a Constitution.

THE PURPOSE OF A CONSTITUTION

A written constitution is an instrument which enumerates and defines the rights and duties of government, distributes its powers, prescribes the manner of their exercise, and limits them to the end that the liberties of the citizens may be preserved. Since the purpose of government is to protect human rights, not to destroy them, it follows that the charter by which a government operates cannot contain a grant of unlimited power. For the exercise of such power would be tyranny, inasmuch as it would tend to destroy rights which both the natural and the positive laws of God place beyond the jurisdiction of men. Hence, in the commonly accepted American doctrine, a constitution vests the government with such rights and powers as are necessary for the proper exercise of its just functions, and at the same time forbids it to encroach upon rights of a higher order which come to men, not from the people, nor from the State, nor from any aggregation of States, but from the Creator of both men and States, almighty God. This conception is wholly in keeping with the teaching of the Catholic Church.

---

[7] Previous to this date, the State endeavored to make the bishops and priests political appointees, and to legislate in Church affairs.

[8] *Diario Official,* November 21, 1918. Bill to modify Article 3. *Ibid.,* December 17, 1918. Bill to modify paragraphs VII, VIII and XVI of Article 130.

There can be no possible doubt, then, that protection of the natural and inalienable rights of the individual is essential to the very notion of a constitution. Unlimited power would need no constitution, for a constitution is a guarantee of liberty, not an engine of tyranny. No such document, whatever its origin, can win respect or exact obedience when it destroys these rights or enacts statutes which make their exercise morally impossible. For such an instrument is not in accord with that right reason which vindicates man's natural rights. "Human law is law only by virtue of its accordance with right reason," says St. Thomas Aquinas, "and thus it is manifest that it flows from the eternal law. And in so far as it deviates from right reason it is called an unjust law; in such case it is no law at all, but rather a species of violence."[9]

MAN HAS INALIENABLE RIGHTS

This, indeed, is the force of the Declaration of Independence, a document rightly regarded by all Americans as the cornerstone of this government. With the signers, we hold certain truths "to be self-evident." We agree that "all men," Mexicans included, "are endowed by their Creator with certain unalienable rights; that among these are Life, Liberty, and the pursuit of Happiness. That to secure these rights governments are instituted among men. . . ." Plainly, then, these rights are held by every man, not by the tolerance or grant of any State, but by the immutable decree of almighty God. It is not within the authority of any government to destroy or to hamper them. On the contrary, it is the solemn duty of the government "to secure" them; and the government which attacks them must be repudiated by all right-minded men. In the words of St. Thomas, its action is not law "but rather a species of violence." On this teaching St. Thomas and the Declaration of Independence are in complete accord.

Now, while it is not easy, as the Supreme Court has recently declared, to enumerate all the rights which are comprehended under the primal right "to Life, Liberty and the pursuit of Happiness," it is certain, as the same court has held, in a very important case,[10] that among them is the right to worship almighty God according to the dictates of conscience. Let it be further observed that the constant and unvarying interpretation of the federal Constitution by the court bears out our contention that the government exists to protect the

---

[9] *Summa*, Ia, IIae, Q. xciii, Art. 3.
[10] Meyer *vs.* Nebraska, 262, U. S., 390.

citizen in the exercise of his natural and unalienable rights, and that it may enact no law which destroys them.

THE STATE MUST PROTECT THESE RIGHTS

Constantly, too, has the Catholic Church upheld this conception of government under whatever form it may be exercised. Unlimited power over the liberty of the citizen is not Christian teaching. It is not the teaching of the Fathers of this Republic. It is not the doctrine of our courts, which have again and again rejected it. To frame a constitution or to enact legislation which makes impossible man's enjoyment of his natural heritage of liberty is not within the legitimate power of any civil government, no matter how constituted. For this heritage descends to him by the natural law which "is coeval with mankind" and, since it "is dictated by God Himself," as Blackstone writes in his celebrated *Commentaries*,[11] "it is of course superior in obligation to any other. . . . No human laws are of any validity if contrary to this; and such of them as are valid derive their force and all their authority, mediately or immediately, from this original." The legislator, opposing the dictates of this law, cannot prescribe a course which is reasonable, or which is profitable to the community, and since his act in no way reflects the wisdom of the natural law, which is the wisdom of the Eternal Lawgiver, it is not law, and can impose no obligations upon any citizen. It merits respect from no just man, and least of all from Americans whose theory of government it outrages. Thus it is seen that the wisdom of Christian teaching has not failed to impress itself on the minds of distinguished men whose studies and writings on law have won for them deserved eminence before their fellows. In this connection we recall words written in our Pastoral of 1919: "The end for which the State exists, and for which authority is given it, determines the limit of its powers. It must respect and protect the divinely established rights of the individual and the family. It must safeguard the liberty of all, so that none shall encroach upon the rights of others. But it may not rightfully hinder the citizen in the discharge of his conscientious obligations, and much less in the performance of duties he owes to God."

MAN CANNOT SUSPEND GOD-GIVEN RIGHTS

These words are in accord with both the natural and the positive laws of God. They are in accord with the recognition of these laws by

---

[11] *Commentaries*, Intro., Sec. 2.

the founders of our Republic. To give practical effect to them the First Amendment to the Constitution, forbidding Congress to prohibit the free exercise of religion, was adopted, and by degrees a similar prohibition was inserted into the constitutions or bills of rights of the several states. These guarantees are more than part of the federal Constitution and of the constitutions of the respective states. They are part of the constitution of the rights of free men. The Church has never been in disaccord with them, for, while she has been careful always to safeguard peace and oppose discord by protecting legitimate authority, she has not failed to point out to the civil authority its duties to the people as well as its responsibilities to God. Through her theologians, among whom may be cited St. Thomas Aquinas, Blessed Robert Bellarmine, and Suarez, she has indicated the rights of the people with which no State and no ruler may interfere, insisting that they are beyond and above the statutes made by kings and senates, because deriving their sanction, not from the will and power of earthly authority, but from the authority of God and the dignity of man as an intelligent being.

It is not possible to hold that modern progress has antiquated or set aside this truth of the divine source of all authority, for it is not within man's power to destroy that which is true, nor yet within his power to change that which is unchangeable. Truth is fixed and immutable. It is possible to discover new beauty in truth so that it shines brighter to the eyes of man, but its light cannot be extinguished. Light does not fight light but dissolves into it according to the universal law of its essential unity. Nor is it possible to hold that, under exceptional circumstances, a nation may acquire or take the right to set aside the principles upon which just government is built and thus interfere with the fundamental rights of conscience for the supposed good of the State. The State cannot benefit by wrong, and rights given by God are beyond the legitimate power of man to suspend or to cancel.

The Inviolable Sanctuary of the Soul

The individual citizen does not then resign to society all the rights that he possesses as a free man, as some would have it appear, receiving back only a portion of them as a gift from the State, while nominally retaining in himself a sovereignty that actually is exercised by those who rule in his name. This doctrine, well known to the Fathers of the Republic, was nevertheless rejected by them. The government of Mexico, by insisting on obedience to a constitution made without reference to justice by a handful of military rulers, contrary to human rights and never submitted to the people for ratification, insists that the individual citizen has no rights that his government is bound to respect; that there are no limits to the powers of government. No doctrine could be more certain than that to sweep out of existence the sturdy self-reliance of a people, to sow discord within and enmity without. The power of the State, coming from God, may be bestowed by the people, but when thus bestowed, it does not and cannot include what is not within the competency of the State to accept. Had God ordained the rule of the State over the soul and conscience, He would have given the State the means to direct conscience and control the operations of the soul, since He gives means to the end. The sanctuary of the soul and of conscience the State cannot invade. It is precisely this the government of Mexico seeks to do, and then to justify, before a people whose national ideals are in direct contradiction to the evil spirit of despotism and tyranny that actuates the laws and the rulers now making of Mexico a shocking example of wrong to the whole civilized world. It is plain, then, that there was no exaggeration in the language of Pope Pius XI when he characterized these laws as "diabolical."

American Recognition of the Rights and Utility of Religion

Passing now from consideration of the constitutions themselves, we may, with better informed minds, contrast the laws founded upon them by Mexico and by our own Republic.

American laws recognize the right of the citizen to worship God "according to the dictates of his conscience," and, in order that this freedom may be assured him, religious societies are recognized as corporate legal entities having power to possess what property they need to carry out their mission. Furthermore, that mission is recognized as being, not only religious in root and trunk, but as bearing powers and fruit in works of education and social welfare. Religious societies may, therefore, own land and upon it erect such buildings as are necessary for their purposes. They may establish, own, and direct schools, colleges, universities, asylums, hospitals, and other institutions of education and social welfare. They may, as legal entities, protect their property rights by due process of law. They may possess endowments for the benefit of these activities and receive bequests. They may have seminaries wherein their clergy are trained and educated. Over and above all this, property owned by them, when used for purposes of worship, charity, or education, almost universally with us is specially exempt from taxation; not only because it is recognized as of utility to the public welfare, but also in order to carry into effect the spirit of the national will which, expressing itself through the Continental Congress, says: "Religion, morality and knowledge, being necessary to good government and the happiness of mankind, schools and the means of education shall forever be encouraged."[12] In this connection the words of our first president are eloquent: "And let us with caution indulge the supposition that morality can be maintained without religion. Whatever may be conceded to the influence of refined education on minds of peculiar structure, reason and experience both forbid us to expect that national morality can prevail in exclusion of religious principle."[13]

This condition has obtained since the formation of the Republic. It has worked out for the benefit of the State and of the people. No one now seriously believes that it could be changed. It has become an accepted and highly esteemed part of our national life, because it recognizes the rights of conscience, encourages private initiative in the establishing of useful agencies for learning and charity, promotes peace, contentment, and good will among citizens, encourages the enforcement of wise and good laws as well as the practice of the civic virtues, and allows to religion freedom in its own sphere for its teachings and for the cultivation of the spiritual life of the people. It has stood the test of nearly one and a half centuries, and the American people today are undoubtedly more than ever convinced of the desirability of its continuance. While with us there is no union of Church and State, nevertheless there is full and frank recognition of the utility of religion to good government. Hence the American State encourages religion to make greater and greater contributions to the happiness of the people, the stability of government, and the reign of order.

Mexico's Attempt to Destroy Religion

In contrast with this, according to the present Constitution of Mexico, no religious society may enjoy the right of corporate legal existence.[14] Officially, there are no Churches in Mexico; for a Church cannot possess anything, lacks the right of petition for redress of grievances, cannot sue or be sued in the civil courts, and in general is entirely without legal standing. Clergymen are disfranchised by the

---

[12] Northwest Ordinance, Art. 3.
[13] Farewell Address.
[14] Constitution of 1917, Art. 130. Law of November 25, 1926, Art. 5.

fact of ordination.[15] A Church cannot own the buildings in which its
public worship is held.[16] It cannot possess endowments.[17] It cannot
take up a collection or a subscription outside the doors of the building
used for religious services. That building, however, is owned by the
government, though paid for and supported by the people. The government merely allows the rightful owner to use it at the good pleasure
of State officials.[18] All Churches in Mexico, therefore, have to be supported by collections during the services. Now, Churches are mainly
supported everywhere by subscriptions accepted apart from the acts of
worship themselves. With us, nearly all church building is paid for in
that way. This is forbidden in Mexico, not by a mere regulation, but by
constitutional enactment.[19]

In order to make this enactment effective, a Church is not allowed
to possess houses for its bishops, priests, ministers, teachers, or super-
intendents. Its future may not be provided for, because it cannot have
a seminary in which a clergy may be trained to take places made
vacant by death or incapacity. The fact that a Church uses a building
is considered good ground for holding that it really belongs to that
religious body. It may then be seized and confiscated. If a clergyman
even rents a home for himself, the law provides that it may be seized
on mere suspicion. Relatives of clergymen are threatened with the
loss of their own personal property by confiscation on the ground that
such property really belongs to a Church, for the law decrees that mere
suspicion in such a case is full ground for the presumption that the
property is held for the Church.[20] All property devoted by religious
bodies to education or charitable purposes is subject to confiscation.[21]
In order to make it impossible for a Church to secure a building of
any kind, it is provided that, in case of seizure, no trial by jury shall
be allowed should its real owner appeal for justice.[22]

WORKS OF EDUCATION AND CHARITY DESTROYED

A Church, therefore, cannot own anything, cannot provide for its
current expenses, cannot provide for a future clergy. A native clergy

---

[15] Const. 1917, Art. 37, § III.
[16] Const. 1917, Art. 27. Law of November 25, 1926, Art. 6.
[17] Const. 1917, Art. 27, § II. Law of June 21, 1926, Art. 21. Law of November 25,
1926, Art. 6.
[18] Const. 1917, Art. 27, § II. Law of June 21, 1926, Art. 22.
[19] Const. 1917, Art. 130. Law of November 25, 1926, Art. 14.
[20] Const. 1917, Art. 27, § II.
[21] Const. 1917, Art. 27, § III. Law of June 21, 1926, Art. 4.
[22] Law of November 25, 1926. Const. 1917, Art. 130.

is thus made impossible, a fact which ordinarily would throw the burden of the religious care of the people upon strangers. To prevent the possibility of that happening, however, the law provides[23] that no clergyman but a native-born Mexican may officiate in any act of worship; and in consequence foreign clergy have been expelled. Thus the law first makes it impossible for the people to have a native clergy and then impossible to have a foreign clergy; while the government keeps assuring the world of its liberality and that there is no religious persecution in Mexico.[24]

The effect of such laws is felt in more than the spiritual work of the Church. It is also the ruin of works of education and charity. Religion fosters education. Practically all the great universities of the United States, for example, were founded by religious organizations, except the State universities, and even some of these owe their beginnings to clergymen or to religious bodies, while all owe to them the inspiration that gave them birth. It would be true to say that not one third of the colleges and universities of the United States would be in existence today had it not been for the educational activity of the Churches. Almost every American-born statesman and scholar up to 1840 was educated in schools established under religious auspices. Now the Mexican Constitution provides[25] that no clergyman may teach in a primary school or manage higher schools except on conditions impossible for him to accept. No college under private control may give a degree recognized by the State.[26] All religious teaching orders have been suppressed[27] and the formation of such orders made illegal.

Sadder still is the effect of such laws on works of charity, a special field for religious efforts. Churches have always been, and still are, the principal sources of relief for the sick and the poor. More than 60 per cent of the hospital beds in the United States are in religious institutions. To make it certain that Churches will not engage in such corporal works of mercy, the Mexican law confiscates institutions of charity and forbids the existence of any religious band of self-

---

[23] Law of June 21, 1926, Art. 1. Law of November 25, 1926, Art. 8. Const. 1917, Art. 130.

[24] *Foreign Affairs* for October, 1926, "The Policies of Mexico Today," by Plutarco Elias Calles, p. 4. "In conclusion, I wish to lay stress upon the fact that a real religious problem does not exist in Mexico. I mean that there is no such thing as persecution of a religious character against religious creeds or opposition on the part of the government to the dogmas or practices of any religion."

[25] Const. 1917, Art. 3. Law of June 21, 1926, Art. 4.

[26] Const. 1917, Art. 130. Law of November 25, 1926, Art. 15. Law of June 21, 1926, Art. 4.

[27] Const. 1917, Art. 5. Law of June 21, 1926, Art. 6.

sacrificing men and women devoted to their service. In consequence, Mexico is today full of ruined institutions of charity, and its sick and poor are without protectors.

Again, under the Mexican law the religious press is permitted to exist only on condition of giving up its liberty. The laws and even the acts of public officials cannot be criticized by a religious paper under severe penalties, not even by secular papers betraying a religious bias.[28] Several religious papers have already been suppressed, and even certain daily papers of large circulation that were not religious but were at least sympathetic with religion. How far such laws depart from the American ideal is shown by the Virginia Bill of Rights and other similar acts.

The Persecution a Product of New Paganism

It is scarcely necessary to set down the conclusions that naturally flow from the contrast we have made. They are at once apparent and must convince right-thinking men and women that there can be no relationship between the principles upon which the Mexican Constitution is built, the laws that embody them, the spirit with which it is proposed they shall be enforced, and the principles, laws, and spirit that are held sacred by the American people.

In fact, such laws hark back to paganism. Were they to prevail they would show civil society to have been marching, not in advance, but in a circle; and again arriving, in this our day, at the point from which it started with the dawn of Christianity. Such laws, in reality, embody the pagan plan of government, for they differ from it not at all in effect, but only in the manner and form of attaining the result. The ancient pagan gave despotic authority to the State by deifying it in its origin, and often in its rulers and its actions. The founders of Rome were supposed to be the children of the gods. Her emperors were saluted as "divine" and altars erected to them. Great men of Greece were honored likewise. Even to this day some earthly rulers receive quasi-divine honors. The legendary benefactor of the ancient tribes of Mexico and Central America is said to have been a white man worshiped as a god.[29] Thus paganism united earthly and divine power in a deified state. The program of this new paganism eliminates the divine so as to leave the earthly in full possession. But the result of

---

[28] Const. 1917, Art. 130. Law of June 21, 1926, Art. 13. Law of November 25, 1926, Art. 16.

[29] Orozco y Berra, *Hist. Ant.*, v. 1, pp. 63–67.

both extremes is the same — the slavery of the individual. How far all this is from our convictions as Americans and Christians is immediately apparent.

PART II

WHAT THE CHURCH HAS DONE FOR MEXICO

A cause that has to be defended before the American people by concealing its underlying motives will not hesitate at having recourse to falsehoods and even to suppressing facts of history. Hence it is no surprise to find charges unproved and unprovable urged against the part played by Catholic missionaries in the task of planting religion and civilization in Mexico. This is all the more easily done because the great majority of the people who read and hear such charges have neither the time nor the leisure to give further attention to them, and, therefore, accept them as undisputed statements of historic facts. In consequence, it is believed by some, and the belief has been encouraged by propaganda efforts of the Mexican government especially in our colleges, that these missionaries destroyed a superior civilization in Mexico to build on its ruins a national monument to ignorance and superstition. The popular mind has been fed with the falsehood that the Church not only gave nothing of value to the Mexican people, but planted amongst them what was harmful; refusing to improve their condition by establishing schools, and meriting their hatred for thus keeping them illiterate and backward for centuries.

THE CHURCH AND THE MEXICAN INDIAN

Fair and honest consideration of the facts will show the frail foundation upon which such charges are built. There was once, in all probability, a pagan civilization in Mexico superior to the social and political condition of any other part of this hemisphere at the time, possibly excepting Peru; but it had disappeared long before the missionaries set foot on Mexican soil. Its depths we cannot probe. What the missionaries found, however, was not the fantastic Empire of the Aztecs, a creation of the imagination,[30] but a degraded land in which

---

[30] José María Luis Mora, *Mexico y sus Revoluciones,* Paris, 1836, v. 4, p. 2 et seq. Mora explains that the aid of the masses for the revolt could not be enlisted with abstract ideas about independence, so it was necessary to inflame their passions with "fables" about the greatness of the Aztecs and the "barbarity" of the conquest and "three hundred years of slavery."

Hidalgo's rallying cry was defense of King and Religion. Alaman, v. I, p. 379.

murder and cannibalism[31] had reached the dignity of religious rites. The old civilization, long since passed, had left part of its story preserved in legends and in ruins. The new civilization brought by the Spanish missionaries has its monuments still standing, and its deeds set down in historic writings. Its Laws of the Indies have been pronounced the most just code ever made for the protection of an aboriginal people.[32] If we contrast the condition of the Mexican Indian at the beginning of the nineteenth century with that of his northern neighbor, we see at a glance that the work of the Catholic missionaries was well done. We find even that the work has not failed to show results down to our own day. The praises and honors showered on Juarez, for example, are not undeserved so far as his intelligence and ability are concerned; but these praises and honors are reflected back to the Church that he persecuted, the Church that had made a Juarez possible. Such an Indian as Juarez would be a wonder here, but he was no wonder in Mexico where great men came out of the Indian population, and are still coming out of it, because the Church, before her work was hampered and injured, had laid the foundation. Miguel de Cabrera was Mexico's greatest painter, but an Indian. Panduro and Velazquez were worthy of a place in the same hall of Indian fame. Altamirano was at once a great orator, novelist, poet, and journalist, but likewise an Indian. Juan Esteban, a simple lay Brother of the Society of Jesus, was so great as a primary teacher that families of Spain sent children across the ocean to secure for them the foundation of this Indian's original and most effective methods of instruction. Among orators, an Indian bishop, Nicolas del Puerto, holds a place of distinction. In the realms of profound philosophy the world has produced few greater than Archbishop Munguía of Michoacán. Francisco Pascual García was a great lawyer; Ignacio Ramirez, a distinguished journalist; Rodriguez Gavan, a fine poet as well as a journalist; Bartolomé de Alba, a winning and solid preacher; Diego Adriano and Augustín de la Fuente were expert printers; Adriano de Tlaltelolco, a Latinist as well. All these were Indians, as were the historians Ixtlilxochitl and Valeriano. Rincón wrote the best grammar in the Aztec tongue. He was, like De Alba himself, a descendant of the

[31] Cortés, Third Letter to Charles V. Dead are devoured after battle. Bodies of roasted children found in provisions of enemy.
Las Casas, *Brevisima Relación*. Dead and prisoners are devoured after battle.
Sahagun, Lib. II, Caps. II, XX, XXI, XXXII. Durán, Cap. LXXXI. Mendieta, Lib. II, Cap. XVI. Motolinia, Caps. 17, 19, 27. Pomar, *Relación*, p. 17. *Recopilación de Indias*, 1–1–7. (Law forbidding cannibalism.)
[32] Lummis, *Awakening of a Nation*, Introduction.

kings of Texcoco. A bibliography of the books written by Mexicans before the First Revolution fills many large volumes and in it the Indian has no small place. To whom the credit? To the Church which the Mexican government informs the world gave nothing to its country.

EDUCATIONAL PROGRESS UNDER THE CHURCH IN MEXICO

Baron von Humboldt testified thus of the Mexico he visited: "No city of the new continent, without even excepting those of the United States, can display such great and solid scientific establishments, as the capital of Mexico."[33] Why, then, did Mexico advance to such a high place from the depths of savagery, there stop and begin to retrograde, while the United States went on and climbed to her present eminence? Ask that question of the closed university, the suppressed colleges, the empty schools, the confiscated monasteries and convents, students scattered in other lands, the muzzled press, the Laws of Reform, the sword, the gun, the violated ballot box. One of these alone might have the power only to whisper the answer, but together they shout it so that the whole world may hear. It is an eloquent testimony to the wonderful work of the persecuted Church that to her, and to her alone, the credit is due that, at the beginning of the nineteenth century, Mexico had proportionally more colleges and more students in them, as well as less illiteracy, than even Great Britain, a testimony given her by a writer in a recent number of a London magazine.[34]

That fine picture fades and is replaced by one of sadness when, more than a century ago, Mexico's internal troubles began. In two generations, she had lost what three centuries of peace and cultivation had won for her; her churches seized; her wealth, formerly dedicated to education and social welfare, turned over to the looter. The worst elements rose to power and for them power was merely the road to riches. The subversive Jacobin doctrines, an evil legacy carried like a taint in the blood from generation to generation, yet prevail; but the buildings of the Church, monuments of education and social betterment, still stand, changed, alas, to other and often ignoble uses. Solidly, often beautifully constructed, many remain as barracks, prisons, hotels,

---

[33] *Political Essay on the Kingdom of New Spain.* Translated from the original French by John Black, New York, 1811, v. 1, p. 159. "The capital and several other cities have scientific establishments which will bear a comparison with those of Europe" (p. 139).

[34] The *Month,* Oct., 1926, "Church and State in Mexico."

and offices. To Mexico goes the glory of the first book, the first printing press, the first school, the first college, and the first university in
the New World,[35] and to Mexico's Catholic missionaries should go her
gratitude for these distinctions. To the evil philosophy of the Red
Terror goes only the sad credit for a century of destruction. A French
writer on social science said that "Private initiative begins where the
intervention of power ends." In Mexico it is proposed never to permit
it to begin since the power of the State is to have no end. Yet the
State owes all its progress and success to the individual. All advance
in education, for example, such as the science of pedagogy, the planning of methods, the proper division of studies, the balanced curriculum, are the contributions of individuals. Surely these neo-Jacobins
must see the force of the words of a French writer who said of people
under such a regime, that they "judged liberty to lie in restricting the
liberty of others."

THE WEALTH OF THE CHURCH IN MEXICO

The charge that the Church accumulated an undue proportion of
the land of Mexico and gathered to herself vast estates as well as
money, on examination has been found to be a gross exaggeration.
When the facts are examined in the cold light of history, and the
actual figures are given to show of what this wealth consisted, the
charge falls to the ground, for the so-called wealth of the Church was
chiefly in the endowments of Mexican education and works of social
welfare. Little land was owned by the Church,[36] and in part only did

---

[35] Icazbalceta, *Bibliografia Mexicana del Siglo XVI*, p. xvi. First Printing Press,
1536. First Book, *La Escala Espiritual*, 1537. First School, 1522. (Justo Sierra, *Mexico
— Its Social Evolution*, p. 478.) First College, 1533. (Cuevas, *Historia de la Iglesia
Mexicana*, v. 1, p. 386.) First University, 1553. (Cavo, *Tres Siglos*, Lib. IV, 12.)

[36] Humboldt, *Political Essay on the Kingdom of New Spain*, New York, 1811,
v. 1, p. 174. "The lands of the Mexican clergy (bienes raices) do not exceed the value
of 12 or 15 millions of francs" ($2,285,714.28 to $2,857,152.85).

Colección Dávalos, v. 2, Doc. 361. Abad y Queipo says: "Mas: la poca propiedad
de la iglesia y clero de América no consiste en posesiones." And in Doc. 363: "El valor
de los bienes de estos piadosos destinos (capellanias y obras pias) se puede estimar
prudencialmente en dos y medio ó tres millones de pesos."

Mora (*Obras Sueltas*, v. 1, p. 372) quotes a report made by the Minister for
Ecclesiastical Affairs, 1833, showing 129 farms and 3331 city properties belonging to
the religious orders of both sexes. The total income from these properties is given
respectively as $147,047 and $631,762. The members of these orders, according to that
same report numbered 3160. Mora's estimate of Church wealth (minus its fictitious
values) totals less than $120,000,000.

Duarte, *Curiosidades Historicas*, p. 82, lists 861 farms and 22,649 city properties
valued at $184,614,000. Various colleges and hospitals, even the guild of silversmiths,
appear as owners.

See also note 41.

even the wealth gathered for the endowments of education and social welfare come from the gifts of the people during a period covering three centuries in one of the richest countries in the world; for these endowments represented also the labor and self-sacrifice of thousands of religious men and women, working for nothing but their bread and raiment. The greater part of the wealth was, as we have stated, not that of the Church but of the country's educational and charitable agencies, and the amount itself has been greatly exaggerated for the purposes of propaganda.

When figures revealing the actual extent of these endowments are shown, and when they are contrasted with like endowments for educational and social welfare institutions here in the United States, it is plain that the charge that they constituted an undue part of the wealth of Mexico is not well founded. Three American universities[37] alone have endowments greater than all the educational and charitable institutions under the care of the religious orders of Mexico. A certain single non-Catholic religious denomination here, and that not the largest, has far more invested funds than the Catholic Church in Mexico possessed, with all her works of education and charity, at the period of her greatest prosperity.[38] That particular denomination in

---

[37] *World Almanac,* 1926, p. 392.

Harvard	$69,689,840
Columbia	57,456,803
Chicago	31,992,620

$159,139,263

165 institutions possess $794,231,462 in endowments of $1,000,000 or more.

[38] The Baptists are referred to for purposes of comparison, because the number of their communicants in 1916 happens nearly to equal the number of Mexicans in 1810. The comparison is as follows:

	Baptists (a)	Mexicans
Population	6,107,686	6,122,354 (b)
Churches	51,248	10,112 (c)
Clergy	36,926	7,341 (b)
Unproductive property	$173,705,800	$52,331,894 (d)
Productive property	$98,453,844	$64,073,180 (e)
Income	$43,055,007	$5,682,153 (f)
Total values	$272,159,644	$116,405,074 (g)

a) *Baptist Year Book,* 1916.

b) 1810 — Navarro y Noriega, *Memoria,* in *Boletín de la Soc. de G. y E.,* 2a Ep., v. p. 281. Based on census of 1793 and Humboldt, 1803.

c) Romero, *Mexico and the U. S.,* p. 97.

d) Mora, *Obras Sueltas,* v. 1, p. 372. Citing report of Minister for Eccl. Affairs, 1833, including 213 conventual establishments, valued at $21,300,000.

this country today has twenty times the number of clergy, in proportion to its membership, and five times the number of church buildings.[39] Moreover, the history of the rise and development of educational and social welfare endowments here is almost identical with
those in Mexico, at least in so far as religious motives entered into
the effort. The whole foundation of popular and higher education in
the United States was built by the religious denominations that had
found a place in American life, as we already pointed out; so that
if we took from American life all the educational and social welfare
values that these pioneers put in it, we would have today less than
half our present equipment. But here in the United States zeal began
and encouragement builded; while Mexico's "patriots" destroyed and
ate up her own substance and sold her birthright as, one by one, her
schools were closed, her teachers driven out, and her welfare institutions turned over to other uses. Many of these were sold at nominal
prices to enrich the families of the revolutionists.[40] Those that stand
today are monuments to a zeal and devotion that promised great
things for the Mexican people, but which is now fast becoming a
memory of a light that once astonished by its brilliancy and power;
for the early progress of Mexico under the care of its missionaries was
the admiration of the world. But figures speak louder than words.

---

e) Ibid. less his fictitious values; for example: Dr. Mora assumes $600 as the
income of each parish priest, multiplies this by 20, and charges the product to capital.

f) Ibid. less his fictitious values: and includes the tithes for 1829 amounting to
$2,341,152. Does not include alms or fees.

g) Ibid. less his fictitious values.

Including his fictitious values, Mora's figures show $181,116,754 total values and
$7,456,593 total income.

According to Abad y Queipo the funds held in trust by the secular and regular
clergy (1807) totaled $44,500,000. *Representación Colección Dávalos*, v. 2, Doc. 263.

Mora estimates them to amount to $80,000,000 (*Mexico y sus Revoluciones*, v. 1, p.
121). But in his *Obras Sueltas*, v. 1, p. 372, he follows Bishop Abad y Queipo
($44,500,000).

These funds were known as "capellanias y obras pias." Their disposition is indicated by $256,000 of "capellanias" and $220,630 of "obras pias" being listed with
the funds belonging to the girls' college of San Ignacio in Mexico City. *Boletín, etc.*, 3a
Epoca, v. 5, p. 652.

[39] This is based on the present population of Mexico, 14,234,799 (Census 1921;
World Almanac, 1926) and the present number of priests, which is about 4000.

[40] Monjardin, *Ocurso, etc.* (Mexico: Murguia Imprenta, 1862). This is an account
of a lawsuit in which it is shown that a certain citizen purchased 50 confiscated properties, valued at $525,528 (in 1859 at $587,419), for $1,832.40 in cash, and government
due bills that had cost him $40,077.90.

Romero, *Mexico and the United States*, p. 363. "The Church property . . . was
sold . . . at a nominal price, payable partially in national bonds then selling at . . .
about five per cent of their face value."

The highest estimate of the wealth of the Church in Mexico ever offered even by her enemies was $250,000,000, including all the endowments. Without such educational and social welfare endowments, the property devoted to religion in the United States is estimated by the Federal Trade Commission at $2,820,220,000. With the endowments, it is estimated at seven billions of dollars. Proportionately the Mexican figure might well be one fourth of the American. It was actually not even one tenth. When it was confiscated the Government realized far less than half of its estimated value.[41]

The history of the decline of education in Mexico begins with the expulsion of the Jesuits in 1767. Shortly after came the debacle that has been going on ever since. There were few to take the place of the old teachers. College after college had to be given up, most of them closed by the predecessors of President Calles. Gomez Farias closed the University of Mexico, the first university on this continent, in 1833. Reopened by Catholics, it was closed again by Comonfort in 1857. Again reopened one year later, Juarez closed it in 1861. The Liberal Cabinet of the weak Maximilian put an end to it in 1865. Later it descended to about the grade of a high school and, with some exceptions in certain departments, it has scarcely more than that rank today.

The Church and the Poor in Mexico

Bitter indeed was the lot of the people who had to witness, not only the confiscation of the educational and charitable foundations that were their own in every sense of the word, but to see, in the sweeping away of their endowments, the rise of usury and the exploitation of poverty in order to increase the wealth of a new moneyed class that revolution had made. The endowments of the Church institutions were almost exclusively invested in the development of Mexico's great agricultural resources at low rates of interest. The revenues from these investments went to the support of the country's educational and charitable institutions, the schools, the colleges, the orphan asylums, the homes for the aged, and the hospitals. The investments themselves increased agricultural and industrial prosperity, even as the returns furthered intellectual and social progress. The very profession of the churchman made of his debtors his friends. But let an enemy tell the tale. We take it from a speech on the subject by Juan A. Mateos in the Mexican Chamber of Deputies, delivered on October 20, 1893. "In

---

[41] In April, 1866, the office reported a total of $62,365,516.41 of confiscated values. *Boletin de la Sociedad de Georgrafia y Estadistica*, 2a Epoca, v. 2, p. 388.

the days of the old regime, when the clergy possessed a great number of city and country properties, year after year went by without the shameful evictions to which so many families are the victims today. The sordid avarice of the landlords of today has no compassion in contrast to the clergy who, animated by a spirit truly Christian, overlooked and excused. The Church loaned its capital at a low rate of interest, 4, 5, or 6 per cent, which was called the legal rate, a rate unknown today. Very rarely was a foreclosure notice published against a property pledged for a loan from these funds. For this reason I proposed, at the time of their confiscation, that a bank for the poor be established from the millions of the clergy, but my voice was drowned in the passions of the revolution. Because of this, the selfish interests and exactions of today have left homeless the many families who formerly enjoyed the tolerance and charity of the clergy." It was the revolutionary leader, President Juarez, who repealed the laws against usury by his decree of March 15, 1861. The work done for the people by this use of endowments practically constituted a land bank for the Mexican agriculturists.[42] Only a few years ago our own government had to found such a bank in the United States for the relief of the farmers.

The Church and Social Uplift in Mexico

The charge has been made that the Church in Mexico had no definite program of social action, that her attitude has been one of opposition. The record of Catholic Spain in this respect toward Mexico was such as to justify the statement by a recognized authority on the history of the Mexican people that: "No other nation has founded so extensively such beneficences in the colonies."[43] The Church was the first organization in Mexico to devote herself to the solving of the social question. But for sixty and more years she has not been free; yet, even before the revolution of 1910–1911 broke out, she had already a program of social action, progressive, advanced, and comprehensive, free of the spirit of caste, and not leading to turbulence and to unjust confiscation. This program of the Church was one of loyalty to the people of Mexico, generous, disinterested, and inspired by no political passion.

As early as 1903, Catholic delegates in the National Congress of

---

[42] Mora, *Mexico y sus Revoluciones*, v. 1, p. 121; Ramos Arizpe, in *Boletin de la Soc. de G. y E.*, 1a Ep., v. 1, p. 137; José Guadalupe Romero, *Boletin de la Soc. de G. y E.*, 2a Ep., v. 3, p. 556; Matias Romero, *Mexico and the United States*, p. 96; Bustamante, *Suplemento á Los Tres Siglos de Mexico*, § 63.

[43] Lummis, *The Awakening of a Nation*.

Mexico introduced bills providing for the creation of rural co-operative banks. That year a Mexican Catholic convention was held in the city of Puebla, and, among other problems, it discussed those of labor unions, of the Indians, and of industrial education. Similar congresses were held in succeeding years. In that of 1906, no less than twenty-nine reports were presented covering distinct phases of social action in which the Church was at that time engaged in Mexico. At the Congress held in 1909, in the city of Oaxaca, practically the entire time of the Congress was devoted to the discussion of the Indian problem.[44]

It was a group of Catholic delegates to the Congress of Mexico that introduced bills giving legal status to labor unions, providing for Sunday rest, and a workmen's compensation act. In the State of Jalisco, where in 1912 the Catholic members constituted a majority in the state legislature, statutes were enacted protecting the property rights of wives and children, protecting the rights of minorities, and granting a legal status to labor syndicates. One needs but read Catholic publications of that time to know with what zeal the Catholic people and the Catholic clergy of Mexico were devoting themselves to social questions in that country when their action was free. In March, 1913, the National Catholic Party, assembled in Guadalajara, discussed a program which included such points as municipal autonomy, the land problems, rural co-operative banks, and the property rights of wives and children; the mere enumeration of which shows how far not only the Party, but the Catholic people of Mexico, had advanced in the solution of the social problems of that day. The Catholic labor unions of Mexico, at their convention held in 1913 in the city of Zamora, adopted resolutions demanding every just thing contained in Article 123 of the Constitution of Queretaro and even went further than this Article in the protection of workingmen's rights.[45]

It would not be hard, but for limitations of space, to enlarge on the story of the effort of the Church along social lines to better the condition of the people; and, at the same time, to insist that the Catholics of Mexico have never failed to contribute their best to all the demands made on them for intelligent, patriotic action.

THE CHURCH AND POLITICS IN MEXICO

The charge that comes easiest to the tongue or pen of the Mexican politician is that the Church interfered in politics. The answer is even easier to give than the charge was to make, for no one ever tries to

---

[44] *Policy of the Catholic Church in Mexico*, 1925, p. 3.
[45] *Ibid.*, pp. 4, 5, 6, 7, 8.

offer proofs that it is true. It is taken for granted that it will be believed without proofs. When and how was the Mexican Church in politics? If the charge refers to Spanish times, it is true that men like Bishop Las Casas, to whose memory revolutionary Mexico has recently erected a public monument, were in "politics" to the extent of fighting the Spanish officials in the colony, even to the foot of the throne of the King, to secure justice and education for the Indian. It is true also to the extent that, because of a none too ideal union of Church and State in those times, the latter often went beyond its rights granted under the Concordat, to encroach upon those of the Church, and was for that rebuked and opposed. It is true again to the extent that individuals sometimes sought to use the union for their own self-aggrandizement. It is true in no other way.

If the charge refers to the early revolutionary times, it is true to the extent that priests led the fight against Spain, but that the Church condemned them for deserting their spiritual activities to mix in the only kind of politics men then understood — warfare.[46] It is true to the extent that the bishops tried to preserve religious rights against the assaults of the revolutionists of the day. It is true in no other way.

If the charge refers to more recent revolutionary history, it is true that the Church is the only defender the country could find against assaults by communists and atheists on civil, political, and religious liberties. It is not true that the Church engaged in merely partisan politics. The Catholic Party of Madero's day was a party of laymen organized to win for Mexico by constitutional means a more just and equitable code of laws. Madero welcomed it as "the first fruits of my revolution." To this extent, and not to any other, Catholics, not the Church, were in politics. What of it? Does not the democratic State proclaim the legitimacy of constitutional methods to redress grievances? If that method is wrong, then we Americans do not understand democracy. And if these grievances, by the deed of the enemies of religion, lie in the realm of religious rights, are the friends of religion forbidden by that fact to work for their redress, because by so doing they would be mixing in politics?

THE CHURCH AND STATE IN MEXICO

The statement of the government of Mexico that it is now only try-

---

[46] One hundred and fifty-five clergymen are listed in *Através de los Siglos,* v. 3, p. 775, as taking an active part in the revolution of 1810–1821.

Hidalgo and his followers were condemned in proclamation issued by Bishop-elect of Michoacan, Abad y Queipo, September 24, 1810. *Colección Dávalos,* v. 2, Doc. 44.

ing to dissolve a union between Church and State, and that the Church is seeking temporal power, finds an obvious answer in the history of the Mexican nation. There has been no union of Church and State in Mexico since 1857. Even before that, however, when, in 1821, a revolutionary Mexican government desired to retain some part of the union in the ancient right of "patronage," formerly enjoyed by the Spanish Crown, so as to have the appointment of bishops in its hands, it was met with a refusal from the Archbishop of Mexico. When the demand was made the following year, it was again rejected, this time by the whole body of the Episcopate.[47]

The Constitution of 1857 declared the union of Church and State to be dissolved.[48] That instrument, however, recognized the Church as a legal, though separate, entity. According to the "liberal" doctrine then in vogue, no "legal person" was such by its own inherent right, and became so only by grant of the State, which by a legal fiction created it. What the State makes, however, it can unmake, and this the Constitution of 1917, by a logical conclusion from a false premise, attempted to do. It recognizes[49] "no juridical personality in the religious institutions known as churches," thus depriving them of any legal protection against the encroachments of tyrants, whose real and often expressed purpose in Mexico was, and is, not to separate the Church from the State but to subject the Church to the control of the State.[50] The Church in Mexico, on the other hand, is not asking for the union of Church and State to be restored, but for the American system of freedom of religion to be introduced. This may easily be learned from the words[51] of the Mexican bishops addressed to the legislature: "What is it that we petition? Not tolerance, not complacency, much less privileges or favors. We demand liberty and we demand nothing but liberty, we demand liberty for all religions. . . . A regime of restrictions against religion is the denial of liberty."

SLANDERS AGAINST THE CLERGY IN MEXICO

Equal in falsehood with the slander against the Church in reference to education and wealth is that concerning extortion on the part of the

---

[47] Concilio III Mexicano, p. 569.

Succeeding governments attempted to arrange for, or to assert, the right to appoint the bishops and priests, until in 1857 when the Constitution declared the separation of Church and State and the policy of expropriation was adopted.

[48] Art. 3.

[49] Art. 130.

[50] Law of November 25, 1926, Art. 1.

[51] September 7, 1926.

Mexican clergy.[52] Those who have seen the poverty in which the clergy
of our generation have lived need no proof drawn from statistics to
know that they have been slandered. It suffices to say for those of
other days that the total offerings collected in the churches by the
Mexican clergy never represented a donation of even as much as one
peso from each member of the flock per year. Offerings on the occasions
of baptisms and marriages are smaller than those made to clergymen
in the United States.[53] Works of education and charity have been supported chiefly by those whose means enabled them to be generous, as
in our own country. The poor paid nothing but the copper dropped
into the collection basket on Sunday. In Spanish times it is quite
true that the revenues of the bishops were often large,[54] but it is also
quite true to say that the surplus was spent on the great institutions
to which we have already referred. Indeed, the building of hospitals
and orphanages seems to have been the favorite work of many bishops,
who paid for them out of the revenues not needed for the support of
their households and the cost of managing their large dioceses.[55] The

[52] The Indians were exempt from the payment of the tithing during the colonial
period (Alaman, v. 1, p. 23). On the other classes only the tithing and first fruits were
obligatory, anything else being voluntary (Concilio III Mexicano, Lib. III, Tit. XII,
§ III). The fees which the parish priests were permitted to receive were fixed; those
accepting more were fined double the excess. Marriages in the parish church occasioned
no offering. The customary offering for baptism was one peso; burials, five to twelve
pesos. For Indians the customary offerings were one half those expected from the
Spaniards (Arancel, 1767).

[53] The *Churchman,* a Protestant Episcopal publication, in an editorial, February 6,
1915, quoted William Watson (a non-Catholic, who had lived some eight years in
Puebla, Oaxaca, Guadalajara, and Mexico) on offerings as follows: baptisms, 33 to
69 cents; marriages, $2.50 to $3.00; and nothing for baptisms and marriages during
missions.

[54] Humboldt (*Political Essay on the Kingdom of New Spain* [New York, 1811],
v. 1, p. 173) gives the revenues of the bishops as follows: Mexico 130,000 double
piastres (evidently pesos or dollars); Puebla 110,000; Valladolid 100,000; Guadalajara
90,000; Durango 35,000; Monterey 30,000; Yucatan 20,000; Oaxaca 18,000; and
Sonora 6000. The last was from the government treasury.

The tithing for the twenty-year period 1771–1789 averaged $1,584,048.90 per year
according to a tabulation given by Humboldt (*Political Essay on the Kingdom of
New Spain,* 1822 edition, v. 3, p. 96). The tithing was divided as follows: one fourth
to the bishop, one fourth to the cathedral chapter; the remaining half was divided
into nine parts, of which two ninths went to the King, three ninths to the cathedral
building fund and hospital, and four ninths to the parish priests (*Recopilación de
Indias,* Lib. I, Tit. XVI, Ley XXIII).

[55] It was customary for the bishops to devote any surplus to works of public benefit.
This accounts for the numerous schools and hospitals founded by them. The San
Andres Hospital is an example. It was founded in 1779, by Archbishop Haro who
secured the building, which had been a Jesuit college, from the government. He
equipped it with 400 beds, all endowed. By February, 1790, his donations had totaled
$459,586. The hospital's funds amounted to $1,454,657. Some of the properties belonging to it appear in the list of the confiscated properties referred to in note 40.

hospitals in particular were the best that the times knew and superior to those of Europe. Some of those still standing are considered models for such a climate as that of Mexico, even at this day. Notable amongst such wonderful buildings is one in Guadalajara which is still visited by physicians, even from the United States, to study its construction and its plans for the care of patients; yet it is three centuries old and the gift of a bishop. Where the revenue of Bishop Zumárraga went is indicated by one of his letters[56] to the King of Spain written in 1537: "That which occupies my thoughts, to which my will is most inclined and my small forces strive, is that in this city and in every diocese there shall be a college for Indian boys learning grammar at least, and a great establishment with room for a large number of the daughters of the Indians." Before his death the Bishop had seen to it that a goodly part of his wish was made a reality. Nor should we pass without attention the letter of Geronimo Lopez to the King in which, as early as 1541, he complained against the Church because her clergy had taught the Indians too faithfully, even to the point of making them excellent writers and expert Latinists.[57]

It must be remembered that the bishops were the responsible trustees of funds for works other than those of the parishes and missions. In their zeal for progress, however, they often went far afield to make Mexico a progressive nation, for we find them building public roads and even aqueducts.[58] If the poor of Mexico have been systematically robbed by the extortion of their clergy, surely it will be hard to explain a devotion on their part to the Church and to their pastors which not even rigid censorship succeeds in concealing from those who today read what is happening in Mexico.

THE CHURCH TURNS TO PRAYER NOT ARMS

Even Catholics have asked why the Church in Mexico does not use its undoubted power to bring this persecution to a speedy end and take measures to prevent its recurrence, since it is admitted that the overwhelming majority of the Mexican people are of its fold. They forget that there are but two human means to that end: the ballot and the sword. The first is hopeless in Mexico, because there the ballot is not respected and governments are unaffected by it. Few citizens use

---

56 Zumárraga, *Estudio Biografico*. Garcia Icazbalceta, p. 215.
57 *Colección de Documentos para la Historia de Mexico*, Garcia Icazbalceta, v. 1, p. 148.
58 Aqueduct at Durango, 1728. *Gaceta* of April, 1728.
Aqueduct at Valladolid (Morelia), 1788, *Bol., etc.*, 3a Ep., v. 1, p. 627.

it, because their votes are counted only when they favor the ruling powers or when these powers, for effect or deception, are willing to admit the existence of a small minority. An outstanding proof of this is found in the rejection, by a vote of every member save one, of the petition for relief addressed by the Mexican bishops to the Congress, though the petition was supported by the people. Congress, senate, and courts do the bidding of the president; and this condition has been the rule and not the exception since "liberty" came to Mexico by force of arms. It will continue to be the rule while that kind of "liberty" stays. Ballots are less powerful than bullets when they are the playthings of tyranny.

The second human remedy is equally hopeless, for Christian principles forbid the Church founded by the Prince of Peace to take up the sword or rely upon such carnal weapons as the inflamed passions of men would select. If the Church has learned many things in her life of two thousand years the principal lesson came from the patience of the divine Founder. She is not fated to die, but she has learned how to suffer. With Him she will be crucified but with Him also she will rise. The weapons of men are not for her. But, if these human weapons the Church will not use, she has one that well fits her hand, armored as it is in justice and in truth. She has prayer. Never in the history of the trials of the Church in Mexico has that weapon been so firmly held as now, thanks to the paternal counsels of the Sovereign Pontiff. Because of these, no longer does the quivering voice of the afflicted Church of Mexico rise alone to the Comforter. From end to end of the earth the answer to the appeal of Pius goes upward to the throne of God. The hatred of men may spurn it. The malice of men may curse it. The unbelief of men may mock it. But its hope is in a Promise and its power is in a Faith.

This Is No Appeal for Political Intervention or Action of Any Sort

What, therefore, we have written is no call on the faithful here or elsewhere to purely human action. It is no interposition of our influence either as bishops or as citizens to reach those who possess political power anywhere on earth, and least of all in our own country, to the end that they should intervene with armed force in the internal affairs of Mexico for the protection of the Church. Our duty is done when, by telling the story, defending the truth and emphasizing the principles, we sound a warning to Christian civilization that its foundations are again being attacked and undermined. For the rest, God will bring His will to pass in His own good time and in His own good way. Mexico will be saved for her mission whatever it may be. That this mission is now to give a great example of Christian patience and to demonstrate the force of faith undaunted, we may well believe. For the future we may take confidence from the examples of other nations that went through the same fiery furnace of persecution and emerged, triumphantly prepared for great things. The Mexican nation once proved its inherent worth by its rapid advancement in Christian civilization. For the days of De Gante and Zumárraga, Las Casas and Motolinia, as well as those of Junípero Serra, who carried the work of the missionaries into what is now our own land, Mexico has no need to offer apology.

Mexico's Debt to the Church

For the sad days of decline, the Church, forbidden by law to teach and robbed of the means to carry on her mission of enlightenment, has only to show her chains, and say to her enemies: "You blame me for poverty, yet you took from me the endowments for my hospitals, my orphanages, my countless works of mercy. You blame me for ignorance, yet you closed my schools, and stole my colleges, the first to light the torch of learning on this continent. You say that I have added nothing to science and art, but you destroyed the art I brought with me and developed, burned my books and scattered the results of my labor for science to the four winds of heaven. You blame me for lawlessness, yet you destroyed my missions among a peaceful and thriving Indian population, and gave to them, in place of Christ's Gospel, the thirty pieces of silver with which you bribed them to murder their fellows. You took the cross out of their hands to replace it with a torch and a gun. Show me one good thing in Mexico I did not give you. Show me one genius for whom I was not responsible. Show me one step toward the light that I did not help you to make. Take out of your country all that I put in it, and see what remains. You may thrust me out, exile my bishops, murder my priests, again steal my schools and desecrate my sanctuaries, but you cannot blot out history, you cannot erase the mark I made on you — not in a century of centuries."

"For My Name's Sake"

If the gaining of the whole world does not recompense the individual for the loss of his soul, then what shall it profit a nation? There was a soul in Mexico, a spirit manifesting its presence by the impulse that sent her missionaries of civilization along a way unmarked, save for the print of their sandals, but now the great Royal Road of California — the Camino Real. It was a spirit that, building on its faith and its inspiration, left monuments to tell Mexico's story in the old missions of Texas, Arizona, New Mexico, and along the shores of the Pacific from San Diego to San Francisco. For us of the North, these buildings, landmarks of the first Christian missions within our borders, beacons of the light of religion and civilization on our soil, fonts and fertile sources of a distinctive literature touched and tinted with colors and values all its own, are treasures honored as a rich legacy, noble and ennobling. The old records speak in the Spanish tongue to tell us that it was not really Spain but Mexico that sent the padres to the North. Their Castilian speech is passing; nor are there left many descendants of the brave souls who came with them to write the first chapter, the chapter of beauty, into the history of our California. But the memories are not dead, nor has the trail been lost that was marked by the discoverers who gave to the Far Western country the first martyrs as well as the first teachers in all our nation. Through them we share in the glory of the initial gesture of Christian civilization on this continent. We have not denied, nor shall we deny, our debt to Mexico for this. Already it has been acknowledged by voices which, if they do not all sing the old hymns, yet do all understand something of the message of the singers; if they do not all worship at the old altars, yet do all hold sacred the spots upon which the padres built them, and give to the new cities that grew around them the old names, to keep for the great West its traditions, its character, and its charm. If the mother should forget what the sons and daughters love, shall not these sons and daughters take shame instead of glory from her? For you of your own flock in this happy land, where the rights of conscience are recognized and upheld by the laws, and respected by her people, we re-echo the appeal of our Holy Father, Pope Pius XI, and ask the charity of your prayers — a memento in the daily Masses of the priests, and a remembrance in the daily devotions of the faithful — for your afflicted brethren in Mexico, recalling to you words of our Lord to show that your practical sympathy thus expressed will be pleasing in His sight: "Blessed are they that suffer persecution for justice sake: for theirs is the Kingdom of Heaven."[59]

To the bishops, the clergy, and the faithful of Mexico we inscribe this defense of their history and their rights, not alone as a duty to

[59] Matt. 5:10.

the faith we hold in common, but as a testimony of their fortitude under trial and to the justice they preach in their dignified and legitimate demands. We bid them be of good cheer, for to Mexico in affliction may the significant words of the Master to the Apostle of the Gentiles be once more applied: "This man is to me a vessel of election, to carry my name before the Gentiles, and Kings, and the children of Israel. For I will show him how great things he must suffer for my name's sake."[60]

Given, this twelfth day of December, in the year of our Lord, MCMXXVI, feast of Our Lady of Guadalupe.

---

[60] Acts 9:15, 16.

3. THE HIERARCHY OF THE UNITED STATES

PASTORAL LETTER ON THE CATHOLIC CRUSADE FOR CHRISTIAN DEMOCRACY, THROUGH THE CATHOLIC UNIVERSITY OF AMERICA*

October 14, 1938

At the annual meeting of the archbishops and bishops of the United States held at the Catholic University, October 12, 13, and 14, 1938, the following letter was issued by the hierarchy. The letter was signed by Cardinal Dougherty in his own name and in the name of all the bishops present at the meeting.

To the Priests and Faithful of the United States:

On the occasion of the Golden Jubilee Year of the Catholic University of America, His Holiness, Pope Pius XI, has addressed a pontifical letter of grave import to Church and nation.**

The Holy Father, alarmed by the revolutionary conditions prevailing in most countries, charges us in a special manner to prepare for what may be a turning point in the history of the world. We must face the fact that the dangers of which His Holiness speaks threaten our own democratic institutions. The Pope emphatically calls upon us "to assume still greater and more momentous responsibilities than in the past."

When fifty years ago the bishops of America, with great foresight and courage, besought Pope Leo XIII to establish a Catholic university with a pontifical charter at the capital of the nation, they proposed to make it a citadel of truth and Christian culture, where inquiring minds could confidently move truthward and expose error, however subtle or insidious.

---

* *Catholic Action* (December, 1938), 7–8.
** *Solemnia jubilaria,* Sept. 21, 1938. See *Acta Apost. Sedis,* 30 (1938), 340–341.

The history of the Catholic University during a half century records the efforts and sacrifices of bishops, rectors, professors, priests, and religious communities, and the noble generosity of an appreciative laity.

If the Catholic world looks with approval upon our school system as the most extensive and best organized to be found anywhere, a large measure of credit is due the Catholic University. This organization has not been effected without laying a heavy financial burden upon the shoulders of the laity. The sacrifices of the founders, promoters, and teachers of our grammar schools, high schools, and colleges in our respective dioceses can never be adequately described. But the contribution made by the University to this school system is not widely known outside educational circles. We, however, who are familiar with the University, realize how effective have been its inspiration and work in building up Catholic education in the dioceses of our country.

Concerned as we naturally are with the educational needs of our own dioceses, the Catholic University may seem remote and, consequently, its influence on diocesan education may be underestimated, even overlooked. We must regard it, however, as an element essential to the completion of our educational system, and one which requires our unfailing and generous support. The Catholic University must be sustained by unanimous Catholic public opinion in order to assume its rightful supremacy in the field of Catholic education.

We must not think of the Catholic University as an isolated unit. Its progress will benefit all of us. Under its guidance our diocesan institutions can go forward, strengthened by Christian principles and standards and assured of timely warning against the dangers of secularism in education.

The work of the University proper during fifty years has progressed as steadily as its resources permitted. These resources, in comparison with those of other universities and in consideration of the vast possibilities in the field of higher Catholic education, have been sadly inadequate despite the generous gifts of many Catholics and the annual University collection taken up by order of the Holy See. The process of establishing a great center of learning and culture in our day and in our country is a slow one — too slow, indeed, in view of the pressing need of such an educational center. Let us, therefore, frankly acknowledge that after fifty years we are still building a Catholic University.

It is, then, with a sense of our grave pastoral responsibility that we beg all our people to be mindful of the urgent needs of the Catholic University and to heed the plea of our Holy Father to make the Jubilee Year an occasion not only of retrospect and commemoration but also and chiefly of prospect and dedication.

In that prospect and dedication we, the shepherds of souls, cannot but realize our need in these crucial days of outstanding leaders among the clergy and laity. Our seminaries and colleges are doing excellent work in laying solid foundations for this leadership. It is upon these foundations that the Catholic University, through graduate studies, would build with living stones the city of truth and Christian culture. Signal success has been achieved by Catholic universities in countries small in extent and meager in resources. Shall we, blessed in a vast country with more abundant resources and freedom to hearten us, do less for our University?

The Holy Father in his Jubilee letter lays special emphasis upon the sublime mission of the University in guarding the social heritage of man in the natural and supernatural order.

Pope Pius XI knows better than any other living person how that heritage is endangered today. "The world has entered," he says, "upon one of those periods of unrest, of questioning, of disorientation, and of conflict which have been well described as turning points of history. Christian doctrine and Christian morality are under attack from several quarters; dangerous theories which a few years ago were but whispered in the secret conventicles of discontent are today preached from the housetops, and are even finding their way into action; private immorality and public subversion have in many places raised the banner of revolt against the Cross of Christ."

We bishops, shepherds of souls, whose duty it is to guard the sheep of Christ and to seek other sheep not of His Fold, are seriously alarmed by the spread of subversive teaching and by the audacity of subversive action in our country. We are witnesses today of proclamations and programs which, if translated into action, would destroy all that is just and ennobling in liberty-loving America. When, therefore, Pope Pius XI says that the Catholic University "must, because of the exigencies of the present age, give special attention to the sciences of civics, sociology, and economics," His Holiness calls us to the defense of our democratic government, framed in a Constitution that safeguards the inalienable rights of man. The Pope explicitly instructs the Catholic University to "evolve a constructive program of social action, fitted in its details to local needs, which will command the admiration and acceptance of all right-thinking men."

This charge solemnly approves the American hierarchy's traditional position of unswerving allegiance to our free American institutions.

To carry out the injunction of the Holy Father it is necessary that our people, from childhood to mature age, be ever better instructed in the true nature of Christian democracy. A precise definition must be given to them both of democracy in the light of Catholic truth and tradition and of the rights and duties of citizens in a representative republic such as our own. They must be held to the conviction that love of country is a virtue and that disloyalty is a sin.

To foster this Christian concept of citizenship, the bishops in their annual meeting have charged the Catholic University of America to compile at once a more comprehensive series of graded texts for all educational levels. On the foundation of religious training, which is the distinctive characteristic of our schools, these texts will build an enlightened, conscientious American citizenship.

We, therefore, entreat all the faithful of every walk in life to unite in this Catholic crusade for better citizenship, which will bring to every individual wider opportunities for sound social education.

Through its own proper agencies, the Catholic University will put before the people its financial plea, which we earnestly endorse. We trust that all will respond generously to the appeal of the Holy Father and thus enable our University to render our country the priceless service of a more enlightened and vigorous Catholic citizenship.

During the Jubilee Year we entreat all committed to our pastoral care to join with us in making it possible for the Catholic University to render a greater measure of service to education and to religion. We ask for the University from all the children of our schools, from the communities of our Sisterhoods and Brotherhoods, and from the faithful the gift of a daily prayer, and from our priests a daily memento in Holy Mass.

May the divine Teacher deign to make our Catholic center of learning at Washington a providential exponent of the principles of a Christian social order which will command the acceptance of all right-thinking American citizens.

(In his own name and in the name of the bishops present at the annual meeting at Washington, 1938.)

✝ DENNIS CARDINAL DOUGHERTY,
Archbishop of Philadelphia

4. THE HIERARCHY OF THE UNITED STATES

STATEMENT OF THE BISHOPS OF THE UNITED STATES ON THE CRISIS OF CHRISTIANITY*

November 14, 1941

A statement of the Administrative Board of the National Catholic Welfare Conference, deputed by the bishops of the United States meeting in annual session at Washington, D. C., November 12–13, 1941, to express their mind on the historic position of the Catholic Church regarding the solution of problems incident to the present international and national situation.

Christianity faces today its most serious crisis since the Church came out of the catacombs.

We, the members of the Administrative Board of the National Catholic Welfare Conference, deputed in the annual meeting of the bishops of the United States to express their mind on the crisis of Christianity, declare, as shepherds of souls, that our concern is the supreme interest of religion. Our thoughts, therefore, turn to the two greatest evils of today, which would destroy all spiritual values. We find two subversive forces, both in control of powerful governments, both bent on world dominance. They are Nazism and Communism.

However plausible their constitutions and their propaganda, the alarming reality is that neither system understands nor permits freedom in its true Christian sense. Both systems usurp arbitrary power over the lives and destinies of men; their dictators assume a power which belongs to God alone.

Our late Holy Father significantly issued his epochal encyclicals on Nazism and Atheistic Communism within five days of each other.

---

* May be had in pamphlet form at the N.C.W.C. Headquarters, Washington 5, D. C.

SYSTEMS AND THEIR VICTIMS

His Holiness condemned the aberrations of Nazism, its denial of God in the true Christian sense, its deification of the State, its usurpation of the powers of God, of religion, and of parents, its falsification of Christian terminology, its betrayal of the eternal principles of objective morality, and its rejection of the rights and dignity of every human being. Pope Pius XI, with prophetic vision, declared that "its (Nazism) machinations, from the beginning, had no other aim than a war of extermination." He branded the Nazi oppressors of the Church in Germany as "the nullifiers and destroyers of the Christian West."

The late Holy Father, while condemning the Nazi system, expressed his love for the German people in these words: "Before our eyes stands the countless throng of faithful sons and daughters for whom the suffering of the Church in Germany, and their own suffering, has in no way diminished their devotion to the cause of God . . . nor diminished their cheerful readiness to remain true to what they have believed and have received from their forefathers as a sacred inheritance. From a heart that is deeply moved, we send them our paternal greeting."

The Holy See has condemned atheistic Communism. Popes Pius IX, Leo XIII, and Pius XI pronounced their solemn condemnations of the system. Exercising their God-given commission, the Roman pontiffs could take no other course than to condemn the errors, the tactics, the satanic designs of Communism. At no time can there be any possibility of compromising with an ideology that proclaims and acts upon the denial of a personal and omnipotent God, rejects contemptuously the divine Saviour of the world, all Christian principles and Christian culture, ruthlessly persecutes religion, and brutally murders its ministers. The leaders of atheistic Communism have done this nefarious work. Under them only anti-God and anti-Christian propaganda can have liberty of action.

POPE PIUS XI'S CONDEMNATION OF COMMUNISM

Pope Pius XI, who pronounced the most explicit condemnation of atheistic Communism, expressed in the same encyclical his paternal and compassionate benevolence for the people of Russia in these words:

"In making these observations it is no part of Our intention to condemn *en masse* the peoples of the Soviet Union. For them We cherish the warmest paternal affection. We are well aware that not a few of them groan beneath the yoke imposed on them by men who, in very large part, are strangers to the real interests of their country. We recognize that many were deceived by fallacious hopes. We blame only the system, with its authors and abettors who consider Russia the best field for experimenting with a plan elaborated decades ago, and who from there continue to spread it from one end of the world to the other."

AIMS FOR JUST PEACE

We, the bishops, who here express, at this critical hour, our judgment in these matters of gravest import, while enjoying, as we do, a well-ordered liberty in a free country, declare our devotion to His Holiness, Pope Pius XII, and our loyalty to his leadership as the Vicar of Christ and the Common Father of all nations and peoples. We unite with our Holy Father in praying for the attainment of a peace that will be accepted by all right-thinking governments and individuals as permeated by justice and charity. We earnestly ask our priests and people to continue their prayers that the violence of the war tempest may soon be spent, and that a just peace and an ordered prosperity may be restored to a distracted world.

POPE PIUS XII's FIVE POINTS

In a Christmas message to the world, His Holiness, Pope Pius XII, on December 4, 1939, laid down five points for a just and honorable peace. In our own statement of April, 1941, we urged the consideration of these conditions proposed by our Holy Father.

Again, in his message delivered on Christmas Eve, 1940, His Holiness reiterated these five indispensable prerequisites for the right kind of a new order in the world. He called them triumphs — the triumph over hate, over mistrust, over the spirit of ruthless selfishness, over the conflict in world economy, over the false principles that might makes right.

FUNDAMENTAL VALUES IN WORLD RECONSTRUCTION

Observing the fiftieth anniversary of the Magna Charta of labor, the *Rerum Novarum* of Leo XIII, His Holiness, Pope Pius XII, on June 1, 1941, spoke of "three fundamental values" which must be kept in mind for the reconstruction of the world after the present devastating war.

The first of these values has to do with the use of material goods. His Holiness quotes from the letter which he addressed to the American hierarchy, *Sertum Laetitiae,* on November 1, 1939, in which he stated that "the goods which were created by God for all men should flow equitably to all, according to the principles of justice and charity."

VALUE OF HUMAN LABOR

The second fundamental value considered by His Holiness is human labor. He says: "The duty and the corresponding right to work are imposed on, and conceded to, the individual in the first instance by nature and not by society. . . . The duty and the right to organize the labor of the people belong above all to . . . the employers and the workers. It devolves upon the State to intervene in the field of labor and in the division and distribution of work according to the form and measure that the common good, properly understood, demands. Every legitimate and beneficial interference of the State in the field of labor should be such as to safeguard and respect its personal character."

The third "value" emphasizes the importance of the possession of private property by the family. His Holiness insists that, of all goods which can be held as private property, "none is more conformable to nature than the land." The Holy Father lays stress on the social significance of widespread ownership of land in the form of the family homestead. To him, the function of the family as the root of a nation's greatness and power is bound up with family ownership of "the holding on which it lives, and from which it draws all or part of its subsistence." Without that "stability which is rooted in its own holding," the family cannot be the "cell of society" which nature destined it to be.

Domestic progress and peace depend on securing vital space for the rural family, as world progress and peace depend on securing living space for all the nations of the world. Accordingly, an adequate solution of the problems of emigration is of major importance in bringing tranquillity to a confused world.

HOPE FOR TOMORROW

Our Holy Father, despite the horrors of war which sadden his paternal heart, and the crushing burdens which his pontificate has laid upon him, is full of hope. His Holiness is looking, as he tells us, to that tomorrow "when the ruin of this world hurricane is cleared, and when the onset of a reconstruction of new social order (which is a desire worthy of God and of man) will infuse new courage and a new wave of profusion and growth in the garden of human culture." The words of the Pope of Peace regarding the conditions he lays down for peace and the triumphs to be achieved in the reconstruction of a world order in which justice and charity are to prevail deserve our most careful study.

PRAYERS FOR SUFFERING AND OPPRESSED

With apostolic liberty and with fraternal charity we send our greetings and sympathy to our suffering brother bishops and their flocks in all countries where subversive forces are persecuting religion and denying freedoms of conscience. Our fervent prayers are offered for their liberation, for their freedom to worship God according to the dictates of their conscience, for their freedom of education, their freedom of assembly, their freedom from the slavery of tyranny; the freedom of the sons of God.

Our sympathy goes out again to the peoples of those countries who have been crushed under the heel of the invader, and, indeed, to all upon whom war has imposed so heavy a burden of suffering and sacrifice. We cannot too strongly condemn the inhuman treatment to which the Jewish people have been subjected in many countries.

In the hour of cruel torture, we are mindful, daily at God's altar, of all the innocent victims of the war, of the homeless, the exiled, the imprisoned, and all who are suffering because of hunger or disease. We ask the faithful to unite with us in offering daily prayers and sacrifice in their behalf.

DEFENSE OF OUR COUNTRY

We support wholeheartedly the adequate defense of our country. Thoughtful statesmen are perplexed, patriotic citizens are divided in their opinions as to the procedure our country should follow. In these crucial times, when the civil fabric of every country is threatened and when dictators would destroy all religion, we herewith restate the position of the Catholic Church in the language of the immortal Pope Leo XIII:

"The Almighty has appointed the charge of the human race between two powers, the ecclesiastical and the civil: the one being set over divine, and the other over human things. Each in its kind is supreme; each has fixed limits within which it is contained, limits which are defined by the nature and special object of the province of each, so that there is, we may say, an orbit within which the action of each is brought into play by its own native right.

"But inasmuch as each of these two powers has authority over the same subjects, and as one and the same thing, under different aspects but still remaining identically the same, might chance to fall under the jurisdiction and determination of both powers, God, who foresees all things and is Author alike of these two powers, has marked out the course of each in correlation to the other. 'For the powers that are, are ordained of God' (Rom. 13:1). Were this not so, deplorable contentions and conflicts would often arise, and not infrequently men, like travelers at the meeting of two roads, would hesitate in anxiety and doubt, not knowing what course to follow. Two powers would be commanding contrary things, and it would be a dereliction of duty to disobey either of the two. But to judge thus of the wisdom and goodness of God would be most repugnant. . . . One of the two has for its proximate and chief object the well-being of this mortal life; the other, the joys of heaven. Whatever, therefore, in things human is of a sacred character, whatever belongs, either of its own nature or by reason of the end to which it is referred, to the salvation of souls, or to the worship of God, is subject to the power and judgment of the Church. Whatever is to be under the civil and political order is rightly subject to the civil authority. Jesus Christ has Himself given command that what is Caesar's is to be rendered to Caesar, and that what belongs to God is to be rendered to God."

RESPECT FOR AUTHORITY

Pondering this solemn teaching of Pope Leo XIII, we must recognize that all lawful authority is from God. "Let everyone be subject to the higher authorities, for there exists no authority except from God" (Rom. 13:1). Disrespect for authority, both ecclesiastical and civil, must be condemned. In the confusion of the hour, we deplore the presumption of those who, lacking authority, strive to determine the course of action that the Church should take within her clearly defined field. Recognizing the liberty of discussion, and even of criticism, which our democratic form of government guarantees, we urge and commend respect and reverence for the authority of our civil officials which has its source in God.

CONDUCT DURING THE WAR

At the present moment, in varying degrees, in every part of the world, the peaceful course of events is disturbed. People are called upon to make sacrifices and to suffer. Comparing our conditions in the United States with those of other lands, we must recognize that our country is singularly blessed. But we cannot avoid the repercussions of a world cataclysm. Our faith in a Divine Providence ruling the universe should inspire us to have confidence in the benevolent designs of a loving God who permits suffering to correct evil and to bring forth the fruits of justice and charity and peace.

URGE SPIRIT OF RESTRAINT

In this solemn hour when fateful decisions are to be made, it is evident that a spirit of exemplary restraint should characterize our priests and people. In every national crisis and every danger, our priests have been an inspiration. We are confident that their good example of strong faith and courage, founded on the virtue of fortitude, will not be lacking now. As moral teachers, they show that freedom has its limitations. It is limited, first of all, by the rights of God, and next, by the rights of others and by the interests of the common good.

As shepherds of souls, we are gravely concerned about the future of supernatural religion in our country. Here, as elsewhere, it is seriously threatened by growing evils of which our Holy Father has but recently warned the world. These are the evils of "false doctrine, immorality, disbelief and reborn paganism." The threat is to our youth, above all. Not only must we have a thorough understanding of the thoughts of the youth of our day, of its urge for action, of its fixed purpose to put teaching into practice, but pre-eminently, we must encourage youth to realize the constructive need of Christian doctrine and Christian discipline.

HOPE FOR LABOR PEACE

We are hopeful that priests and leaders among the laity will show an ever increasing interest in the cause of the multitudes who, in order to eke out a mere existence, are so largely taken up with the material things of life.

We express again our sympathy for labor and we appreciate the difficulties of maintaining family life with the mounting cost of living. In union with the Holy See, we have, on many occasions, condemned the evils of unrestrained capitalism. At the same time, in union with the Holy See, we hold that "our first and most fundamental principle, when we undertake to alleviate the condition of the masses, must be the inviolability of private property."

PAPAL APPROVAL OF UNION LABOR

Pope Leo XIII declared: "Religion teaches the laboring man and the workman to carry out honestly and well all equitable agreements freely made; never to injure capital nor to outrage the person of an employer; never to employ violence in representing his own cause, nor to engage in riot and disorder; and to have nothing to do with men of evil principles, who work upon the people with artful promises, and raise foolish hopes which usually end in disaster and repentance, when too late. Religion teaches the rich man and the employer that their work-people are not their slaves; that they must respect in every man his dignity as a man and as a Christian."

Popes Leo XIII and Pius XI expressed their approval of unions for the workers. As we think of the present difficulties in labor and trade unionism, we express the hope that the leaders will be well advised for the welfare of the workers of the nation; that they will keep before them the common good of the country; that they will refrain from doing anything that is harmful to the general welfare, and that they will come forth from the emergency of national defense united in closer co-operation with all right-minded employers and deserving the commendation of the general public.

Prayer for Unity and Guidance

If we trust in God we shall be constant in prayer. We shall pray for all the world, but especially for our own country; for the well-being of the Church, and for unity among our citizens. We shall pray that the Holy Spirit may enlighten, guide, and strengthen our Chief Executive, the Congress, and all who bear the grave responsibilities of government in these difficult days.

Signed:

✝ Most Rev. Edward Mooney, *Chairman, Archbishop of Detroit*

✝ Most Rev. John T. McNicholas, *Archbishop of Cincinnati*

✝ Most Rev. Samuel A. Stritch,   ✝ Most Rev. Hugh C. Boyle,
Archbishop of Chicago   *Bishop of Pittsburgh*

✝ Most Rev. John Gregory Murray, ✝ Most Rev. John F. Noll,
Archbishop of St. Paul   *Bishop of Fort Wayne*

✝ Most Rev. Francis J. Spellman, ✝ Most Rev. Edwin V. O'Hara,
Archbishop of New York   *Bishop of Kansas City*

✝ Most Rev. John Mark Gannon, ✝ Most Rev. John A. Duffy,
Bishop of Erie   *Bishop of Buffalo*

Administrative Board
National Catholic Welfare Conference

Washington, D. C.
November 14, 1941

5. THE HIERARCHY OF THE UNITED STATES

STATEMENTS ISSUED BY THE ARCHBISHOPS AND BISHOPS OF THE UNITED STATES ON VICTORY AND PEACE*

November 14, 1942

Our country has been forced into the most devastating war of all time. This war, which is the absorbing interest of all the world, involves unquestionably the most important moral issue of today. Some nations are united in waging war to bring about a slave world — a world that would deprive man of his divinely conferred dignity, reject human freedom, and permit no religious liberty. We are associated with other powers in a deadly conflict against these nations to maintain a free world. This conflict of principles makes compromise impossible.

While war is the last means to which a nation should resort, circumstances arise when it is impossible to avoid it. At times it is the positive duty of a nation to wage war in the defense of life and right. Our country now finds itself in such circumstances.

Even while we meet here, the exigencies of war have driven our armed forces into unexpected areas of conflict in Africa. Our President, in letters addressed to the rulers of all the friendly nations concerned, has given solemn assurance that the United States has no designs of permanent conquest or sordid interest. Our aim, he pledged, is to guarantee to countries under temporary occupation as well as to our own the right to live in security and peace. We bishops are confident that the pledge of our Chief Executive, not lightly made, faithfully mirrors the mind and conscience of the American people. That pledge is in full harmony with the expression of high purpose which

---

* May be had in pamphlet form at the N.C.W.C. Headquarters, Washington 5, D. C. Cf. N.C.W.C. pamphlet, *Victory and Peace* (Pope's messages, 1941–1942), 8–19; N.C.W.C. "News Release," 11/16/42–S, pp. 2–2a.

the President made to the Catholic bishops of the United States when our own country was plunged into war: "We shall win this war and in victory we shall seek not vengeance but the establishment of an international order in which the spirit of Christ shall rule the hearts of men and of nations."*

From the moment that our country declared war we have called upon our people to make the sacrifices which, in Catholic doctrine, the virtues of patriotism, justice, and charity impose. In every section of this nation the voices of our bishops have been heard. Their instructions, their pastorals, their counsels, their appeals for prayers are an encouragement and an inspiration to their flocks. Our priests as chaplains on the war front have inspired confidence in the men whom they so zealously serve. Our men in the armed forces deserve unstinted gratitude for their heroic services to our country and high commendation for the faithful practice of their religion.

In every diocese prayers have been incessantly offered, asking God's pardon for the sins of individuals and nations, begging divine mercy for all, pleading for a victory which will have the sanction of infinite justice and for an enduring peace founded on the love of God and the love of all men. Priests and people have earnestly prayed that the Holy Spirit may guide our President and all who share with him the heavy responsibilities of directing the war efforts and of winning the victory from which all peoples will derive a just and lasting peace.

In the discharge of our pastoral responsibility, we are gravely concerned about the world peace of tomorrow.

Secularism cannot write a real and lasting peace. Its narrow vision does not encompass the whole man, it cannot evaluate the spirituality of the human soul and the supreme good of all mankind.

Exploitation cannot write a real and lasting peace. Where greedy might and selfish expediency are made the substitutes of justice there can be no securely ordered world.

Totalitarianism, whether Nazi, Communist, or Fascist, cannot write a real and lasting peace. The State that usurps total powers, by that very fact, becomes a despot to its own people and a menace to the family of nations.

The Spirit of Christianity can write a real and lasting peace in justice and charity to all nations, even to those not Christian.

In the epochal revolution through which the world is passing, it is very necessary for us to realize that every man is our brother in

---

* See *Doc. 77b*.

Christ. All should be convinced that every man is endowed with the dignity of human personality, and that he is entitled by the laws of nature to the things necessary to sustain life in a way conformable to human dignity. In the postwar world, the profit element of industry and commerce must be made subservient to the common good of communities and nations if we are to have a lasting peace with justice and a sense of true brotherhood for all our neighbors. The inequalities of nations and of individuals can never give to governments or to the leaders of industry or commerce a right to be unjust. They cannot, if they follow the fixed principles of morality, maintain or encourage conditions under which men cannot live according to standards befitting human personality.

Unfortunately, in our day we must wage a global war to secure peace. War is abnormal and necessarily brings on abnormal conditions in the life of a nation.

During the war crisis free men must surrender many of their liberties. We ask our people to be united and prepared to make every sacrifice which our government deems necessary for a just and enduring peace through the victory of our armed forces. We are confident that they will perform their wartime duties gladly because they know that our country has been the defender, not the destroyer, of liberties and has in the past always re-established the full measure of peacetime freedom, on the conclusion of hostilities.

Our government has announced that the war emergency makes it necessary to employ an unprecedented number of women in industry. While we are wholeheartedly co-operating with our government in the prosecution of the war, we must, as shepherds of souls, express our grave concern about the Christian home in our beloved country in these crucial days. When mothers are engaged in industry a serious child care problem necessarily arises. Every effort must be made to limit, as far as necessity permits, the employment of mothers in industry, particularly young mothers. Due provision in harmony with American traditions should be made for the day care of the children of working mothers. The health and moral welfare of mothers employed in industry should be thoroughly safeguarded. With a full realization of the role which women must play in winning the war and of the extreme measures that our government must take, we ask that all try to realize the dangers involved, especially the moral dangers. We urge that there be a wholesome moral atmosphere wherever women are employed.

We know that patriotic mothers are generous in giving their sons to the defense of our country. We express their concern, and ours, about youths of eighteen years of age who are now to be called to the armed forces. We hope that special moral safeguards will shield them, so that they may serve their country without moral blemish.

We express our deepest sympathy to our brother bishops in all countries of the world where religion is persecuted, liberty abolished, and the rights of God and of man are violated. Since the murderous assault on Poland, utterly devoid of every semblance of humanity, there has been a premeditated and systematic extermination of the people of this nation. The same satanic technique is being applied to many other peoples. We feel a deep sense of revulsion against the cruel indignities heaped upon the Jews in conquered countries and upon defenseless peoples not of our faith. We join with our brother bishops in subjugated France in a statement attributed to them: "Deeply moved by the mass arrests and maltreatment of Jews, we cannot stifle the cry of our conscience. In the name of humanity and Christian principles our voice is raised in favor of imprescriptible rights of human nature." We raise our voice in protest against despotic tyrants who have lost all sense of humanity by condemning thousands of innocent persons to death in subjugated countries as acts of reprisal; by placing other thousands of innocent victims in concentration camps, and by permitting unnumbered persons to die of starvation.

The war has brought to the fore conditions that have long been with us. The full benefits of our free institutions and the rights of our minorities must be openly acknowledged and honestly respected. We ask this acknowledgment and respect particularly for our colored fellow citizens. They should enjoy the full measure of economic opportunities and advantages which will enable them to realize their hope and ambition to join with us in preserving and expanding in changed and changing social conditions our national heritage. We fully appreciate their many native gifts and aptitudes which, ennobled and enriched by a true Christian life, will make them a powerful influence in the establishment of a Christian social order.

We recall the words of Pope Pius XII expressing his paternal solicitude for the colored people of our country. In a letter addressed to the American bishops on the occasion of the 150th anniversary of the establishment of the American hierarchy, His Holiness said: "We confess that we feel a special paternal affection which is certainly inspired of heaven for the Negro people dwelling among you; for in the field of religion and education we know that they need special care and comfort and are very deserving of it. We, therefore, invoke an abundance of heavenly blessing and we pray fruitful success for those whose generous zeal is devoted to their welfare" (*Sertum Laetitiae*, 1939).

We send our cordial greetings to our brother bishops of Latin America. We have been consoled by recent events which give a sincere promise of a better understanding by our country of the peoples of Mexico, Central and South America. Citizens of these countries are bound to us by the closest bonds of religion. They are not merely our neighbors; they are our brothers, professing the same faith. Every effort made to rob them of their Catholic religion or to ridicule it or to offer them a substitute for it is deeply resented by the peoples of these countries and by American Catholics. These efforts prove to be a disturbing factor in our international relations. The traditions, the spirit, the background, the culture of these countries are Catholic. We bishops are anxious to foster every worthy movement which will strengthen our amicable relations with the republics of this continent. We express the hope that the mistakes of the past which were offensive to the dignity of our southern brothers, their culture and their religion, will not continue. A strong bond uniting in true friendship all the countries of the Western Hemisphere will exercise a most potent influence on a shattered postwar world.

We urge the serious study of the peace plans of Pope Pius XII which insist that justice be inspired by love — first, love of God and then, love of every human being. "The command of love among individuals found in the Gospels," said Benedict XV, "differs in no respect from that which should reign among states and peoples" (*Pacem Dei*, Benedict XV, 1920). If we are not to have a Christian peace, then we shall be given only an armistice, and we shall begin to prepare for a third world conflict.

We conclude by urging, again, unceasing prayers: the prayer of all prayers by priests, the Holy Mass; prayers addressed to the Blessed Virgin that she will intercede with her divine Son for mercy on a war-blighted world. We ask that Tuesday, December 8, the feast of the Immaculate Conception of our Blessed Mother, the Patroness of our country, be set aside as a special day of prayerful supplication. In its observance, the priests and faithful of every diocese will follow the timely instruction of their bishop. We recommend the recitation of the Rosary in common, both in our churches and in our homes. We trust that the children of our country will, in response to the many appeals of our Holy Father, offer their innocent prayers to God for peace. Let us all unite in praying for a victory and for a peace acceptable to God.

Signed by the members of the Administrative Board, N.C.W.C., in the name of the bishops of the United States:

✠ EDWARD MOONEY,
Archbishop of Detroit

✠ JOHN T. MCNICHOLAS,
Archbishop of Cincinnati

✠ SAMUEL A. STRITCH,
Archbishop of Chicago

✠ JOHN J. MITTY,
Archbishop of San Francisco

✠ JOSEPH F. RUMMEL,
Archbishop of New Orleans

✠ FRANCIS J. SPELLMAN,
Archbishop of New York

✠ JOHN MARK GANNON,
Bishop of Erie

✠ JOHN F. NOLL,
Bishop of Fort Wayne

✠ KARL J. ALTER,
Bishop of Toledo

✠ JOHN A. DUFFY,
Bishop of Buffalo

6. THE HIERARCHY OF THE UNITED STATES (THROUGH THE ADMINISTRATIVE BOARD) ON THE

ESSENTIALS OF A GOOD PEACE*

November 11, 1943

In the spirit of a free nation, whose rights and security have been wantonly attacked, our country is putting into its war effort the whole weight of our resources, our ingenuity, and our patriotism. We must be as determined to reap the full fruits of victory in a just peace as we are to win the war. We know that the sword cannot make peace. It can remove obstacles to peace, and it can impose its terms. But peace must be made first of all in the minds and wills of the victors. Unless we have the vision of a good peace and the will to demand it, victory can be an empty, even a tragic thing.

It is with these thoughts in mind that we deem it timely again to focus attention on the first essentials of a good peace. The responsibility for the postwar social reconstruction will fall on the victors. Many serious men have misgivings that there may be tragic com-

---

* Reprinted from *Catholic Action*, 25:12 (December, 1943).

promises and a fateful repudiation of sound principles. These men are not pessimists or obstructionists, but they know the forces at play in the world about us. The declarations of the Moscow Conference do, indeed, open the way to necessary international co-operation for peace as well as for war. In this they represent a definite step in the right direction. They do not, however, dispel the fear that compromises on the ideals of the Atlantic Charter are in prospect. Some things these documents imply by statement and, more significantly still, by omission leave an uneasiness in minds intent on peace with justice to all.

Not to enter the domain of statesmanship, but speaking as pastors of souls and teachers of religion, we wish to emphasize some fundamental social truths, deriving from religion, and to plead for their general recognition. It is heartening to note the wide agreement on the moral postulates of a just peace among religious leaders, otherwise divided by the deep cleavage of fundamental doctrinal differences. This significant and hopeful agreement has recently been evidenced in three parallel statements on World Peace issued by American religious groups. This pattern for peace fashioned on the moral law has attracted nationwide attention and will, we hope, be carefully studied by all men of good will. It is our purpose here to go deeper into our Catholic heritage of truth in faith and reason and to indicate the application of primary religious truth to the problems of peace and the planning of a right social order.

Without doubt the root of the maladies which afflict modern society and have brought on the catastrophe of world war is the social forgetfulness and even the rejection of the sovereignty of God and of the moral law. There is written in human reason the law of good and evil, which calls to God for its authority and its sanctions. When this moral law is cast aside in social life, every principle, every right, every virtue rests on the shifting sands of mere human conventions. Human dignity, human solidarity become, then, not endowments from the Creator but mere fictions of man-made systems. In the quest for some principle for social stability, the authority of the State is exaggerated and its function of protecting and defending the rights of the citizens in the pursuits of the common good cedes to a tyrannical violation and invasion of these rights. In the name of realism the rights of the weak and the helpless are sacrificed. A first principle for a sane reconstruction of society is the social recognition of God's sovereignty and of the moral law.

What reason tells us about God and His moral law is complemented and supplemented, is made definite and achievable in the Gospel of

Christ. It is significant that when the Western peoples socially ostracized the Saviour and put their faith in secularism, they lost a clear vision of the moral law. They found no effective inspiration to civic virtue in materialism and naturalism, which despite signal advances in science, invention, and administrative techniques, closed the avenues of genuine social progress. We shall go back to God and the moral law when we re-establish Christ in our social life.

The recognition of the sovereignty of God and of the moral law, as treasured in the Christian tradition, is basic to the right ordering of international relations. In creation God gave to the human race its essential unity and bound all men together in a brotherhood as comprehensive as humanity itself. In the plan of Divine Providence the human family was divided into nations and races, but this division in no way impaired the essential unity of mankind. When sin broke man's right relation with God and brought disunion between man and man, nation and nation, our blessed Saviour restored, perfected, and ennobled human brotherhood. The ideal of human brotherhood must inspire international relations. Only when this ideal is accepted by men and nations will the exploitation of the weak cease and jungle exaltation of might be outlawed.

This does not mean that national rights and national sovereignties, rightly interpreted, must be surrendered to a world government. It does mean that every nation and every people must recognize and satisfy its obligations in the family of nations. The discharge of these duties is entirely compatible with national differences which give a happy variety of cultural treasures in human unity. Indeed these differences must be respected and defended, and every effort must be made to assist peoples now in tutelage to a full juridic status among the nations of the world.

In the circumstances of our times it is imperative that the nations in satisfaction of their responsibilities unite in setting up international institutions for the preservation of world peace and mutual assistance. Such institutions, rightly conceived, are in full harmony with the divine plan of human solidarity and should be helpful to rightly interpreted sovereignty and independence.

The social recognition of the sovereignty of God and of the moral law must be a first norm for the right ordering of the internal life of nations. Circumstances of history, differences of culture, and economic inequalities create differences of political forms. But all nations, if they are to conform to the moral law, must embody in their political structures the guaranty of the free exercise of native human rights, encouragement in the practice of virtue, an honest concern for the common good, and a recognition of the inviolability of the human person. No nation has under God authority to invade family freedom, abrogate private ownership, or impede, to the detriment of the common good, economic enterprise, co-operative undertakings for mutual welfare, and organized works of charity sponsored by groups of citizens. It is only when nations adhere to right principles in their domestic administration that they will co-operate for the common good of the family of nations.

Where God and the moral law are not given social recognition, human laws lose their stability and binding force. Ours is a tradition of government under law. In that tradition, law is not the expression of the will even of the majority, but of right reason, which reflects the law of Nature and of God. We ourselves have seen in the sorry experiences of other countries the tyranny and injustice which come from government by decree under a dictator or a party. When civil law conforms to the moral law and seeks its greatest sanction in that law, there is social stability, and the common good is promoted. It would be a tragic mistake to forsake our tradition of law even to achieve a greater efficiency in administration. It would be a greater tragedy to forsake our tradition of law for a currently popular philosophy which fails to base law on the eternal maxims of justice and disregards the inalienable rights of the citizen which derive from God.

It troubles us to see in the publication of crime statistics that there is a widespread disrespect for law, particularly in the youth of our country. No graver indictment of our social behavior could be written. A greater effort to protect the stability and the sanctity of the home and to inculcate moral discipline will contribute much to the solution of this problem. A better supervision of recreational activities in our communities will likewise be helpful. But more than all, we must instill in the soul of youth deeper respect for authority and greater devotion to the common good. How can these things be done unless there is a frank social recognition of God and the moral law? Certainly no system of thought and action based on a materialistic concept of life offers any promise of better things.

In God's plan the family is a social institution with its own rights and dignity. Its stability, unity, and sanctity are as necessary to a right social order as the proper constitution of government itself. If in the family right order prevails, and the children are trained in virtue, there is a guaranty for social well-being. Where the State violates family rights and makes light of family stability and parental responsibility, no amount of welfare work carried on or promoted by public authority will adequately provide for social well-being. The political authority which earnestly seeks the common good of all citizens will not fail to lend itself to the establishment of a just family wage, in order that family income may be commensurate with the discharge of family duties. Nor will the prudent, wise, political authority, for any seeming temporary advantage, fail to recognize the function and dignity of woman in society and to warn her against the false economy of our times, which turns her mind and heart away from the home, thereby depriving the family, State, and Church of her proper contribution to the common welfare.

We voice a grave warning against the propaganda of so-called planned parenthood, which violates the moral law, robs the family of its nobility and high social purpose, and weakens the physical and moral fiber of the nation. We plead for a return to the Christian concept of marriage, in which sex has such a high and noble function. We condemn the prevalent perverted teaching on sex which is degrading our youth, destroying the sanctity of the home, and prostituting the social function of the family to individual caprice. God is not mocked with impunity. Neopagan views on marriage which are being propagated with misguided zeal in our country can lead only to moral ruin and national decadence.

It would be inconsistent to promote a world reconstruction in which all nations, great and small, powerful and weak, would enjoy their rights in the family of nations, unless in our own national life we recognize an equality of opportunity for all our citizens and willingly extend to them the full benefits of our democratic institutions.

In the Providence of God there are among us millions of fellow citizens of the Negro race. We owe to these fellow citizens, who have contributed so largely to the development of our country, and for whose welfare history imposes on us a special obligation of justice, to see that they have in fact the rights which are given them in our Constitution. This means not only political equality, but also fair economic and educational opportunities, a just share in public welfare projects, good housing without exploitation, and a full chance for the social advancement of their race. When given their rights in fact as in law, they will prize with us our national heritage and not lend ear to agitators whose real objective is not to improve but to destroy our way of living.

In many of our great industrial centers acute racial tensions exist. It is the duty of every good citizen to do everything in his power to

relieve them. To create a neighborhood spirit of justice and conciliation will be particularly helpful to this end. We hope that our priests
and people will seek opportunity to promote better understanding of
the many factors in this complex problem and strive for its solution
in a genuine Catholic spirit.

And we plead as well for a generous interest in the welfare of our
Spanish-speaking population. Many of them go back through a long
line to the first settlers who came into our Southwest, and others have
come in recent years from Mexico. They also have a right to expect
the full enjoyment of our democratic institutions and that help in
social life which is accorded to others. The sincerity of our Good
Neighbor Policy with Latin America, so Christian in its spirit and so
well calculated to foster right international relations, will be attested
by our attitude toward our fellow citizens of Latin-American origin or
descent.

If the responsibility faced by the victors is great, the opportunity
is historical. Now there comes the chance not in hatred or vengeance
but in justice and charity to base a social reconstruction on truth and
right. The men of our fighting forces, in whose gallantry and heroism
we rejoice: their loved ones whose anxiety we share will be satisfied
with nothing less. The peoples of the world, the simple peoples, the
fathers of families, the toilers and laborers, the people who have the
same interests and the same ambitions which we cherish are looking
to us, to this great land of freedom. We must not disappoint them.
It is our historic opportunity to do our full duty in the family of
nations. The causes of war must be removed, the honest needs of
people must be met, their rights recognized. This must be a good peace
which our victory will achieve. But first let us make ourselves in very
truth peacemakers. Let us recognize the problems in our own social
life and courageously seek the solution of them. A first principle must
be the recognition of the sovereignty of God and of the moral law in
our national life and in the right ordering of a new world born of the
sacrifices and hardships of war.

7. THE HIERARCHY OF THE UNITED STATES (THROUGH THE ADMINISTRATIVE BOARD)

STATEMENT ON INTERNATIONAL ORDER*

November 16, 1944

The Catholic bishops of the United States at the close of their annual meeting in Washington, D. C. (November 16–19, 1944) issued the following statement on International Order. It was signed in their names by the Administrative Board of the National Catholic Welfare Conference.

We have met the challenge of war. Shall we meet the challenge of peace?

This is the question uppermost in the minds of men everywhere who in suffering and hardship have stood out against ruthless aggression. The men of our armed forces, the masses of our citizens, our leaders, all want to be true to our heroes who have given so much, some even their lives, in this war for freedom. They want to be true, as well, to future generations on whom we have been forced to place a heavy burden as the price for their freedoms. Honestly, earnestly we want to garner from the sacrifices, hardships, and losses which have gone into this war, the full fruits of victory, in a good peace. The foremost problem in postwar planning is how to secure for ourselves and all the world a just and lasting peace.

Recently representatives of the United States, the United Kingdom, the Soviet Union, and China at Dumbarton Oaks formulated and presented to their governments broad tentative proposals for an international organization for "the maintenance of peace and security and the creation of conditions which make for peace." These proposals have been given to the public for full study and discussion by peoples of all countries. Our own Secretary of State has expressed the hope that leaders of our national thought and opinion will discuss them in the spirit of constructive effort.

---

* Published by the Administrative Board of the N.C.W.C., Washington 5, D. C. N.C.W.C. "News Release," November 19, 1944.

FREEDOM FROM HATRED, GREED

Public opinion in our country can exert a tremendous influence in making the peace and determining the manner of international collaboration for its maintenance. If public opinion is indifferent or uninformed, we shall run the risk of a bad peace and perhaps return to the tragedy of "power politics," which in the past divided nations and sowed the seeds of war. If public opinion is alert and informed, we can have a lasting peace and security. It is imperative that all our citizens recognize their responsibility in the making and maintenance of the peace. They must inform themselves on the issues and form their judgments in the light of sound reason and our Christian democratic traditions. They must free themselves from hatred, from distrust, from the spirit of mere expediency, from national greed, and from indifference to right in the use of might, and they must form their judgments on the basis of stern objective realities.

This war came largely from bad education. It was not brought on by primitives or unlettered peoples. The contemporary philosophy which asserts the right of aggression is the creation of scholars. Discarding moral principles and crowding God out of human life, scholars produced the monstrous philosophies which, embodied in political and social systems, enslave human reason and destroy the consciousness of innate human rights and duties. In these systems the notion of the common good is utterly distorted; it is no longer conceived as the consequence of the common enjoyment of rights and the common discharge of duties, but the creation of the caprice of a dictator or a group or a party. The gilded dreams of a new era, which these systems heralded, have proved to be a hideous nightmare. If we are to have a just and lasting peace, it must be the creation of a sane realism, which has a clear vision of the moral law, a reverent acknowledgment of God its Author, and a recognition of the oneness of the human race underlying all national distinctions.

ATLANTIC CHARTER, WITHOUT EQUIVOCATIONS

We have no confidence in a peace which does not carry into effect, without reservations or equivocations, the principles of the Atlantic Charter. We feel, too, that it should provide assistance for prostrate nations in reconstructing their economic, social, and political institutions. If justice is compromised, if unreasonable concessions are made to might, grievances will rankle in the bosom of aggrieved nations to endanger the peace of the world. If prostrate nations are not assisted in giving to their people fair economic opportunities, they will become the arena of civil strife and turmoil. No international organization will be able to maintain a peace which is unfair and unjust.

There is an international community of nations. God Himself has made the nations interdependent for their full life and growth. It is not, therefore, a question of creating an international community but of organizing it. To do this we must repudiate absolutely the tragic fallacies of "power politics" with its balance of power, spheres of influence in a system of puppet governments, and the resort to war as a means of settling international difficulties.

MIGHT MUST YIELD TO LAW

After the last world war an attempt was made to organize the international community. It failed not because its objective was mistaken but because of inherent defects in its charter and more especially perhaps because the nations were not disposed to recognize their duty to work together for the common good of the world. International law must govern international relations. Might must be subordinated to law. An international institution, based on the recognition of an objective moral obligation and not on the binding force of covenant alone, is needed for the preservation of a just peace and the promotion of international co-operation for the common good of the international community. The common good of every nation is inseparably connected with the common good of the international community.

The international institution must be universal. It must seek to include, with due regard to basic equality of rights, all the nations, large and small, strong and weak. Its constitution must be democratic. While it is reasonable to set up a Security Council with limited membership, this Council must not be an instrument for imperialistic domination by a few powerful nations. Before it every nation must stand on its rights and not on its power. It must not allow any nation to sit in judgment in its own case. Frankly it must recognize that for nations as well as individuals life is not static. It must therefore provide in its charter for the revision of treaties in the interest of justice and the common good of international community, as well as for the recognition of a people's coming of age in the family of nations.

STRONG NATIONS MUST HELP WEAK

The function of the international organization must be the maintenance of international peace and security, the promotion of international co-operation and the adoption of common policies for the solution of common economic, social, and other humanitarian problems. In the maintenance of peace it is reasonable that the organization have at its disposal resources for coercing outlaw nations even by military measures.

In fostering and promoting international co-operation it must seek to guarantee to the weak and poor nations economic opportunities which are necessary to give their peoples reasonable standards of living, and it must seek to prevent selfish monopolistic control of raw materials which are needed for the economic stability of other nations. Effective international co-operation lays definite duties on favored nations. No nation may view with unconcern conditions that permit millions of workers in any country to be without the opportunity to secure from their labor adequate family support. Nations rich in natural resources must remember that ownership of property never dispenses from the social obligations of stewardship. Nations gifted with inventive and productive genius are obligated to serve the reasonable needs of other nations. Nations should open, under effective guarantees, world lanes of commerce and world avenues of communication to all law-abiding countries. Protective national legislation for legitimate national economic interests must not impede the flow of international commerce and the right social function of international exchange.

TEETH FOR WORLD COURT

In the international organization there should be a world court to which justiciable disputes among nations must be submitted. Its authority should not be merely advisory but strictly judicial. A condition for the right functioning of this court is the proper development and codification of international law. Competent international authority must enact into positive law the principles of the moral law in their international references, and to these will be added positive treaty provisions and the charter and legislation of the international organization.

The world court should be empowered to render decisions in cases submitted to it either by any party in interest or by the international organization. It must have authority to refer its decisions to the international organization for execution. It would be useless to set up a world court and either deny it the right to demand the execution of its decisions or make the execution of them subject to the discretion of the international organization. Nations which refuse to submit their international disputes which constitute a threat to the peace or the common good of the international community should be treated by the international organization as outlaw nations. Moreover, obligatory arbitration of international disputes which threaten world peace would mark a signal advance in international relations.

INSIST ON INNATE RIGHTS OF MAN

The international organization must never violate the rightful sovereignty of nations. Sovereignty is a right which comes from the juridical personality of a nation and which the international organization must safeguard and defend. However, national sovereignty may not be interpreted as absolving a nation from its obligations in the international community. Moreover, even within the State, national sovereignty is limited by the innate rights of men and families. Since civil authority does not confer these God-given rights, it may not violate them.

The ideology of a nation in its internal life is a concern of the international community. To reject this principle is tantamount to maintaining that the violation of the innate rights of men in a country by its own government has no relation to world peace. Just at this moment, in the interest of world peace, our nation is exerting itself to root out some ideologies which violate human rights in the countries we are liberating. We hold that if there is to be a genuine and lasting world peace, the international organization should demand as a condition of membership that every nation guarantee in law and respect in fact the innate rights of men, families, and minority groups in their civil and religious life. Surely our generation should know that tyranny in any nation menaces world peace. A nation which refuses to accord to its own people the full enjoyment of innate human rights cannot be relied upon to co-operate in the international community for the maintenance of a peace which is based on the recognition of national freedom. Such a nation will pursue its own selfish international policies, while paying lip service to international co-operation.

FREE MEN, FREE NATIONS

We have it within our power to introduce a new era, the era for which peoples have been longing through the centuries, the era in which nations will live together in justice and charity. It is a Christian hope we want to realize, the hope of a world at peace, a world of sovereign states co-operating in assuring all men the full enjoyment of their rights, a world of free men and free nations with their freedom secured under law. War may come, but if our hope is realized it will be a war of punishment meted out to outlaw nations. Through all the sufferings and sacrifices of this war we have remembered and we recall today the words of our Chief Executive, written at its beginning: "We shall win this war and in victory we shall seek not vengeance but the establishment of an international order in which the spirit of Christ shall rule the hearts of men and of nations."

Signed by the members of the Administrative Board, N.C.W.C., in the names of the bishops of the United States:

✠ Edward Mooney, *Chairman,*
  Archbishop of Detroit

✠ Samuel A. Stritch, *Vice-Chairman,*
  Archbishop of Chicago

✠ Francis J. Spellman, *Secretary,*
  Archbishop of New York

✠ John T. McNicholas,
  Archbishop of Cincinnati

✠ John Gregory Murray,
  Archbishop of St. Paul

✠ John J. Mitty,
  Archbishop of San Francisco

✠ Joseph F. Rummel,
  Archbishop of New Orleans

✠ John F. Noll,
  Bishop of Fort Wayne

✠ Karl J. Alter,
  Bishop of Toledo

✠ James H. Ryan,
  Bishop of Omaha

8. THE HIERARCHY OF THE UNITED STATES (THROUGH THE ADMINISTRATIVE BOARD)

BETWEEN WAR AND PEACE*

November 18, 1945

The war is over but there is no peace in the world. In the Atlantic Charter we were given the broad outline of the peace for which we fought and bled and, at an incalculable price, won a great martial victory. It was that ideal of peace which sustained us through the war, which inspired the heroic defense of liberty by millions driven underground in enslaved countries. It made small, oppressed nations con-

---

* Cf. N.C.W.C. "News Release" for November 18, 1945.

fide in us as the trustee of their freedoms. It was the broad outline of a good peace. Are we going to give up this ideal of peace? If, under the pretext of a false realism, we do so, then we shall stand face to face with the awful catastrophe of atomic war.

Since the Moscow Conference of 1943, the United States, Great Britain, and Russia have undertaken to shape gradually the peace which they are imposing on the nations. From the conferences of these victorious powers there is emerging slowly their pattern for the peace. It is disappointing in the extreme. Assurances are given us in the announced peace principles of our country but so far results do not square with these principles. We are in perhaps the greatest crisis of human history. Our country has the power, the right, and the responsibility to demand a genuine peace, based on justice which will answer the cry in the hearts of men across the world.

We want to work in unity with other nations for the making of a good peace. During the war perhaps, it may have been necessary for strategic reasons to postpone final decisions on many questions mooted at the conferences of the three great powers. Now we must face the facts. There are profound differences of thought and policy between Russia and the Western democracies. Russia has acted unilaterally on many important settlements. It has sought to establish its sphere of influence in eastern and southeastern Europe, not on the basis of sound regional agreements in which sovereignties and rights are respected, but by the imposition of its sovereignty and by ruthlessly setting up helpless puppet States. Its Asiatic policy, so important for the peace of the world, is an enigma.

The totalitarian dictators promise benefits to the masses through an omnipotent police State which extends its authority to all human relations and recognizes no innate freedom. Their theories, moreover, look to the realization of world well-being as ultimately to be secured by the inclusion of all countries in their system. Sometimes Russia uses our vocabulary and talks of democracy and rights but it attaches distorted meanings to the words. We think in terms of our historic culture. We see God-given, inviolable human rights in every person and we know democracy as the free collaboration under law of citizens in a free country.

There is a clash of ideologies. The frank recognition of these differences is preliminary to any sincere effort in realistic world co-operation for peace. The basis of this co-operation must be mutual adherence to justice. It would be unjust for us to be an accomplice in violating the rights of nations, groups, and individuals anywhere in the world.

A first step toward effective negotiation for peace is to have a plan. A good plan states principles in terms of all the specific questions at issue. Instead, so far we have compromised and sought to make mere piecemeal settlements. Instead of honest, promising discussion even on diverging plans, we are witnessing a return of the tragedy of power politics and the danger of balance of power arrangements which, with the substitution of mere expediency for justice, have begotten war after war. We must indeed aim at collaborating with all of our allies in the making of a good peace. There are, however, concessions which we dare not make because they are immoral and destructive of genuine peace.

Peace Program

Our peace program envisions a world organization of nations. The charter which emerged from the San Francisco Conference, while undoubtedly an improvement on the Dumbarton Oaks proposals, does not provide for a sound, institutional organization of the international society. The Security Council provisions make it no more than a virtual alliance of the great powers for the maintenance of peace. These nations are given a status above the law. Nevertheless, our country acted wisely in deciding to participate in this world organization. It is better than world chaos. From the provision in the charter for calling a constituent assembly in the future, there comes the hope that in time the defects may be eliminated and we may have a sound institutional organization of the international community which will develop, not through mere voluntary concessions of the nations, but from the recognition of the rights and duties of international society.

While peace is in the making, there are urgent issues which we can no longer evade. At Yalta we gave a pledge to the Polish people and assumed responsibility before the world that they would be unhampered in setting up their own independent, democratic government. Are we working to the fulfillment of that pledge in the full measure of our responsibility and our power? What apology can be offered for the failure of the protagonists of democracy to protest the absorption by force and artifice of the Baltic countries into the Union of Soviet Republics? We are shocked by the news which is leaking out from Slovakia, Croatia, Slovenia, and other southeastern European countries. Religious persecution which is both brutal and cunning rages in many lands. No reason of policy justifies our silence. What is happening behind the blackout of eastern and southeastern Europe is a stark contradiction to the high ideals which inspired our fighting to save the world from totalitarian aggression.

No one can fail to see the importance of a reconstructed, revitalized Europe which is the cradle of Western culture. We deplore the tragic indifference to the plight of the Italian people who threw off the chains of a Fascist regime, who fought side by side with us in ardent loyalty. For over two long years of agony the friends of democracy in that country have had to stand by in impotence while we have toyed with the vital problems of relief and rehabilitation and deferred the fulfillment of our own solemn promises.

MERCY TO ENEMIES

Our own national interest, as well as the cause of world peace, and the fate of Christian culture are at stake in Italy. Today it is an outpost of Western civilization. We are fully confident that the Italian people, if we save them from despair by our helpful interest, will stand fast against the deceitful appeal of alien and subversive ideologies and shape their future in the spirit of their own noble tradition.

We cannot be unconcerned about the future of Germany, Austria, and Hungary. Whatever period of probation must be imposed on the vanquished nations, we must help them to take their rightful place in the family of nations. To treat them in a spirit of vengeance is neither right nor politic. Justice demands the punishment of the guilty and reasonable reparations of damage done. But we cannot forget, or allow our representatives to forget, that our traditional system of punitive justice is anchored to the concept of individual responsibility. The inhumanities which now mark the mass transference of populations, the systematized use of slave labor, and the cruel treatment of prisoners of war should have no place in our civilization.

Acute suffering is the daily lot of whole populations in many wartorn lands. Every report indicates that unless heroic measures are taken at once, millions will die from starvation and exposure during the coming winter. The feeding and clothing and sheltering of these suffering people is not a work which can be left to some future convenient date. Our country, because of our greater resources, must do the major part of this work of relief. In it we have the right and duty to insist on the leadership which corresponds to our sacrifices and contributions. It is imperative that Congress make adequate appropriations for this work from the public treasury.

PRIVATE RELIEF

It is equally imperative that private relief agencies be given a full opportunity to carry on their beneficent work among all suffering peoples. And relief must envision something larger than merely feeding the starving and sheltering the homeless. Help must be given to peoples whose economies are ruined. They have the right to assistance in getting back to normal economic life. Neither the prosperity of the greater nations nor their might will prevent war unless conditions are removed in which poor, helpless peoples are denied the opportunity of a decent living standard. The world is one only insofar as men live together as brothers under God.

Ours is a grave responsibility. The heart and hand of America are called upon in a way that is unique, not only in the history of our country but even in the annals of mankind. We know that democracy is as capable of solving the admittedly difficult problems of peace as it has shown itself in war. We must be true to ourselves. We must hold fast to our own free institutions. We must resolutely oppose the few amongst us who are trying to sabotage them. We may well pity those who in their half-veiled sympathy for totalitarianism are playing with the thought that perhaps in this great emergency its day is at hand. On bended knees let us ask God in His blessed Providence to help us to be the vigorous champion of democratic freedom and the generous friend of the needy and oppressed throughout the world.

Signed by the members of the Administrative Board, N.C.W.C., in the names of the bishops of the United States:

✠ SAMUEL A. STRITCH,
   Archbishop of Chicago
✠ JOHN GREGORY MURRAY,
   Archbishop of St. Paul
✠ FRANCIS J. SPELLMAN,
   Archbishop of New York
✠ JOHN MARK GANNON,
   Bishop of Erie
✠ JOHN J. MITTY,
   Archbishop of San Francisco

✠ JOSEPH F. RUMMEL,
   Archbishop of New Orleans
✠ RICHARD J. CUSHING,
   Archbishop of Boston
✠ JAMES H. RYAN,
   Archbishop of Omaha
✠ JOHN F. NOLL,
   Bishop of Fort Wayne
✠ KARL J. ALTER,
   Bishop of Toledo

9. THE HIERARCHY OF THE UNITED STATES (THROUGH THE ADMINISTRATIVE BOARD) ON

MAN AND THE PEACE!*

November 17, 1946

At the bottom of all problems of the world today is the problem of man. Unless those who bear the responsibility of world leadership are in basic agreement on what man is, there is no way out of the confusion and conflict which block the road to real peace. Clashes on the question of boundaries, national security, minority safeguards, free movement of trade, easy access to raw materials, progressive disarmament, and the control of the atomic bomb, important as these are, take a second place to the need of unity in protecting man in the enjoyment of his God-given native rights. The struggle of the small nations for their indisputable rights and the stalemate among the strong nations in a contest of power would admit of bearable, even though hard, compromise if the fate of man, as man, did not hang in the balance.

To be more explicit, it is a question whether national governments are disposed to protect or to hinder the individual in the exercise of rights and in the discharge of duties which are proper to him prior to any action by the State. The words of our own Declaration of Independence express no new doctrine but voice the basic tradition of Christian civilization: "We hold these truths to be self-evident, that all men are created equal, that they are endowed by their Creator with certain unalienable rights, that among these are life, liberty, and the pursuit of happiness." Respect for the rights and duties of man as an individual and as a member of civic and domestic society we hold to be the first obligation of any government to its citizens. The State has a just claim on the co-operation of its citizens for the common good, but not to the point of coercion in violation of their personal political, social, and religious rights. What a government cannot do in the exercise of its own sovereignty it cannot approve or abet on the part of

---

* Published by the N.C.W.C., Washington 5, D. C.; cf. N.C.W.C. "News Release," November 18, 1946.

another government in the settlement of complicated issues such as confront the nations in making peace and planning for its preservation.

THE CONFLICT BETWEEN RUSSIA AND THE WEST

The menace to man as man looms large in the outstanding questions which engage the attention of the victorious allies. It hangs in the background of the conflict between Russia and the West which has so long delayed the making of the peace. Eighteen months have passed since the surrender and occupation of Germany and fifteen months since the capitulation of Japan. There have been continuous negotiations among the three great victors, the United States, Britain, and Russia, for the conclusion of agreements on stable peace and reconstruction. These negotiations have brought out in the clear the tragic lack of unity among the peacemakers on fundamental issues. In some instances agreements which were pointed to the safeguarding of basic human rights, reached in conferences, have been repudiated unilaterally by the action of one of the victors, and these repudiations have been tolerated by the other nations which were parties to the agreements. In an effort to preserve unity, fatal compromises have been made, either explicitly or by tolerance of shocking aggressions. In so difficult a task it is understandable that there should be differences and a clash of interests. Some sort of sacrifice of particular national advantages for the common good of the international community, and therefore for the ultimate good of all nations, must be made. But the tragic fact is that the cleavage touches on issues on which there can be no compromise. While it is stated that the Western democracies and Russia with her satellite governments in the countries of eastern Europe are at a stalemate over questions of security against aggressions, the fact is that underlying these questions there is the question of man, as man. Throughout the war our battle cry was the defense of native freedoms against Nazi and Fascist totalitarianism. The aftermath of war has revealed victorious Soviet totalitarianism no less aggressive against these freedoms in the countries it has occupied. Totalitarianism does not acknowledge and respect these freedoms. It persecutes the citizen who dares assert his native rights. It imposes on peoples its philosophy of life, in which there is no authority above the State, and in which all values in life are derived from human conventions. The corollary of such philosophy is the police State, which terrorizes its citizens and dominates them in all fields of human behavior. Before we can hope for a good peace there must come an agreement among the peacemakers on the basic question of man, as man.

If this agreement is reached, then secondary, though important, defects in the peace may be tolerable in the hope of their eventual correction. Misrepresentations, deceitful promises, the use of equivocal language, and violation of agreements only widen the cleavage between nations. In the charter of the United Nations the signatories have contracted to co-operate "in promoting and encouraging respect for human rights and for fundamental freedoms for all without distinction as to race, language or religion." Let the nations in the making of the peace do even more and in solemn covenants actually secure men everywhere in the enjoyment of their native rights. Then there will be the beginnings of peace, and the fear of war will be banished from men's minds.

PLEA FOR PRISONERS OF WAR

Considerations of human dignity are deeply involved in the fate of prisoners of war. The strict observance of international law does not oblige the victorious nations to repatriate prisoners of war until after the conclusion of the peace, but owing to the circumstance of the long delay in making the peace, the contention of our country for the speedy repatriation of these prisoners is admirably humane and almost a dictate of justice. There are millions of them separated from their families and kept from their normal occupations, engaged in forced labor, and in many cases underfed. They are needed at home for the work of reconstruction. The use of prisoners of war as slave laborers in alien lands should not be any part of reparations levied by the victors. They are men, and they should be treated as men. So large is their number, estimated as high as 7,000,000, that even with every effort put forth for their speedy repatriation, it will take years to transport them back to their own countries in an orderly way. It is the strict obligation of all nations to treat these prisoners as we demanded that our combatants, who fell into the hands of the enemy, be treated. It is unworthy of the victors to revenge injustices by violating human rights and heaping insults on human dignity. As things are now, future generations may well charge the victors with guilt of inhumanities which are reminiscent of Nazism and Fascism.

HUMANE TREATMENT OF DISPLACED PERSONS

A serious problem which challenges the nations is finding a way rightly to provide for the hundreds of thousands of refugees from persecution and dire danger now in camps in central Europe. These victims of injustice have the right of refuge — a right that is sacrosanct in our history and culture. To provide for them and to give them an opportunity to begin life anew in useful pursuits without fear is the inescapable responsibility of the nations. All of them, the displaced persons and the persecuted peoples, must be treated humanely without discrimination. A perfect solution of the problem would be to give them the full guarantee for the enjoyment of their native rights in their countries of origin. Since this solution is not forthcoming, the nations must extend to them the help which their very human rights demand. It is plain that to continue indefinitely to support them in camps is not a solution of the problem and is, in fact, an injury to them. To force them against their will to return to their countries of origin, where, with reason, they fear that grave dangers await them, is stark inhumanity. By agreement among the victors those in the displaced persons camps allegedly guilty of crimes must be returned to their countries of origin. If guilty, they should be punished but they should not be made the victims of political persecution with the co-operation of the authorities of the military occupation. Before honoring demands for the return of these persons to their countries of origin the military authorities are obligated to give the accused honest juridical preliminary hearings to prevent grave injustice. Tragic indeed was the decision of the United Nations Committee on Refugees that "all measures be taken" to repatriate child refugees to their countries of origin. Nor can we condone with any sense of humanity the alternative of either returning refugees against their will to their countries of origin or throwing them on the economy of an already overcrowded and impoverished Germany. With justice to all these unfortunate men, women, and children, and without discrimination in favor of any group of them, the nations must find a way to resettle them in countries where opportunities to begin life anew await them. It is heartening that the President of the United States has pledged himself publicly to ask our Congress to enact a law which will permit the entry of considerable numbers of them into the United States. If this is done, the generosity of our country will stir other nations to give these unfortunate people a haven and a chance to live in the enjoyment of their God-given rights. The problem is admittedly very difficult, but the difficulty in it should be a challenge to the nations to solve it in a constructive, humane way, in which charity will do even what justice does not compel.

Ruthless Herding of Uprooted People

Something has been happening in Europe which is new in the annals of recorded history. By agreement among the victors, millions of Germans who for centuries have lived in eastern Europe are being forced from their homes, without resources, into the heart of Germany. The sufferings of these people in their weary travels, the homelessness of them, and the hopelessness, make a sad story of the inhumanity of their transplantation. Had there prevailed in the councils of the victor nations a right appreciation of the dignity of man, at least arrangements would have been made for transplanting these people in a humane way. We boast of our democracy, but in this transplantation of peoples we have perhaps unwittingly allowed ourselves to be influenced by the herd theory of heartless totalitarian political philosophy.

The reports of the deportation of thousands in areas of Soviet aggression to remote and inhospitable regions just because they cannot subscribe to Communism tell of a cruel violation of human rights. These men are men and have the rights of men. Our sympathy also goes out to the technicians and skilled workers in enemy countries who have been seized and forced to work for the strengthening of the economy of victorious nations. It is not in this way that peace is made and the nations are united in mutual co-operation. No lasting good can ever come from the violation of the dignity of the human person.

Continued Relief Imperative

In many lands, men, women, and children are in dire need of the very necessaries of life. In some large measure this need is the consequence of the stoppage of that normal interchange of goods between the industrial and agricultural areas of Europe, which for centuries has been at the base of European economy. In some places it is the result of political, racial, and religious persecution. For many millions it is the heavy penalty of war. In our charity we must not be insensible to the misery of our fellow men. Human solidarity, as well as Christian brotherhood, dictates the sharing of our substance with our brothers in distress. We may well be proud of the generosity of the people of the United States in their relief work in war-torn lands. The want, however, is so great that, without continued governmental aid, private charity will be inadequate to relieve it. A way must be found for the nations to continue their work of relief until the danger of widespread starvation and disease is gone and peoples are able to provide for at least their own basic needs. The winter before us will be a hard, bitter winter for millions, and the charity of individuals and governments must be very large to prevent an awful catastrophe. But charity is not a substitute for justice. The continuance of widespread want is largely due to the delay of the nations in making the peace. Justice demands that they make promptly a peace in which all men can live as men.

DIGNITY OF HUMAN PERSON

In the aftermath of war, public opinion tends to overlook the sacredness of human life. We have just been through our first experience with mechanized war, in which the manhood of the world has been in battle on fields of combat and in industry, agriculture, and transportation. Our enemies, with utter disregard for the sacredness of human life, committed brutalities that horrified us and unfortunately we used weapons which brought widespread, unspeakable suffering and destruction. Day after day there were the accounts of the killing and the maiming of thousands. Never before did the human family suffer so large a number of casualties. It was hard always to be mindful of the sacredness of the life of the individual. There was the temptation to think only in terms of mass killings and mass murders. Out of it all, many have failed to interpret in terms of the human sufferings which they connote, the headlines in our daily press which even now tell of race and religious persecution, of the transplantation of millions of people from one area to another and of the seizure of political control by the liquidation of opposition. How can there be a beginning of even a tolerable peace unless the peacemakers fully realize that human life is sacred and that all men have rights?

PRAYER FOR PEACEMAKERS

And for us who profess the Christian name, human life is even more precious and sacred, because for every man the Saviour shed His Blood in bitter anguish on Calvary. We know that in His Sacred Blood all men are called to be brothers. We are our brothers' keepers. It is not possible for us to be complacent and inactive while any of our brothers in the human family groan under tyranny and are denied the free exercise of their human rights. In Christian solidarity, with humble hearts, we confess our sins and the sins of our race, and pleadingly beg, through the merits of Christ, merciful forgiveness from our Father who is in heaven. Mindful of the sacred promise of the Saviour, we pray for light and strength for those who in our country bear the heavy responsibility of making decisions for us in the peace conferences; and, indeed, for all the peacemakers. May the Saviour enlighten and strengthen them to imitate His blessed example and, in sacrifice and unselfishness, in the clear light of reason, secure for all men the enjoyment of their God-given rights, so that they may follow their vocation as sons of God and brothers in Christ.

Signed by the Members of the Administrative Board, N.C.W.C., in the names of the bishops of the United States:

✝ SAMUEL CARDINAL STRITCH,
    Archbishop of Chicago
✝ FRANCIS CARDINAL SPELLMAN,
    Archbishop of New York
✝ JOHN GREGORY MURRAY,
    Archbishop of St. Paul
✝ JOHN J. MITTY,
    Archbishop of San Francisco
✝ JOSEPH F. RUMMEL,
    Archbishop of New Orleans

✝ RICHARD J. CUSHING,
    Archbishop of Boston
✝ JAMES H. RYAN,
    Archbishop of Omaha
✝ JOHN MARK GANNON,
    Bishop of Erie
✝ JOHN F. NOLL,
    Bishop of Fort Wayne
✝ KARL J. ALTER,
    Bishop of Toledo

10. THE HIERARCHY OF THE UNITED STATES (THROUGH THE ADMINISTRATIVE BOARD) ON

SECULARISM*

November 14, 1947

No man can disregard God — and play a man's part in God's world. Unfortunately, however, there are many men — and their number is daily increasing — who in practice live their lives without recognizing that this is God's world. For the most part they do not deny God. On formal occasions they may even mention His name. Not all of them would subscribe to the statement that all moral values derive from merely human conventions. But they fail to bring an awareness of their responsibility to God into their thought and action as individuals and members of society.

This, in essence, is what we mean by secularism. It is a view of life that limits itself not to the material in exclusion of the spiritual, but to the human here and now in exclusion of man's relation to

---

*Published by the N.C.W.C., Washington 5, D. C.

God here and hereafter. Secularism, or the practical exclusion of God from human thinking and living, is at the root of the world's travail today. It was the fertile soil in which such social monstrosities as Fascism, Nazism, and Communism could germinate and grow. It is doing more than anything else to blight our heritage of Christian culture, which integrates the various aspects of human life and renders to God the things that are God's. Through the centuries, Christian culture has struggled with man's inborn inclination to evil. The ideals of Christianity have never been fully realized — just as the ideals of our Declaration of Independence and of our Constitution have never been fully realized in American political life. But for that reason these ideals can neither be ignored nor discarded. Without doubt, Christians have often failed to meet their responsibilities and by their transgressions have permitted ugly growths to mar the institutions of their culture. But wherever, despite their lapses, they have held steadfastly to their Christian ideals, the way to effective reform and progress has been kept open. The remedy for the shortcomings and sins of Christian peoples is surely not to substitute secularism for godliness, human vagaries for divine truth, man-made expedients for a God-given standard of right and wrong. This is God's world and if we are to play a man's part in it, we must first get down on our knees and with humble hearts acknowledge God's place in His world. This, secularism does not do.

The Individual

Secularism, in its impact on the individual, blinds him to his responsibility to God. All the rights, all the freedoms of man derive originally from the fact that he is a human person, created by God after His own image and likeness. In this sense he is "endowed by his Creator with certain unalienable Rights." Neither reason nor history offers any other solid ground for man's inalienable rights. It is as God's creature that man generally and most effectively recognizes a personal responsibility to seek his own moral perfection. Only a keen awareness of personal responsibility to God develops in a man's soul the saving sense of sin. Without a deep-felt conviction of what sin is, human law and human conventions can never lead man to virtue. If in the privacy of his personal life the individual does not acknowledge accountability to God for his thought and his action, he lacks the only foundation for stable moral values. Secularism does away with accountability to God as a practical consideration in the life of man and thus takes from him the sense of personal guilt of sin before God. It takes account of no law above man-made law. Expediency, decency, and propriety are, in its code, the norms of human behavior. It blurs, if it does not blot out, the ennobling and inspiring picture of man which the Christian Gospel paints. In divine revelation, man is the son of God as well as God's creature. Holiness is his vocation, and life's highest values have to do with things of the soul. "For what does it profit a man, if he gain the whole world, but suffer the loss of his own soul? Or what will a man give in exchange for his soul?" Secularism may quote these words of Christ, but never in their full Christian sense. For that very reason secularism blights the noblest aspirations in man which Christianity has implanted and fostered. Unfortunately, many who still profess to be Christians are touched by this blight. The greatest moral catastrophe of our age is the growing number of Christians who lack a sense of sin because a personal responsibility to God is not a moving force in their lives. They live in God's world, quite unmindful of Him as their Creator and Redeemer. The vague consciousness of God which they may retain is impotent as a motive in daily conduct. The moral regeneration which is recognized as absolutely necessary for the building of a better world must begin by bringing the individual back to God and to an awareness of his responsibility to God. This, secularism, of its very nature, cannot do.

THE FAMILY

Secularism has wrought havoc in the family. Even the pagans saw something sacred in marriage and the family. In Christian doctrine its holiness is so sublime that it is likened to the Mystical Union of Christ and His Church. Secularism has debased the marriage contract by robbing it of its relation to God and, therefore, of its sacred character. It has set the will and convenience of husband and wife in the place that Christian thought gives to the will of God and the good of society.

A secularized pseudo science has popularized practices which violate nature itself and rob human procreation of its dignity and nobility. Thus, selfish pursuit of pleasure is substituted for salutary self-discipline in family life.

Secularism has completely undermined the stability of the family as a divine institution and has given our country the greatest divorce problem in the Western world. In taking God out of family life, it has deprived society's basic educational institution of its most powerful means in molding the soul of the child. Public authority and the press are constantly emphasizing our grave problem of juvenile delinquency. On all sides is heard the cry that something be done about the problem. Our profound conviction is that nothing much will ever be done about it unless we go to the root of the evil and learn the havoc that secularism has wrought in the family. In vain shall we spend public moneys in vast amounts for educational and recreational activities if we do not give more thought to the divinely ordained stability of the family and the sanctity of the home.

God planned the human family and gave it its basic constitution. When secularism discards that plan and constitution it lacerates the whole social fabric. Artificial family planning on the basis of contraceptive immorality, cynical disregard of the noble purposes of sex, a sixtyfold increase in our divorce rate during the past century, and widespread failure of the family to discharge its educational functions are terrible evils which secularism has brought to our country. What hope is there of any effective remedy unless men bring God back into family life and respect the laws He has made for this fundamental unit of human society?

Education

In no field of social activity has secularism done more harm than in education. In our own country secularists have been quick to exploit for their own purposes the public policy adopted a century ago of banning the formal teaching of religion from the curriculum of our common schools. With a growing number of thoughtful Americans, we see in this policy a hasty and shortsighted solution of the very difficult educational problem that confronts public authority in a nation of divided religious allegiance. But it should ever be kept in mind that the original proponents of the policy did not intend to minimize the importance of religion in the training of youth. Erroneously, however, secularists take this policy, adopted as a practical expedient in difficult circumstances, and make it the starting point in their philosophy of education. They positively exclude God from the school. Among them are some who smile indulgently at the mention of the name of God and express wonder that inherited illusions last so long. Others are content with keeping God closeted in the inner chambers of private life.

In the rearing of children and the forming of youth, omission is as effective as positive statement. A philosophy of education which omits God, necessarily draws a plan of life in which God either has no place or is a strictly private concern of men. There is a great difference between a practical arrangement which leaves the formal teaching of religion to the family and to the Church, and the educational theory of the secularist, who advisedly and avowedly excludes religion from his program of education. The first, reluctantly tolerated under certain conditions as a practical measure of public policy, may actually serve to emphasize the need of religious instruction and training, and to encourage public school administrators to co-operate with home and Church in making it possible. The other strikes at the very core of our Christian culture and in practice envisions men who have no sense of their personal and social responsibility to God. Secularism breaks with our historical American tradition. When parents build and maintain schools in which their children are trained in the religion of their fathers, they are acting in the full spirit of that tradition. Secularists would invade the rights of parents, and invest the State with supreme powers in the field of education; they refuse to recognize the God-given place that parents have in the education of their children. God is an inescapable fact, and one cannot make a safe plan for life in disregard of inescapable facts. Our youth problems would not be so grave if the place of God in life were emphasized in the rearing of children. There would be less danger for the future of our democratic institutions if secularism were not so deeply intrenched in much of our thinking on education.

THE WORLD OF WORK

Economic problems loom large in the social unrest and confusion of our times. Research students of varying shades of opinion are seeking the formula for a sound program of economic reform. Their common objective is a beneficent social order that will establish reasonable prosperity, provide families with an adequate income, and safeguard the public welfare. The Christian view of social order rejects the postulate of inexorable economic laws which fix recurring cycles of prosperity and depression. It lays the blame for instability in our social structure on human failure rather than on blind and incontrollable economic forces. It faces the plain fact that there is something gravely wrong in our economic life and sees in secularism, with its disregard of God and God's law, a potent factor in creating the moral atmosphere which has favored the growth of this evil. Pointedly, indeed, has an eminent modern economist called attention to the fact that "in one hundred and fifty years economic laws were developed and postulated as iron necessities in a world apart from Christian obligation and sentiment." He adds: "The early nineteenth century was full of economic doctrine and practice which, grounded in its own necessity and immutability, crossed the dictates of Christian feeling and teaching with only a limited sense of incongruity and still less of indignation."

God created man and made him brother to his fellow man. He gave man the earth and all its resources to be used and developed for the good of all. Thus, work of whatever sort is a social function, and personal profit is not the sole purpose of economic activity. In the Christian tradition, the individual has the right to reasonable compensation for his work, the right to acquire private property, and the right to a reasonable income from productive invested capital. Secularism takes God out of economic thinking and thereby minimizes the dignity of the human person endowed by God with inalienable rights and made responsible to Him for corresponding individual and social duties. Thus, to the detriment of man and society, the divinely established balance in economic relations is lost.

In Christian thought the work of man is not a commodity to be bought and sold, and economic enterprise is an important social function in which owner, manager, and workman co-operate for the common good. When disregard of his responsibility to God makes the owner forget his stewardship and the social function of private property, there comes that irrational economic individualism which brings misery to millions. Helpless workers are exploited; cutthroat competition and antisocial marketing practices follow. When men in labor organizations lose the right social perspective, which a sense of responsibility to God gives, they are prone to seek merely the victory of their own group, in disregard of personal and property rights. The Christian view of economic life supports the demand for organization of management, labor, agriculture, and professions under government encouragement but not control, in joint effort to avoid social conflict and to promote co-operation for the common good. In default of this free co-operation, public authority is finally invoked to maintain a measure of economic order, but it frequently exceeds the just limits of its power to direct economic activity to the common good. In the extreme case, where Marxian Communism takes over government, it abolishes private ownership and sets up a totalitarian State capitalism, which is even more intolerable than the grave evils it pretends to cure. Surely it ought to be plain today that there is no remedy for our economic evils in a return either to nineteenth-century individualism or to experiments in Marxianism. If we abandon secularism and do our economic thinking in the light of Christian truth, we can hopefully work for economic collaboration in the spirit of genuine democracy. Let us be on our guard against all who, in exiling God from the factory and the market place, destroy the solid foundation of brotherhood in ownership, in management, and in work.

The International Community

In the international community there can be only one real bond of sane common action — the natural law which calls to God, its Author, and derives from Him its sanctions. There is objective right and objective wrong in international life. It is true that positive human law which comes from treaties and international conventions is necessary, but even these covenants must be in accord with God-given natural law. What may seem to be expedient for a nation cannot be tolerated if it contravenes God's law of right and wrong. In the international community that law has been flouted more openly, more widely, and more disastrously in our day than ever before in the Christian centuries. Shocking crimes against weak nations are being perpetrated in the name of national security. Millions of men in many nations are in the thralldom of political slavery. Religion is persecuted because it stands for freedom under God. The most fundamental human rights are violated with utter ruthlessness in a calculated, systematic degradation of man by blind and despotic leaders. Details of the sad and sickening story seep through the wall of censorship which encloses police States. Men long for peace and order, but the world stands on the brink of chaos. It is significant that godless forces have brought it there. Nazism and Fascism and Japanese militarism lie buried in the debris of some of the fairest cities of the world they vowed to rule or to ruin. Atheistic Communism, for a time thrown into alliance with democratic nations through Nazi aggression against Russia, stands out plainly today as the force which, through violence and chicanery, is obstructing the establishment of a right juridical order in the international community. That is plain for all to see. But thoughtful men perceive as well that secularism, which over the years has sapped the divinely laid foundations of the moral law, bears a heavy burden of responsibility for the plight of the world today.

Secularism which exiles God from human life clears the way for the acceptance of godless subversive ideologies — just as religion, which keeps God in human life, has been the one outstanding opponent of totalitarian tyranny. Religion has been its first victim; for tyrants persecute what they fear. Thus secularism, as the solvent of practical religious influence in the everyday life of men and nations, is not indeed the most patent, but in a very true sense the most insidious hindrance to world reconstruction within the strong framework of God's natural law. There would be more hope for a just and lasting peace if the leaders of the nations were really convinced that secularism which disregards God, as well as militant atheism which utterly denies Him, offer no sound basis for stable international agreements for enduring respect for human rights or for freedom under law.

In the dark days ahead we dare not follow the secularist philosophy. We must be true to our historic Christian culture. If all who believe in God would make that belief practical in their workaday lives, if they would see to it that their children are definitely imbued with that belief and trained in the observance of God's way of life, if they would look across the real differences which unfortunately divide them, to the common danger that threatens, if they would steadfastly refuse to let a common enemy capitalize on those differences to the detriment of social unity, we might begin to see a way out of the chaos that impends. Secularism holds out no valid promise of better things for our country or for the world. During our own lives it has been the bridge between a decaying devotion to Christian culture and the revolutionary forces which have brought on what is perhaps the gravest crisis in all history. The tragic evil is not that our Christian culture is no longer capable of producing peace and reasonable prosperity, but that we are allowing secularism to divorce Christian truth from life. The fact of God and the fact of the responsibility of men and nations to God for their actions are supreme realities, calling insistently for recognition in a truly realistic ordering of life in the individual, in the family, in the school, in economic activity, and in the international community.

Signed by the members of the Administrative Board, N.C.W.C., in the names of the bishops of the United States:

✠ DENNIS CARDINAL DOUGHERTY,
    Archbishop of Philadelphia
✠ EDWARD CARDINAL MOONEY,
    Archbishop of Detroit

✠ SAMUEL CARDINAL STRITCH,
    Archbishop of Chicago
✠ FRANCIS CARDINAL SPELLMAN,
    Archbishop of New York

✠ John T. McNicholas, O.P.,
Archbishop of Cincinnati

✠ Robert E. Lucey,
Archbishop of San Antonio

✠ Richard J. Cushing,
Archbishop of Boston

✠ Joseph E. Ritter,
Archbishop of St. Louis

✠ James H. Ryan,
Archbishop of Omaha

✠ John Mark Gannon,
Bishop of Erie

✠ John F. Noll,
Bishop of Fort Wayne

✠ Emmet M. Walsh,
Bishop of Charleston

✠ Karl J. Alter,
Bishop of Toledo

✠ Michael J. Ready,
Bishop of Columbus

11. THE HIERARCHY OF THE UNITED STATES ON

THE CHRISTIAN IN ACTION*

November 21, 1948

Human life centers in God. The failure to center life in God is secularism — which, as we pointed out last year, is the most deadly menace to our Christian and American way of living. We shall not successfully combat this evil merely by defining and condemning it. Constructive effort is called for to counteract this corrosive influence in every phase of life where individual attitudes are a determining factor — in the home, in the school, at work, and in civil polity. For as man is, so ultimately are all the institutions of human society.

To combat secularism, the individual Christian must get the full vision of Christian truth. It is not divisible. One cannot pick and choose from it. Either it is accepted as a whole or it counts for little in real life. When the Christian does get this full vision, he becomes enthusiastic in trying to share it with the world about him. It is a wonderful vision which gives new meaning to human

---

* Published by the N.C.W.C., Washington 5, D. C.

life and an impelling urge to selfless action. The sorry fact is that many, very many Christians see this vision only dimly and vaguely and miss its impact on reality. They hold themselves to be Christians and are accepted as Christians, but they have never been thrilled by the glory of the truth of Christ in action. By their apathy they actually abet those who work for destruction and chaos. They criticize and even deplore the decay of morality and the spread of corruption in public life, but they feel no obligation to do anything about it. They simply do not realize that the great wonder of Divine Love is that it brings the divine into human life and that godliness in living is giving self to God. The great Christian paradox is that to find you must lose, to get you must give. Much of the confusion and chaos about us is attributable more directly to the inaction of Christians than to the effectiveness of the feverish efforts of the destroyers. The destroyers are definitely a minority, and yet the work of destruction goes on. The crisis is at hand. Today every Christian must face the full Christian vision and with no thought of compromise must seek vigorously to live it. Every day he must ask himself: What am I doing to build a Christian world? No matter what his condition or state, there is much that he can do. The reconstruction must start with the individual. He must be vigorously Christian in thought and in action — in the home, in the training of his children, in his office or workshop, and in his community.

RELIGION IN THE HOME

In the full Christian vision, there is the divine ideal of the home — the basic social institution. It is not enough to profess the Christian truths of the stability and sanctity of the marriage bond and to keep in mind the purposes of marriage. The Christian must make his home holy. It remained for modern history to record the first experiment in secularizing the home, an experiment which is at the root of so many of our greatest social evils. The Christian home must realize the Christian ideal. The whole atmosphere of the home must be impregnated with genuine Christian living. The domestic virtues must be practiced and family prayer made a daily exercise. It is in the home that the children learn their responsibility to God and in this responsibility their duty to others. The home is the child's first school, in which he is taught to make the vision of Christian truth the inspiration of all living. We strongly commend organized effort to make the home more truly Christian. Our Catholic

Family Life Bureau plans and offers programs which make for a veritable apostolate of the Catholic home. It is gratifying to see the use that is being made of these programs by our Catholic lay organizations and the spread of this work in our dioceses. These activities serve as a powerful antidote to the venom of secularism and withstand its withering effect on piety and virtue in the American home. All of us are familiar with the problems which the family faces in our complex and maladjusted society. In trying to solve these problems we must not compromise our Christian principles. The solution of these problems is only a part of the solution of the wider social problems of our day. To do their part, our homes must be thoroughly Christian and must let the glory of the full vision of Christian truth illumine them.

RELIGION IN EDUCATION

We know the sacrifices made by our people to educate their children in schools in which the "superabundant wisdom" is the Gospel of Christ. Catholic parents closely associate their schools with their Christian homes, because they know that human living must center in God. Year after year we are making wider provisions for the education of our Catholic youth. At a time when secularism has captured the minds of very many leaders in education, it is heartening that Catholic parents are becoming more insistent in their demand for schools in which the best standards of instruction and training are integrated in the teaching of religion. It behooves us to see that we enable our schools to work out fully the Christian educational ideal. The field of higher education in particular demands a wider and more active interest. Our institutions of higher learning are the natural training grounds for Christian leadership. The ranks of Christian leadership will draw recruits largely from the undergraduate schools, but these ranks will not be filled without the Christian scholars who are formed in graduate schools. Perhaps much of the success of the secularist is due to the fact that the number of excellent Christian scholars is inadequate for the needs of our times. We ask a deeper appreciation of the contribution our institutions of higher learning are making to a Christian reconstruction of society, and we urge a more generous support of their work. For if we as Christians are to do our part in restoring order to a chaotic world, Christ must be the Master in our classrooms and lecture halls and the Director of our research projects.

RELIGION IN ECONOMIC LIFE

Christian principles should be put into action in economic life. It is not enough to find fault with the way our economic system is working. Positive, constructive thought and action are needed.

The secularist solutions proposed by eighteenth-century individualism or twentieth-century statism issue either in perpetual conflict or deadening repression. Christian social principles, rooted in the moral law, call insistently for co-operation, not conflict, for freedom, not repression in the development of economic activity. Co-operation must be organized — organized for the common good; freedom must be ordered — ordered for the common good. Today we have labor partly organized, but chiefly for its own interests. We have capital or management organized, possibly on a larger scale, but again chiefly for its own interests. What we urgently need, in the Christian view of social order, is the free organization of capital and labor in permanent agencies of co-operation for the common good. To insure that this organization does not lose sight of the common good, government as the responsible custodian of the public interest should have a part in it. But its part should be to stimulate, to guide, to restrain, not to dominate. This is perfectly in line with our federal Constitution which empowers government not only "to establish justice" but also to "promote the general welfare."

Catholic social philosophy has a constructive program for this organic development of economic life. Pope Pius XI, rounding out the social principles formulated by Leo XIII, laid down the broad outlines of this program seventeen years ago. In line with that constructive program we advocate freely organized co-operation between the accredited representatives of capital and labor in each industry and in the economy as a whole under the supervision but not the control of government. The agencies of this freely organized co-operation have been called by various names: Occupational Groups, Vocational Groups, or, more recently, Industry Councils. American Catholic students of the Social Encyclicals have expressed their preference for the name "Industry Councils" to designate the basic organs of a Christian and American type of economic democracy into which they would like to see our economic system progressively evolve. This evolution can come only as the fruit of painstaking study and effort to safeguard in justice and charity, the rightful interests of property and the rightful interests of labor in the pursuit of the dominant interest of all, which is the common good.

Such a constructive program of social order seems to us to be the answer to the questionings of high-minded leaders of industry and to the explicit proposals of sound and responsible leaders of organized labor. We bespeak for it in these critical times dispassionate consideration and calm, open discussion in an atmosphere of good will and in a disposition to seek solutions by agreement rather than by force, whether political or economic. We call upon men of religious faith and principle, both in management and labor, to take the lead in working out and applying, gradually if need be, a constructive social program of this type. For the moral and social ideals which it would realize are their heritage.

RELIGION AND CITIZENSHIP

The inroads of secularism in civil life are a challenge to the Christian citizen — and indeed to every citizen with definite religious convictions. The essential connection between religion and good citizenship is deep in our American tradition. Those who took the lead in establishing our independence and framing our Constitution were firm and explicit in the conviction that religion and morality are the strong supports of national well-being, that national morality cannot long prevail in the absence of religious principle, and that impartial encouragement of religious influence on its citizens is a proper and practical function of good government. This American tradition clearly envisioned the school as the meeting place of these helpful interacting influences. The third article of the Northwest Ordinance passed by Congress in 1787, re-enacted in 1790, and included in the Constitutions of many states enjoins: "Religion, morality and knowledge being necessary to good citizenship and the happiness of mankind, schools and the means of education shall forever be encouraged." This is our authentic American tradition on the philosophy of education for citizenship.

In the field of law our history reveals the same fundamental connection between religion and citizenship. It is through law that government exercises control over its citizens for the common good and establishes a balance between their rights and duties. The American concept of government and law started with the recognition that man's inalienable rights — which it is the function of government to protect — derive from God, his Creator. It thus bases human law, which deals with man's rights and their correlative duties in society, on foundations that are definitely religious, on principles that emerge from the definite view of man as a creature of God. This view of man anchors human law to the natural law, which is the moral law of God made clear to us through the judgments of human reason and the dictates of conscience. The natural law, as an outstanding modern legal commentator has written, "is binding over all the globe, in all countries and at all times; no human laws are of any validity if contrary to this." Thus human law is essentially an ordinance of reason, not merely a dictate of will on the part of the State. In our authentic American tradition this is the accepted philosophy of law.

On this basically religious tradition concerning the preparation of the citizen through education and the direction of the citizen through law, secularism has in the past century exercised a corrosive influence. It has banned religion from tax-supported education and is now bent on destroying all co-operation between government and organized religion in the training of our future citizens. It has undermined the religious foundations of law in the minds of many men in the legal profession and has predisposed them to accept the legalistic tyranny of the omnipotent State. It has cleverly exploited, to the detriment of religion and good citizenship, the delicate problem of co-operation between Church and State in a country of divided religious allegiance. That concrete problem, delicate as it is, can, without sacrifice of principle, be solved in a practical way when good will and a spirit of fairness prevail. Authoritative Catholic teaching on the relations between Church and State, as set forth in papal encyclicals and in the treatises of recognized writers on ecclesiastical law, not only states clearly what these relations should normally be under ideal conditions, but also indicates to what extent the Catholic Church can adapt herself to the particular conditions that may obtain in different countries. Examining, in the full perspective of that teaching, the position which those who founded our nation and framed its basic law took on the problem of Church-State relations in our own country, we find that the First Amendment to our Constitution solved the problem in a way that was typically American in its practical recognition of existing conditions and its evident desire to be fair to all citizens of whatever religious faith. To one who knows something of history and law, the meaning of the First Amendment is clear enough from its own words: "Congress shall make no laws respecting an establishment of religion or forbidding the free exercise thereof." The meaning is even clearer in the records of the Congress that enacted it. Then, and throughout English and Colonial history, an "establishment of religion" meant the setting up by law of an official

Church which would receive from the government favors not equally accorded to others in the co-operation between government and religion — which was simply taken for granted in our country at that time and has, in many ways, continued to this day. Under the First Amendment, the federal government could not extend this type of preferential treatment to one religion as against another, nor could it compel or forbid any State to do so. If this practical policy be described by the loose metaphor "a wall of separation between Church and State," that term must be understood in a definite and typically American sense. It would be an utter distortion of American history and law to make that practical policy involve the indifference to religion and the exclusion of co-operation between religion and government implied in the term "separation of Church and State" as it has become the shibboleth of doctrinaire secularism.

Within the past two years secularism has scored unprecedented victories in its opposition to governmental encouragement of religious and moral training, even where no preferential treatment of one religion over another is involved. In two recent cases, the Supreme Court of the United States has adopted an entirely novel and ominously extensive interpretation of the "establishment of religion" clause of the First Amendment. This interpretation would bar any co-operation between government and organized religion which would aid religion, even where no discrimination between religious bodies is in question. This reading of the First Amendment, as a group of non-Catholic religious leaders recently noted, will endanger "forms of cooperation between Church and State which have been taken for granted by the American people," and "greatly accelerate the trend toward the secularization of our culture."

Reluctant as we are to criticize our supreme judicial tribunal, we cannot but observe that when the members of that tribunal write long and varying opinions in handing down a decision, they must expect that intelligent citizens of a democracy will study and appraise these opinions. The Journal of the American Bar Association, in a critical analysis of one of the cases in question, pertinently remarks: "The traditionally religious sanctions of our law, life and government are challenged by a judicial propensity which deserves the careful thought and study of lawyers and people."

Lawyers trained in the American tradition of law will be amazed to find that in the McCollum case the majority opinions pay scant attention to logic, history, or accepted norms of legal interpretation. Logic would demand that what is less clear be defined by what is more clear. In the present instance we find just the reverse. The carefully chiselled phrases of the First Amendment are defined by the misleading metaphor "the wall of separation between Church and State." This metaphor of Jefferson specifies nothing except that there shall be no "established Church," no state religion. All the rest of its content depends on the letter of the law that sets it up and can in the concrete imply anything from the impartial co-operation between government and free religious bodies (as in Holland and traditionally in our own country) all the way down to bitter persecution of religion (as in France at the turn of the century). As was pointedly remarked in a dissenting opinion: "A rule of law cannot be drawn from a metaphor."

A glance at the history of Jefferson's own life and work would have served as a warning against the broad and devastating application of his "wall of separation" metaphor that we find in this case. The expression first appears in a letter written by Jefferson in 1802 and, significantly enough, in a context that makes it refer to the "free exercise of religion" clause rather than to the "establishment of religion" clause of the First Amendment. Twenty years later Jefferson clearly showed in action that his concept of "separation of Church and State" was far different from the concept of those who now appeal to his metaphor as a norm of interpretation. As the rector of the State University of Virginia, Jefferson proposed a system of co-operation between the various religious groups and the university which goes far beyond anything under consideration in the case at hand. And Mr. Madison, who had proposed the First Amendment and who led in carrying it through to enactment by Congress, was one of the visitors of the University of Virginia who approved Jefferson's plan.

Even one who is not a lawyer would expect to find in the opinion of the court some discussion of what was in the mind of the members of Congress when they framed and adopted the First Amendment. For it would seem that the intent of the legislator should be of capital importance in interpreting any law when a doubt is raised as to the objective meaning of the words in which it is framed. In regard to the "establishment of religion" clause, there is no doubt of the intent of the legislator. It is clear in the record of the Congress that framed it and of the State legislatures that ratified it. To them it meant no official Church for the country as a whole, no preferment of one religion over another by the federal government — and at the same time no interference by the federal government in the Church-State relations of the individual states.

The opinion of the court advances no reason for disregarding the mind of the legislator. But that reason is discernible in a concurring opinion adhered to by four of the nine judges. There we see clearly the determining influence of secularist theories of public education — and possibly of law. One cannot but remark that if this secularist influence is to prevail in our government and its institutions, such a result should in candor and logic and law be achieved by legislation adopted after full popular discussion, and not by the judicial procedure of an ideological interpretation of our Constitution.

We, therefore, hope and pray that the novel interpretation of the First Amendment recently adopted by the Supreme Court will in due process be revised. To that end we shall peacefully, patiently, and perseveringly work. We feel with deep conviction that for the sake of both good citizenship and religion there should be a re-affirmation of our original American tradition of free co-operation between government and religious bodies — co-operation involving no special privilege to any group and no restriction on the religious liberty of any citizen. We solemnly disclaim any intent or desire to alter this prudent and fair American policy of government in dealing with the delicate problems that have their source in the divided religious allegiance of our citizens. We call upon our Catholic people to seek in their faith an inspiration and a guide in making an informed contribution to good citizenship. We urge members of the legal profession in particular to develop and apply their special competence in this field. We stand ready to co-operate in fairness and charity with all who believe in God and are devoted to freedom under God to avert the impending danger of a judicial "establishment of secularism" that would ban God from public life. For secularism is threatening the religious foundations of our national life and preparing the way for the advent of the omnipotent state.

Signed by the members of the N.C.W.C. Administrative Board in the names of the bishops of the United States:

✠ DENNIS CARDINAL DOUGHERTY,
Archbishop of Philadelphia

✠ EDWARD CARDINAL MOONEY,
Archbishop of Dertoit

✠ SAMUEL CARDINAL STRITCH,
Archbishop of Chicago

✠ FRANCIS CARDINAL SPELLMAN,
Archbishop of New York

✠ FRANCIS P. KEOUGH,
Archbishop of Baltimore

✠ JOHN T. McNICHOLAS,
Archbishop of Cincinnati

✝ Robert E. Lucey,
Archbishop of San Antonio

✝ Richard J. Cushing,
Archbishop of Boston

✝ Joseph E. Ritter,
Archbishop of St. Louis

✝ John Mark Gannon,
Bishop of Erie

✝ John F. Noll,
Bishop of Fort Wayne

✝ Emmet M. Walsh,
Bishop of Charleston

✝ Karl J. Alter,
Bishop of Toledo

✝ Michael J. Ready,
Bishop of Columbus

12. THE HIERARCHY OF THE UNITED STATES (THROUGH THE ADMINISTRATIVE BOARD) ON THE

CHRISTIAN FAMILY*

November 21, 1949

The world's horizons are those of time, not of eternity. Its interests are material, not spiritual. The world acknowledges God with an occasional word of reference, but it is not truly interested in God, His purposes, or His law. It wishes God to stay in His heaven; as occasion permits, it is willing to salute Him there. But it resents intervention of God in affairs on earth. It is irritated by any assertion of God's rights here, any demand for service to God, any exaction of reliance upon God's Providence.

The Western world today still proclaims human dignity. But in the main it treats man, physically, as the product of materialistic and mechanical evolution. It tends more and more to treat man, socially, as the creature of the State or of control groups within the State. Again, the world recognizes a vaguely conceived spiritual institution which it calls the Church. Yet, practically, the Church is treated as a collection of welfare centers, a human thing throughout and not divine, which is to be formed into a unified instrument

* N.C.W.C. "News Release," November 21, 1949.

of social action by general concession and compromise. The world makes no quest for divinely revealed truth. It seeks no divine guidance, no divine indication of duty and spiritual allegiance. It ignores ultimates, and restricts its vision to the here and now. In all this, there is inversion and disorder. Out of such disorder it is not reasonable to expect the emergence of human security, prosperity, and peace.

For God comes first. God has revealed His purposes regarding man not only through the light of natural reason but also through the gift of supernatural revelation, which we accept by faith. Paradoxically, as a brilliant modern writer observes, if you take away the supernatural, you have left, not the natural, but the unnatural.

Perhaps the most evident and devastating effect of the disregard of supernatural faith in human society is to be found in what it has done to family life. The world which discounts supernatural faith in God's revelation, praises family life, declares its place and function essential to human well-being, and speaks with high sentiment of the sacredness of the home. Yet by countless acts and agencies it moves steadily to disrupt family life and to destroy the home. It approves and facilitates divorce as a cure for domestic ills. It accepts multiple marriages which usually mean a hopeless entanglement of the infelicities of a plurality of broken homes. It sponsors planned parenthood by use of unnatural and morally degrading means, thus infusing poison into the heart of family life by destroying in husband and wife the self-respect and mutual reverence on which alone are built enduring love and patient fidelity. It is unconcerned, for the most part, about its manifest duty of removing the great difficulties that lie in the way of those who wish to marry and establish homes. Its social legislation in point of suitable housing, decent material facilities, security in income and prospects, is slow, fumbling, and inadequate. An unbelieving world professing recognition of the essential value of family life, actually discounts that value and moves to destroy what it claims to cherish.

All this amounts to a calculated attack upon family life. To counteract this attack it is urgent to have the clear knowledge which faith gives of what the family is, and of what it means to the individual man and to human society.

In the view of faith the family is, first of all, a divine institution. A divine institution is not within man's control to abrogate or alter. It is God's own work. Attack upon it is even humanly speaking disastrous. It strikes tragically at the even balance of right human relations, and ends in calamitous disorder.

Faith merely confirms reason in holding that husband and wife constitute conjugal society. When their union is blessed with offspring, this society becomes a family. It is a divinely founded natural society. It is prior, in existence and in its nature, to every other human society, to every state or nation. It is the basic social unit. It has its own native rights which no civil power can take away or unduly limit. To serve and protect the family and its life, States are formed and governments established.

Social philosophers, as well as the great mass of mankind schooled only in sanity and common human experience, agree upon the importance of the family to individual man. The formative years of life are normally passed in the bosom of the family. Family life encircles the child with no mere casual set of surroundings. It is his constant school; it is his realm, his world. Even through his adolescence he returns to it as to the moorings of his soul. Family life, far beyond any other external influence, molds lastingly the tastes, the temperaments, the attitudes, the personality of the child. No human social influence can compare with the family in power to form and to direct the individual lives of men.

The importance of family life for individuals is discerned in the service it renders to father and mother as well as to the child. Husband and wife find fulfillment in their fruitfulness, and find strength and comfort in the home. Family life gives dignity and peace and security to the mother. It exercises an ennobling and steadying influence upon the father. In both it awakens and develops a sense of responsibility, and fosters their growth in selflessness, sacrifice, and patience.

The State measures its true strength by the stability of family life among its citizenry. For the family is the social cell. It is the family that produces the citizen. No nation can be greater than its families. In vain does the world that disregards the injunction of God loosen family ties and break up family life and then look to state schools to produce good citizens. At its best the school is only a strong aid to the home. Good citizens must first be good persons. School courses in civics and political science, and inspirational studies of the lives and works of patriotic leaders, meet a practical need. But these alone never make good citizens. Virtue is best developed in a good home where God is held in reverence. And virtue is the basis of good citizenship. The State which weakens the family inflicts deep injury upon itself. Any attack of the State on family life is suicidal.

No less important is the role of the family for the Church. The Son of God, when He walked among men, set up His one Church as a kind of family, and its members call that Church their Holy Mother. Only those who know and live the family life of that Church can appreciate the glory and the solace of soul that abides in this earthly home of the human spirit. The Church, through the Sacrament of Matrimony, constantly channels the essential grace of God to her faithful children in the home. But history proves that it is God's will and providence that the Church should depend for her continuity and growth, as well as for the devotion of the faithful, upon Christian family life.

Since family life is thus essential to the individual, to the State, and to the Church, it follows that whatever protects or promotes good family life is to be diligently fostered. It is of paramount concern to all mankind that family life be preserved in full soundness and moral health.

To exist in full effectiveness, family life must have permanence. This permanence depends chiefly upon the permanence of marriage. Strictly requisite is marriage that is monogamous and indissoluble: the marriage of one man with one woman in divorceless union that is broken only by the death of one of the spouses. Such a marriage is requisite, not for the mere begetting of offspring, but for the rearing and training of children until they come to full maturity. Any marriage which looks to dissolution or divorce, even as a possibility, cannot give to children the security they need; cannot surround children with the enduring atmosphere of home; cannot breathe into children the spirit of true family life. Nor can such a marriage give to husband and wife the complete reliance on each other which is requisite for their peace and happiness under the exacting conditions of marital duty.

Further, family life must have freedom. There must be no undue intervening of the civil power in the domain of husband and wife. This requirement involves two points of obligation. Freedom implies that rights be respected. The State must respect the rights of the family. It must not therefore fail to provide opportunities for the adequate housing of families, for the requisite schooling of children for the use of common benefits supplied through the taxing of citizens. On the other hand, the State must not oppress the family. It must not discount parental authority by invading the home and legislating upon matters which are of strictly domestic concern. It must be neither arbitrary nor tyrannous. It must not usurp the right which belongs to parents, of educating their children. On this score, the part of the State is to furnish opportunity for schooling, and to see that parents are not recreant in making use of the opportunity on behalf of their children. The State cannot force a child to attend this school or that; it cannot prescribe courses of study that may involve intellectual or moral dangers for pupils. Nor can the State make discrimination among families, distributing common benefits to some and withholding them from others.

To the Church belongs the pre-eminent right to guide the child's spiritual and moral formation; to the parents belongs the natural right to govern and supervise the child's nurture and general education; in society is vested the right to transmit, generally by means of schools, the cultural heritage of successive generations.

The function of the State is to assist these three agencies to discharge harmoniously their responsibilities in the best interest of the public welfare. The State must ever keep in mind that children belong to their parents before they belong to the State; the resources to develop them into their full stature as human beings destined for eternal union with God are not the property of political government; these constitute the treasury of families and the Church.

Again, the family, to exercise its good influence in full effectiveness, needs a just measure of economic security. When, in a wealthy and prospering nation, diligent and willing parents are forced to live in grinding poverty; when parents have no opportunity of owning their own home; when the aid of government is extended to those who raise crops or build machines but not to those who rear children; there exists a condition of inequity and even of injustice. Social legislation and social action must concur to improve man's economic opportunity, to enable him to marry early, to free him from the peril of unnaturally limiting his family, and to afford him some certainty of sufficiently gainful employment and some assurance that death or accident will not reduce his dependence to the status of public charges.

Finally, the family needs religion. It requires the high morality and the unvarying standards of duty which only the spirit of religion can supply to family life. It needs the strong quality of stanch loyalty to God and to His commandments, to His Church and to her precepts. It needs the filial piety which has its source and support in piety toward God. It needs prayer and the example of prayerfulness. We are consoled by the evident growth of pious practices in the home, the enthronement of the Sacred Heart, regular family prayer, and the wide variety of Catholic devotions, which have given to Christian homes the character of sacred sanctuaries.

The family needs to gather again around its hearths and rekindle there the fires of religious fervor. The home must again become a shrine of fidelity, a place where God is the unseen Host. We commend the program of the Catholic Family Life Conference as one means of meeting the evident present need for better and happier homes. Family retreats, Cana conferences, courses on family life in schools and colleges, and study groups concerned with preparation for family life, should be widely encouraged and zealously promoted throughout our country. The press, radio, motion pictures, and all agencies of public opinion should give constant aid in emphasizing the ideals of worthy family life. These powerful forces should be an unfailing support for the virtues which safeguard the home and give nobility to the nation.

These, then, are the requisites for family life if it is to produce its wondrous benefits in full measure and effectiveness: it must be permanent in its establishment and prospects; it must be free from unwarranted interventions; it must have economic security; it must be religious. Yet even when these requisites are not perfectly realized, family life, though hampered, is productive of incalculable good. In the Providence of God it is the best of existing human agencies for social benefit. There is grave danger, however, that, if a Godless philosophy be still permitted to prevail, family life among us will not only be further hampered but ultimately destroyed.

We have, indeed, supernatural knowledge that God's Church will not be destroyed, and while the Church endures family life will still, in some measure, exist and fruitfully function. But viewing our country and the world by and large, and noting the growing tendency to ignore God and His rights in society, the lethal danger to the family is neither chimerical nor remote. It is a present danger, more fearsome than the atom bomb.

After thirty-five years of war and its effects which have wrought incalculable injury to family life, we call for an intensive effort to restore the virtues and practices guaranteeing family stability and peace.

With confidence in the help of God, through Jesus Christ, His Son, and with constant faith in the intercession of His Mother, the Immaculate Mary, we urge all families to strive by their prayers for the restoration of pure family life. Let all recite the family Rosary. Let there be a renewal of devotion, a frequency in the reception of the Sacraments, a rebirth of all those virtues which make family life a mirror of the Holy Family of Nazareth. Joseph, the honest workman, is still the guardian of families. Mary, the Mother of God, is the blessed Mother of every Catholic home. And Jesus, subject to them, His creatures, is the model of every child. To Jesus, Mary, and Joseph, we commit your hearts, your souls, and your homes.

Statement issued November 21, 1949, by the bishops of the United States and signed in their names by the members of the Administrative Board, N.C.W.C.:

✝ DENNIS CARDINAL DOUGHERTY,
Archbishop of Philadelphia

✝ EDWARD CARDINAL MOONEY,
Archbishop of Detroit

✝ SAMUEL CARDINAL STRITCH,
Archbishop of Chicago

✝ FRANCIS CARDINAL SPELLMAN,
Archbishop of New York

✝ FRANCIS P. KEOUGH,
Archbishop of Baltimore

✝ JOHN T. McNICHOLAS, O.P.,
Archbishop of Cincinnati

✝ ROBERT E. LUCEY,
Archbishop of San Antonio

✝ RICHARD J. CUSHING,
Archbishop of Boston

✝ JOSEPH E. RITTER,
Archbishop of St. Louis

✝ PATRICK A. O'BOYLE,
Archbishop of Washington

✝ JOHN MARK GANNON,
Bishop of Erie

✝ JOHN F. NOLL,
Bishop of Fort Wayne

✝ EMMET M. WALSH,
Coadjutor Bishop of Youngstown

✝ MICHAEL J. READY,
Bishop of Columbus

13. THE HIERARCHY OF THE UNITED STATES (THROUGH THE ADMINISTRATIVE BOARD) ON

THE CHILD: CITIZEN OF TWO WORLDS

November 17, 1950

In the present grim international struggle, the American people have resolutely championed the cause of human freedom. We have committed ourselves to oppose relentlessly the aggressions of those who deny to man his God-given rights and who aim to enslave all mankind under the rules of Godless materialism. The responsibilities which we have thereby assumed are both grave and continuing. They deserve conscientious consideration.

It is of primary importance for our people to realize that human freedom derives from the spiritual nature of man and can flourish only when things of the spirit are held in reverence. Our present principles of action need to be evaluated in the light of that truth. But we must go even further. Small comfort to be successful today if tomorrow the world finds us unworthy of the trust reposed in us. We need, therefore, to examine carefully what spiritual direction we are giving to our children to prepare them to fulfill their future moral responsibilities to God and to their fellow man.

In recent decades, striking advances have been made in meeting the child's physical, emotional, and social needs; but his moral and religious needs have not been met with the same solicitude and understanding. As a result, many of our children today betray confusion and insecurity because these unmet needs are fundamental to the harmonious development of their whole nature.

The child must be seen whole and entire. He must be seen as a citizen of two worlds. He belongs to this world surely, but his first and highest allegiance is to the kingdom of God. From his earliest years he must be taught that his chief significance comes from the fact that he is created by God and is destined for life with God in eternity.

The child's prospects for fulfilling this great hope which God has reposed in him must be viewed realistically. He will come to maturity in a society where social, moral, intellectual, and spiritual values are everywhere disintegrating. In such a society, he will urgently need the integrating force of religion as taught by Christ. Such a force will give him a complete and rational meaning for his existence.

First of all, it will arouse in him a consciousness of God and of eternity. His vision will be opened out upon a supernatural world revealed by faith which differs from the world of nature his senses reveal. Thus he will discover a higher life than this daily one and a brighter world than he sees. Second, it will give him a continuing purpose in life, for it will teach him that he was made to know, love, and serve God in this world as the condition for meriting eternal happiness. Third, it will induce in him a deep sense of responsibility for those rights and obligations he possesses by reason of his citizenship in heaven as well as on earth. Finally, religion will challenge him to sanctify whatever walk of life he chooses and to seek and accept the will of God in whatever way it may be manifested. Thus, as a principle of integration, religion will help the child to develop a *sense of God,* a *sense of direction,* a *sense of responsibility,* and a *sense of mission* in this life.

I. Sense of God

The child is not complete in himself. He will find his completion only in life with God; and that life must begin here upon earth. Parents, therefore, should make early provision for their child's growth in God. This is not something to be postponed for nurture by school authorities. It must begin in the home through simple and prayerful practices. Morning and evening prayers, grace before and after meals, the family rosary, the saying of a short prayer each time the striking clock marks the passage of another hour nearer eternity, the reverential making of the Sign of the Cross, the inculcation of respect for the Crucifix and other religious objects — all these are practices which should be encouraged in the religious formation of the child. No one can doubt that there is a readiness on his part to receive such formation, and if parents are remiss in giving it they will lose a splendid opportunity to develop in their child that habitual awareness of God which is vital to his full growth.

Only two courses are open to the child — either he will be God-centered or self-centered. He is made and destined for God, but he bears in his nature the lingering effects of original sin which incline him to seek the satisfaction of every selfish whim. To correct this bend in his will so that God, rather than self, will occupy the center of his life is one of the most challenging tasks facing parents.

In meeting this challenge, let parents make use of the strong, supernatural motivation which can be drawn from the life of Christ. Let them encourage the imitation of Him, particularly in His obedience, patience, and thoughtfulness of others; and let them foster the emulation of that spirit of unselfish giving so characteristic of Christ. This can be done in many practical ways, particularly through providing the child with frequent opportunities for making acts of self-denial in the home. If he is taught to deny his selfish whims for the sake of Christ, he will not only discover a supernatural motive for his actions, but he will learn to give God that central place in his affections which God must occupy if the child is to come to his full spiritual stature.

Little point would be served in intensifying the child's awareness of God during his preschool years, if later his schooling were to rob him of that. The child's education during school years should be of a piece with his education at home. Catholic parents, clearly grasping this essential truth, have undergone great sacrifice and enormous expense to establish and maintain schools which will continue and enlarge the spiritual development of the child that was begun at home. In doing this, parents have acted within their competence, because it is they, and not the State, who possess the primary right to educate.

This natural right of parents is one which has ever been recognized in our American traditions. As recently as 1944, the highest court in our land confirmed it in these words: "It is cardinal with us that the custody, care, and nurture of the child *reside first in the parents* whose primary function and freedom include preparation for obligations the State can neither supply nor hinder."

In helping parents to exercise this right, the Church stands ready at hand with all her material and spiritual resources. At infancy she initiates the child into the life of grace and for the rest of his days she stands by his side ready to minister to his needs. She recognizes his pre-eminent need for God and she meets it by providing Catholic schools for each stage of his educational development. She does this in virtue of the sublime teaching office conferred upon her by Jesus Christ.

When it is impossible for parents to take advantage of the God-centered education which Catholic schools offer, they have a grave obligation to provide for their child's religious instruction in some other way. At least they must see that their children attend Catechism classes and vacation schools and receive the benefit of other activities of the Confraternity of Christian Doctrine.

Nor should the State, which has demonstrated a genuine interest in so many aspects of the child's welfare, be indifferent to the inherent value of religious instruction and training for the child attending tax-supported schools. The continuance and well-being of a State based on democratic principles require that it show a lively concern for moral principles and practices which are firmly grounded only in religion. For the child who is not receiving thorough religious education, the State should look with favor on released-time programs for his religious instruction.

Many important services have been rendered by governmental agencies to the child who has been deprived of the care and support of his parents by death, illness, or misfortune. However, it is a source of growing concern to us that in certain parts of our country there is a trend to regard this whole field of foster care as falling within the exclusive province of governmental authorities. It surely lies within their province to set up and enforce legitimate minimum standards of care for the dependent child; but the responsibility for his care should not be entirely assumed by them. There is a definite place in America for the voluntary agencies of mercy — particularly those operating under religious auspices, which are equipped to safeguard and develop the religious life of the dependent child. Certainly the child bereft of the immediate care of his parents is entitled to those opportunities for a religious upbringing, which his parents were obligated to give him. These opportunities can be best supplied by an agency operating under religious auspices.

II. SENSE OF DIRECTION

The child whose eyes have been opened to the vision of God must be encouraged to walk by the steady light of that vision; otherwise he will follow wandering fires. He is too young and immature to be left to himself. His impulses and desires, so largely unregulated because of his tender years, need to be given a sure direction by religious training, if he is to achieve that great purpose for which he was made: to know, to love, and to serve God.

The child must *know* God. There is a vast difference between "knowing about God" and "knowing God." The difference is made by personal experience. It is not enough that the child be given the necessary truths about God. They ought to be given in such a way that he will assimilate them and make them a part of himself. God must become as real to him as his own father or mother. God must not remain an abstraction. If He does, He will not be loved; and if

He is not loved, then all the child's knowledge about Him will be sterile. Where love is, there too is service. "If you love me, keep my commandments." That is Christ's test and it must be applied to the child. He should be brought to see God's commandments and precepts as guideposts which give an unerring direction to his steps. In this work, the Church, the family and the school all have a part to play.

From the time that the Church pours the waters of Baptism over his forehead, until she surrenders him at death to God, there is no period when she does not provide the child, through her sacraments and teachings, with a steady inspiration to serve God. The inculcation of virtues, both natural and supernatural, the repeated warnings against succumbing to the demands of his lower nature, the balm with which she alleviates the wounds caused by sin in his life, and the channels of grace she holds constantly open for him — all these are aids which the Church gives the child in directing his steps toward God.

Parents are obligated to see that he makes ample use of these helps; and in addition they must inspire him to love and service of God by their own daily actions. The home will be his first school. He will be quick to imitate what he sees and hears there. Let them turn this impulse to imitate, which can be the source of much mischief and lasting harm, to the child's advantage by giving him at home a good example of Christian living.

If this example is not forthcoming, the child will become confused by the contradiction between what he is taught and what he sees practiced. This confusion will be compounded when he goes to a school where religion is taught. There he will be taught to reverence the name of God, but at home he will hear God's name used irreverently in petulance and anger. At school he will learn to co-operate and get along with his fellow pupils, but at home he will be allowed to offend and wrangle with his brothers and sisters. At school he will be taught strict precepts of honesty and justice, while at home he will hear his parents boast of sharp business practices and clever evasions of the truth. Disturbed by these contradictions and torn by conflicting loyalties to home and school, the child will lose confidence in his parents' and teachers' powers to give him effective direction.

A close association between home and school should be maintained by parents and school authorities so as to facilitate an exchange of views and confidences regarding the child. In this way, home and school life can be better integrated and there will be a reduction of those conflicts which very often are at work in his life, and which do not receive the understanding and attention they deserve.

When we speak of parents' responsibilities, it should be remembered that they do not devolve entirely upon the mother. The father has his responsibilities, too, and he must not shirk them. It is not enough for him to provide the material means of support for the family. He also has the obligation to identify himself with the interests and activities of his child. If the full benefits of parental direction are to be reaped by the child, such direction should include that steadying and stabilizing influence which it is the father's duty to exert.

Fathers and mothers have a natural competence to instruct their children with regard to sex. False modesty should not deter them from doing their duty in this regard. Sex is one of God's endowments. It should not be ignored or treated as something bad. If sex instruction is properly carried on in the home, a deep reverence will be developed in the child and he will be spared the shameful inferences which he often makes when he is left to himself to find out about sex. We protest in the strongest possible terms against the introduction of sex instruction into the schools. To be of benefit such instruction must be far broader than the imparting of information, and must be given individually. Sex is more than a biological function. It is bound up with the sacredness and uniqueness of the human personality. It can be fully and properly appreciated only within a religious and moral context. If treated otherwise, the child will see it apart from the controlling purpose of his life, which is service to God.

Many unsalutary influences are at work in modern society which must not be allowed free play upon the personality of the growing child. Parents should carefully regulate the company and the hours which their child keeps. They should not treat him as an adult. He needs to be warned against, even forbidden, certain associations. Particularly during adolescence, this is extremely important. A vigilant watch should be kept over the type of entertainment in which he indulges, the motion pictures he attends, the books he reads, the radio and television programs to which he is exposed in the home.

III. Sense of Responsibility

A common complaint registered against the home and the school today is that they do not sharpen the child's sense of responsibility. He is made conscious of his rights, to be sure; but he also has obligations which are correlates of those rights. His education and training are defective in the proportion that those obligations are not impressed on his young mind.

No point is urged with greater insistency by religion than the accountability of each individual before God. It is the duty of parents to see to it that their child develops a deep sense of personal responsibility; learning at the earliest possible period that he is accountable to God for his thoughts, his words, and his actions. His home training must reinforce this teaching in every practical way. He should be held to strict account for the performance of chores and tasks which are given to him by his parents. He must be made to see that each member of the family has a part to play in the service of God by carrying out an assigned role. The child, thus enlightened, will be enabled to see in later life how the faithful discharge of his duties as a citizen can be related to the service of God.

Part of the boredom affecting our society today is due to the unsound separation which has developed between work and spiritual growth. The concept of work as a means of furthering sanctification has largely been lost. It remains for parents to recover that concept and apply it to the child's daily experience. From the consciousness that even the smallest household task when faithfully carried out draws him closer to God, the child will derive a continuing motivation for relating all that he does to God. And thus every task, no matter how trivial or menial, can take on a significance which will yield rich spiritual returns.

In this way the child will have learned at home a great lesson which will make it easier for him to adjust to the demands of school life. As he takes his place in that larger community, he will do so as a responsible individual. He will see his homework, his attention in class, and his participation in school activities as part of the same divine plan learned in the home, whereby each action has its significance in God's eyes. This mindfulness throughout his daily life of the supernatural value of his actions will be a safeguard against the careless performance of any duty. The greater his talent, the more he will be conscious of his obligation to serve God by a rightful exercise of that talent.

If the child is constantly aware that his time and his talents belong to God he will want to use them properly and will avoid those harmful associations and pastimes which frequently lead to juvenile delinquency. This implies however that adequate recreational facilities and opportunities for the development of his interest in hobbies, games and other activities are available so that his abounding energy can find wholesome channels for expression.

The spiritual helps which the child has for deepening his sense of responsibility must not be neglected. Parents should encourage the practice of nightly examination of conscience and weekly confession.

The child who goes over his thoughts, speech, and actions at the end of each day, seeking out what has been displeasing to God, will gradually develop a sensitivity to God's claims upon his life. The practice of weekly confession will make him conscious of the manner in which he has misused his time and talents. It will heighten in him that sense of accountability to God which is necessary if he is to show proper contrition for his failings and proper amendment of them.

IV. Sense of Mission

In learning the valuable lesson that he is accountable to God for the use of his time and talents the child will acquire not only a sense of responsibility, but a sense of mission as well. For his religious training will remind him that his future happiness lies not in the indulgence of selfish desires, but in the complete dedication of his whole personality to God's service. "I am come to do the will of him who sent me." This must be the keynote of the child's mission in this world. For him the will of God must come to be more important than any personal consideration. Only when he masters this truth will he be given to see how all things, even disappointments and setbacks, can be turned to good account in the service of God.

Since everyone is not called to serve God in the same way or in the same capacity, great care should be exercised in the child's vocational guidance. Otherwise, aimlessness in his training will leave him without permanent direction for his talents and aptitudes. Parents and teachers must help him to choose and to follow a calling for which he is fitted and in which he can best serve God. A deeper awareness in the child of his mission in life will do much to reduce the shocking waste of time and energy which in so many instances characterizes his formative years today, and later prevents him from taking his full place in civic life.

Among the boys and girls of our land, God has destined some to carry on the work of His Church for the salvation of souls. To these He has given a religious vocation. Here indeed is a challenge to the generosity of American parents. If in all sincerity they have impressed upon their child that he has a mission in life to do God's will, they in turn will want to co-operate with that will and aid in its fulfillment. God's claims are prior to every human consideration. If He calls the child to His special service, parents should not shrink from the sacrifice often entailed by such a call. The pain of severing home ties will be more than offset by the spiritual joy given to those who labor in the vineyard of the Lord.

In emphasizing the supreme importance of religion in the spiritual development of the child, we are but applying to the circumstances of today the eternal principles which the Church received from her divine Founder. For nineteen centuries, the Church has lingered lovingly over Christ's tribute to the child: "Suffer little children to come unto me and forbid them not; for of such is the kingdom of God." The implications of that tribute should be recognized by all who have care of the child. Theirs is the great vocation to show him that he is a citizen, not only of this world, but of that other world which lies beyond with God whose kingdom is the kingdom of children.

Statement issued November 17, 1950, by the bishops of the United States and signed in their names by the Administrative Board of the National Catholic Welfare Conference, whose members are:

✚ DENNIS CARDINAL DOUGHERTY,
Archbishop of Philadelphia

✚ EDWARD CARDINAL MOONEY,
Archbishop of Detroit

✚ SAMUEL CARDINAL STRITCH,
Archbishop of Chicago

✚ FRANCIS CARDINAL SPELLMAN,
Archbishop of New York

✚ FRANCIS P. KEOUGH,
Archbishop of Baltimore

✚ ROBERT E. LUCEY,
Archbishop of San Antonio

✚ RICHARD J. CUSHING,
Archbishop of Boston

✚ JOSEPH E. RITTER,
Archbishop of St. Louis

✚ PATRICK A. O'BOYLE,
Archbishop of Washington

✚ JOHN M. GANNON,
Bishop of Erie

✚ JOHN F. NOLL,
Bishop of Fort Wayne

✚ MICHAEL J. READY,
Bishop of Columbus

✚ EMMET M. WALSH,
Coadjutor Bishop of Youngstown

SECTION B

RESOLUTIONS AND
LETTERS OF THE HIERARCHY
SENT TO
INDIVIDUALS

14.
LETTER OF THE HIERARCHY OF THE UNITED
STATES SIGNED BY JAMES CARDINAL GIBBONS
AND ADDRESSED TO PRESIDENT WOODROW
WILSON, APRIL, 1917, REGARDING THE

ESTABLISHMENT OF THE
NATIONAL CATHOLIC WAR COUNCIL*
AND PLEDGE OF CATHOLIC LOYALTY

When war was declared in 1917 by the United States against the German Empire, every part of the organization of the Church immediately became solicitous to do its share in assisting the Government. Shortly after the declaration of war, the loyalty of the Catholic hierarchy, clergy, and people was pledged anew to the country, its government, and its supreme executive in a letter to President Woodrow Wilson, drawn up by the archbishops of the United States at their annual meeting in April, 1917, at the Catholic University of America.

The following is the complete text of this important document, presented to the President by Cardinal Gibbons:

Standing firmly upon our solid Catholic tradition and history from the very foundation of this nation, we affirm in this hour of stress and trial our most sacred and sincere loyalty and patriotism toward our country, our government, and our flag. Moved to the very depths of our hearts by the stirring appeal of the President of the United States and by the action of our national Congress, we accept wholeheartedly and unreservedly the decree of that legislative authority proclaiming this country to be in a state of war. We have prayed that we might be spared the dire necessity of entering the conflict. But now that war has been declared, we bow in obedience to the summons to bear our part in it, with fidelity, with courage, and with the spirit of sacrifice, which as loyal citizens we are bound to manifest for the defense of the most sacred rights and the welfare of the whole nation. Acknowledging gladly the gratitude that we have always felt for the protection

---

* Cf. *Handbook of the National Catholic War Council*, pp. 7–8 (N.C.W.C., Washington 5, D. C.).

of our spiritual liberty and the freedom of our Catholic institutions under the flag, we pledge our devotion and our strength in the maintenance of our country's glorious leadership in those possessions and principles which have been America's proudest boast. Inspired neither by hate nor fear, but by the holy sentiments of truest patriotic fervor and zeal, we stand ready, we and all the flock committed to our keeping, to co-operate in every way possible with our President and our national government, to the end that the great and holy cause of liberty may triumph, and that our beloved country may emerge from this hour of test stronger and nobler than ever. Our people, as ever, will rise as one man to serve the nation. Our priests and consecrated women will once again, as in every former trial of our country, win by their bravery, their heroism, and their service new admiration and approval. We are all true Americans, ready, as our age, our ability, and our condition permit, to do whatever is in us to do, for the preservation, the progress, and triumph of our beloved country. May God direct and guide our President and our government, that out of this trying crisis in our national life may, at length, come a closer union among all citizens of America, and that an enduring and blessed peace may crown the sacrifices which war inevitably entails.

15. LETTER OF THE HIERARCHY OF THE UNITED STATES TO MICHAEL CARDINAL LOGUE, ARCHBISHOP OF ARMAGH, PRIMATE OF IRELAND, SEPTEMBER 22, 1921, ON THE

FATE OF IRELAND*

This letter was addressed to Michael Cardinal Logue, Primate of Ireland, by the archbishops and bishops of the United States at their annual meeting, September 21 and 22, 1921, on the occasion of conferences held between the Irish and English governments.

His Eminence,
    Michael Cardinal Logue,
        Archbishop of Armagh,
            Primate of Ireland.

Your Eminence:

In this solemn and portentious hour of Ireland's history, we, the bishops of the United States, gathered in annual conference, feel it a duty incumbent on us to extend to Your Eminence and your brethren of the Irish hierarchy the assurance of our sympathy, our prayers, and our united good wishes for the happy outcome of the conference in which the representatives of your people are now engaged.

Particularly at this time we are not unmindful of the tremendous debt the Church in this country owes to Ireland and its people. For more than a century millions of your race have come to our shores and by their strong faith and their loyal generous help, have built up a Church which has become the pride of Christendom and the glory of the country in which we dwell. And even though they have become loyal Americans, faithful to the flag under which they dwell, time has never been able to extinguish in their souls the love they bore to the land of their fathers, to the little island from which they parted as exiles destined never to return.

And particularly during these recent years, with anxious and ex-

---

* *N.C.W.C. Bulletin,* December, 1929, p. 7. Cf. footnote, No. 51 of the Foreword.

pectant hearts, they have watched the trend of events, ever hopeful that Providence in its wisdom might ordain that at last Ireland was to take its place among the nations of the earth.

And indeed, during these latter weeks their hearts were filled with pride when they saw the representatives of their race conduct themselves with a statesmanship that has challenged the admiration of the world.

Therefore, in this fateful hour, when the future of Ireland trembles in the balance, it is not our desire, Your Eminence, by any word of ours to peril the outcome of those deliberations upon which a world waits with bated breath. Rather, in the true spirit of our holy Faith, united with our people from every race and every station, our prayers ascend from every altar in the land that God in His Wisdom may bring Ireland's misery of seven hundred years to an end, that this most apostolic race among all of God's peoples may receive the reward for what they have done for the Church of America and elsewhere by obtaining the fulfillment of their national aspirations.

And finally, that God may grant you and your colleagues to live to see Ireland's golden age, and find your people even more faithful to their Church in the sunburst of their new freedom than ever they were in the years of their exile and expectancy.

Your Eminence's devoted servants in Christ,

THE ARCHBISHOPS AND BISHOPS OF THE UNITED STATES

16. RESOLUTIONS OF THE HIERARCHY OF THE UNITED STATES SENT TO ARCHBISHOP AUSTIN DOWLING OF ST. PAUL IN

APPRECIATION OF DEVOTED SERVICES*

November 24, 1929

The archbishops and bishops of the United States, meeting in November, 1929, at the Catholic University of America, Washington, D. C., adopted the following resolution expressing regret upon Archbishop Austin Dowling's retirement from the Committee and appreciation of his devoted services to the Conference since its inception in 1919:

His Grace, the Most Reverend Austin Dowling, Archbishop of St. Paul, has been a member since its organization of the Administrative Committee, N.C.W.C.;

He has been also the Episcopal chairman of its Department of Education, and for an equal length of time has served as treasurer of the N.C.W.C.

His thorough understanding of the questions and problems of the day: his zeal in the work of his office: his devoted interest in the promotion of the spiritual welfare of the Catholic body, have made him a leader and a guide in this work of ours. Only his own conviction that through ill-health he can no longer serve has led us to accept his resignation.

This resolution is a testimony of our appreciation. We hope and pray that our Lord in His great goodness may restore health and strength to the Archbishop of St. Paul, that he may yet and for years to come personally give of his wisdom and his devotion to our deliberations.

---

* *N.C.W.C. Bulletin,* December, 1929, p. 7. Cf. footnote 15 of Foreword.

17.

LETTER OF THE MOST REV. SAMUEL A. STRITCH, D.D., ARCHBISHOP OF MILWAUKEE, AND MOST REV. EMMET M. WALSH, D.D., BISHOP OF CHARLESTON, IN THE NAME OF THE HIERARCHY OF THE UNITED STATES TO DR. THOMAS W. TURNER, HAMPTON INSTITUTE, PRESIDENT

FEDERATED COLORED CATHOLICS OF THE U.S.A.

(15?) November, 1939

My dear Dr. Turner:

We have learned in greater detail from your letter of August 8th the admirable work of the Federated Colored Catholics of the United States in helping to right the social wrongs of our brothers by promoting a wider and deeper knowledge and practice of Christian social justice and charity.

Indeed, your activities foster the hope in us that you will be a great force, gathering strength with the years, to break down customs and practices, born of selfish individualism and arrogant false assumptions, which have placed on our colored brothers the ugly burden of crushing social injustices. With satisfaction we read in his recent letter to the hierarchy of the United States, the words of the Holy Father: "We confess that we feel a special paternal affection, which certainly is inspired of Heaven, for the Negro people dwelling among you." When the father of the whole Church holds our colored brothers in special affection, surely the Christian family will emulate his charity. It were a sham Christianity were we to try to exclude from the embrace of justice any man, or to make our charity narrower than the outstretched arms of Christ on Calvary.

We pray that your noble efforts will be fruitful of abundant good and win the brotherly support of all good men.

Sincerely yours in Christ,

The Administrative Board
National Catholic Welfare Conference

✝ Samuel A. Stritch
Archbishop of Milwaukee
✝ Emmett M. Walsh,
Bishop of Charleston

Dr. Thomas W. Turner, President
The Federated Colored Catholics of the United States
1727 Thirteenth Street, Northwest
Washington, D. C.

18. BRIEF OF THE HIERARCHY OF THE UNITED STATES ADDRESSED TO THE HON. PAUL V. MC NUTT, CHAIRMAN

WAR MANPOWER COMMISSION*

November 30, 1942

This brief is directed by the archbishops and bishops of the Catholic Church in the United States representing over twenty-five million Catholics for the purpose of respectfully requesting the inclusion of religious facilities and services in the War Manpower Commission's "List of Essential Activities."

Religious facilities and services for this purpose include: churches; convents; orphanages; infant asylums; homes for the aged; homes for the poor; homes for delinquents; day nurseries; administrative buildings; publications; seminaries; monasteries and cemeteries. Hos-

---

* N.C.W.C. Archives under date of November 30, 1942. Attachment 3, re: "List of Essential Activities."

pitals and schools have been purposely omitted because they are explicitly included at present in the "Essential Activities List."

THE NECESSITY OF RELIGION

It is hoped that there is no need in this country of proving the necessity of religion and of its facilities and services as "essential to the support of the war program and necessary to the maintenance of the health, safety, morale, and security of the civilian population." In his message to Congress on January 4, 1941, the President of the United States declared: "Storms from abroad directly challenge free institutions indispensable to Americans now as always. The first is religion. It is a source of the other two — democracy and international good faith. . . . There comes a time in the affairs of men when they must prepare to defend not their members alone, but the tenets of faith and humanity on which their churches, their governments, and their very civilization are founded. The defense of religion, of democracy, and of good faith among nations is all the same fight. To save one we must now make up our mind to save all."

It is with grave concern that we note that the mention of religion with its facilities and agencies is omitted completely from the "List of Essential Activities" issued at the direction of the War Manpower Commission. It is admitted that the List is "not to be regarded as a final list of essential activities" and "the list must necessarily be flexible to permit the addition or deletion of other activities as warranted by changing war conditions." To us it is obvious that religion must be included from the outset in any "List of Essential Activities" and its inclusion or deletion must not depend on changing war conditions; otherwise not only are the President's words false but the government of the United States would appear to assume an essentially materialistic attitude. We prefer to believe that the omission of religious facilities and services from the "List of Essential Activities" was an oversight which will be remedied immediately when the fact is called to the attention of the War Manpower Commission.

NECESSITY OF RELIGIOUS FACILITIES AND SERVICES

Obviously religion cannot function without the existence of its necessary facilities and services, which are enumerated broadly in the beginning of this Brief. Each of these facilities and services contributes essentially to the support of the war program and is necessary for the maintenance of national interest and morale. In a time of crisis our citizens turn closer to their religion, looking for the consolation and guidance necessary to sustain them in their hour of peril, whether in the armed forces, in war production plants, or in ordinary civilian life. Each of the religious facilities and services enumerated above is necessary for the proper pursuance of the war effort, and therefore the means necessary to accomplish these ends must be made available. In our seminaries are trained the ministers of religion who not only contribute their services on the home front but serve as well as chaplains, accompanying our armed forces; if our seminaries are not allowed to operate, the efficiency of the war program will be seriously impaired. Our orphanages, infant asylums, homes for the aged, institutions for the protection and care of delinquent youth, etc., are performing in most cases the functions which are in reality public functions which would otherwise be the necessary duty of government. The operation and maintenance of our cemeteries is not only necessary from the viewpoint of public health but is a necessary part of religion; if the operation of our cemeteries is curtailed, both civilian population and in many instances our armed forces will quickly be demoralized and the war effort will be seriously affected.

Necessity of Occupational Deferment of Necessary Men

Some large religious institutions will suffer a "serious loss in effectiveness" — will even find it impossible to operate at all without the occupational deferment under the provisions of the Selective Service Act of some "necessary men" "with the required degree of training, qualification, or skill for the performance of the duty involved." Examples of such critical occupations are: stationary engineer; electrical engineer; civil engineer; skilled mechanic; trained, experienced maintenance man in large institution; shop engineer; superintendent or sexton of large cemetery.

It is admitted that the need of occupational deferment under the provisions of the Selective Service Act *will be rare*, but without a listing as an "essential activity," it is most difficult to obtain consideration for the comparatively *very few necessary* men from local draft boards.

Manpower Shortage

Obviously it is impossible to operate these religious facilities and services without an adequate supply of manpower; some very few skilled, some semiskilled, and most unskilled. At present because we have no listing as "essential activities" our needs suffer badly in the United States employment offices. The danger is not merely that we are not able to obtain adequate manpower without a listing as essential, but that our necessary supply, not rated at present as being engaged in an essential activity, will be drained to fill the needs of those activities which are rated as essential.

THE REMEDY

The only solution to our problem lies in the classification of religious facilities and services in the "List of Essential Activities" which is officially declared "to be used as a guide by the local Selective Service Board in connection with problems of occupational deferment and by the United States Employment Service in determining which type of activities should be regarded as having prior claims to the workers available for referral to the job opening."

Although we realize that the "List of Essential Activities" as well as National Headquarters Selective Service System's Local Board Release No. 115 explicitly states that consideration should also be given to activities and occupations which are not listed as essential, nevertheless our nonclassification as essential will lead in *practical* application in many important instances in local Selective Service boards and in United States employment offices to the conclusion that we are actually not essential and therefore not deserving of prior consideration with other activities of a recognized essential nature.

It is our patriotic wish to do everything within our power to support our beloved country in the war effort. We are already using women to replace men whenever possible and will continue to do so at a rapidly increasing rate. We are unable to determine with any degree of accuracy the exact number of men in the category referred to in this brief, but we are determined to keep it as low as possible and we are convinced that *only in relatively very rare instances* will it be necessary to seek occupational deferment for anyone under the provisions of the Selective Service Act. We shall continue to co-operate patriotically with every need of our country in wartime, but we feel that we would be seriously neglecting our duty as Churchmen and patriotic citizens if we did not point out the vital necessity that religion must play in any successful prosecution of our war effort.

SECTION C

RESOLUTIONS AND STATEMENTS
OF THE
HIERARCHY OF THE UNITED STATES
ON
EPISCOPAL COMMITTEES
ON
VARIOUS TOPICS

19. STATEMENT OF THE AMERICAN HIERARCHY ON

DISARMAMENT*

September, 1921

This statement was prepared by the American hierarchy in September, 1921, on the eve of the Disarmament Conference called by President Warren G. Harding. The conference met in Washington, D. C., in November, 1921.

Following, not merely dutifully, but with a full conviction of its supreme importance, the expressed desire of our Holy Father, Pope Benedict XV, that steps should be taken to lift the crushing burden of heavy armaments from the overburdened shoulders of the peoples and nations of the world, and gratefully recalling the fact that the Father of Christendom first proclaimed the necessity of united action to secure this end, we commend most heartily the spirit and the measures so far adopted by the President of the United States in summoning the representatives of the great nations to meet in Washington in November to discuss and carry into effect a limitation of armaments by all the nations, and we call upon the Catholic people of the United States to set apart Armistice Day, November 11, the day of the opening of the Conference, as a day of special prayer that God's blessing may rest upon the Conference and that His Holy Spirit may guide its deliberations toward hastening that era of peace and good will for which the stricken peoples of the earth hope and pray and labor.

---

* *N.C.W.C. Bulletin,* October, 1921, p. 4.

20. RESOLUTION OF THE HIERARCHY OF THE UNITED STATES REGARDING

CONDITIONS IN RUSSIA*

September 25, 1924

This resolution was adopted at the annual meeting of the American hierarchy, held at the Catholic University of America on September 24 and 25, 1924.

We view with pain and deep anxiety the extremely sad plight of the Christian communities of Russia. To them today, in the throes of a religious persecution surpassing in studied cruelty the fearful sufferings of the early Christians, we extend our heartfelt sympathy.

Speaking in the name of twenty millions of Catholics of this republic, and supported, we are sure, in this, our action, by the liberty-loving Christian millions of America, we condemn the wholly unjust attitude of the present Russian government, opposed as it is to the fundamental principles of justice and repugnant to the best sentiments of all Christian people. We furthermore declare that we are ready to aid in every way possible our suffering brethren, bishops, priests, and people of Russia.

---

* *N.C.W.C. Bulletin,* October, 1924, p. 5.

21. RESOLUTION OF THE HIERARCHY OF THE UNITED STATES DEALING WITH THE CHURCH SITUATION IN

GUATEMALA*

SEPTEMBER 25, 1924

Resolution adopted at the annual meeting of the American hierachy, held at the Catholic University of America on September 24 and 25, 1924.

The hierarchy of the Catholic Church in the United States of America observes with profound distress that the situation of the Church in Guatemala has grown worse instead of better in the past twelve months, and that the enemies of Christianity, who have fastened a terroristic regime upon that unhappy country, not content with the expulsion of the hierarchy and a final and sweeping pillage of the Church, have now resorted to the ill-treatment and exile of nuns and the proscription of the crucifix; therefore, be it unanimously

Resolved, That formal expression of the sincere sympathy of the entire Catholic Church in the United States, as represented by the hierarchy now assembled in Washington, with the Catholic clergy and people of Guatemala upon the prolonged anguish of their harrowing persecution be conveyed to the Catholic clergy and laity of each of the other countries of this hemisphere, and brought to the attention of all right-minded people throughout the civilized world.

---

* *N.C.W.C. Bulletin,* October, 1924, p. 5.

22. LETTER OF SYMPATHY FROM THE HIERARCHY OF THE UNITED STATES TO THE ARCHBISHOPS, BISHOPS, PRIESTS, AND LAITY OF

MEXICO*

September 16, 1926

At their annual meeting held on September 15–16, 1926, at the Catholic University of America, Washington, D. C., the cardinals, archbishops, and bishops of the United States drafted and sent the following message of "sympathy and affection" to the Episcopate and laity of Mexico:

Archbishops, Bishops, Priests, and Laity of Mexico:

In these days of your severe trials and persecutions, we, the bishops of the United States of America, assembled in conference, send our greetings of sympathy and affection to you, dear brethren, bishops of the United States of Mexico, and to your heroic people. We, our clergy and laity, are watching with eagerness and entire sympathy your magnificent fight against a tyrannical government. We applaud your wisdom, moderation, and firmness; and are filled with admiration of the calmness, courage, and endurance of the Mexican people. You are showing to the whole world the true spirit of martyrs, ready to endure and suffer all for the sake of Christ. You are also showing yourselves the real champions in Mexico of religious and civil liberty. You are fearlessly resisting armed force in defense of the inalienable rights of man.

The fight may be long; it may give many martyrs to the Church and to mankind. It will end only with the victory of liberty and justice. The long-suffering and peace-loving Mexican people, too long the victim of ruthless militarism, will emerge from this trial a stronger and purer nation, with a constitution founded on the true principles of

---

* *N.C.W.C. News Bulletin,* October, 1926, p. 18; cf. also Nos. 2, 29, 31, 34, 58, 63.

justice and liberty, and a government that honestly respects the rights of the people.

Be comforted, therefore, dear brethren. We, the Catholic bishops and priests and people of America, pledge you our prayers and our deepest sympathy in this your hour of sorrow. With God's blessing, we shall be with you to the end and to victory.

23. RESOLUTION OF THE HIERARCHY OF THE UNITED STATES REGARDING

HOME AND FOREIGN MISSIONS*

September 15, 1927

This resolution was adopted at the general meeting of archbishops and bishops, Catholic University of America, Washington, D. C., September 14–15, 1927.

Whereas, The Holy See has given its approval to plans for organizing parish and diocesan units for the purpose of promoting interest in, and for aiding the Home Missions, plans which have had the unanimous support of three separate meetings of the American Episcopate, followed by the appointing of a board to carry such plans into action throughout the entire country:

To make clear the import of these actions, both on the part of the Holy See and of the American Episcopate, as well as to support still more strongly this much-needed movement in favor of our Home Missions —

Resolved, That each bishop should immediately proceed to organize in his diocese a society for the Home and Foreign Missions, with a minimum monthly offering of ten cents per month or one dollar per year for all adult members, and five cents per month or fifty cents per

* *N.C.W.C. Bulletin*, October, 1927, p. 6.

year for junior members, besides taking up a collection on Mission Sunday.

2. Wherever a mission society already exists in a diocese, that its monthly dues be raised to the same minimum.

3. That Mission Sunday be an opportunity given to those who have failed to make their full contribution for the year, to make up for it at one time, or for those who have given nothing, to pay up their membership dues in one offering, at the rate of ten cents a month.

4. The Diocesan Director of Societies thus organized or re-organized be instructed to send 60 per cent of the total membership receipts to the national director of the Society of the Propagation of the Faith, and 40 per cent to the treasurer of the American Episcopate of Catholic Missions.

5. That the bishops further direct the diocesan directors to so arrange their appeals for missions and so direct their influence, that designated gifts be made as nearly as possible to conform to the 60 – 40 basis stated above.

6. That an executive secretary be appointed by the American Board of Catholic Missions to carry out the purposes of the organization under the direction of the said Board.

7. That it is the sense of this meeting that the work of the American Board of Catholic Missions be organized on lines similar to the Society of the Propagation of the Faith in the United States, and

8. That one month previous to the annual meeting of the American Board of Catholic Missions a written notice be sent to all bishops requesting the remittance of the Home Mission allotment to the treasurer.

24. STATEMENT OF THE HIERARCHY OF THE UNITED STATES (THROUGH THE ADMINISTRATIVE BOARD) CONCERNING

UNEMPLOYMENT*

November 12, 1930

In accordance with the authorization given by the cardinals, archbishops, and bishops of the United States at their meeting in Washington during November, 1930, the Most Rev. Edward J. Hanna, Archbishop of San Francisco and Chairman of the Administrative Committee of the National Catholic Welfare Conference, issued the following statement dealing with the grave situation of unemployment.

Again the United States is suffering the tragedy of millions of men and women who need work, who want work, and who can find no work to do. May God give the country His wisdom and grace to throw off this yoke of suffering, unlike famine only in that men themselves inflict it in the midst of plenty.

The workless must indeed be cared for. We thank the men and women, both lay and religious, in our institutions, organizations, and parishes who give food to the hungry, clothe the naked, harbor the harborless during this lengthening year of unemployment. We thank those also who either directly or indirectly, through either money or supplies, make it possible for them to care for the poor who flock to them. God will reward them. There can be no respite in this generosity. More and more money and goods will be needed, it seems certain, to meet during the cold of the coming winter only the call for alms from the poorest of the poor.

More than temporary alms is necessary. Justice should be done. This unemployment returning again to plague us after so many repetitions during the century past is a sign of deep failure in our

* *N.C.W.C. Review,* January, 1931, pp. 5–6; cf. Nos. 25, 52, 60, 62, 66, 68, 71.

country. Unemployment is the great peacetime physical tragedy of the nineteenth and twentieth centuries, and both in its cause and in the imprint it leaves upon those who inflict it, those who permit it, and those who are its victims, it is one of the great moral tragedies of our time. The failure is not due to lack of intelligence nor any more to ignorance. It is due to lack of good will. It is due to neglect of Christ.

We call upon Catholics, and we ask all, to do more than give alms and more even than take measures to provide work and reduce the present army of the unemployed. Both are imperative. People are suffering, and we are obliged to help them. But our country needs, now and permanently, such a change of heart as will, intelligently and with determination, so organize and distribute our work and wealth that no one need lack for any long time the security of being able to earn an adequate living for himself and for those dependent upon him.

Co-operation of Catholics in their organizations and as individuals with the federal, state, and city efforts to reduce unemployment is most commendable. They have already done much. We ask them to do still more. But let them also look to the long-time, deeper-seated, and harder task of allowing the likeness of the Saviour of the world to shine through our country's economic institutions. Let them begin with their own work and wealth, and their own relations to property, to employees, to employers, to customers, to their corporation and organization associates. Let the spirit of Christ shine there.

In a world based in its work and wealth upon the neglect of Christ's teachings, there is, of course, a limit and a boundary to what Catholics of the best of spirit may do. This is not said to discourage or suggest excuses for inaction. The limit must be further extended; the boundary stretched to the utmost. We are ever under the call to do more and more and as one tries the best he can to live his Catholic morals, to try also to remold the institutions that surround work, ownership, and trade to the image of the Saviour of the world.

To this purpose we commend particularly Pope Leo's great encyclical on the Condition of Labor, now nearly forty years with us, the Bishops' Program of Social Reconstruction issued shortly after the war* and the passages on industrial relations in the last joint pastoral letter of the American bishops. They give a guide, even

---

* No. 51, this volume.

in many details, to the remaking in Christ's likeness of the property relations and working life of our times. Catholics should read and study these three. We invite all to read and study them.

And as a proof of their practical value both in this period of unemployment and at all other times, we quote briefly from one of them: "A living wage is not necessarily the full measure of justice. All the Catholic authorities on the subject explicitly declare that this is only the *minimum* of justice. In a country as rich as ours, there are very few cases in which it is possible to prove that the worker would be getting more than that to which he has a right if he were paid something in excess of this ethical minimum. Since our industrial resources and instrumentalities are sufficient to provide more than a living wage for a very large proportion of the workers, why should we acquiesce in a theory which denies them this measure of the comforts of life? Such a policy is not only of very questionable morality, but is unsound economically. The large demand for goods which is created and maintained by high rates of wages and high purchasing power by the masses is the surest guarantee of a continuous and general operation of industrial establishments. It is the most effective instrument of prosperity for labor and capital alike."*

Had this passage been heeded during the dozen years since it was written, it would in itself have gone far to prevent the calamity we now undergo. "The human and Christian, in contrast to the purely commercial and pagan, ethics of industry," to quote again, will both cure our country of our present malady and prevent its cruel recurrence.

We add our earnest appeal for the use of what is the most efficacious of means — prayer. Pray daily that the needy may be relieved; that the suffering and the consequent moral tragedies may be lessened; that a greater energy may enter into the hearts of all to build a social structure which in far greater measure than the present will voice practically the teachings of Christ and His Church, and bring a larger measure of justice unto men.

---

* See No. 52, p. 251 for this quote.

25. STATEMENT OF THE HIERARCHY OF THE UNITED STATES ON THE

ECONOMIC CRISIS*

November 12, 1931

This statement on the economic crisis was issued at the annual meeting of hierarchy, November 11–12, 1931, Catholic University of America, Washington, D. C.

Urged by the charity of Christ, of whose Church we are the shepherds, we seek always to extend to the multitude that spiritual food which alone sustains the life of the soul and all that the soul means to man, both here and hereafter. To the multitude we seek also to give that material food essential to the life and well-being of the individual, of the family, of all society. In this day of world-wide depression and of hardship, we voice our deep paternal sympathy for those millions of Americans, of whatever creed or race, who, victims of the present industrial crisis, must rely on their more fortunate brethren for food, clothing, and shelter.

We urge the reading, the study, and the application to everyday business, occupational, and social life, of the encyclical of our Holy Father, Pius XI, "On the Reconstruction of the Social Order." In keeping with the recommendations of the Holy Father, we have enlisted the services of our clergy and laity in a "crusade of charity," either in co-operation with approved relief agencies or independently of them, as varying local conditions suggest.

Since we are all bound together as brothers in Christ, it is our duty to insist that the wealthy are obligated in conscience to contribute for the relief of those who suffer, and the more so because the system under which they suffer has yielded wealth to others.

While co-operating in these private efforts, we are convinced, be-

---

* *N.C.W.C. Review,* December, 1931, p. 8; cf. Nos. 24, 52, 60, 62, 66, 68, 71.

cause of the vastness of the number suffering, that federal and state appropriations for relief in some form will become necessary.

Our economic system should be so improved that the laboring man, suddenly thrown out of employment, would not be deprived of sustenance during a period of severe business depression.

We deem it our duty also to quote the Holy Father on the relationships of armament to the present crisis:

"The unbridled race for armaments is on the one hand the effect of the rivalry among nations and on the other the cause of the withdrawal of enormous sums from the public wealth and hence not the smallest of contributors to the current extraordinary crisis."

The unemployment crisis is deep-rooted in the avarice of human nature which for a century and more has caused disorganization of the processes of production and distribution. This has run its course through unlimited individual and organized competition and is climaxed now by an ineffective economic rule. We ask a living wage for the family; a proper proportion between the wages of the different kinds of workers; an ample sufficiency for all. We ask for wages that will provide employment to the greatest extent possible; and for an equitable sharing of the goods produced so abundantly by industry.

And to avoid unjust and inequitable wage reductions, we ask for joint conferences of employers and their associations and labor and their unions, supplemented and assisted by government. Indeed all economic life needs such common counsel to deal with the present depression. Through such common counsel and organization, industry may proceed, animated by a sense of justice and good will to all. Thus will it care for the common good; meet the desire to solve a great problem of the present age; properly use the material resources and talents God has given us; and secure an equitable distribution of the income and wealth of our country and the world.

Only on these lines will the problem of how best to form a system of unemployment insurance, reserves, and old-age pensions be successfully worked out. There is dire need that our country and all its citizens bring the competence of every element, versed in the complexities of our industrial and social life to the solution of this great crisis and the avoidance of its like in the future. There is supreme need that our country be guided and enlightened in all these things by the full teaching of Christ.

The present crisis should urge everyone to careful thought and courageous action. We urge Catholic organizations to study the social teaching of the Church so as to help prepare Catholics to take their full part in this great task of our times. Fidelity to the teachings of Christ and of His Church, both as individuals and as a social body, is the foundation on which sure and permanent social justice and happiness must be built. What we seek, here as elsewhere, is a fuller measure of the Kingdom of God on earth as it is in heaven.

26. RESOLUTION OF THE HIERARCHY OF THE UNITED STATES ON

RELIEF MOBILIZATION*·

November 17, 1932

In view of the most extraordinary conditions which threaten so many of our fellow citizens with want and misery during the coming winter, the bishops of the National Catholic Welfare Conference urge upon their people in the United States full co-operation with the effort of the National Citizens Committee of the Welfare and Relief Mobilization to avert the worst consequences of the economic depression. They pledge themselves to sincere and effective co-operation with the committee in its work and they pray that Almighty God may bless and prosper its every endeavor.

---

* *Catholic Action*, December, 1932, p. 3.

27. RESOLUTION OF THE HIERARCHY OF THE UNITED STATES REGARDING THE

RIGHT USE OF LEISURE TIME*

November 17, 1932

Complete text of the resolution adopted by the archbishops and bishops at their general meeting at the Catholic University of America, Washington, D. C., November 16–17, 1932, regarding the right use of leisure time.

Unemployment has imposed upon millions of men and women more leisure time. While we pray the scourge of unemployment be lifted, we cannot but fear that the lesser hours of labor for many will continue. The problem, therefore, of the use of leisure time becomes more and more acute. It is one of the gravest problems at present facing our country. The individual is easily demoralized by idleness and aimlessness. Yet the door to both is held open by circumstances to millions of our young and our adult.

The public entertainments are therefore more widely patronized. Commercialism, which our Holy Father has named as the root of modern evils, practically controls the theater of today, the spoken drama and the screen. Apart from a very small number of worthy plays and moving pictures, the stage and the movie have abandoned all reserve, mocked every finer human feeling, every higher taste, and show themselves as the panderers of this day and age.

For those who are idle, the government — city, state, or federal — has, unfortunately, small moral concern. Yet it is the duty of government to aid in the moral well-being of its citizens. Government oftentimes does not protect its idle citizens; it leaves them to be the prey of the theater and movie-house owner, who exhibits by virtue of government authority, by virtue of a government license. The nation is debauched through the sanction of government. That

---

* *Catholic Action,* December, 1932, p. 4.

our citizens permit this is no encouraging sign for the future moral and mental stamina of the nation. Yet both will be required in abundance, if we are to weather the storm that no one now seems able to control.

We earnestly appeal to the conscience of our country to rouse itself for the sake of the unemployed, for the sake of the entire nation, to a sense of, and to action on, this far-reaching public evil.

Leisure time should be used only for wholesome enjoyment and entertainment, such as one may look back to with a good conscience and a satisfied heart.

To our own people we appeal that they should further resolve to use part at least of their leisure time in attendance at daily Mass; in frequenting the other services of the Church and endeavoring to acquaint themselves with the meaning and the message to them of the liturgical year. To our Catholic organizations, particularly to our St. Vincent de Paul Councils, we earnestly recommend a personal service, personal contact with the individual unemployed. He may be facing the crisis of his life. Personal encouragement, even when financial aid is impossible, is of the greatest value.

In like manner, Catholics of professional training, such as doctors, nurses, might most worthily give of their free time in service to the sick poor. Such service is effectively done by orderly, local organization.

Spiritual help, personal companionship are the human chords by which we are sustained and helpfully bound one to another. To pastors, under the Ordinary of course, we recommend the holding of extra Church devotions that further opportunity be given to the unemployed to pass well their leisure time. Thus can we promote that Christian, Catholic consciousness which will help ourselves and our fellows over all barriers into the power and the victory of Christ and of His Church.

28. RESOLUTION OF THE HIERARCHY OF THE UNITED STATES IN

CONDEMNATION OF INDECENT LITERATURE*

November 17, 1932

Resolution adopted at the general meeting of archbishops and bishops of the United States, Catholic University of America, Washington, D. C., November 16, 17, 1932.

Much has been said and written on the causes of the present depression. Undoubtedly those causes are in the main economic, but it would be blindness not to recognize the looseness and laxity of morals which both hastened the economic chaos of the world and now plays its part in extending laxity in public morals, loss of public decency, and consequently, a lowering of the standards of citizenship.

One of the most potent factors in this debasing of the individual and the public conscience is the increasing flood of immoral and unmoral books, periodicals, pamphlets, which are widely advertised throughout the country. Great metropolitan dailies, literary journals, carry laudatory advertisements of books that have always been known as obscene. Publishers repeatedly issue new books outdoing the old ones in obscenity. Public opinion has influenced the courts of the nation to such an extent that it is now almost impossible to have the most obscene of books debarred from the customs or from the mails.

Literature has its uplifting, human mission. Wholesome, healthy reading promotes both entertainment and education. Talented men and women are today producing worthy literature, devoting themselves to it as one of the greatest of the arts. A practical guide to such literature may be found in the lists of the Cardinal Hayes Literature Committee, published in our Catholic press.

It is further undeniable that many writers, beggared of talent and

---

* *Catholic Action,* December, 1932, p. 5; cf. Nos. 30, 31, 37, 44.

of true literary gifts, are playing up the sexual, the sensational, and the superficial, and these books are exploited by many reviewers as literary productions. They speak of the flesh rather than of the mind.

We call upon our own Catholic people, young and old, to maintain valiantly the standards of worthy, clean literature. We ask them to make it part of that crusade of Catholic Action, of which the Holy Father speaks. Catholic organizations can and should express publicly to daily newspapers, magazines, their protest against this corrupt and corrupting reading and picture matter. Co-operation by committees of Catholic organizations with the local public library would be conducive of much good. Our people should not be misled by books written under the cloak of medical advice, instruction on matters of sex, many of which are indecent beyond expression.

The corruption of private and public morals wears away more surely than any other agency the foundations of a nation. The publication and unobstructed distribution of indecent books and periodicals is, at the present time, one of the greatest menaces to our national well-being.

29. PROTEST OF THE HIERARCHY OF THE UNITED STATES (SUBCOMMITTEE IN CONJUNCTION WITH THE ADMINISTRATIVE BOARD) AGAINST THE

CONTINUED PERSECUTION OF THE CHURCH IN MEXICO*

January 12, 1933

"The right of religious liberty, of freedom of worship, is native to the thought of our own country. We feel, therefore, we are justified in asking all our fellow citizens actively to interest themselves in the restoration in Mexico of religious freedom for its citizens." (*Statement prepared by a subcommittee of bishops, which, with the Administrative Committee, N.C.W.C., had been charged with its issuance by and in behalf of the Catholic bishops of the United States.*)

The cardinals, archbishops, and bishops of the United States, assembled in conference at Washington, D. C., renew their emphatic protest against the sustained persecution of the Church in Mexico, and the persistent refusal of the Mexican government to grant religious liberty to its citizens. The facts of the continued active persecution have been admirably set forth in the recent encyclical on Mexico, of our Holy Father, Pope Pius XI. Nor does that encyclical by any means cover the entire list of definite acts of injustice and persecution of the Church by the present Mexican government.

The government summarily exiled the apostolic delegate. To limit, as the federal and the state governments of Mexico have limited, the number of priests to one for every fifty thousand, is practically to aim at the destruction of the Church and the eradication of the Faith from the hearts of the people.

The admirable patience of the Holy Father in asking the faithful of Mexico to bear with these evils, to employ only the limited legal

---

* *Catholic Action*, February, 1933, p. 5; cf. also Nos. 2, 22, 31, 34, 58, 63.

ways open to them to secure justice, offers a unique example to the entire world.

We extend our appreciation, our praise, and our support to the bishops of Mexico and to its suffering, faithful people. The example of a neighboring nation denying religious liberty to its citizens cannot but be a matter of serious concern to all right-thinking people and a detriment to the amicable understanding and friendship that should exist between our own country and all the nations of both American continents.

30. PLANS OF THE EPISCOPAL COMMITTEE ON MOTION PICTURES TO EXTEND THE

LEGION OF DECENCY*

June 21, 1934

Meeting in Cincinnati, June 21, 1934, the Episcopal Committee on Motion Pictures announced plans to extend the Legion of Decency drive to every city and town in the United States and heard promises to reform from representatives of the film industry sent to confer with the bishops. While expressing pleasure at these promises and offering their co-operation, the bishops, nevertheless, reiterated their unfailing opposition to evil motion pictures and asserted that support of the Catholic campaign of protest "must be maintained" so that the producers of films may be "constantly aware" of the demand for clean pictures. To aid in this work the bishops appointed a national committee of priests on the subject of motion picture decency. Following is the text of the statement issued at the Cincinnati meeting by the Episcopal Committee on Motion Pictures, the members of which were the Most Rev. John T. McNicholas, O.P., Archbishop of Cincinnati,

---

* *Catholic Action*, July, 1934, pp. 17–18; cf. also Nos. 28, 32, 37, 44.

episcopal chairman of N.C.W.C. Department of Education; the Most Rev. John J. Cantwell, Bishop of Los Angeles and San Diego; the Most Rev. Hugh C. Boyle, Bishop of Pittsburgh and episcopal chairman of the N.C.W.C. Press Department; and the Most Rev. John F. Noll, Bishop of Fort Wayne and secretary to the N.C.W.C. Administrative Committee and chairman of the Catholic Action Department of the Conference.

During the past several months, the Catholic Bishops' Committee on Motion Pictures, in co-operation with authorities of all the dioceses of the country, has been waging a campaign of protest against the destructive moral influence of evil motion pictures.

There has been no wish to harm or destroy the motion-picture business. But the evil character of portions of many motion pictures, and the low standards of some motion pictures, have forced the bishops to take direct and aggressive action in safeguarding the moral well-being of their people.

These recent activities against motion pictures which offend decency and morality were launched only after years of vain hope that the producers of these pictures would realize the harm being done and take positive steps to correct the trend.

The committee is not hostile to the entertainment business. In fact, it recognizes entertainment as a virtual necessity in modern life. But such entertainment must be of a wholesome character, and to that objective the committee has earnestly addressed its efforts.

The Legion of Decency, whose members pledge themselves not to patronize theaters showing offensive films, has gathered to its banner many thousands of adherents wherever it has been introduced. Plans are being developed to extend its membership to every town and city in the United States and to invite all persons in sympathy with its purpose to lend their support.

The committee has been informed that, through the loyal co-operation of our Catholic people, together with a widespread response on the part of many others who believe that a purification of the cinema is an outstanding moral issue of the day, the motion-picture theaters have suffered a severe curtailment of patronage. This curtailment has prompted the Motion Picture Producers and Distributors of America, Inc., to send Mr. Martin Quigley of New York City and Mr. Joseph I. Breen of Hollywood to the meeting of the Episcopal Committee today.

The companies which are members of the above-named organization are reputed to be responsible for approximately 90 per cent of the films produced in the United States. These companies are R.K.O. Pictures Corporation, Fox Film Corporation, Metro-Goldwyn-Mayer Corporation, Paramount Pictures Corporation, Warner Brothers, First National Pictures Corporation, Columbia Pictures Corporation, Hal Roach, Education Pictures, Inc., Universal Pictures Corporation, United Artists, Inc., Walt Disney Productions, Pathe, Inc., Principal Pictures, Inc.

The representatives of the association submitted a proposal covering certain specific revisions of the industry's plan of self-regulation.

The committee has been pleased to receive these representatives and to learn from them of the renewed efforts toward enforcement of the industry's plan of self-regulation, effective as of July 1, 1934, which has been decided upon. The committee is informed that the producers' jury in Hollywood, a part of the original machinery for enforcement of the production code, which was adopted in April, 1930, has been abandoned and that additional local authority has been assigned to the code administration, which administration is to be given an amplified personnel. In the past, the producers' jury has functioned ineffectively.

The final responsibility for the character of the motion pictures to be issued by the organized industry has been accepted by the board of directors of the organized industry. The court of last resort in the settlement of any disputes which may arise between the studios and the code administration will be this board of directors.

The Episcopal Committee views with favor the renewed efforts of the organized industry to discharge its responsibility of issuing only such motion pictures as may conform with reasonable moral standards. The committee believes that the production code, if given adequate enforcement, will materially and constructively influence the character of screen entertainment. Hence it is disposed to render encouragement and co-operation to these efforts, which it hopes will achieve the promised results.

Our Catholic people, however, are counseled that in the long run the desired results of a wholesome screen can be assured only through unfailing opposition to evil motion pictures. The widespread interest in and loyal support of our campaign of protest must be maintained in order that the producers of motion pictures may constantly be aware of the demand for clean entertainment. The salacious and otherwise objectionable type of motion picture must be avoided.

The Episcopal Committee hopes that the results of the organized industry's renewed efforts looking toward adequate self-regulation will be followed by an adequate moral improvement in the pictures shown. And thus it is hoped that the Catholic bishops may be relieved of what otherwise will be the imperative necessity of continuing indefinitely and of extending the campaign of protest.

The Episcopal Committee approved of a national committee of priests, members of which are as follows: the Rt. Rev. Msgr. Hugh L. Lamb, D.D., chancellor, archdiocese of Philadelphia; the Rev. Edward Roberts Moore, Ph.D., head of the Division of Social Action, Catholic Charities of the archdiocese of New York; the Rev. George Johnson, Ph.D., associate professor of education, Catholic University of America, Washington, D. C., and executive secretary, Department of Education, National Catholic Welfare Conference; the Rev. F. G. Dineen, S.J., rector of St. Ignatius Church, Chicago, Ill.; the Rev. John J. Devlin, St. Victor's Church, West Hollywood, Calif.

31. STATEMENT OF THE HIERARCHY OF THE UNITED STATES ON

ANTI-CHRISTIAN TYRANNY IN MEXICO*

November 15, 1934

Seventy-eight cardinals, archbishops, and bishops of the United States, assembled in annual meeting at the Catholic University of America, Washington, D. C., November 14–15, 1934, issued a vigorous statement deploring anti-Christian tyranny in Mexico and citing the progressive steps in the persecution directed against Catholics and all religion in that country. Calling upon the faithful for a special crusade of prayer for the ending of persecution of the Church in Mexico, the bishops as American citizens requested their fellow citizens to urge that representatives of the United States be guided by true American principles with

---

* Catholic Action, December, 1934, pp. 3, 4, 5; cf. also Nos. 2, 22, 29, 34, 58, 63.

respect to Mexico — principles that recognize liberty of conscience, of religious worship, of education, of the press, of assembly and petition.

In 1926, the cardinals, archbishops, and bishops of the United States issued in their own names a pastoral letter, protesting against the persecution of the Church in Mexico.

Since that pastoral was issued, the bishops of Mexico restored public worship in Mexico, under an agreement involving handicaps and restrictions that should never have been imposed. But even that inadequate agreement whereby liberty of worship was promised, the juridical identity of the Church was recognized, and the severity of the laws against the Church and her institutions was to be mitigated, a new policy has repudiated.

In our pastoral of 1926, we stated what is even more evident today: "The present conflict, as one part of a war against religion in Mexico which had its inception almost a century ago, to a greater degree than any preceding it, comes from an attempt at nothing less than the destruction of the divine Constitution of the Church by reducing her to the status of a State-controlled body, without the right to form, train, and educate her own clergy, to have a sufficient number of them for the care of souls, to find means for her support, to develop works in accord with her mission of charity and enlightenment, and to apply the teachings of the Gospel to the formation of a public conscience. Sad experience, as well as right reason, tells us what would follow the success of such an attempt, and what it would mean to Church as well as to State."*

We spoke then not only as bishops having primarily with us the care of souls, we spoke also as American citizens. We said then what we repeat with fuller justification. "We have a duty to speak as Americans attached to the institutions of our country and loving them for the benefits they have conferred upon us all." Present conditions made it necessary that we should no longer guard silence. War on religion has extended beyond national boundaries through organized propaganda in many countries.

Beginning systematically at the end of 1931, the priests permitted to minister to the people in Mexico were decreased to such a ridiculously small number as to make of liberty of religious worship a mockery. In the Federal District comprising over one million, three hundred thousand Catholics, only twenty-five priests are permitted to minister.

---

* See p. 67, this volume.

Many states have prohibited priests altogether: for example, Tabasco, Zacatecas, Sonora, Chiapas, Vera Cruz, Campeche, Querétaro.

Without due process of law, church buildings, residences of bishops and of priests, even dwellings owned by others in which bishop or priest may be temporarily living, educational and charitable institutions have been closed and confiscated. No trial by jury is permitted in case of any appeal.

Catholic citizens are denied the right of assembly and the right of freedom of the press.

Any religious society is denied the right of corporate legal existence.

To hear the duly executed and duly presented petition of citizens is refused.

The right of franchise is denied a clergyman simply because he is a clergyman.

Any and every Church is denied the right to hold property or the right to present a petition for the redress of grievances.

Any and every Church is denied the right to possess endowments.

The right of any Church to have a seminary or a preparatory school for the training of candidates for the ministry is denied.

Schools in which native citizens may be trained for the priesthood are outlawed. Any foreign-born clergyman is forbidden to serve in Mexico. Therefore, according to present policies neither a native nor a foreign-born clergy is permissible in Mexico.

Secular papers with any policy favorable to religion are prohibited from criticizing any acts of the government or the government officials.

Journals and publications are suppressed at will; the use of the mail is denied them.

Citizens in Mexico are denied those inalienable rights which the Constitution of the United States asserts belong to every man.

The liberty of education is denied. It is maintained that the State must possess the mind of the child.

Bishops, priests, nuns, and lay citizens who desire to have the privilege of religious life must exile themselves.

Liberty of religious worship, of education, of speech, and of the press are denied all who live in Mexico.

We need not repeat that we protest with our whole heart and soul against this anti-Christian tyranny, and again call upon all the faithful in our country to pray that such a reign may cease, and to do everything in their power by word and by act to make the fact of such tyranny known.

No upholder of the rights of man and of liberty of conscience can view complacently the exercise of such tyranny, even though it be in a country other than our own. They who suffer in Mexico, they who suffer in exile, are our fellow faithful, all members of our beloved Church, which is one Body. The Church in our country, the Church throughout the world, suffers with the suffering Church in Mexico. We implore the faithful to pray most earnestly, to offer their self-denials and their special acts of devotion for the ending of the persecution of the Church in Mexico. We ask them to make themselves apostles proclaiming to the world the iniquity and the tyranny that mutilate and despoil the Body of Christ.

And again, as American citizens we present our plea that justice may be done, that all our fellow Americans may make themselves advocates of that common justice for man, which is the security of every man and every nation.

We sincerely deplore the evident indifference on the part of many to the life and worth of those principles upon which our American Republic is founded. We cannot, we would not wish to impose those principles as political principles upon any other nation. But to us they are as true outside as inside the physical territory of our country. Propaganda in this country that would weaken our principles is abhorrent to us. Compromise at home and abroad on the part of any of our fellow citizens with regard to those principles is, to us, most reprehensible.

As we declared in our pastoral of 1926, our own country cannot view with indifference the persecution of religion, the exiling of its citizens by a neighboring country. We need not say we would wish most earnestly to live on terms of peace with every nation. We wish to say again, as we said in 1926: "What we have written is no call on the faithful here or elsewhere to purely human action. It is no inter-position of our influence either as bishops or as citizens to reach those who possess political power anywhere on earth, and least of all in our own country, to the end that they should intervene with armed force in the internal affairs of Mexico for the protection of the Church."*

We wish for Mexico prosperity in its national life, in its economic and social life. We wish it the more honestly when we ask primarily a fidelity to the fundamental rights of liberty of conscience, freedom of religious worship, freedom of education, freedom of the press, and freedom of assembly and petition.

We respectfully request our fellow citizens to advocate that these

---

* See p. 94, this volume.

principles be ever the guide for our American representatives. The full consequences of the persecution of the Church and of Catholics in Mexico can scarcely be foreseen at the present time. They cannot but eventually be very grave. Those who must flee from their own country into ours bring with them a problem to which we cannot be indifferent. It is not without significance that in the present turmoil of the world and distress of nations, the basic truths of religion from which has sprung the stability of nations are flouted and denied by those who seek absolutism in government. The struggle, therefore, which arises from the persecution of the Church in Mexico today is an illustration of a crisis which may have far-reaching consequences.

No man's voice should sound an uncertain note. We cannot but deplore the expressions unwittingly offered, at times, of sympathy with and support of governments and policies which are absolutely at variance with our own American principles. They give color to the boast of the supporters of tyrannical policies, that the influence of our American government is favorable to such policies. We do not believe, for a moment, that it is. It could not be. We would wish on the part of the entire American public, of our great secular press, a fuller knowledge of the actual conditions in Mexico. All would then more fully realize that we are pleading not only the cause of the Catholic Church, but the cause of human freedom and human liberty for all the nations of the world.

32. STATEMENT OF THE HIERARCHY OF THE UNITED STATES ON THE

GENERAL MOVING-PICTURE SITUATION*

November 15, 1934

At the annual meeting of the American hierarchy at the Catholic University of America, November 14–15, 1934, the following statement was made regarding the general moving-picture situation and the Legion of Decency.

The action of the bishops at their spring meeting in deciding to take vigorous steps in opposition to obscene and debasing moving pictures has been overwhelmingly justified by the support it has received from all classes in every part of the country. It is especially gratifying to note that our Protestant brethren, judging by the official utterances of their leaders, are unanimous in their denunciation of the moving-picture menace and untiringly zealous in their efforts to bring it to an end.

In undertaking this campaign the Catholic hierarchy had no desire to deprive the public of any legitimate source of recreation, nor to set themselves up as a universal board of censors. No group of men are less inclined than the Catholic bishops to interfere with legitimate amusements, or, in these times of trial and uncertainty, to deprive people of any pleasure that may bring joy into their lives. Nobody can deny the tremendous potentialities, recreational and educational, to be found in moving pictures, but there is nobody who will assert that these potentialities can be realized unless those who control the production and distribution of these pictures aim at high standards in taste and morals.

The moving picture has become a force second only to school in forming the taste, the minds, and the morals of youth. In many respects the influence of moving pictures is greater than that of the

---

* *Catholic Action*, December, 1934, p. 5; cf. also Nos. 30, 37, 44.

schools because their appeal is directly to the senses and the emotions. Moving pictures must not be permitted to counteract or to nullify the purposes for which schools are established and maintained. They must not be allowed to hold up ideals to young and old which are destructive of the finest things in life and which are frequently incentives to crime, disorder, and immorality.

It is just as inconceivable that the educational system of the country should be placed under the direction of the men who control the moving-picture industry, as that their standards of life should dominate an agency which is equally potent in its influence on minds and morals. The campaign against the crimes and transgressions of the makers of moving pictures has been undertaken with no other purpose than to show that a clear line must be drawn between what is elevating and instructive and what is debasing and degrading. The campaign will go on, and, if the producers should return to their old ways and the moving-picture industry is made to suffer, the responsibility must be placed at the door of those who failed to understand the inherent decency of the American character.

33. STATEMENT OF THE HIERARCHY OF THE UNITED STATES ON

CATHOLIC ACTION*

November 14, 1935

At the 1935 general meeting of the cardinals, archbishops, and bishops of the United States, the following statement calling attention to the distinction between "Catholic Action" and "Catholic activity" was issued:

The bishops of the National Catholic Welfare Conference in the general meeting at Washington, November 14, 1935, call attention of all Catholic groups in the United States to the distinction between

---

* *Catholic Action,* December, 1935, p. 8; cf. also No. 36.

Catholic activity and Catholic Action. The bishops remind all groups according to the instruction of our Holy Father, Pope Pius XI, that there is no such thing as Catholic Action until there is an episcopal commission. For a diocese there must be a commission from the bishop of a diocese, for a province from the bishops of a province, and for the country from the bishops of the United States. The Holy Father only can give a commission for the universal Church on Catholic Action. When His Holiness does so he communicates with the bishops.

34. LETTER OF APPEAL BY THE HIERARCHY OF THE UNITED STATES FOR THE

TRAINING OF MEXICAN PRIESTS*

September 20, 1936

Responding to the appeal of the Committee of Bishops on the Mexican Seminary, collections in behalf of such an institution for the training of Mexican clergy were taken up in a large number of dioceses on "Mexican Seminary Sunday," September 20, 1936. This action followed an appeal from the committee, of which the Most Rev. John Mark Gannon, Bishop of Erie, was chairman and whose other members were the Most Rev. Arthur J. Drossaerts, Archbishop of San Antonio, vice-chairman; The Most Rev. Francis C. Kelley, Bishop of Oklahoma City and Tulsa, secretary-treasurer; the Most Rev. Rudolph A. Gerken, Archbishop of Santa Fe; the Most Rev. James A. Griffin, Bishop of Springfield in Illinois; and the Most Rev. Peter L. Ireton, Coadjutor Bishop of Richmond.

The urgent needs of the suffering Church in Mexico cry out to us for help and assistance. For many years some unholy force in Mexico has not only persecuted the Church but has sought to

---

* *Catholic Action,* October, 1936, p. 14; cf. also Nos. 2, 21, 29, 31, 58, 63.

destroy the means whereby the Church in Mexico might train and educate candidates for the sacred priesthood.

Catholic schools, Catholic colleges, Catholic seminaries are confiscated and prohibited in Mexico. This tyranny has now continued for many years. In their desperate need the hierarchy of Mexico appealed to their fellow bishops in the United States to aid them in the education of their young seminarians for the holy priesthood.

Your Committee, appointed at the last general meeting of the bishops of the United States, have not only carefully studied the problem, but have taken definite steps whereby we might answer readily, generously, and effectively the plea of the bishops of Mexico.

In answer to the request sent to all the bishops of the United States, asking if they (a) approved the petition sent to us by the Mexican hierarchy for a proposed seminary in the United States; (b) would they authorize the Bishops' Committee to proceed with the establishment of said seminary; (c) would they promise a diocesan collection for the same — 87 Ordinaries of the United States have, up to date, answered "Yes" to all three questions.

We therefore announce Sunday, September 20, 1936, as Mexican Seminary Sunday. We recommend the official collection in behalf of the seminary be taken up on that day. We request a report on all collections be filed with the Committee before November 1, in order to afford the Committee time to prepare an official report to the annual meeting of the American hierarchy. It is of great importance that the bishops at their next meeting know how much money is available for the Mexican Seminary project so that they may cast sound judgment in their instruction to your Committee for future policies.

We are happy to add that the Holy Father, since His Holiness knows this work is one on which the hierarchy of the United States has set its will and heart, will honor the work by a personal, substantial contribution.

Your committee has taken steps to see to it that (a) the property and title thereto will always remain with the hierarchy of the United States; (b) that proper and definite arrangements will be made with duly appointed representatives of the Mexican hierarchy; (c) that the supervision of the seminary will be in charge of the Mexican hierarchy and under a religious community to be approved by the Holy See; (d) that expenses for site, building, repairs, maintenance, indeed all expenditures, will be under the charge and authority of your Committee — that the number of students to be accepted will be determined by your Committee in accordance with the moneys received.

It has already been agreed upon with the Mexican bishops that the bishops of Mexico pay as generously as their means will allow for the maintenance of the seminary.

We are pleased to inform you that His Excellency, the Most Reverend James A. Griffin, Bishop of Springfield, has kindly agreed to supply free envelopes if desired for this collection. Bishop Griffin has sent a letter to all the members of the hierarchy. The returns of the collection itself should be sent to His Excellency, the Most Reverend Francis C. Kelley, 1000 North Lee Avenue, Oklahoma City, Oklahoma.

35. MESSAGE OF THE HIERARCHY OF THE UNITED STATES URGING PRAYERS FOR CHURCH IN

WAR-TORN SPAIN*

November 19, 1936

Eighty-nine members of the American Hierarchy gathered in annual session at the Catholic University of America, Washington, D. C., extended their "sympathy and comforting encouragement" in a message sent to the bishops, priests, and faithful of Spain.

We pray that, in spite of the terrors to which the Catholics of Spain have been subjected, the cruelties they are forced to endure, and the sorrows constantly heaped upon them in the torture and murder of so many of their clergy and people, God will grant them the fortitude to stand fast and struggle on for the faith of Jesus Christ and the liberty of His Holy Church.

The Catholics of America and a legion of their right-minded fellow

---

* *Catholic Action*, December, 1937, p. 5; cf. also No. 38.

citizens have been horrified at the savage extremes to which irreligion and inhumanity have been carried. They deplore the horrible carnage the more deeply because of the conviction that the sufferings of the Spanish Church are but the agony of civilization, battling for its spiritual and cultural heritage over the prostrate body of Spain. They know well that the Spanish Catholics are the victims of a studied oppression; and that men like-minded with their oppressors have constantly misrepresented here their struggle.

In all these injustices and sufferings our saddened hearts go out to the Church in Spain in sympathy and comforting encouragement. Already in answer to the appeal of our Holy Father, Pope Pius XI, and in filial endeavor to bear with him the burden of sorrow which the tragedy of Spain lays upon his paternal heart, our bishops have led their flocks in prayer for that afflicted nation. Again we exhort our people to turn to God in persevering prayer for the liberty of His Church and the deliverance of the Spanish people from the thralldom of forces that are the foes of God as well as of all religion.

36. STATEMENT OF THE HIERARCHY OF THE UNITED STATES

AFFILIATION OF LAY GROUPS WITH THE NATIONAL CATHOLIC WELFARE COUNCIL*

November 19, 1936

A statement of general principles and of their particular application promulgated at the 1936 annual general meeting of the bishops of the United States.

I. GENERAL PRINCIPALS

The bishops of the United States in establishing the National Catholic Welfare Conference provided a means whereby Catholic

---

* *Catholic Action,* December, 1936, pp. 18 and 21; cf. also No. 33.

organizations of the country might act in co-operation with the hierarchy on all matters of national interest and particularly those requiring definite Catholic leadership and definite expression of Catholic thought. The departments of the Conference welcome affiliation of Catholic societies and of other Catholic groups.

The following principles set forth in terms that refer specifically to the Department of Lay Organizations are equally applicable to affiliation with any department of the Conference.

The Department of Lay Organizations includes the National Council of Catholic Men and the National Council of Catholic Women. Affiliation with these enables Catholic lay organizations to know the mind of the hierarchy which must ever be the common guide of all. Through such affiliation, therefore, it is easy for any Catholic organization in the United States to know whether its common effort is in harmony with the mind of the bishops before publicity is given.

A Catholic organization is acting out of harmony with the principles of Catholic Action if, without this readily available guidance, it takes a public position on a matter — legislative or otherwise — which affects Catholic interests. Even a just claim to expert knowledge in any particular field does not qualify an organization to speak for the Church. The authoritative voice of the Church in matters of common interest is the voice of the bishop.

It is, of course, clear that diocesan organizations are entirely subject to the Ordinary of the diocese. The Ordinary is the proper authority to which they should look for guidance and direction. The fact that they may be diocesan units of the National Council of Catholic Men or the National Council of Catholic Women, and that as such they seek guidance from these councils on certain matters does not in any way lessen their responsibility to, and their dependence on their Ordinary.

Catholic societies that are interstate or national may, by affiliating themselves with the proper department of the National Catholic Welfare Conference, develop their activities in such a way as definitely to promote Catholic unity. For their action within a diocese they should, of course, submit their plans to the Ordinary of that diocese. But for their action in a wider field which would affect the Catholics of many dioceses, they should first of all ascertain whether their program be in line with the common mind of the bishops. That common mind of the bishops may be ascertained from the Administrative Board, National Catholic Welfare Conference.

Any organization that fails to observe this procedure runs the risk of having its announced program disavowed, to the chagrin of the society; to the embarrassment of the bishops; and to the detriment of the Church. Questions of gravest import have faced the Church in this country and will continue to face it. The Bishops, therefore, hold a yearly conference to safeguard the interests of the Church, and expect that all Catholic organizations work together in union with them and under their guidance. By the appointment of the Administrative Board the bishops of the National Catholic Welfare Conference have supplied the means whereby each and every organization can assure itself of the Catholic position on any matter of national import.

Far from diminishing Catholic lay activity, or discouraging lay initiative, this co-operation of lay organizations with the National Catholic Welfare Conference is designed to guide such activity and make it effective in common action. It must be evident, therefore, to all that when a Catholic organization, without seeking to know the mind of the bishops, speaks categorically on a question that affects general Catholic interests, it is doing a disorderly thing. While it would indeed be lamentable to limit Catholic effort even on national matters to the Administrative Board, National Catholic Welfare Conference, it is nonetheless lamentable for a Catholic organization not to make sure beforehand that any action it proposes to take is in conformity with the mind of the bishops.

II. Particular Application

1. In the case of diocesan organizations the contact with the National Catholic Welfare Conference is through the Ordinary or through the agency designated by him.

2. In the case of an organization functioning in more than one diocese, whether it be state, interstate, or national, contact with the N.C.W.C. should be made through an authorized and acceptable agent. It is to be noted, however, that even in this case action of any such organization within a given diocese must be carried out subject to the Ordinary of that diocese.

3. The Administrative Board, National Catholic Welfare Conference, shall direct the particular organizations to the proper department for affiliation.

Note: At their general meeting in 1935, the archbishops and bishops of the United States issued an important statement calling attention to the distinction between "Catholic Action" and "Catholic activity." This statement, made at the annual general meeting of the bishops in 1936, is a more detailed explanation of the subject (cf. No. 33).

37. STATEMENT OF THE HIERARCHY OF THE UNITED STATES CONDEMNING

IMMORAL FILMS, UNCLEAN SHOWS, AND UNWISE DRINKING*

November 17, 1937

Statement issued at annual meeting, November 17–19, 1937.

The bishops of the United States, in annual meeting assembled, voice their deep concern over the evils arising from the all-too-prevalent, promiscuous, and unwise use of intoxicating liquors. They feel that the dangers inherent to such intoxicants, under the present-day customs, critically threaten our growing youth, particularly girls. With the same fervor with which they condemn immoral and unclean movies, the bishops condemn the suggestive, sensuous, and unclean floor shows connected with many drinking places and urge all clean-minded people to co-operate in their suppression.

---

* *Catholic Action,* December, 1937, p. 11; cf. Nos. 30, 32, 44.

38. LETTER OF THE HIERARCHY OF THE UNITED STATES ADDRESSED TO THE

SPANISH HIERARCHY*

November 18, 1937

On the occasion of their annual meeting in Washington in November, 1937, eighty-two members of the American hierarchy assembled thereat took occasion to sympathize with their episcopal brothers in Spain. The American bishops express their horror at the terrible events that have accompanied the persecution there and recall that the hierarchy of Spain once helped to save the Western world from the menace of Islamism. The bishops deplored the fact that "some Christian leaders unwittingly have allowed themselves to be sponsors of principles which, if given wide sway, would destroy the last vestige of Western civilization."

To Their Eminences and Excellencies of the Spanish Hierarchy:

With profound emotion we read the pastoral letter written in your hour of sorrow to your brothers, the bishops of the world. You did this gracious and invaluable service to let us know the true state of religion in your country.

Poignant has been our sorrow, for we could not but realize the suffering of the venerable Church of Spain to which the world is so deeply indebted for its countless contributions to everything summed up by the words "Christian culture." In the midst of great political and economic conflicts, you have been maligned before the world as though, unmindful of your great traditions and fine achievements, you had forgotten the sorry plight of peasants and workers. Clever propaganda, maliciously used by those who would promote atheism and chaos, has beclouded the real facts in the contemporary life of the Church in Spain. It has sought to make prevail the notion that this Church no longer represents the very heart of the Spanish people. Human rights have been violated and the Church in Spain outrageously

---

* *Catholic Action,* 1937, pp. 12–13; cf. also No. 35.

persecuted, not because it had forgotten the rights of the lowly and weak in human society, but because it dared even with martyr blood to stand witness to the Christian principles of a great people.

Tragic are the true facts of the religious persecution in Spain by men who before the world sought to appear in the role of vindicators of human rights. You tell us that ten bishops, thousands of priests and religious, and tens of thousands of laymen have been put to death, often with unspeakable cruelty, because they were active in teaching the world to promote the works of the gospel. Your words horrify us who are wont to accept liberty of conscience and freedom of speech as an axiom.

Irreligion and atheism, whatever be their changing cloak, are things with which bishops may not temporize. Pitiable indeed is the fact that many men, right-minded and honest, have fallen victims to the mis-shapen news which has been given the world about the Church in Spain. Worse still, some Christian leaders unwittingly have allowed themselves to be the sponsors of principles which, if given wide sway, would destroy the very last vestige of Western civilization.

You have spoken clearly as followers of the Prince of Peace, and we thank you for your letter. It is particularly pleasing to us that your words show a realism which is not inconsistent with the high idealism that has been through the ages an outstanding characteristic of the Church in Spain. Nowhere in your gratefully appreciated letter may honest men gather the thought that you have advocated any social philosophy which refuses to recognize the salient problems of our times. There comes to us from your letter the assurance of the insistent effort of the Catholics of Spain, with a courage equal to that of the Crusaders, to promote the principles of the Social Encyclicals of our Holy Father.

As a hierarchy in a great democracy, ever alert to defend and protect for all men the fundamental principles of our American Constitution, we know from our past the sorry difficulties before the forum of world opinion which face you. To none do we yield the honor of a greater and more loyal adherence to the great democratic principles on which our government is founded. These principles are basically a thing of sound reason and wholly consonant with Christian teachings. We know full well that Your Eminences and Excellencies with your truly admirable clergy, religious, and courageous laity are laboring with a disinterestedness which compels the sympathy and support of all informed men, to inculcate the principles of social justice and charity so fully and so clearly enunciated in the Social Encyclicals of our

Holy Father. In your effort we want you to know that in common with the Catholic bishops of the world we stand beside you and thank you for your clear, calm, dignified statement on the condition of the Church in Spain. Without leaving your field of action as the pastors of the flocks given to your care, you have done a great service by your pastoral letter. The very restraint of its wording and its clear statement of facts by qualified witnesses, gives the lie to the assertions of propagandists of atheistic systems and should compel all right-thinking men to appreciate your work for all men and thank you for high courage and resolution.

We offer you our sympathy and assure you that we are deeply afflicted and moved by your tribulations. Day by day we pray with our priests, religious, and people that the land of Ferdinand and Isabella will find a solution of its pressing problems without deserting the Christian principles which have made it great in the past. As Americans we owe you a great debt of gratitude. In our Far South, Southwest, and West there still is told the story of the heroic Spanish priests and friars who did a work which is part of our national glory. Once before, the hierarchy of Spain helped to save the Western world from the menace of Islamism. God grant that once again you may be a powerful force to stem the tide of atheism, translated into social language and disguised with diabolical ingenuity! In your sorrows and tribulations you may be comforted to know that we understand and sympathize with you. The day is dark for you but the darkness of Calvary in the history of the Church has always been followed by the Light of Easter Morn.

In behalf of the bishops of the United States of America, at their annual meeting, Washington, D. C., November 18, 1937.

Fraternally in the charity of Christ,

✠ EMMET M. WALSH,
Bishop of Charleston

✠ DENNIS CARD. DOUGHERTY,
Archbishop of Philadelphia

39. LETTER OF THE HIERARCHY OF THE UNITED STATES TO THE

GERMAN HIERARCHY*

November 18, 1937

On the occasion of their annual meeting in Washington in November, 1937, eighty-two members of the American hierarchy took occasion to sympathize with their episcopal brothers in Germany. In their letter to the German hierarchy the bishops of the United States referred to the "satanic resourcefulness" and the "incredible excesses" of the leaders of modern paganism in Germany which have outraged "the sense of all religious-minded men and women throughout the world." The bishops commended their German brethren for the encouragement and support the latter have given their heroic people.

Venerable Brethren:

In this your hour of sorrow and trial, we, your brother bishops of the United States of America, pledge you and your persecuted people our unceasing prayers.

We are intimately bound to the hierarchy of Germany in the bond of holy faith and by many other sacred ties. The German blood that flows in the veins of many of our fellow citizens has enriched the Catholic and national life of our country. We American bishops, therefore, wish to bear witness to our solidarity with you, our brethren in Germany; in this hour of tribulation, we assure you of our genuine sympathy, our sincere admiration, and our deep affection.

Having followed the development of the persecution in your country through four years, we realize that in carrying on their nefarious work the oppressors of supernatural religion have in very truth been "wiser than the children of light." Beginning with petty restrictions, this persecution, according to the well-worked-out plan of its authors, has

---

* *Catholic Action,* December, 1937, pp. 13–14.

increased in violence. Today the sense of all religious-minded men and women throughout the world is outraged by the satanic resourcefulness of these leaders of modern paganism and by the incredible excesses committed by them in their attempt to exterminate religion and to blot out from the minds of the German people all true knowledge and love of God. In the words of Pope Pius XI, their "machinations from the beginning had no other aim than a war of extermination."

The Holy Father, in his encyclical letter of March 14, while paternally counseling you, the vigilant and courageous shepherds of the German people, recalled the unchangeable principles of the religion of Jesus Christ and the fixed code of Catholic morality. His Holiness comforted and encouraged you, Venerable Brethren, your clergy, and the Catholic people of your afflicted nation. Indicating the firm foundations on which civilization must rest, the Vicar of Christ pointed out the means to be taken to insure social order and the public weal and how to withstand successfully both Bolshevism and every enemy of peace. All right-thinking men are grateful to the Holy Father for taking that occasion to give a new and solemn proof of his great love for the country whose Christian faith is being tried so severely by a new paganism, destructive of the glorious Christian treasures of the German race.

We realize that an attempt is being made to destroy the very work of the redemption of all men by Jesus Christ, to take away the prestige of the Church, to deprive the Vicar of Christ, and yourselves as well, of all authority, and to besmirch the honor of the priesthood. We recognize in this a deliberate attempt to destroy gradually the faith of your people by denying them the nourishment of the life-giving sacraments, by depriving them of Christian education, and by destroying confidence in their religious leaders. The attempt to vilify priests and to destroy their reputations in indecent and frequently unjustified trials has produced in our country just the contrary effect. It has shown us and the world the degradation of governmental agencies in Germany today.

We join you in your pastoral sorrow over the ruin that is caused especially amongst the young, by means of newspapers, reviews, books, and the radio. We know that the weapons of scorn and calumny are freely used, the most sacred rights of liberty of conscience and of citizenship are denied; that your people, among the best citizens of Germany, are forbidden to unite for their own protection, while religious newspapers have been ruthlessly suppressed. It seems inconceivable that Catholic and all other religious groups in Germany upholding a supernatural religion are refused the legitimate means of defense allowed in every free nation.

But in spite of the present inhuman struggle, systematic and cruel as it is, faith still lives and will ever live, and will finally triumph over its persecutors.

We know that pressure of every kind is used to recruit an army of traitors to religion, who will be asked to serve as Church haters, Christ haters, and God haters. We know how all privileges, even the most fundamental natural rights of liberty, of work, advancement, and legitimate protection of family and individual interests, are denied to those who remain steadfast to Christ and to the Church. As our Holy Father has pointed out, there are "among the spokesmen many who, by reason of their official position, seek to create the impression that leaving the Church, and the disloyalty to Christ the King which it entails, is a particularly convincing and meritorious form of profession of loyalty to the present state."

Praised be God, the number of heroes steadily increases, and the example of their virtue and their heroism is daily more appreciated. They are the hope of the German people, and an inspiration to the believing world. It is your glorious privilege to encourage and to sustain them. The Church of America, the Catholic world, and all who believe are with them and with you.

Fraternally yours in Christ,

✠ Emmet M. Walsh,
Bishop of Charleston

✠ Dennis Card. Dougherty,
Archbishop of Philadelphia

40. STATEMENT OF THE HIERARCHY OF THE UNITED STATES REGARDING

PEACE AND WAR*

November 16, 1939

This statement was made by the American hierarchy at their annual meeting in Washington, D. C., at the Catholic University of America, November 14, 15, and 16, 1939. It voices gratitude to Pope Pius XII for his efforts to restore peace to the world and to the government of the United States for its determination to adhere to a program of peace. An expression of sympathy for all those who must bear the burden of suffering during time of war is also found in this statement, which was hailed by both secular and religious press as a sincere prayer for peace.

From the first moment of his pontificate, our Holy Father, Pope Pius XII, labored unceasingly to prevent the outbreak of war. When, despite his entreaties, his prayers, and his diplomatic counsels the dread conflict was finally initiated, he set himself resolutely to mitigate its horrors. For such devotion to the cause of peace we desire to offer the august Pontiff the expression of our profound gratitude and to recommend that our people, emulating his example, join in the effort of their Common Father.

We note with gratification the efforts of our government to save Europe from the cruelty of war and of its expressed determination to pursue the ways of peace.

To all who in time of war must bear a heavy burden of suffering in soul and body, we express our prayerful sympathy.

Conscious of the Christian duty to raise our prayers to God, that in His providence He may lead the rulers of men to seek and work for peace, we are nonetheless mindful that our charity must transcend the form of words. Effective sympathy must be expressed in deed. While war and rumors of war, coupled with dire forebodings of yet greater

---

* *Catholic Action,* December, 1939, pp. 8–9.

disaster, haunt the minds of men, it is all the more imperative that they should focus their attention not on war, but upon salvaging the remnants of peace. In the present crisis it is necessary for all men to devote their mightiest efforts to the reconstruction of a just order in society whose disruption has brought the world to its present pass.

Accordingly, we plead for a spirit of calm deliberation in our own nation. We beg our people neither to be carried away by intemperate emotion, nor to become victims of hate mongers who set loose the evils of cupidity, anger, envy, and revenge. The first line of defense against the involvement of our nation in the misery of war is aloofness from emotional entanglements. Our primary duty is that of preserving the strength, stability, and security of our own nation, not, indeed, in a spirit of selfish isolation, but rather in a spirit of justice and charity to those people whose welfare is our first and chief responsibility.

Perhaps the most appalling thing in modern warfare is the fact that its tragic sufferings are visited not only upon combatants, but as well upon women and children, the weak and infirm, young and old. No longer do armies alone march in battle, but whole nations are mobilized for total and unrestricted warfare.

Peace with justice is the stated objective of combatants in the present strife. But no peace can endure unless justice be tempered with charity. Peace achieved through outright victory and defeat may easily be nothing more than an armed peace. We recognize that the sanctity of international contracts must be restored, but there must be first a sanctity in the contract itself, generated by free negotiation and free acceptance. If force is made the instrument of acceptance of a contract, then force is inevitably invited as an instrument of its rejection.

As in the steward of great gifts from Divine Providence, our nation has the moral task to minister to the common welfare of the people of the Western hemisphere, especially through the preservation of peace and the cultivation and promotion of those high moral principles which give vigor to political and social life.

Materialism excites greed. From greed stems hatred, rivalry, envy, war. Faith in God, recognition of the inviolable character of human rights are noble Christian ideals embodied in our Declaration of Independence. By standing fast to those high principles we can best serve our national defense and preserve our cherished ideals.

Particularly appropriate is it, then, that at this season of Thanksgiving, we should raise our hearts in gratitude to our heavenly Father that among the many blessings He has vouchsafed to us, we can number the precious gifts of peace and security.

41. STATEMENT OF THE HIERARCHY OF THE UNITED STATES ON

POLAND*

November 16, 1939

This statement was issued at the same time that the announcement was made of the Bishops' Committee for Polish Relief (No. 42). This action was taken at the annual meeting of the bishops at the Catholic University, Washington, D. C., November 14, 15, and 16, 1939. In this message the sympathy, charity, and prayers of the Catholics of the United States are extended to the people of Poland.

The bishops of the United States, mindful of the stanch faith and bloodstained valor of the Church in Poland, voice their brotherly compassion with the Polish hierarchy, its clergy and people in this its hour of bitter sorrow. Like a mighty champion this noble Christian people has stood at the outpost of Christian Europe to witness and defend the Cross. Only yesterday, amidst the mysterious changes of the times, the Cross in Poland seemed the bulwark of Western Christian traditions against upsurging atheistic hordes. Like darkness came to Calvary, sorrow and suffering have settled on the Church in Poland.

As our Holy Father says: "The blood of countless human beings, even noncombatants, raises a piteous dirge over a nation such as our dear Poland, which for its fidelity to the Church, for its defense of Christian civilization, written in indelible characters in the annals of history, has a right to the generous and brotherly sympathy of the whole world, while it awaits, relying on Mary, Help of Christians, the hour of resurrection in harmony with the principles of justice and true peace."

Poland's faith, which Divine Providence wills to appear more lustrous in storm and tempest, looks confidently to an approaching

---

* *Catholic Action,* December, 1939, p. 9; cf. Nos. 42, 47.

Easter Morn of Peace in justice and charity. We, the bishops of the
United States, extend our sympathy to our brothers of the Episcopate
of Poland. We shall not forget them and their flocks in our charity
and with the people we suppliantly beg the Virgin of Czestochowa to
bring peace and succor to the suffering in Poland and once more
confound the world by making the bloodstained, devastated Church of
Poland, like Calvary's bloodstained Cross, the portent of new triumphs
for Christ, our King.

42. PLEA OF THE HIERARCHY OF THE UNITED STATES FOR

POLISH RELIEF*

November 16, 1939

*The Committee of Bishops for Polish Relief was authorized at the
annual general meeting of the American hierarchy in Washington,
D. C., at the Catholic University of America, on November 14, 15,
and 16, 1939.*

Your Committee on Polish Relief is convinced that immediate action
is important if the tragic condition of Polish refugees, and of Poles
still living inside their country, is to be relieved. In this afflicted country if anywhere in the world today, he doubles the effectiveness of his
gift who gives quickly. It is the intent of the Committee to fortify the
Polish ecclesiastical authorities in Europe but outside Poland, who
have informed minds on conditions inside its borders, in order that they
may use whatever remains of the Church organization there to reach
the most necessitous of their people. To that end, it is the plan of the
Committee at this moment to send money as it comes in to Cardinal
Hlond, and to leave to him the finding of agents and of agencies to
use this money for food and clothing and shelter for his despairing

---

* *Catholic Action,* January, 1940, p. 7; cf. Nos. 41, 47.

fellow countrymen, and our own brethren in the Household of the Faith.

There is no time to build a collecting organization even if such an agency were desirable. The Committee is persuaded that the usual diocesan organization is equal to the task of securing funds, and that the plight of millions of our fellow Christians is a sufficient spur to the generosity of our people everywhere in this country. The Committee, therefore, releases the campaign in each diocese to its bishop, and its mechanism to his designing. It asks only that the effort be made at the earliest moment, and that the moneys collected be started on their errand of mercy as soon as they are available. The Committee asks people and priests and bishops to pray that almighty God may add His comfort to this stricken people and that He may ward off from the Western world the threat to its civilization, now the guardian of its gateway is fallen.

The joint resolution adopted by Congress, November 4, 1939, Section Eight, regulating solicitation and collection of funds and contributions has been complied with.

Will you send, as soon as your contributions reach a sizable amount, a check to the Most Rev. Stephen S. Woznicki, D.D., Auxiliary Bishop of Detroit, 3151 Farnsworth Avenue, Detroit, Michigan? The balance can be turned over when your campaign is completed, or in partial amounts in the interval.

This letter was signed by the Committee, the members of the Bishops' Committee for Polish Relief being the Most Rev. Hugh C. Boyle of Pittsburgh, chairman; the Most Rev. Samuel A. Stritch, Archbishop of Chicago; the Most Rev. Paul P. Rhode, Bishop of Green Bay; the Most Rev. Joseph C. Plagens, Bishop of Marquette; the Most Rev. Stanislaus V. Bona, Bishop of Grand Island; the Most Rev. John A. Duffy, Bishop of Buffalo; the Most Rev. James A. McFadden, Auxiliary Bishop of Cleveland; the Most Rev. William D. O'Brien, Auxiliary Bishop of Chicago; and the Most Rev. Stephen S. Woznicki, Auxiliary Bishop of Detroit, treasurer.

43. RENEWAL OF LOYALTY BY THE HIERARCHY OF THE UNITED STATES TO THE

IDEALS OF THE AMERICAN REPUBLIC*

November 13, 1940

In a statement which called attention to the appeal of His Holiness Pope Pius XII for universal prayers for peace on Sunday, November 24, 1940, the archbishops and bishops of the United States, at their twenty-second annual meeting in Washington took cognizance of the nation's extraordinary peacetime efforts to defend American institutions and pledged themselves and their flocks to "give themselves unstintingly" to the country's "defense and its lasting endurance and welfare." Following is the text of the bishops' statement:

In an extraordinary personal appeal, our Most Holy Father, Pope Pius XII, has designated Sunday, November 24, as a day of universal prayer for the war afflicted of all nations and for the establishment of just peace and the reign of charity uniting all men in brotherly love.

Our nation, too, determined to perpetuate its traditional devotion to peace and the prosperity of its people, has been forced by tragic and threatening world events to resort to extraordinary peacetime measures to defend our free institutions and protect our liberties. The ready acceptance of this defense program is a heartening example of national solidarity. Whatever sacrifices may be involved in defense of the Americas will be loyally borne in generous unanimity.

Confident that the prayers of our Holy Father with his united Christian people and the peace proposals of our President and fellow citizens must prevail, the bishops of the Catholic Church in the United States, with the flock committed to their keeping, renew their most sacred and sincere loyalty to our government and to the basic ideals

---

* *Catholic Action,* December, 1940, p. 8.

of the American Republic. Standing ever securely upon their unswerving allegiance to our nation since its foundation, they are again resolved to give themselves unstintingly to its defense and its lasting endurance and welfare.

44. WARNING OF EPISCOPAL COMMITTEE OF THE HIERARCHY OF THE UNITED STATES ON

MOTION PICTURES*

November 13, 1940

The following statement was issued in November, 1940, by the Episcopal Committee on Motion Pictures during the annual meeting of the archbishops and bishops of the United States.

The statement notes efforts made by producers in the recent past to improve the moral character of motion-picture entertainment, but warns that "some of the good ground gained has been lost."

The Episcopal Committee consisted of the Most Rev. John T. McNicholas, O.P., Archbishop of Cincinnati, chairman; the Most Rev. John J. Cantwell, Archbishop of Los Angeles; the Most Rev. Hugh C. Boyle, Bishop of Pittsburgh; the Most Rev. John F. Noll, Bishop of Fort Wayne, and the Most Rev. Stephen J. Donahue, Auxiliary Bishop of New York.

While in the recent past it has been our pleasure to note the efforts which cinema producers have made to improve the moral character of motion-picture entertainment, and to express our appreciation of results obtained, it now becomes our duty to warn our people that some of the good ground gained has been lost. Evidence is accumulating that there is a partial return to practices against which the voice and authority of the Catholic Church in the United States vigorously protested in 1934.

In this protest concurred multitudes not of the Catholic Faith who

---

* *Catholic Action,* December, 1940, p. 5; cf. also Nos. 30, 32, 37.

also were deeply concerned about films which threatened the morals of the young, the family, and the nation.

Our responsibility for the welfare of souls makes it incumbent upon us to do everything in our power to prevent the exposure of our people to the incalculable evil of the immoral cinema. We therefore register our strong protest against the increasing objectionable tendencies which lately have become manifest in films.

We urge our Catholic people, especially parents, to renew their vigilance against the pernicious influence of films which disregard the moral law and subvert the foundations of Christian society.

We call upon priests and people to maintain and strengthen diocesan organization of the Legion of Decency in each diocese, and to coordinate efforts with the National Office of the Legion in New York, so that a united front may stand firmly against films morally objectionable.

The Bishops' Committee expressed gratitude to the press generally, for the support given the movement for decency in motion pictures. The Committee likewise thanked the National Catholic Welfare Conference News Service for its distribution of the Legion motion picture qualifications, the Catholic Press for its publication of these ratings, and the Motion Picture Department of the International Federation of Catholic Alumnae for its motion-picture reviewing activities.

45. STATEMENT OF THE BISHOPS' COMMITTEE ON THE

POPE'S PEACE POINTS* CONCERNING THE "LAW OF NATIONS" (JUS GENTIUM)

January 3, 1942

In his peace message of Christmas Eve our Holy Father, Pope Pius XII, elaborating in the midst of this terrific world catastrophe on what he had written in his first encyclical letter, captures the attention of honest minds in all the world. Daily as this calamity

---

* *Catholic Action,* January, 1942, p. 19.

becomes more and more widespread and intense, it is clearer and clearer that the prime necessity for a righteous peace is the sincere, honest, earnest acceptance by all the nations, large and small, of the Law of the Nations. This Law is basically nothing more than right and wrong in international relations. In our cultural heritage there is a wealth of precious thought on the Law of Nations, or as it was called in other days, *jus gentium*, which should be studied now, diligently and profoundly, by all who want to make the victory of our country in this war the beginning of sound world prosperity, a price well worth our sufferings and sacrifices.

The Law of the Nations does not impose on any nation the surrender of legitimate sovereignty or the abandonment of its cultural resources. It envisions all nations living under the Law of the all-just God and prizes righteousness above material aggrandizement, without however overlooking the temporal happiness of peoples. When hate and passion and pride are cast aside, human reason easily discovers the fundamental provisions of the Law of Nations. With happily opportune reference to large details our Holy Father calls to the leaders of men everywhere to make this Law the basis of their peace structure.

Let it not be said that all this is mere idealism, something to be hoped for and yet something very impractical in this world of ugly, cruel international realities. Truth is the greatest reality, and to lose heart in the power of truth is to confess that all our noblest aspirations, world peace in righteousness, are futile, and human reason itself capable of nothing finer than doubt and helplessness. Let it never be said that that which is the desire and ardent hope of all good men is beyond realization. There was a time when the Law of Nations was in force in the Christian West and, although nations may have sinned against it, the conscience of right and wrong in international life was alive and alert.

There is genuine optimism in the words of our Holy Father. He, through the clouds and terrors of this universal calamity, envisions a world in which sovereign peoples, proud of their heritages, will live together under the Law of the Nations. Our own country is contending against strong, resourceful, clever enemies, precisely for a world order under the Law of Nations. Without surrender of our sovereignty or injury to our free institutions, proud that we have been accused by an enemy nation of idealism, we are ready to make hard sacrifices and to give generously of our abundant resources to outlaw forever the domination of international life by brute force, lying propaganda, and privileged nationalism. The things which the Pope points out as requisites for the peace, which our victory will establish, we place in our war aims and make the very prime reason for our hardships and sacrifices, disappointments and triumphs.

46. RESOLUTION OF THE HIERARCHY OF THE UNITED STATES ON

COMPULSORY MILITARY TRAINING*

November 17, 1944

The Administrative Board, N.C.W.C., opposes the immediate passage of a bill (either the Wadsworth-Gurney or May bills — H.R. 1806–H.R. 2497) looking toward compulsory military training of all the male youth of the United States on the grounds that:

    a) this problem should not be settled until after the end of the war and we know what the international situation shall be;

    b) that those now serving in the Army and Navy should be given an opportunity to express their views on this measure before it is enacted;

    c) that military requirements until the end of the war can be met by the extension of the Selective Service Act.

---

* Taken from the General Minutes of the Bishops' Meeting November, 1944, cf. p. 7.

47. RESOLUTION OF THE HIERARCHY OF THE UNITED STATES ON

RELIGIOUS FREEDOM IN POLAND AND BALTIC STATES*

November 17, 1944

RESOLUTION

The bishops of the United States in Christian solidarity share the sufferings, misery, and fears of their brother bishops, the clergy, the

---

* Taken from the Archives of N.C.W.C.; cf. also Nos. 41, 42.

religious, and the faithful of all the war-torn countries of Europe. The circumstances of the moment excite in them a particular anxiety for the fate of religion among their fellow Christians in Poland, the Baltic States, and neighboring Catholic lands. They recall how centuries ago the Western Slavs, later joined by the Lithuanians, associated themselves with the peoples of Europe in weaving and embellishing the fabric of Western Christian civilization. History records their heroic exploits in the defense of the West against Tartar and Moslem. Mighty tyrants enslaved them and even in their shackles they fought and bled in the sacred cause of freedom. Never losing their identity, they chose ever to shed martyr blood rather than deny or dilute their Christian Faith. Cruel, inhuman aggressors are now heaping upon them frightful atrocities and unprecedented barbarities. The exercise of their religion is either denied them or is so thwarted as to be practically impossible. And dark fear is now in them that when our victory comes their hope for a better day with security in the enjoyment of their civil and religious freedoms will not be realized. To them the bishops of the United States, with their clergy and people, extend deep sympathy with the prayerful hope that the strong, victorious nations in charity and justice will give them succor in their sufferings and the full enjoyment of their indisputable rights.

American Catholics would ever resent their country's being made a party to the de-Christianization of historic Catholic peoples.

48. STATEMENT OF THE HIERARCHY OF THE UNITED STATES REGARDING

FEDERAL AID FOR EDUCATION*

November 17, 1944

The Department of Education of the National Catholic Welfare Conference opposes:

1. A federal department of education;

---

* From the Archives of the N.C.W.C. — Department of Education.

2. Federal control of education;
3. Any form of federal aid which cannot be demonstrated as needed to meet the minimum educational requirements in areas where resources are inadequate.

Under present economic conditions, areas of certain states of the Union do not provide an education that is defensible on the basis of even minimum standards. We recognize that these states cannot find taxable wealth available to provide adequate educational opportunity for all their children.

The Department of Education, National Catholic Welfare Conference, recommends the acceptance of the following basic principles which are a necessary condition for the just granting of federal aid:

1. The aid given by the federal government for education should be distributed according to a law or plan that will bring this aid only to areas in which it is needed, and will be equitable to all children in that area without regard to color, origin, or creed, and in any school that meets the requirements of compulsory education. If necessary to achieve this purpose because of any state constitutional prohibition, then the federal authority should distribute the funds directly and not through state channels.
2. The federal aid given should be distributed in all areas where the need is proved.
3. Where federal funds are distributed for education, they must supplement the state, local, or private funds; they must not entirely supplant them. State, local, and private funds should be used to the utmost before invoking federal assistance.
4. Federal aid should never impose in our country federal control of education either in law or in practice. The American tradition of local boards in control of education would be more responsive to the parent or to the family that has the primary and imprescriptible right in the education of children.

The Department of Education, National Catholic Welfare Conference, has in the past opposed bills which were undemocratic, discriminatory, and wasteful of public funds. It has opposed federal measures which were so worded as to defeat the purpose of equalizing educational opportunity for all children in those areas where such equalization was really needed. It cannot support bills now pending before the United States Senate or the House of Representatives for use of federal funds to equalize educational opportunity because these are objectionable bills.

It is un-American to offer, as an argument for federal aid, the poverty and need of many children, and at the same time to exclude millions of other children, equally poor and in need, because of religious or racial considerations.

All fair-minded citizens, if not misinformed by propaganda, will oppose any bill advocating federal aid which is not fair to all American children regardless of color, origin, or creed.

49. RESOLUTION OF THE HIERARCHY OF THE UNITED STATES ON

COMPULSORY MILITARY TRAINING*

November 15, 1945

The following resolution on compulsory military training was passed November 14, 1945, by the Catholic bishops of the United States assembled at their annual general meeting at the Catholic University of America, His Eminence Dennis Cardinal Dougherty, Archbishop of Philadelphia, presiding.

We recognize the imperative need of preparedness for the adequate defense of our country in all circumstances.

In determining what constitutes national defense in our present circumstances, our government, we feel, should explore the possibility of having military conscription abolished in all countries, and, to that end, might well consider how our control of economic assistance to other countries may be used to lend weight to our plea for such abolition.

If a wide extension of military training is found necessary for pres-

---

* From the N.C.W.C. "News Release" for November 15, 1945 (Press Dept.); cf. No. 46.

ent adequate defense of our nation, we feel that such training should be in keeping with American traditions, and that, specifically:

1. Voluntary enlistments in the armed forces should be stimulated as much as possible, to provide our first line of defense;

2. Any period of enforced training should be integrated with normal school life; and,

3. The War and Navy Departments should work with recognized moral leadership to correct certain policies and attitudes which have wrought grave moral damage to great numbers of young people in the armed services during the past five years.

50. RESOLUTION OF THE HIERARCHY OF THE UNITED STATES ON

APATHY REGARDING IRON CURTAIN RELIGIOUS PERSECUTION*

November 15, 1950

The bishops of the United States, one in faith and human sympathy, salute with admiration the Christian heroism, the stanch loyalty to freedom, and the unconquered spirit of their brother bishops, the clergy, the religious, and the faithful, who live and suffer in all those countries of Asia and Europe behind the Iron Curtain and under the influence of a Godless persecution.

With horror in this so-called civilized age, we view the martyrdom, the exile and imprisonment of their shepherds; the dispersion of religious; the denial and thwarting of divine worship; the closing of schools; the suppression of the press; the imposition of false teaching and the insidious capture of their youth. All is of a pattern that follows stark fear, planned starvation, the displacement and massacre of millions of innocent people. All is on a vast scale to outdo the most violent barbarism in history.

These good people have known persecution in other years. Gallantly have they fought against other tyrants — the Tartar and the Moslem —

---

* From the N.C.W.C. "News Release" for November 15, 1950 (Press Dept.).

to help defend the freedom of the West. Now in their midst, human rights, human dignity, and human freedom are at their lowest ebb.

With dismay we note the apathy of Christian nations and the futility of their feeble protests in the face of a callous indifference to world opinion that is in its mildest expression inhuman. Again, when all human means seem to fail, we turn inevitably to the God of mercy and united with our clergy and people storm the throne of heaven that the dawn of a new day of peace may brighten the horizon, that out of the blood and misery and tears of our suffering brothers may come hope and strengthened courage, the shattering of the shackles that bind them, and the unhampered enjoyment of all their natural human rights.

51. RESOLUTION OF THE HIERARCHY OF THE UNITED STATES OF

SYMPATHY FOR THE VICTIMS OF IRON CURTAIN PERSECUTIONS*

November 19, 1951

The bishops of the United States of America proclaim before the world their boundless admiration for those heroes of our common Faith, the bishops, priests, religious, and faithful behind the Iron Curtain of Europe and Asia, who are giving their lives and their blood for Christ and for the ideals of human freedom.

In the long history of persecution waged by the absolutists against the followers of Christ, no chapter is more glorious than the one they are now writing.

We mourn our martyred dead in Russia and in the 14 nations which are now captives to communism. We send our fraternal sympathy and the assurance of our fervent prayers to the countless thousands who are now delivered to the torturers in the dungeons of

---

* From the N.C.W.C. "News Release" for November 19, 1951

Europe and of Asia. And we testify at the bar of world opinion, to the sufferings of those indomitable souls, millions and millions of them, who in the midst of this persecution, openly profess their loyalty to God, to Christ, to the Church and to the common ideals of civilized humanity.

Our hearts are filled with sorrow at the indifference of the so-called Christian governments to this frightful persecution, and at the apparent futility of the human means they have thus far employed to stop it. We are no less appalled by the apparent inability of the free secular press to inform the public of the true facts of the persecution. In this new agony of the Church of God, of her modern martyrs and confessors, we are left to tread the wine press alone.

No, not alone. Our help is in the name of the Lord who hath made the heavens and the earth. Inspired by the heroic virtue of these suffering millions and moved by the love of Christ and of our fellow men, we turn to the God of all Mercy; we lift our eyes to the eternal hills from which cometh our help.

In union with the clergy and faithful of the United States, we implore our Common Father to give light and strength and solace to His persecuted children, to open the eyes of the apathetic nations, and to convert the persecutors themselves that His Kingdom of justice and of love and of peace may come to all the people.

Let us call the roll of the nations in which persecution of the Church now rages:

Russia, the Ukraine, Yugoslavia, Hungary, Rumania, Bulgaria, Albania, eastern Austria, Czechoslovakia, Poland, Latvia, Estonia, Lithuania, eastern Germany, Mongolia, and China and northern Korea.

And let us stand in a tribute of reverent admiration and prayer for those churchmen whose names are deathless symbols of all who suffer persecution for the sake of Christ:

Cardinal Mindszenty, Archbishop Stepinac, Archbishop Beran, Bishop Cule, Archbishop Groesz.

PART II

STATEMENTS OF THE ADMINISTRATIVE BOARD* OF THE N.C.W.C.

---

* In the beginning it bore the title of "Administrative Committee."

52. ADMINISTRATIVE COMMITTEE OF THE NATIONAL CATHOLIC WAR COUNCIL

BISHOPS' PROGRAM OF
SOCIAL RECONSTRUCTION*

February 12, 1919

This pronouncement was the most discussed of all the plans for social reconstruction that were drawn up and published by prominent groups in Italy, France, Great Britain, and the United States between February, 1918, and June, 1919. Issued at the end of World War I, it was intended as a guide for solving the problems of social justice on which future peace was seen to depend. Ten of the eleven principal recommendations and proposals contained in this program have since been translated, either wholly or partially, into fact.

FOREWORD

The ending of the Great War has brought peace. But the only safeguard of peace is social justice and a contented people. The deep unrest so emphatically and so widely voiced throughout the world is the most serious menace to the future peace of every nation and of the entire world. Great problems face us. They cannot be put aside; they must be met and solved with justice to all.

In the hope of stating the lines that will best guide us in our right solution the following pronouncement is issued by the Administrative Committee of the National Catholic War Council. Its practical applications are, of course, subject to discussion, but all its essential declarations are based upon the principles of charity and justice that have always been held and taught by the Catholic Church, while its practical proposals are merely an adaptation of those principles and that

---

* Published by the N.C.W.C., 2 ed. (Twentieth Anniversary edition), 1939. Preface by Most Rev. Edward (later Cardinal) Mooney, at that time chairman of the Administrative Board of the N.C.W.C.; cf. also Nos. 24, 25, 60, 62, 66, 68, 71.

traditional teaching to the social and industrial conditions and needs of our own time.

✠ PETER J. MULDOON, *Chairman*,   ✠ PATRICK J. HAYES,
    Bishop of Rockford   *Bishop of Tagaste*
✠ JOSEPH SCHREMBS,   ✠ WILLIAM T. RUSSELL,
    Bishop of Toledo   *Bishop of Charleston*

Washington, D. C.
February 12, 1919

SOCIAL RECONSTRUCTION

"Reconstruction" has of late been so tiresomely reiterated, not to say violently abused, that it has become to many of us a word of aversion. Politicians, social students, labor leaders, businessmen, charity workers, clergymen, and various other social groups have contributed their quota of spoken words and printed pages to the discussion of the subject; yet the majority of us still find ourselves rather bewildered and helpless. We are unable to say what parts of our social system imperatively need reconstruction; how much of that which is imperatively necessary is likely to be seriously undertaken; or what specific methods and measures are best suited to realize that amount of reconstruction which is at once imperatively necessary and immediately feasible.

Nevertheless it is worth while to review briefly some of the more important statements and proposals that have been made by various social groups and classes. Probably the most notable declaration from a Catholic source is that contained in a pastoral letter written by Cardinal Bourne several months ago. "It is admitted on all hands," he says, "that a new order of things, new social conditions, new relations between the different sections in which society is divided, will arise as a consequence of the destruction of the formerly existing conditions. . . . The very foundations of political and social life, of our economic system, of morals and religion are being sharply scrutinized, and this not only by a few writers and speakers, but by a very large number of people in every class of life, especially among the workers."

The Cardinal's special reference to the action of labor was undoubtedly suggested by the now famous "Social Reconstruction Program" of the British Labor Party. This document was drawn up about one year ago, and is generally understood to be the work of the noted economist and Fabian Socialist, Mr. Sidney Webb. Unquestionably, it is the most comprehensive and coherent program that has yet appeared on the industrial phase of reconstruction. In brief it sets up "four pillars" of the new social order:

1. The enforcement by law of a national minimum of leisure, health, education, and subsistence;
2. The democratic control of industry, which means the nationalization of all monopolistic industries and possibly of other industries, sometime in the future, if that course be found advisable;
3. A revolution in national finance; that is, a system of taxation which will compel capital to pay for the war, leaving undisturbed the national minimum of welfare for the masses;
4. Use of the surplus wealth of the nation for the common good; that is, to provide capital, governmental industries, and funds for social, educational, and artistic progress.

This program may properly be described as one of immediate radical reforms, leading ultimately to complete Socialism. Evidently this outcome cannot be approved by Catholics.

PROGRAM OF AMERICAN LABOR

Through its Committee on Reconstruction, the American Federation of Labor has issued a lengthy program of reform proposals and demands which may be grouped under the three heads of trade union action, labor legislation, and general industrial and social legislation. The principal demands under the first head are: the legally guaranteed rights of the workers to organize and to carry on the normal activities of trade unions; a living wage; no reduction in present scales of wages; the right of labor to fix its hours of work; the eight-hour day; equal pay for equal work by the two sexes; exclusive reliance by labor on trade-union effort to maintain fair wages; establishment of co-operative stores; and no organization of a political party by the workers. Labor laws demanded are: prohibition of wage working by children under sixteen years of age; abolition of private employment agencies; prohibition of all immigration for two years; and vocational education which will fit the young for life in an industrial society. By implication both the eight-hour day and the living wage are declared to be subjects for trade-union action, not for legislation. Among the measures of general social legislation recommended are: a special tax on "usable land" not cultivated by the owner, and taxes on land values which would make the holding of idle land unprofitable; government housing; government ownership and operation of docks, wharves, and water powers; taxes on excess profits, incomes, and inheritances; and limitation of the power of the courts to declare laws unconstitutional.

While this program is more practical and more moderate and reasonable than that of the British Labor Congress, its proposal for taxing land into use could easily involve confiscation. On the other hand, it does not give sufficient consideration to the case of the weaker sections of the working class, those for whom trade-union action is not practically adequate; nor does it demand or imply that the workers should ever aspire to become owners as well as users of the instruments of production.

BRITISH QUAKER EMPLOYERS

Probably the most definite and comprehensive statement from the opposite industrial class was put forth several months ago by a group of twenty Quaker employers in Great Britain. In outline their program is as follows: a family living wage for all male employees and a secondary wage in excess of this for workers having special skill, training, physical strength, responsibility for human life; the right of labor to organize, to bargain collectively with the employer, and to participate in the industrial part of business management; serious and practical measures to reduce the volume and hardship of unemployment; provisions of such working conditions as will safeguard health, physical integrity, and morals; the reduction so far as practicable of profits and interest until both the basic and the secondary wage have been paid, and transfer to the community of the greater part of surplus profits.

The spirit and conception of responsibility that permeate every item of the program are reflected in this statement: "We would ask all employers to consider very carefully whether their style of living and personal expenditure are restricted to what is needed in order to insure the efficient performance of their functions in society. More than this is waste, and is, moreover, a great cause of class divisions."

AMERICAN EMPLOYERS

The only formal statements on the subject of social reconstruction that have yet come to our attention from an important group of American employers, are a declaration of principles and certain proposals by the National Chamber of Commerce. The declaration of principles was made at a convention of the organization, in Atlantic City, December 6, 1918. Beyond a general commendation of peaceful and friendly relations between employers and employees, it included nothing of importance on the labor phase of reconstruction. It condemned government operation and ownership of railroads, telegraphs, and telephones, and demanded more moderate taxes and a modification of the Sherman Anti-Trust Law. More recently the executive officials of the Chamber have submitted to a referendum vote of its membership a statement, "with a view to furnishing a basis on which American industry can build a national labor program." The main specific proposals in this statement are: recognition of the right of workers to organize; adequate representation of both parties in the determination of employment conditions; a decent home and proper social conditions; no reduction in wages until all other costs of production have been brought down to the lowest possible level; and a system of national employment offices. Inasmuch as this organization represents more employers than any other association in the country, the vote of its members on these proposals will be of the greatest significance.

An Interdenominational Statement

In Great Britain an organization known as the Interdenominational Conference of Social Service Unions, comprising ten religious bodies, including Catholics, spent more than a year formulating a statement of Social Reconstruction. (See the summary and analysis contained in the *Catholic Social Year Book* for 1918.) This statement deals with principles, evils, and remedies. Presuming that Christianity provides indispensable guiding principles and powerful motives of social reform, it lays down the basic proposition that every human being is of inestimable worth, and that legislation should recognize persons as more sacred than property, therefore the State should enforce a minimum living wage, enable the worker to obtain some control of industrial conditions; supplement private initiative in providing decent housing; prevent the occurrence of unemployment; safeguard the right of the laborer and his family to a reasonable amount of rest and recreation; remove those industrial and social conditions which hinder marriage and encourage an unnatural restriction of families, and afford ample opportunity for education of all children industrially, culturally, religiously, and morally. On the other hand, rights imply duties, and the individual is obliged to respect the rights of others, to cultivate self-control, to recognize that labor is the law of life, and that wealth is a trust. Finally, the statement points out that all social reform must take as its end and guide the maintenance of pure and wholesome family life.

Such in barest outline are the main propositions and principles of this remarkable program. The text contains adequate exposition of the development and application of all these points, and concrete specifications of the methods and measures by which the aims and principles may be brought into effect. In the latter respect the statement is not liable to the fatal objection that is frequently and fairly urged against the reform pronouncements of religious bodies: that they are abstract, platitudinous, and usually harmless. The statement of the Interdenominational Conference points out specific remedies for the evils that it describes; specific measures, legislative and other, by which the principles may be realized in actual life. Especially practical and valuable for Catholics are the explanations and modifications supplied by the *Year Book* of the Catholic Social Guild.

No Profound Changes in the United States

It is not to be expected that as many or as great social changes will take place in the United States as in Europe. Neither our habits of thinking nor our ordinary ways of life have undergone a profound disturbance. The hackneyed phrase: "Things will never again be the same after the war," has a much more concrete and deeply felt meaning among the European peoples. Their minds are fully adjusted to the conviction and expectation that these words will come true. In the second place, the devastation, the loss of capital and of men, the changes in individual relations, and the increase in the activities of government have been much greater in Europe than in the United States. Moreover, our superior natural advantages and resources, the better industrial and social condition of our working classes still constitute an obstacle to anything like revolutionary changes. It is significant that no social group in America, not even among the wage earners, has produced such a fundamental and radical program of reconstruction as the Labor Party of Great Britain.

A Practical and Moderate Program

No attempt will be made in these pages to formulate a comprehensive scheme of reconstruction. Such an undertaking would be a waste of time as regards immediate needs and purposes, for no important group or section of the American people is ready to consider a program of this magnitude. Attention will therefore be confined to those reforms that seem to be desirable and also obtainable within a reasonable time, and to a few general principles which should become a guide to more distant developments. A statement thus circumscribed will not merely present the objects that we wish to see attained, but will also serve as

an imperative call to action. It will keep before our minds the necessity for translating our faith into works. In the statements of immediate proposals we shall start, wherever possible, from those governmental agencies and legislative measures which have been to some
extent in operation during the war. These come before us with the
prestige of experience and should therefore receive first consideration
in any program that aims to be at once practical and persuasive.

The first problem in the process of reconstruction is the industrial
replacement of the discharged soldiers and sailors. The majority of
these will undoubtedly return to their previous occupations. However,
a very large number of them will either find their previous places
closed to them, or will be eager to consider the possibility of more
attractive employments. The most important single measure for meeting this situation that has yet been suggested is the placement of such
men on farms. Several months ago Secretary Lane recommended to
Congress that returning soldiers and sailors should be given the opportunity to work at good wages upon some part of the millions upon
millions of acres of arid, swamp, and cut-over timber lands, in order
to prepare them for cultivation. President Wilson in his annual address to Congress endorsed the proposal. As fast as this preliminary
task has been performed, the men should be assisted by government
loans to establish themselves as farmers, either as owners or as tenants
having long-time leases. It is essential that both the work of preparation and the subsequent settlement of the land should be effected by
groups or colonies, not by men living independently of one another
and in depressing isolation. A plan of this sort is already in operation
in England. The importance of the project as an item of any social
reform program is obvious. It would afford employment to thousands
upon thousands, would greatly increase the number of farm owners
and independent farmers, and would tend to lower the cost of living
by increasing the amount of agricultural products. If it is to assume
any considerable proportions it must be carried out by the governments of the United States and of the several states. Should it be
undertaken by these authorities and operated on a systematic and
generous scale, it would easily become one of the most beneficial
reform measures that has ever been attempted.

UNITED STATES EMPLOYMENT SERVICE

The reinstatement of the soldiers and sailors in urban industries will
no doubt be facilitated by the United States Employment Service.
This agency has attained a fair degree of development and efficiency

during the war. Unfortunately there is some danger that it will go out of existence or be greatly weakened at the end of the period of demobilization. It is the obvious duty of Congress to continue and strengthen this important institution. The problem of unemployment is with us always. Its solution requires the co-operation of many agencies, and the use of many methods; but the primary and indispensable instrument is a national system of labor exchanges, acting in harmony with state, municipal, and private employment bureaus.

WOMEN WAR WORKERS

One of the most important problems of readjustment is that created by the presence in industry of immense numbers of women who have taken the places of men during the war. Mere justice, to say nothing of chivalry, dictates that these women should not be compelled to suffer any greater loss or inconvenience than is absolutely necessary; for their services to the nation they have been second only to the services of the men whose places they were called upon to fill. One general principle is clear: no female worker should remain in any occupation that is harmful to health or morals. Women should disappear as quickly as possible from such tasks as conducting and guarding streetcars, cleaning locomotives, and a great number of other activities for which conditions of life and their physique render them unfit. Another general principle is that the proportion of women in industry ought to be kept within the smallest practical limits. If we have an efficient national employment service, if a goodly number of the returned soldiers and sailors are placed on the land, and if wages and the demand for goods are kept up to the level which is easily attainable, all female workers who are displaced from tasks that they have been performing only since the beginning of the war will be able to find suitable employments in other parts of the industrial field, or in those domestic occupations which sorely need their presence. Those women who are engaged at the same tasks as men should receive equal pay for equal amounts and qualities of work.

NATIONAL WAR LABOR BOARD

One of the most beneficial governmental organizations of the war is the National War Labor Board. Upon the basis of a few fundamental principles, unanimously adopted by the representatives of labor, capital, and the public, it has prevented innumerable strikes and raised wages to decent levels in many different industries throughout the country. Its main guiding principles have been a family living wage for all male adult laborers; recognition of the right of labor to organize and to deal with employers through its chosen representatives; and no coercion of nonunion laborers by members of the union. The War Labor Board ought to be continued in existence by Congress, and endowed with all the power for effective action that it can possess under the federal Constitution. The principles, methods, machinery, and results of this institution constitute a definite and far-reaching gain for social justice. No part of this advantage should be lost or given up in time of peace.

Present Wage Rates Should Be Sustained

The general level of wages attained during the war should not be lowered. In a few industries, especially some directly and peculiarly connected with the carrying on of war, wages have reached a plane upon which they cannot possibly continue for this grade of occupations. But the number of workers in this situation is an extremely small proportion of the entire wage-earning population. The overwhelming majority should not be compelled or suffered to undergo any reduction in their rates of remuneration, for two reasons: first, because the average rate of pay has not increased faster than the cost of living; second, because a considerable majority of the wage earners of the United States, both men and women, were not receiving living wages when prices began to rise in 1915. In that year, according to Lauck and Sydenstricker, whose work is the most comprehensive on the subject, four fifths of the heads of families obtained less than $800, while two thirds of the female wage earners were paid less than $400. Even if the prices of goods should fall to the level on which they were in 1915 — something that cannot be hoped for within five years — the average present rates of wages would not exceed the equivalent of a decent livelihood in the case of the vast majority. The exceptional instances to the contrary are practically all among the skilled workers. Therefore, wages on the whole should not be reduced even when the cost of living recedes from its present high level.

Even if the great majority of workers were now in receipt of more than living wages, there are no good reasons why rates of pay should be lowered. After all, a living wage is not necessarily the full measure of justice. All the Catholic authorities on the subject explicitly declare that this is only the minimum of justice. In a country as rich as ours, there are very few cases in which it is possible to prove that the worker would be getting more than that to which he has a right if he were paid something in excess of this ethical minimum. Why, then, should we assume that this is the normal share of almost the whole laboring population? Since our industrial resources and instrumentalities are sufficient to provide more than a living wage for a very large proportion of the workers, why should we acquiesce in a theory which denies them this measure of the comforts of life? Such a policy is not only of very questionable morality, but is unsound economically. The large demand for goods which is created and maintained by high rates of wages and high purchasing power by the masses is the surest guarantee of a continuous and general operation of industrial establishments. It is the most effective instrument of prosperity for labor and capital alike. The principal beneficiaries of a general reduction of wages would be the less efficient among the capitalists, and the more comfortable sections of the consumers. The wage earners would lose more in remuneration than they would gain from whatever fall in prices occurred as a direct result of the fall in wages. On grounds both of justice and sound economics, we should give our hearty support to all legitimate efforts made by labor to resist general wage reductions.

Housing for Working Classes

Housing projects for war workers which have been completed, or almost completed by the government of the United States, have cost some forty million dollars, and are found in eleven cities. While the federal government cannot continue this work in time of peace, the example and precedent that it has set, and the experience and knowledge that it has developed, should not be forthwith neglected and lost. The great cities in which congestion and other forms of bad housing are disgracefully apparent ought to take up and continue the work, at least to such an extent as will remove the worst features of a social condition that is a menace at once to industrial efficiency, civic health, good morals, and religion.

Reduction of the Cost of Living

During the war the cost of living has risen at least 75 per cent above the level of 1913. Some check has been placed upon the upward trend by government fixing of prices in the case of bread and coal and a few other commodities. Even if we believe it desirable, we cannot ask that the government continue this action after the articles of peace have been signed; for neither public opinion nor Congress is ready for such a revolutionary policy. If the extortionate practices of monopoly were prevented by adequate laws and adequate law enforcement, prices would automatically be kept at as low a level as that to which they might be brought by direct government determination. Just what laws, in addition to those already on the statute books, are necessary to abolish monopolistic extortion is a question of detail that need not be considered here. In passing, it may be noted that government competition with monopolies that cannot be effectively restrained by the ordinary antitrust laws deserves more serious consideration than it has yet received.

More important and more effective than any government regulation of prices would be the establishment of co-operative stores. The enormous toll taken from industry by the various classes of middlemen is now fully realized. The astonishing difference between the price received by the producer and that paid by the consumer has become a scandal of our industrial system. The obvious and direct means of reducing this discrepancy and abolishing unnecessary middlemen is the operation of retail and wholesale mercantile concerns under the ownership and management of the consumers. This is no Utopian scheme. It has been successfully carried out in England and Scotland through the Rochdale system. Very few serious efforts of this kind have been made in this country because our people have not felt the need of these co-operative enterprises as keenly as the European working classes, and because we have been too impatient and too individualistic to make the necessary sacrifices and to be content with moderate benefits and gradual progress. Nevertheless, our superior energy, initiative, and commercial capacity will enable us, once we set about the task earnestly, even to surpass what has been done in England and Scotland.

In addition to reducing the cost of living, the co-operative stores would train our working people and consumers generally in habits of saving, in careful expenditure, in business methods, and in the capacity for co-operation. When the working classes have learned to make the sacrifices and to exercise the patience required by the ownership and operation of co-operative stores, they will be equipped to undertake a great variety of tasks and projects which benefit the community immediately, and all its constituent members ultimately. They will then realize the folly of excessive selfishness and senseless individualism. Until they have acquired this knowledge, training and capacity, desirable extensions of governmental action in industry will not be attended by a normal amount of success. No machinery of government can operate automatically, and no official and bureaucratic administration of such machinery can ever be a substitute for intelligent interest and co-operation by the individuals of the community.

The Legal Minimum Wage

Turning now from those agencies and laws that have been put in operation during the war to the general subject of labor legislation and problems, we are glad to note that there is no longer any serious objection urged by impartial persons against the legal minimum wage. The several states should enact laws providing for the establishment of wage rates that will be at least sufficient for the decent maintenance of a family, in the case of all male adults, and adequate to the decent individual support of female workers. In the beginning the minimum wages for male workers should suffice only for the present needs of the family, but they should be gradually raised until they are adequate to meet future needs as well. That is, they should be ultimately high enough to make possible that amount of saving which is necessary to protect the worker and his family against sickness, accidents, invalidity, and old age.

Social Insurance

Until this level of legal minimum wages is reached the worker stands in need of the device of insurance. The State should make comprehensive provision for insurance against illness, invalidity, unemployment, and old age. So far as possible the insurance fund should be raised by a levy on industry, as is now done in the case of accident compensation. The industry in which a man is employed should provide with all that is necessary to meet all the needs of his entire life. Therefore, any contribution to the insurance fund from the general revenues of the State should be only slight and temporary. For the same reason no contribution should be exacted from any worker who is not getting a higher wage than is required to meet the present needs of himself and family. Those who are below that level can make such a contribution only at the expense of their present welfare. Finally, the administration of the insurance laws should be such as to interfere as little as possible with the individual freedom of the worker and his family. Any insurance scheme, or any administrative method, that tends to separate the workers into a distinct and dependent class, that offends against their domestic privacy and independence, or that threatens individual self-reliance and self-respect, should not be tolerated. The ideal to be kept in mind is a condition in which all the workers would themselves have the income and the responsibility of providing for all the needs and contingencies of life, both present and future. Hence all forms of State insurance should be regarded as merely a lesser evil, and should be so organized and administered as to hasten the coming of the normal condition.

The life insurance offered to soldiers and sailors during the war should be continued, so far as the enlisted men are concerned. It is very doubtful whether the time has yet arrived when public opinion would sanction the extension of general life insurance by the government to all classes of the community.

The establishment and maintenance of municipal health inspection in all schools, public and private, is now pretty generally recognized as of great importance and benefit. Municipal clinics where the poorer classes could obtain the advantage of medical treatment by specialists at a reasonable cost would likewise seem to have become a necessity. A vast amount of unnecessary sickness and suffering exists among the poor and the lower middle classes because they cannot afford the advantages of any other treatment except that provided by the general practitioner. Every effort should be made to supply wage earners and their families with specialized medical care through development of group medicine. Free medical care should be given only to those who cannot afford to pay.

LABOR PARTICIPATION IN INDUSTRIAL MANAGEMENT

The right of labor to organize and to deal with employers through representatives has been asserted above in connection with the discussion of the War Labor Board. It is to be hoped that this right will never again be called in question by any considerable number of employers. In addition to this, labor ought gradually to receive greater representation in what the English group of Quaker employers have called the "industrial" part of business management — "the control of processes and machinery; nature of product; engagement and dismissal of employees; hours of work, rates of pay, bonuses, etc.; welfare work; shop discipline; relations with trade unions." The establishment of shop committees, working wherever possible with the trade union, is the method suggested by this group of employers for giving the employees the proper share of industrial management. There can be no doubt that a frank adoption of these means and ends by employers would not only promote the welfare of the workers, but vastly improve the relations between them and their employers, and increase the efficiency and productiveness of each establishment.

There is no need here to emphasize the importance of safety and sanitation in work places, as this is pretty generally recognized by legislation. What is required is an extension and strengthening of many of the existing statutes, and a better administration and enforcement of such laws everywhere.

VOCATIONAL TRAINING

The need of industrial, or as it has come to be more generally called, vocational training, is now universally acknowledged. In the interest of the nation, as well as in that of the workers themselves, this training should be made substantially universal. While we cannot now discuss the subject in any detail, we do wish to set down two general observations. First, the vocational training should be offered in such forms and conditions as not to deprive the children of the working classes of at least the elements of a cultural education. A healthy democracy cannot tolerate a purely industrial or trade education for any class of its citizens. We do not want to have the children of the wage earners put into a special class in which they are marked as outside the sphere of opportunities for culture. The second observation is that the system of vocational training should not operate so as to weaken in any degree our parochial schools or any other class of private schools. Indeed, the opportunities of the system should be extended to all qualified private schools on exactly the same basis as to public schools. We want neither class divisions in education nor a State monopoly of education.

CHILD LABOR

The question of education naturally suggests the subject of child labor. Public opinion in the majority of the states of our country has set its face inflexibly against the continuous employment of children in industry before the age of sixteen years. Within a reasonably short time all of our states, except some of the stagnant ones, will have laws providing for this reasonable standard. The education of public opinion must continue, but inasmuch as the process is slow, the abolition of child labor in certain sections seems unlikely to be brought about by the legislatures of those states, and since the Keating-Owen Act has been declared unconstitutional, there seems to be no device by which this reproach to our country can be removed except that of taxing child labor out of existence. This method is embodied in an amendment to the Federal Revenue Bill which would impose a tax of 10 per cent on all goods made by children.

SUFFICIENT FOR THE PRESENT

Probably the foregoing proposals comprise everything that is likely to have practical value in a program of immediate social reconstruction for America. Substantially all of these methods, laws, and recommendations have been recognized in principle by the United States during the war, or have been indorsed by important social and industrial groups and organizations. Therefore, they are objects that we can set before the people with good hope of obtaining a sympathetic and practical response. Were they all realized a great step would have been taken in the direction of social justice. When they are all put into operation the way will be easy and obvious to still greater and more beneficial result.

ULTIMATE AND FUNDAMENTAL REFORMS

Despite the practical and immediate character of the present statement, we cannot entirely neglect the question of ultimate aims and a systematic program; for other groups are busy issuing such systematic pronouncements, and we all need something of the kind as a philosophical foundation and as a satisfaction to our natural desire for comprehensive statements.

It seems clear that the present industrial system is destined to last for a long time in its main outlines. That is to say, private ownership of capital is not likely to be supplanted by a collectivist organization of industry at a date sufficiently near to justify any present action based on the hypothesis of its arrival. This forecast we recognize as not only extremely probable, but as highly desirable; for, other objections apart, Socialism would mean bureaucracy, political tyranny, the helplessness of the individual as a factor in the ordering of his own life, and in general social inefficiency and decadence.

MAIN DEFECTS OF PRESENT SYSTEM

Nevertheless, the present system stands in grievous need of considerable modifications and improvement. Its main defects are three: Enormous inefficiency and waste in the production and distribution of commodities; insufficient incomes for the great majority of wage earners, and unnecessarily large incomes for a small minority of privileged capitalists. Inefficiency in the production and distribution of goods would be in great measure abolished by the reforms that have been outlined in the foregoing pages. Production would be greatly increased by universal living wages, by adequate industrial education, and by harmonious relations between labor and capital on the basis of adequate participation by the former in all the industrial aspects of business management. The wastes of commodity distribution could be practically all eliminated by co-operative mercantile establishments, and co-operative selling and marketing associations.

CO-OPERATION AND COPARTNERSHIP

Nevertheless, the full possibilities of increased production will not be realized so long as the majority of the workers remain mere wage earners. The majority must somehow become owners, or at least in part, of the instruments of production. They can be enabled to reach this stage gradually through co-operative productive societies and copartnership arrangements. In the former, the workers own and manage the industries themselves; in the latter they own a substantial part of the corporate stock and exercise a reasonable share in the management. However slow the attainments of these ends, they will have to be reached before we can have a thoroughly efficient system of production, or an industrial and social order that will be secure from the danger of revolution. It is to be noted that this particular modification of the existing order, though far-reaching and involving to a great extent the abolition of the wage system, would not mean the abolition of private ownership. The instruments of production would still be owned by individuals, not by the State.

INCREASED INCOMES FOR LABOR

The second great evil, that of insufficient income for the majority, can be removed only by providing the workers with more income. This means not only universal living wages, but the opportunity of obtaining something more than that amount for all who are willing to work hard and faithfully. All the other measures for labor betterment recommended in the preceding pages would likewise contribute directly or indirectly to a more just distribution of wealth in the interest of the laborer.

ABOLITION AND CONTROL OF MONOPOLIES

For the third evil mentioned above, excessive gains by a small minority of privileged capitalists, the main remedies are prevention of monopolistic control of commodities, adequate government regulation of such public service monopolies as will remain under private operation, and heavy taxation of incomes, excess profits, and inheritances. The precise methods by which genuine competition may be restored and maintained among businesses that are naturally competitive cannot be discussed here; but the principle is clear that human beings cannot be trusted with the immense opportunities for oppression and extortion that go with the possession of monopoly power. That the owners of public service monopolies should be restricted by law to a fair or average return on their actual investment, has long been a recognized principle of the courts, the legislatures, and public opinion. It is a principle which should be applied to competitive enterprises likewise, with the qualification that something more than the average rate of return should be allowed to men who exhibit exceptional efficiency. However, good public policy, as well as equity, demands that these exceptional businessmen share the fruits of their efficiency with the consumer in the form of lower prices. The man who utilizes his ability to produce cheaper than his competitors for the purpose of exacting from the public as high a price for his product as is necessary for the least efficient businessman is a menace rather than a benefit to industry and society.

Our immense war debt constitutes a particular reason why incomes and excess profits should continue to be heavily taxed. In this way two important ends will be attained: the poor will be relieved of injurious tax burdens, and the small class of privileged capitalists will be compelled to return a part of their unearned gains to society.

A New Spirit a Vital Need

"Society," said Pope Leo XIII, "can be healed in no other way than by a return to Christian life and Christian institutions." The truth of these words is more widely perceived today than when they were written, more than twenty-seven years ago. Changes in our economic and political systems will have only partial and feeble efficiency if they be not reinforced by the Christian view of work and wealth. Neither the moderate reforms advocated in this paper nor any other program of betterment or reconstruction will prove reasonably effective without a reform in the spirit of both labor and capital. The laborer must come to realize that he owes his employer and society an honest day's work in return for a fair wage, and that conditions cannot be substantially improved until he roots out the desire to get a maximum of return for a minimum of service. The capitalist must likewise get a new viewpoint. He needs to learn the long-forgotten truth that wealth is stewardship, that profit-making is not the basic justification of business enterprise, and that there are such things as fair profits, fair interest, and fair prices. Above and before all, he must cultivate and strengthen within his mind the truth which many of his class have begun to grasp for the first time during the present war; namely, that the laborer is a human being, not merely an instrument of production; and that the laborer's right to a decent livelihood is the first moral charge upon industry. The employer has a right to get a reasonable living out of his business, but he has no right to interest on his investment until his employees have obtained at least living wages. This is the human and Christian, in contrast to the purely commercial and pagan, ethics of industry.

53. STATEMENT OF THE ADMINISTRATIVE COMMITTEE OF THE N.C.W.C.* REGARDING

UNIVERSAL DISARMAMENT**

This statement was prepared by the Administrative Committee, N.C.W.C., in 1921 at the time of the Washington Conference on Disarmament. It was signed by the following members of the American hierarchy: Archbishop Edward Hanna, of San Francisco, chairman; Bishop Peter Muldoon, of Rockford, vice-chairman; Archbishop Austin Dowling, of St. Paul; Bishop Joseph Schrembs, of Toledo; Bishop William Russell, of Charleston; Bishop Edmund Gibbons, of Albany; and His Eminence, Dennis Cardinal Dougherty, of Philadelphia.

Peace among ourselves, peace with all other nations should be not only the earnest desire but the active aim of every Christian. Pope Benedict XV, in his great encyclical on Reconciliation, declared that peace is the very preaching of the law of Christ — the gospel of peace. In that same encyclical the Holy Father emphasized the necessity not only of praying for peace, but of selecting immediate, practical measures that will lessen the danger of war.

It is vain for us to talk of our love of peace and yet to be

---

* Documents 52, 53, 54 were issued under the title of National Catholic Welfare Council; from Document 55 on the correct title is N.C.W. Conference.

** *N.C.W.C. Bulletin,* May, 1921, p. 6. Cf. 57.

promoting differences that are apt to lead to war — to be working for a larger army or a greater navy. If all the nations of the world, while protesting a love of peace, give themselves to such militaristic measures, their people will be burdened with oppressive taxes, the seeds of international discontent and war will be inevitable. Therefore, Benedict asked for "the reduction, if not the abolishment, of the enormous military expenditures which can no longer be borne by the States, in order that in this way murderous and disastrous wars may be prevented."

President Harding, in his first message to Congress, stated: "The Government is in accord with the wish to eliminate the burdens of heavy armament. The United States will ever be in harmony with such a movement toward the higher attainments of peace."

The leaders of the world recognize that peace is the first necessary condition of the nations' and the world's well-being and happiness. The different governments are of themselves unwilling to take the first step. Yet everyone knows the first step must be taken if war is to be made very improbable and almost impossible. The first step is postponed in waiting for some other government to take the lead.

Now it would be foolhardy for one nation to disarm to leave herself defenseless, while other nations are sustaining or increasing their armament. Legislators that would permit a nation so to act would be false to their highest duty. It would be vitally harmful to America's safety and well-being if we were to adopt a policy of disarmament without first having secured the definite, binding agreement of the other nations to a similar policy. And any propaganda for disarmament that does not include this international agreement must be looked upon as unwise and dangerous. Emergencies have often shown that friendships upon which a people have relied proved undependable owing to the absence of definite, binding agreements. It is necessary that all nations act together. "All nations under the influence of Christian benevolence," declares Benedict XV, "should establish a true peace among themselves and join together in one single association which, under the auspices of justice, will be lasting."

The nations must act together. "All States," Benedict XV further asserts, "should put aside mutual suspicion and unite in one sole society or rather family of peoples both to guarantee their own independence and safeguard order in the civil concert of peoples."

And President Harding supported these sentiments in his message to Congress. "The American aspiration, indeed, the world aspiration, was an association of nations based upon the application of justice and right, binding us in a conference and co-operation for the prevention of war and pointing the way to a higher civilization and international fraternity. We wish this association to be conceived in peace in which we would most heartily join and will relinquish no effort to bring the nations of the world into such fellowship."

While, therefore, we must leave the immediate question of disarmament to our national legislators, we should take active means to bring about, for the purpose of general disarmament, a meeting of the representatives of all the leading nations of the world. America should sound such a call and we should do all in our power to make it known that such is the will of the American people.

That is the first necessary step. Without it peace will be but a hope, not a reality. A congress of nations, called at Washington by the American government, backed by popular interest and appeal, will secure undoubtedly practical, effective measures for the promotion of enduring world peace. Thus shall America once again show her leadership on the path of civilization. Such a congress should be the object of our earnest prayers, our active work. For in so working we promote the gospel of the Prince of Peace upon earth and strengthen that message which our Holy Church has ever sought to declare unto the nations.

54. STATEMENT OF THE ADMINISTRATIVE COMMITTEE, N.C.W.C., ON

BIRTH CONTROL*

January 30, 1922

The activity of the advocates of birth control is an affront to all genuine Christians, and to all other persons who cherish the elementary principles and sentiments of morality. We protest against this unholy movement, and we take occasion to reassert the teaching of the Catholic Church.

The Church condemns all positive devices and methods of birth control as necessarily immoral because they are perversions of nature and violations of the moral law. Moreover, they lead inevitably to weakening of character, degradation of conjugal relations, decline of population, and degeneracy of national life.

As a remedy for social and economic ills, birth control is not only mistaken and futile, but tends to divert attention from genuine methods of social betterment.

---

* *N.C.W.C. Bulletin,* February, 1922, p. 7.

55. STATEMENT OF THE ADMINISTRATIVE COMMITTEE N.C.W.C. ON

PATERNALISM IN GOVERNMENT*

February, 1922

The growth of bureaucracy in the United States is one of the most significant aftereffects of the war. This growth must be resolutely checked. Federal assistance and federal direction are in some cases beneficial and even necessary; but extreme bureaucracy is foreign to everything American. It is unconstitutional and undemocratic. It means officialism, red tape, and prodigal waste of public money. It spells hordes of so-called experts and self-perpetuating cliques of politicians to regulate every detail of daily life. It would eventually sovietize our form of government.

The forward-looking forces in our national life must resolutely stand against further encroachments on individual and state liberty. The press, the home, the school, and the Church have no greater enemy at the present time than the paternalistic and bureaucratic government which certain self-seeking elements are attempting to foist upon us.

* *N.C.W.C. Bulletin*, February, 1922, p. 7.

56. RESOLUTION OF THE BISHOPS OF THE N.C.W.C. CONCERNING THE

CATHOLIC PRESS*

September 27, 1923

These resolutions were passed by the unanimous vote of all the bishops of the National Catholic Welfare Conference present at the meeting of September 27, 1923.

I. That the Sunday immediately preceding the feast of St. Francis de Sales, proclaimed by the Holy Father Patron of Catholic Publicity and Press throughout the world, be accepted and approved as Press Sunday in every Catholic Church in the United States of America.

II. That the N.C.W.C. strongly urge all Catholic periodicals to become affiliated as pay subscribers to the N.C.W.C. Press Service and all pastors to use in their parishes, schools, and societies the various periodicals issued by the N.C.W.C. Press Department.

III. That this National Catholic Welfare Conference approve the plan and project of a first-class supplement to be issued each week by the Press Department to all weekly subscribers to the Service, and furthermore authorize such supplement if, and when, the managers of twenty-five of the Catholic weeklies agree to subscribe so as to assure at least the cost of such project; also, that the hope and plan of a Catholic Daily Journal in New York or Washington be hereby approved and kept before the Catholic mind and public opinion for realization in the near future, as soon as conditions permit.

IV. Whereas it is a well-known fact that very serious abuses have grown up among the agencies and agents that solicit subscriptions for Catholic papers, magazines, missionary and Church building projects, among vendors of Church goods, among various persons asking for Mass intentions, and whereas such abuses arise from

---

* *N.C.W.C. Bulletin,* October, 1923, p. 10.

excessive commissions and promises of indulgences and blessings on sacred objects given or sold, be it resolved, (*a*) it is not our wish to restrict reasonable or legitimate private initiative or public enterprise; (*b*) commercialism, however, has invaded religious spheres of action and must be discouraged; (*c*) official diocesan authorization for every Catholic enterprise, association, or periodical is the law and tradition in and of the Catholic Church, hence for all agencies and agents; (*d*) all these abuses are hereby condemned, all priests are urged not to tolerate such agents, and all the faithful are instructed never to subscribe to any such projects or buy such periodicals, unless a clear announcement be made in the Church, authorizing such agents.

57. THE ADMINISTRATIVE BOARD, N.C.W.C.

PLEA FOR WORLD PEACE*

May 4, 1924

This statement was issued by the Administrative Board, N.C.W.C., at the time of President Coolidge's suggestion for a second Limitation of Armament Conference.

The heartening evidences of a more extended and abiding peace among nations who have long been at enmity are a source of joy and hope to every follower of the Prince of Peace. To us also, as Americans, it is a further source of congratulation that, without in any way impairing our sovereignty as a nation or violating the traditions that have so long guided us, we have played an effective and even a leading part in this work of enduring peace.

We cannot but feel that the one great source of inspiration of this truly Christian work among men has been the leadership of the Holy Father, who by his unbounded charity to the needy of all

---

* *N.C.W.C. Bulletin,* June, 1924, p. 3. Cf. 53.

nations has shown good will which should rule our conduct nationally and internationally.

We should, individually, and through organizations, earnestly study to preserve the peace of the world. Our dealings, our thoughts, our aims should be in the path of peace. Peace should be our goal. In our dealings with other nations we should refuse from the very outset to falter in justice or to give offense. We have as a nation our own destiny! We have our own soul to keep. We need not unfairly discriminate against particular peoples and we should exhaust every channel of conference and discussion with other nations on any matter in dispute. In all these conferences we should always keep in mind the fundamental principle of Christian doctrine and action, a right regard for the dignity of the individual man and of the family unit in our civilization.

President Coolidge's recent suggestion of another Limitation of Armament Conference is a step toward a more permanent peace. For the goal of all our national strivings and diplomacy should be a reasonable settlement of international disputes by friendly discussion rather than by resort to arms. Under the providence of God, our country must take the leading place in many fields of world activity. Charity as well as justice to all, ill feeling and discourtesy to none will keep us as a nation in the way of righteousness.

58. FORMAL STATEMENT OF THE ADMINISTRATIVE BOARD, N.C.W.C., ON

MEXICAN INJUSTICE TO THE CHURCH*

April 15, 1926

Statement made at semiannual meeting of archbishops and bishops of the Administrative Committee of the N.C.W.C., April, 1926.

Our fellow Catholics in Mexico are today suffering a most unjust and far-reaching persecution at the hands of the present Mexican government. Churches have been confiscated, priests exiled, the people deprived of religious ministration, the teaching of religion banished from the schools. On March 6, 1926, the Mexican government created a special bureau in the office of the Attorney General to care for the rapid increase of Church property daily being seized by the government.

Much attention is given to the completion of commercial treaties with Mexico. It is far more important, far more essential, that we, as Americans, should actively interest ourselves in securing for the people of Mexico the fundamental rights of religious, educational, and civic freedom.

The Constitution of Mexico, in force since 1917, includes in its antireligious provisions all churches and ministers of every denomination. That those provisions are being carried out almost exclusively against Catholics and the Catholic Church at this time should not blind our fellow citizens to the fact that they are in themselves absolute denials of those principles upon which we, as Americans, believe that just government must be founded.

HISTORY OF PRESENT REGIME

The present government of Mexico won its way to power by revolution, and has been strengthened in its hold upon power by recog-

---

* *N.C.W.C. Bulletin,* May, 1926, p. 4; cf. also Nos. 2, 22, 29, 31, 34, 63.

nition by our own government of the United States. Before such recognition was granted in 1915, the U. S. Secretary of State, Mr. Lansing, at the direction of the United States Senate, interrogated the then provisional government of Mexico as to whether or not that government would guarantee and provide religious liberty for its people. The Mexican government solemnly pledged itself to guarantee religious liberty according to the Constitution of 1857. On that promise our government granted recognition. No sooner was it won that the government of Mexico scrapped the Constitution of 1857; declared a preconstitutional "period"; and by military dictatorship forced, not through popular vote but through picked convention, the Constitution of 1917. The present Constitution of Mexico was imposed on Mexico by a band of insurgents at a time when Mexico was prostrate and when the rest of the world was at war.

Despite the fact that in 1920 our government was again forced to suspend diplomatic relations with Mexico and did not resume them until 1923, the conditions of recognition established in 1915 were still obligatory on Mexico. These conditions, which underlie all negotiations between civilized governments, were postulated as premises to the agreements which were later on entered into by both governments.

Religious Liberty Promised

We are amply justified, and not only justified, but, as is every American, obligated, to call upon our government therefore that its original request upon which recognition to Mexico was granted, be lived up to by the government of Mexico. The United States gave recognition to Mexico on Mexico's specific promise that it would guarantee religious liberty to all its citizens. Mexico has not kept this agreement, but, on the contrary, her government has entered upon a definite campaign of force to destroy religious liberty and is intensifying that campaign by striking at the roots of religion — religious education.

No American can view with indifference the active propaganda of principles that are subversive to our own government; that will, if persisted in, embitter our relations with the whole of Latin America.

Where religious justice is violated, there can be no political, no civic peace.

The situation is so critical that we call upon our Catholic people not only to interest themselves as a body, but to hold meetings with their non-Catholic brethren that will voice the protest of the public;

that will both call upon our own government to use its good offices
to see that justice is restored and that religious and educational
liberty are enjoyed by the people of Mexico.

59. LETTER OF HIS EXCELLENCY, MOST REV. EDWARD J. HANNA, D.D., ARCHBISHOP OF SAN FRANCISCO, CHAIRMAN, ADMINISTRATIVE BOARD, N.C.W.C., TO MOST REV. ISMAELE PERDOMO, D.D., ARCHBISHOP OF BOGOTA, ON THE OCCASION OF THE

CENTENARY OF SIMON BOLIVAR*

The Administrative Committee of Bishops, National Catholic Welfare Conference, at our meeting at Washington, our national capital, on November 10, herewith sends to Your Grace, to all your fellow bishops, and to the people of Colombia our felicitations on the coming centenary, December 17, of your national hero, Simon Bolivar, defender of true liberty and of the principles of just government.

We are pleased to have this opportunity of exchanging mutual sentiments of affection in the one common bond of our holy faith, and of interest and solicitude in the welfare of the Catholic peoples of the United Americas.

Your Simon Bolivar has long been known to and honored by us as a man rich in the heritage of that Catholic faith which came to him through a long line of Catholic ancestors. He was blessed with an education that kept burning within his heart an intelligent devotion to those high principles of duty, justice, and charity as fathered by the Church.

Simon Bolivar persevered when the political world about him bespoke only chaos and despair. Confidently, on the summit of the Aventine in Rome, he pledged wealth, talents, life itself to the sacred cause of liberty in America. On the battlefield, reverses only

---

* N.C.W.C. Review, January, 1931, p. 8.

spurred him to greater effort; victory deepened his conscious dependence on God's Providence. In the halls of legislation, his Catholic mind protected his country and his countrymen from that tyranny which irreligion and the denial of God, of His Christ, and of His Church ever beget.

At the hour of his death, he bequeathed to the nations of America his solemn prayer that they ever hold sacred the holy faith of their ancestors.

To Simon Bolivar we are all indebted. We have often recalled with pride that when, in the hour of gravest need, his representative came to our United States, to plead for help in the fight for liberty, he found both friend and champion in our own Catholic hero — Charles Carroll of Carrollton.

Bolivar is forerunner of co-operation and good will between the nations of America. He is the founder of Pan-Americanism. At his centenary, we renew our hopes and our pledges for a closer union, a more just understanding, a more interested and generous co-operation between the Catholic people of our country and the Catholic peoples of the nations south of us.

We may add that on December 17, this appreciation of your great hero will find echo in the Catholic schools of our country and in the programs carried out by many of our Catholic lay organizations.

In conclusion, we wish to repeat that it is a privilege and a satisfaction to assure Your Grace that we welcome every opportunity to co-operate with you and your fellow bishops in preserving to posterity those Catholic ideals and Catholic principles which ever found a defender in Simon Bolivar.

60. STATEMENT BY THE BISHOPS OF THE ADMINIS-
TRATIVE COMMITTEES OF THE N.C.W.C. ON THE

PRESENT CRISIS*

April 25, 1933

PART ONE

CRUCIAL YEARS

We are passing through crucial years. Hope is the mark of the present moment. We pray that almighty God may give us back our moral, social, and economic life purified and in all ways bettered by the fires through which it has passed. The tragic trials we have endured, which no human power could avert or arrest, have left us nothing on which to lean but the providence of God. Every thoughtful man has had at least a glimpse of the supernatural background upon which the world of material things reposes and to which it must adjust itself if we are not to have over and over again a repetition of these bewildering experiences. It would be a crowning tragedy if we were to learn no lesson from them, if we were to go back to the condition of things out of which the present crisis issued and after a new era of plenty, endure again a new agony. Our most urgent need is God's blessing upon the world and especially upon our own country. We summon all men of good will to pray for that blessing, and, by their works of unselfishness to deserve it, and to advance the commonweal.

We have been witnesses of a great social and political catastrophe, the causes of which are not to be found in one place or in one nation, but in all places and among all peoples, and the effects of which are devastating and world wide. Through the mysterious and just dispensations of Divine Providence, the world has been shaken to its very foundations as a consequence of the World War. While

---

* Printed by the N.C.W.C., Washington 5, D. C., 1933; cf. Nos. 24, 25, 52, 62, 66, 68, 71.

the human mind can never measure adequately the monstrous evils which have followed in its wake, we must thank God that it did not overthrow the entire structure of European civilization and the culture of all the Christian centuries.

Universal Distress. Of the evils that have encompassed us, Pope Pius XI, with world vision, said a year ago: ". . . from the Flood on, it would be hard to find spiritual and material distress so deep, so universal, as that which we are now experiencing; even the greatest scourges that left indelible traces in the lives and memories of peoples, struck only one nation at a time. Now, on the contrary, the whole of humanity is held bound by the financial and economic crisis. . . . There is no people, there is no state, no society or family, which in one way or another, directly or indirectly, to a greater or less extent, does not feel the repercussion."[1]

Sacrifices of Our People. Our people, accustomed to standards of living and comforts not enjoyed by other nations, have been called upon to endure grievous hardships. We can speak only words of praise of the long-suffering and disciplined spirit of our Catholic people during the four years of our economic and moral crisis. Their sufferings, their privations, their generosity, especially that shown by the poor to those still poorer, will fill an inspiring page of our history. Noble sacrifices have been made by them to support from their almost exhausted funds our Catholic schools and institutions of charity and our many works of religion.

Alleged Causes of Depression. When considering the causes of the general distress, we hear many lament the material destruction wrought by the World War; the loss of our foreign markets, the extremes of inflation, and the depths of depression; the orgy of speculation and the consequent wiping out of vast fortunes; the collapse of credit; unlimited mass production, disturbing the balance of population between the rural districts and industrial centers; the inexcusable extravagance of government expenditures; and the national crime of maintaining armaments beyond all reasonable limits.

Many, having a materialistic attitude toward life, and therefore without a true moral sense of their obligations, object to any restriction of competition, even that which degrades the dignity of human labor and ignores every principle of justice. Others resent opposition to monopolies and dictatorship in the economic world, and regard as an infringement of their rights any interference with their power-

---

[1] *Caritate Christi Compulsi.*

ful corporations, and mergers, or with lobbies, which have sought to corrupt and to control the State.

Some, with even greater moral callousness, do not hesitate to array the nations one against the other, if thereby their personal power and riches be increased. In the language of Pope Pius, they permit a social order "which spurns no less the laws of nature than those of God."[2]

Greed. In tracing the remote causes of the present misery of mankind, we must listen to him who as a loving father views from an eminence all the nations of the world. Quoting St. Paul, our Holy Father says: " 'The desire of money is the root of all evils.' Is it not that lust of earthly goods that the pagan poet called with righteous scorn 'the accursed hunger for gold,' is it not that sordid egoism which too often regulates the mutual relations of individuals and society, is it not, in fine, greed, whatever be its species and form, that has brought the world to a pass we all see and deplore? From greed arises mutual distrust that casts a blight on all human beings; from greed arises envy, which makes a man consider the advantages of another as losses to himself; from greed arises narrow individualism, which orders and subordinates everything to its own advantage without taking account of others, on the contrary, cruelly trampling underfoot all rights of others. Hence the disorder and inequality from which arises the accumulation of the wealth of nations in the hands of a small group of individuals who manipulate the market of the world at their own caprice to the immense harm of the masses."[3]

A worse condition has been brought about, as the Holy Father says: "In our days not alone is wealth accumulated, but immense power and despotic economic domination is concentrated in the hands of the few, and those few are frequently not the owners but only the trustees and directors of invested funds, who administer them at their good pleasure.

"This power becomes particularly irresistible when exercised by those who, because they hold and control money, are able also to govern credit and determine its allotment, for that reason supplying, so to speak, the lifeblood to the entire economic body, and grasping, as it were, in their hands the very soul of production, so that no one dare breathe against their will. . . .

---

[2] *Quadragesimo Anno.*
[3] *Caritate Christi Compulsi.*

"This concentration of power has led to a threefold struggle for domination. First, there is the struggle for dictatorship in the economic sphere itself; then, the fierce battle to acquire control of the state, so that its resources and authority may be abused in the economic struggles. Finally, the clash between states themselves."

The Pontiff continues to outline the deplorable conditions existing: "Free competition is dead. Economic dictatorship has taken its place. Unbridled ambition for domination has succeeded the desire for gain; the whole economic life has become hard, cruel, and relentless in a ghastly measure. Furthermore, the intermingling and scandalous confusing of the duties and offices of civil authority and of economics have produced crying evils and have gone so far as to degrade the majesty of the state. The state, which should be the supreme arbiter, ruling in kingly fashion far above all party contention, intent only upon justice and the common good, has become instead a slave, bound over to the service of human passion and greed."[4]

And still the worst is to be told — "the ruin of souls." Our Holy Father says that today "the conditions of social and economic life are such that vast multitudes of men can only with great difficulty pay attention to that one thing necessary, namely, their eternal salvation."[5] In the language of St. Paul, "as they liked not to have God in their knowledge, God delivered them up to a reprobate sense."[6]

Our Conditions. If we apply to our own country the weighty words of His Holiness we find that, in common with other nations, we have brought about our present unhappy conditions by divorcing education, industry, politics, business, and economics from morality and religion, and by ignoring for long decades the innate dignity of man and trampling on his human rights. We have failed to realize that these rights are supreme so far as the purpose of human society is concerned; that they include the right of the individual to life, and also to the means of a normal, healthy life of mind and body, so long as man is willing to do his part; that they include likewise his rights as a social being, which rights should ensure sufficient means to provide for himself and his family. And, when speaking of man as a social being, we mean men, women, and children, the husband and wife — in a word, the human family.

An Industrial Nation. That we are an industrial nation is our public boast. Industry is considered to be of more importance than

---

[4] *Quadragesimo Anno.*
[5] *Ibid.*
[6] Rom. 1:28.

the moral welfare of man. The lord of all is Industry. "Save Industry!" is the cry. "Put big business on its feet and all will be well, as it was in the past!"

Industry in our country, through the concentration of wealth, has acquired such complete control that independent operation, even on the part of so-called owners and employers, is practically impossible. The tremendous increase in the output of industry during recent years, due to the natural resources of our country, to inventions and to machinery, especially to the giant machines, has made some enormously rich, has brought many comforts, and has abolished much drudgery, but it has not ensured the worker the proportionate gain to which he is justly entitled. It has, however, vastly increased the incomes of industrialists and capitalists.

False Philosophy. The social philosophy prevailing during recent centuries has carried human society far from its safe moorings. That philosophy — if, indeed, it be worthy of the name — which has ruled governments, groups, and individuals for the past three hundred years has not taken as its guide the moral law, has not considered the rights of man. Money, not man, has been the supreme consideration and the justifying end. That philosophy has aroused opposition and has given rise to errors and exaggerations that are anti-Catholic and anti-Christian.

That same demoralizing philosophy defended, and defends today, unrestrained individual economic freedom and the economic dictatorship that has succeeded it. That philosophy permits individuals, corporations, and nations to accumulate as much wealth as they can, according to the unfair methods of modern business, and to use such accumulated wealth as they see fit. It honors and proclaims as sovereign rulers of economic empires men who have succeeded in amassing unjustly these fabulous fortunes.

That philosophy has broken down or forbidden the establishment of protective organizations. It has broken down or forbidden an organized economic life to administer the production of wealth and its distribution in accordance with social justice and the interdependence of economic relations. It has denied government its right to guard justice and the common good. It has given greed a free hand.

That philosophy denied and denies, in reality, the oneness and the solidarity of mankind. In its light, wealth, business, and the power that material prosperity gives, are in themselves supreme ends. Human rights must be sacrificed to those ends, and humanity itself must become the mere instrument in the production of wealth, not the master controlling it. Such a philosophy has always been and will ever be false and un-Christian in principle and application. It has literally taken God out of the world.

Communism. This extreme of individualism has led to the extreme of Communism. We rightly fear its spread in our country and see an especial menace in its insidious presentation of fundamental truths for its own destructive ends. The brotherhood of man is loudly proclaimed; energetic protest is made against injustice done the working classes; the abuses of the capitalistic system are vigorously condemned; it is insisted that man shall not exploit his fellow man, nor class dominate class, but that all shall be dedicated to a life of service.

A program of social reform couched in such language and with such aims and purposes is unassailable because it is distinctively Christian in origin and purport, but in the hands of the communists it is merely a snare to allure those who are oppressed by the prevailing economic maladjustment into accepting the iniquitous social and religious tenets of Lenin and Stalin. There is very grave and subtle danger of infection from Communism. Special efforts are being made to win the Negroes, who are the victims of injustice. The communists have world vision. They have as their objective a world war on God and the complete destruction of all supernatural and even natural religion. They believe it necessary to inaugurate a merciless class warfare, and they insist, in theory at least, on the complete abolition of ownership of private property.

It is a strange paradox that many who condemn strongly the propaganda of the "Red" and the communist are significantly silent when learned but misguided writers tell us there is no God; when scoffing university professors destroy in the youth of our land belief in God and in the supernatural; when they tell us that man is the plaything of preordained causes; that conscience and sin are myths; that the brotherhood of men, and consequently of nations, is a baseless dream; that morality does not rest upon the immutable and eternal law of God, but is merely a convention of man, subject to the changing conditions of society; that a man's obligations to his fellow man are such only as he is forced to accept by the taxing or police power of the State — in a word, that they are silent when all these destructive forces are preparing the future leaders of Communism in America.

Inevitable Consequences. If, under the plea of liberalism, encouragement or even tolerance be given to the many radical doctrines proposed by teachers, writers, and agitators; if no attempt be made to drag out into the open the secret propaganda that is being carried on; if no consideration be given to the evil consequences that must necessarily follow the divorce of education and economics from morality and religion, what can be expected but that the very foundations upon which our whole social structure rests should be undermined?

Is it not inevitable that in our professional, business, and industrial life the sad effects of this divorce should be evident — that among our lawyers, physicians, teachers, writers, industrialists, and business-men there is to be found too generally an unmoral and un-Christian view of life? This is a terrible indictment which must be laid, at least remotely, at the door of irreligious or nonreligious education and unmoral, or immoral, economics.

In so far as governments, institutions of learning, the press, the theater, and other opinion-forming agencies have been indifferent to or have rejected morality and religion, in that measure have they degenerated. This has been said a thousand times, and yet how far are we from the happy condition which would make all these forces realize the necessity of religion and the obligation of working under its ennobling influence!

Education in Our Country. The educational system of our country, while imposing an unjust and almost impossible tax burden on the general public, is deserving of sympathetic consideration from the standpoint that it is bearing a great responsibility which belongs to the domain of industry. We have in different sections legislation which provides for compulsory education until students reach the age of eighteen, and the further demand is being made today that the age be advanced to twenty years. That our educational institu-tions are nurseries of idleness for millions of our youth, either because they have not the natural gifts to acquire knowledge or because they will not form studious habits, and that the whole system of education is imposing an ever increasing burden, seem to receive little if any consideration. In the eyes of industry, regardless of justice, the one important thing is that students should be kept in school for additional years so as to lessen the number of the unemployed.

Simplify Education. Our whole educational system deserves the most serious consideration of the government and of all thinking and informed men who have at heart the best interests of their country. Great evils are to be corrected. There can be a simplifying of all our educational work without depriving students of essentials and without preventing gifted students from acquiring the education to which native ability entitles them. Approval cannot be given to the spending of so much time in acquiring factual knowledge which should be devoted to training the students to think rightly.

False Principles. The falsity of the principle that education should be made as expensive as possible, which has been accepted by an unsuspecting public, should be everywhere exposed; likewise, the wrong assumption that tax-paid education is the best education, and that big educational units give the best results.

Sacrifices of Catholics. No group in America is making such sacrifices for education as is the Catholic group. No institution in the world has so consistently encouraged sane education as has the Catholic Church, and no institution in the world will as unfailingly support the State in the discharge of its duty to see "that all citizens have the necessary knowledge of their civic and political duties, and a certain degree of physical, intellectual, and moral culture, which, considering the conditions of our times, is really necessary for the common good."[7]

Abnormal Conditions. We are living in abnormal times. We are dealing with abnormal conditions in many fields of endeavor. Hence it is to be expected that we must face abnormal conditions in the field of education.

The State has presumed to take on functions and to discharge duties which in nowise belong to it. From the organization of civil society, which is founded on the natural law, the State receives no commission to teach. When the State exercises the office of teacher, it does so in place of and by the authority of the parents. For, as Pope Pius XI reminds us,[8] parents are in a true sense the vicars of God in the education of their children. Their power is not absolute and despotic, but subject to the natural and divine law, and therefore subject also to the authority of the Church and to the vigilance and administrative care of the State, in view of the common good.

Tax-Paid Education. Despite the decision of the Supreme Court of the United States[9] that "the child is not the mere creature of the State; those who nurture him and direct his destiny have the right, coupled with the high duty, to recognize and prepare him for additional duties," we have a propaganda which assumes the right of the State

---

[7] Pius XI, Encyclical on "Christian Education."
[8] *Ibid.*
[9] Oregon Case.

to a monopoly of education, which takes it for granted that pupils educated in tax-paid schools become better citizens, and that justice demands that they be regarded as privileged children of the State, while those educated in Catholic or private schools are merely tolerated. There is even now an endless and subtle propaganda to strengthen these false ideas in the minds of the people, so that they may continue to bear patiently the necessary burden of excessive school taxation. Of this burden our Catholic people bear their share, while maintaining for conscience' sake and for the good of their country their own schools.

Unfairness to Catholic Schools. Propagandists and school lobbyists have not a sense of fairness to Catholic schools. There is no expression of gratitude on their part for the splendid work that our schools are doing. They are reluctant to give them due recognition, or even that measure of justice which in every other matter the American sense of fairness demands.

Real Purpose of Education. Our Catholic schools today see the folly of attempting to rival the extravagantly conducted tax-paid schools and of regarding them as norms of perfection. Our schools, built by the sacrifices of our poor people, maintained by the even greater sacrifices of our religious Sisterhoods and fostered by the untiring labors of our clergy and the watchful care of our bishops, have the obvious duty to keep ever before them the unchangeable elements of education and its real purpose — to fit men for life in eternity as well as in time; to teach men to think rightly and to live rightly; to instill sound principles in our youth, principles not only of civic righteousness, but of Catholic faith and morality; to educate groups, according to their capacity, so as to make them the best men and the best women of our country — and all this with a thorough training in the secular branches of knowledge.

Rejection of Moral Standards. The failure to instill moral standards during the formative years of childhood and adolescence, and the positive exclusion of moral teaching from the school curricula must always prove disastrous. Our difficulties today are largely efforts to remedy the evils inevitable in any system of education that permits chaotic thinking, pagan license, and uncurbed greed to take the place of that necessary discipline in thought and conduct that produces worthy and upright lives. Because educational needs have been misunderstood and because educational purposes have been so frequently perverted, not only the weak and the backward — the many who lack the qualities that make for business success, and these constitute a large proportion of our population — but the earnest and the industrious and the upright, are the victims of an economic system which is, in itself, the product of unsound thinking and moral disorder.

Undermining the Home. Further evil consequences of the divorce of religion from education and economics have been the rejection of the sacred character of the home, and of marriage as a divine institution. The destruction or serious impairment of home life has brought about a menacing decline in the birth rate and has helped to promote the godless, selfish, and inhuman propaganda of birth prevention. Economic conditions especially are advanced as a justification of what is in reality a criminal marital life. The new paganism of our day has begotten this propaganda. One of the most significant signs of the moral decadence which has taken place in our country is that men speaking from Christian pulpits and writing under the sanction of religion should approve and even actively promote this repellent doctrine. The restoring of the social order, for which we plead, will encourage an increase in the birth rate and will enable parents to make ample provision for the larger family. Malthus a century and a half ago predicted that in a hundred years the population of the world would so increase that the earth would not yield sufficient sustenance to support it. The hundred years have passed, and today our problem is not scarcity but overproduction of food! Our country, so rich in resources, can support comfortably many times its present population. As a matter of fact, the very sparseness of the population is one of the reasons for the severity and the long continuance of our present depression. It must be remembered that children, and especially large families, constitute in themselves great wealth. May our Catholic families courageously and with firm trust in God reject the modern paganism, and seek the priceless riches of large, happy, and blessed families!

The system of social service which has been built up in our country during the past quarter of a century is not without its grave dangers. Social workers, while earnest and well meaning, too often intrude into the sacred sanctuary of conscience and weaken home influence. Some, imbued with an absolutely false and pagan philosophy of life, having no vision beyond the material, do not hesitate to engage in a propaganda that is abhorrent to the Catholic conscience. They assume responsibilities which belong only to parents and to guardians of children. Whatever weakens family ties and lessens the influence of the home is a matter of grave concern to both State and Church.

Economic Nationalism. As the means of communication and transportation become more perfect day by day, the economic interdependence of nations becomes more apparent and presents increasingly difficult international problems. The entire human race has the right of access on reasonable terms to the resources, markets, and settlements of the whole earth. It is entirely reasonable that a government should rigorously exclude all dangerous and unworthy candidates for citizenship, and even temporary visitors of such a character. Economic nationalism may have the gravest consequences, and, if carried to extremes, may be profoundly immoral. International co-operation in debt agreements, markets for finished goods, access to raw materials, and movement of population on a reasonable basis are necessary. Even our country, with its wealth of natural resources and its highly developed industrial technique, cannot stand alone. The oneness and solidarity of mankind make economic isolation impossible. That truth should lead our nation to make such agreements as are necessary for the immediate and future welfare of her own people and for the happiness of mankind. Wars are born of international injustice, isolation, and rivalry. International life, relations, and responsibilities should be recognized and entered into according to the principles of social justice and social charity.

The Farm Problem. For long years the pivotal importance of restoring the purchasing power of those immediately engaged in agriculture, and of developing the farm as the source of the nation's supply of food and clothing has not been recognized. We have failed to acknowledge that six million farms have provided the widest diffusion of privately owned productive property in the United States, as well as the widest diffusion of self-employed families, in contrast to the regimented employment of men in factories and in urban industries generally. Because of our unsound agricultural policy there has been a movement of our rural population to the great industrial centers that is revolutionary in character; there has been serious interference with the economic independence and self-employment of our people, and hundreds of thousands of farm families have been driven from the position of owners and independent tillers of the soil to that of tenants and day laborers on industrialized farms. As a consequence, there has been a serious disturbance of the balance of population between our cities and our rural districts. While during the depression there has been a movement back to the land, there is no assurance of its permanency.

Perhaps the great majority of those living in our cities have not realized that the farm problem is a serious integral part of the national problem; that there can be no permanent restoration of industry on a national scale until the purchasing power of more than thirty million Americans living on the land is materially increased; that the concentration of wealth in the hands of the few has all but crushed agriculture, and has so drained the farm that the farmer finds it increasingly difficult to wrest a decent living from the land; that wheat has been selling at the lowest price in three hundred years; that the wheels of industry in our cities are clogged in no small measure because agriculture lies prostrate.

These are among the problems to which the President and the Congress are now devoting their energy and attention. Much may be accomplished by legislation; but nothing that Congress or the President can do will offer a final solution unless it be accompanied by a revival among the people at large of a firm resolve that any solution, whatever its character, must be an expression of the Christian conception of justice and fair dealing. Business, whether big or little, banking, whether national or international, capital in its relations with labor, and in its relations with capital, must all be made to feel that any departure from the Christian code of morals will bring on those who are guilty universal censure and reprobation.

Unemployment. Unemployment has been our greatest problem in the economic crisis. It has taken from the willing worker the means of earning a livelihood, deprived him of his purchasing power, and made him an object of charity.

In a country so marvelously blessed as ours no man should find it impossible to exercise the right given him by nature to earn his bread in the sweat of his brow. In no part of the globe has nature been more lavish in providing all that men need for their comfort, their well-being, and their prosperity. Rich and fertile soil, varied climatic conditions, mineral resources in abundance, have given opportunity to a people industrious and inventive to provide better and higher standards of living for themselves and their families. The spirit of self-reliance and independence which is almost universal among the people of our country found expression, whenever possible, in an effort to make provision against the uncertainties of illness and old age. The universality of savings banks and building and loan societies gives abundant evidence of the general spirit of thrift and self-helpfulness and of a desire for economic independence.

But, on the other hand, and in spite of these tendencies and efforts among the great mass of the people, the wealth of the nation gradually flowed into the hands of the few. Capitalists and industrialists, driven by greed, monopolized the sources of wealth and gained control of the products and profits made possible by the progress of technological science, to their own enrichment and to the impoverishment and enslavement of the masses. These few, in order to increase their riches and power, have made the machine a curse rather than the blessing it should be, to lighten the toil and shorten the hours of the worker. Being content with a minimum of profit to ensure employment for all and to permit all to share the comforts produced by the machine is far from the thought of these financial magnates, who have been made by our modern economic system, as Pope Pius XI says, "hard, cruel and relentless in a ghastly measure."[10]

His Holiness lays down the principle that in the restoration of the economic world capital should be allowed a reasonable interest only on the amount invested. "In (the) future a just share only of the fruits of production (should) be permitted to accumulate in the hands of the wealthy."[11] If at this moment that principle were accepted by the small group of capitalists and industrialists, perhaps not even a hundred men, who control the financial destinies of our country, if they were to agree to co-operate with the government and with the masses whom they have so wronged, and to have it written into our legislation that capital in the future shall receive a fair return on its investments, and nothing more, it would go far toward setting in motion the wheels of industry and solving the problem of unemployment.

Unemployment and Old Age Pensions. Closely connected with this question are the problems of unemployment insurance and old age pensions. In principle, we should in times of prosperity provide for days of adversity. This is applicable to industry, to the individual, to the family, to the state, and to the nation. This form of insurance should be provided by the employer, the employee, and the government. But in making such provision, the movement of industry and the consequent discharge of workers or their transfer from place to place, with all the loss and hardship that this implies, should be taken into account.

This, however, is a duty belonging to normal times. Sunk in the depths of depression as our people have been for nearly four years, this is not the time to make actual provision for old-age and unemployment pensions. It would be unjust to attempt to force such measures by legislation. Our first concern is to terminate the existing depression. Employment is our first consideration, not insurance against unem-

---

[10] *Quadragesimo Anno.*
[11] *Ibid.*

ployment or old age. Employment can be increased, first, by making drastic cuts in the overhead expenses of industry, by the elimination of bonuses and unreasonably high salaries of officials, by the reduction of excessive taxation, which is a hindrance to the resumption of business; and, second, by increasing the wages of workers, thereby putting money in circulation and causing a demand for the normal products of industry. There is a vicious circle. On the one hand, the employer, especially the small producer, cannot afford to pay a just family wage, considering that he is in competition with those who have no conscience and who do not hesitate to make use of the most inhuman methods in conducting business; and, on the other hand, the reduced scale of wages paid to the ordinary worker does not allow him to purchase the bare necessaries of life, to say nothing of creating a normal demand for the products of industry. We wish to lay special emphasis here on the necessity of higher, that is to say, just wages for the average worker, not only to restore prosperity, but principally because of the moral question involved.

PART TWO

Remedies

Restore Christ. By turning away from Christ, and by rejecting the principles of life and conduct He laid down, human society and human governments necessarily lost sight of the dignity and the rights of man, which, because they were once realized in Christian States, still remain an ideal and a hope even in places where Christianity is merely a tradition. The extent of the denial of Christ in our own country is shocking to the Christian sense. There can be no hope for the restoration of human society without restoring Christ, without striving to accord to man the dignity that He, as God, conferred on every human being. This must be the starting point.

The Authority of Christ. The authority of Christ must be acknowledged. Truly God and truly Man, He is the supreme Ruler of the world, of our country, of our states, cities, and communities. Tribute is due Him not only by individuals and groups, but officially by governments and by the Church. This authority of Christ is from without; it is not within each individual. Moral upheavals, chaos, and ruin have come upon the Christian world because individuals, differing on a thousand points, first presumed to make Christ responsible for their judgments, which made Him a contradiction and an absurdity, then, logically, denied His divinity and rejected His authority.

Authority Rejected. A lamentable sequel to the rejection of the authority of Christ is that authority as a moral force, binding the conscience of men before God and the world, is ignored practically everywhere except in the Catholic Church. Parental authority, as a consequence, carries with it little if any weight. The authority of the State as having its source in God, through the natural law, is derided as a medieval invention. Catholics are often treated with pity because their Church maintains steadfastly the principle of authority; because that Church by a moral force still binds consciences in the court of man and in the court of God; because that Church still faithfully and untiringly carries out the commission given by Christ: "All power is given to me in heaven and in earth. Going, therefore, teach ye all nations . . . teaching them to observe all things whatsoever I have commanded you; and behold, I am with you all days, even to the consummation of the world."[12]

Effects. An unhappy result of the rejection of the principle of authority is that individuals seek to be a law unto themselves. Caprice and emotion determine their judgment of right and wrong. What they like is right; what they dislike is wrong. They presume to act on the anarchistic principle that everyone has the right, as is said, "to lead his own life." They do not regard it as an obligation to inquire: Did the divine Christ determine anything in this matter, or has any delegated authority of Christ a right to determine what should be done or left undone? The authority of the State is accepted as a police power, not as one imposing a moral obligation.

When we consider that for many decades this sad condition has been growing more general in our country, need we wonder that capitalists, industrialists, and business and professional men are not governed by the moral law, and, fearing only the police power of the State, will attempt anything clandestinely that will advance their private interests, provided they are personally secure from exposure or punishment?

Restore Authority. We are demanding a new order, and we are ready to make many changes in the hope of bettering our economic and financial conditions; but we must remember that no legislation can be enacted that will not be circumvented, and no new order will long endure, unless there be a moral force binding our citizens. That moral force must have its source in Christ. The recognition of the authority of Christ is essential for the restoration not only of the moral but also of the economic order.

---

[12] Matt. 28:18–20.

Restore International Confidence. The fear and mistrust of nations should be abolished. International Conferences, the breaking down of tariff barriers, legislation, inflation of credit and currency, may help; but only Christian charity will destroy the suspicion, fear, and mistrust of nations. As the individual life should be governed by charity, which means love of God and neighbor, so should groups and the nations be governed by Christian charity.

Moral Force of Right. The real guarantee of peace among nations is love and forbearance, based on the Christian principle of the brotherhood of man. Charity will labor always for peace; it will seek to settle all matters in dispute between nations by arbitration; it will strive to have all the nations work as members of a family, not as enemies trying to ensnare one another. Charity will make it clear that as justice demands self-defense for the individual, so it also insists that national defense is lawful for national preservation against the aggressor, and also for the restoration of order within its own confines. Charity will condemn as fiendish criminals all those who promote strife between nations in order to acquire individual or national riches. Charity will labor that justice be not violated by exhausting the treasury of a nation and imposing an excessive tax burden upon a people for the building of armaments, which always make war more likely. Charity will, in the thought of Benedict XV, make the moral force of right take the place of the material force of arms, and "set up in the place of armies a court of arbitration."[13]

World Justice, Charity, and Order. Pope Pius XI, in condemning the unbridled race for supremacy in armaments, pleads with the bishops of the world to "employ every means at your disposal, through preaching and through the press, to enlighten men's minds and to incline their hearts to the requirements of right reason, and even more to the law of Christ."[14] We desire world justice, world charity, and world order; but we must realize that the selfishness, rivalry, suspicion, intrigue, and hatred of nations are working against these three great aims. It is our duty to pray for peace and to work for peace, and to pray and to labor that our powerful country may lead all the nations of the world to see the folly of armaments, as they are being augmented by the nations today.

Study. Our priests and selected groups of the laity, members of the professions, employers, and leaders of trade and labor unions

---

[13] Letter to the heads of States engaged in war, August 1, 1917.
[14] Apostolic Letter, *Nova Impendet.*

should study most carefully the plan for the restoration of the social order outlined by our Holy Father, whose voice is the voice of the living representative of Christ upon earth. With providential foresight and more than worldly wisdom he has definitely pointed out the way to the true Christian social order.

Study Groups. Our Catholic economists, sociologists, and moralists have dealt with many of the questions which are of especial interest today. Their work, which is deserving of high commendation, should be made to reach a wider circle of readers. The Catholic press and Catholic societies should look on the dissemination of sound social and economic teaching as a primary and essential part of the apostolate.

Many subjects mentioned in our statement are in need of fuller and more detailed discussion, and these discussions should be made available to wider circles of readers through periodicals and pamphlets. There are other questions which, though treated by Catholic writers, should be restated, owing to their importance today. Such questions are: international peace; world court of arbitration; disarmament; war debts; remission of war debts; the morality of holding companies; injustices of corporations; absentee control; the inflation of stock; dishonest stock promotion; overcapitalization; the true and fictitious value of securities; the immoral transactions of the stock market; deceptive advertising; security of bank deposits; fair interest rates; credit unions; consumers' co-operatives; labor unions; the sound administration of building and loan associations; unjust foreclosures; honest banking; bankruptcy; gambling; last wills and testaments and unjust will contests; unjust chattel mortgages; bribery; price fixing; the minimum wage; the fair price; farmers' marketing co-operatives; the nature and requirements of an organized economic order; distribution of ownership; the moral implications of the new interdependence of economic life; monopolies. These and many other questions receiving public attention can advantageously be studied by leagues, societies, and groups, according to their capacity, but naturally the emphasis will be placed on the moral aspect, which is the supreme concern of the Church. The position of the Church will have an irresistible appeal if stated in simple, forceful language and in an attractive manner. Her concern is the salvation of souls. Her duty is to speak, in season and out of season, where there is a moral question at stake.

Public Opinion. It is our duty as Catholic citizens to share with others the priceless riches of the supernatural treasury of which the Church has been the custodian during all the Christian centuries.

True love of neighbor should impel us to influence public opinion. Many may not accept the whole position of the Catholic Church, but thinking and informed men and women cannot fail to be impressed with her teaching on all questions affecting the commonweal, and especially those engaging the attention of the public mind today.

Defense Against Hostile Legislation. In our study and in our endeavor to form public opinion, we must keep ever in mind what Leo XIII and Pius XI have taught — that the social question is not merely an economic one, but that it is, first of all, a moral and religious question. Governments may not realize that they are failing to promote their own best interests when they fail to regard moral and religious truth, the spiritual and temporal welfare of man, the moral value, therefore, of man and the fullness of his life as a social being, as the pre-eminent ends they should serve. What a sad spectacle to the world that the governments of Mexico, Spain, and Russia should not only reject moral forces, but should become hard and cruel tyrants, persecuting religion. Conditions in these countries and the suffering of our brothers in the Faith are deserving of our serious study. Our daily prayers should be offered that the hand of the persecutor may be stayed.

"No man," wrote Leo XIII, "may outrage with impunity that human dignity which God Himself treats with reverence. . . . Nay more; a man has here no power over himself. To consent to any treatment which is calculated to defeat the end and purpose of his being is beyond his right; he cannot give up his soul to servitude; for it is not man's own rights which are here in question, but the rights of God, most sacred and inviolable."[15] Governments must safeguard these rights and all groups must respect them. All legislation must be framed according to them. Economics, industrialism, taxation, all use of things of the world must be regulated by them.

Our Duty of Voting. In our form of government the obligation of bringing about a reform of the social order rests upon citizens, who by their votes give a mandate to legislators and executives. This makes evident a civic duty, and for us Catholics it is also a religious one governed by the virtue of piety; that is, a certain filial piety toward our country which impels us to promote the reform of the social order by voting for competent and conscientious men of high moral principles.

Battle for Justice. A few individuals, or even several well-meaning

---

[15] *Rerum Novarum.*

corporate entities, owing to unrestrained competition and the rejection of moral principles by their competitors, permitting the "survival of those only who are strongest, which often means those who fight most relentlessly, who pay least heed to the dictates of conscience,"[16] cannot of themselves change a system that is inherently wrong. In a word, because these comparatively few men of conscience cannot do the immoral things and resort to the base and inhuman methods which their competitors in the economic world, without any moral sense, consider merely good modern business, they are helpless of themselves to bring about a reform. They need the militant support of all right-thinking and moral men to fight and to win the battle for justice.

It is, as Pius XI reminds us, "the primary duty of the State and of all good citizens to abolish conflict between classes with divergent interests, and thus foster and promote harmony among the various ranks of society. . . . Just as the unity of human society cannot be built upon class warfare, so the proper ordering of economic affairs cannot be left to free competition alone."[17]

All, therefore, who are governed by justice must continue to do the most they can to influence public opinion in order to secure a general recognition of the rights of man. Our Catholic scholars should do everything possible to promote a serious study of this question.

Rights of Workingman. The workingman is entitled to a family wage, which must be an amount sufficient not only to support husband, wife, and children in frugal and decent comfort, but to provide against sickness, unemployment, infirmity, and old age. His right to organize must not be interfered with. His right to an equitable share in the profits, as a wage earner, must receive due consideration. His right to bequeath and to inherit, and his right to employment under normal moral conditions, should be assured.

Social justice, working in behalf of the common good, requires that the masses not possessing property rise to a degree of ownership. The chasm between owners — the relatively few — and nonowners — the vast majority — must be bridged by a distribution of ownership through thrift and a real sharing of profits, not merely a profit sharing in name. Profit sharing through stock ownership, or through partnership contracts, in our large corporations has in too many instances proved either disastrous or of little value to employees laboring under the disadvantage of being minority stockholders. Indeed, as Pius XI

---

[16] *Quadragesimo Anno.*
[17] *Ibid.*

says,[18] the time seems to have come when the wage contract should itself be somewhat modified by a contract of partnership. This, however, should be a measure of true partnership.

We are reminded here by Pius XI of two important truths. Speaking of St. Paul's teaching,[19] "if any man will not work, neither let him eat," His Holiness says, first, "In no sense does he teach that labor is the sole title which gives a right to a living or to profits,"[20] and, second, that an equitable share of the profits of industry should be given to both capital and labor. Labor and trades unions offer one means of obtaining justice in wages and salaries. The normal working of such organizations, whether singly or as a federation of unions, should be to promote the general welfare and to insure for all workers, whether skilled or unskilled, maximum employment, adequate remuneration, the protection of their rights as men and as citizens, and security against accident and indigence.

Capital and Labor Friends. Our study should make us grasp fully the principle, clearly stated in the *Quadragesimo Anno,* that as labor should not seize, if it were in a position to do so, all the profits, neither should capital. Capital and labor need each other. They should be friends. They should, as brothers, sit down together at the council table. Unlimited, reckless, immoral competition and economic dictatorship will continue until this is done. Capital and labor should be convinced that greed is a vice, and that a just division of profits can and should be a virtue. Capital and labor should work for the common welfare and for their mutual interest should encourage all workers to organize. Unions, embracing all groups of workers, should be governed by good sense. They should endeavor to distribute opportunity to the workers of every class. They should always seek competent and disinterested advisers, that their organizations may ever be characterized by sanity. The individual or personal and social aspect of labor should be well understood. There should be mutual harmony and mutual support. "Unless, above all, brains, capital, and labor combine together for common effort, man's toil cannot produce due fruit."[21]

Large Corporations and Moral Principles. We must recognize that the big corporation has its place, and that, as Pius XI says, "much that was formerly done by small bodies can nowadays be accomplished

---

[18] *Ibid.*
[19] 2 Thess. 3:10.
[20] *Quadragesimo Anno.*
[21] *Ibid.*

only by large corporations."[22] They need, however, to reform; they
need the fullest publicity given in a language that the ordinary man
can understand. The study of our Catholic scholars should put forth
concrete plans that will insist upon the rigorous application of moral
principles to big corporations. These plans of reform should place
limitations on them, so that the rights of smaller units and bodies
will be fully protected. Such small units have not only a right to exist
but are necessary. They should not be crushed by supercorporations
and mergers that fancy it is their right to absorb them. The plans
formulated by our scholars should provide, as Pope Pius XI suggests,
a graded hierarchical order between various subsidiary organizations.
While the big corporations serve a useful purpose, their intolerable
abuses, especially their clandestine manipulation of trust funds and
earned surplus, must cease if we are to restore the social and economic
order. Smaller units of business and production should be encouraged
all over the country. Local communities should take a pride in them.
The law should protect them, and the courts should safeguard them.

Today, as in the past, there is a tendency to place too much reliance
on government to accomplish our economic salvation. This trend arises
from the very individualism that was long dominant. Greed destroyed
economic organization and prevented government from protecting
justice and promoting the common good. Greed enslaved governments.
Now that the whirlwind is being reaped, peoples are relying almost
solely on government to bring a measure of justice and order out of
chaos. One of the greatest dangers facing us is a blind reaction from
our former individualism to a regime of State socialism or State
capitalism.

Government Co-operation. Government in the fulfillment of its
functions should assist in the organization of the various economic
groups. These organized groups, without injustice to themselves, but
seeking always the common good, can be so constituted as to fulfill
properly their own function of production and the distribution of their
services. Such an organization of the various economic groups along
the lines of their separate industries and fields of endeavor should
embrace representatives of every element in the economic group.
Imbued with justice, with love for the common good, and with social
charity, such an organized economic life can free the State from the
danger it faces of become an all-engrossing and all-enveloping power.
As Pope Pius XI says: "The aim of social legislation must be the re-

---

[22] *Ibid.*

establishment of vocational groups. . . . The State should leave to these smaller groups the settlement of business of minor importance. It will thus carry out with greater freedom, power, and success the tasks belonging to it, because it alone can effectively accomplish these, directing, watching, stimulating, and restraining as circumstances suggest or necessity demands."[23] But government, to quote again, should not "arrogate to itself functions which can be performed efficiently by smaller and lower bodies" — bodies that would comprise the organized and autonomous economic life.

Tax Reform. Our Catholic scholars, economists, and moralists should study our crushing burden of taxation, which is, in itself, an indictment of government and of our economic system. Legislators have a serious responsibility whenever they impose taxes. The general welfare of the people should always be kept in mind in performing this duty. To impose taxes unjustly or in a reckless manner or in the interest of special groups or according to the immoral practice of trading votes, too common among legislators, must be regarded as a violation of the oath of office and the betrayal of a sacred trust. Taxation is unjust that favors the strong rather than the weak, the rich rather than the poor. Legislators and men in political life who in imposing taxes sacrifice the general welfare of the people in order to advance their own interests and to continue in office deserve the severest censure.

Fearless Condemnation Necessary. Excessive taxation has been a serious hindrance to the revival of business. Patriotic citizens should fearlessly condemn the extravagant expenditure of the people's money by government agencies and bureaucracies. In recent years the cost of government has mounted to staggering proportions, even though the average income of our citizens has been greatly reduced or practically wiped out. This tremendous increase in government expenditures has not brought any corresponding gain to our people.

Interest in Public Expenditures. In our country, where the responsibility of selecting honest and competent officials and of forming opinion devolves upon the citizens, it is all the more important that thoughtful and informed men become tax-conscious, that they realize that there will be a day of accounting for endless bond issues, and that they exercise their influence to the utmost to arouse and to sustain in the people at large an intelligent interest in public expenditures.

---

[23] *Ibid.*

Intelligible Statement of Tax Methods.   In the simplest language possible taxation, which ultimately is passed on in great measure to the laboring and trades classes, should be explained. to the people. Citizens should be interested in knowing how their money is being spent. They should be informed to what an extent taxation increases the price of the very necessaries of life. Studies on this vital subject should be put out in the most popular form. Public opinion should continue to demand that expenditures by the government for non-essentials be eliminated; that our educational system be simplified; that bureaucracies be limited; that the injustice of favoring special groups at public expense should cease; also, that a clear and simple statement of the cost of government be made available to all our citizens.

We venture to speak on this subject, which may seem to transgress our province, because of the grave injustice that is done to the ordinary taxpayer, the workingman, those who have put most of the earnings of a lifetime into modest homes, and to the farmers who have suffered from the iniquities of officials imposing unnecessary taxes.

Catholic Action.   Our Holy Father from the beginning of his pontificate has insisted on the necessity of Catholic Action, which maintains and develops the Christian life and admits the faithful to a participation in the labors of the hierarchy. Our bishops have frequently laid stress on the work that can be accomplished by an earnest lay apostolate.

The change of thought, of temper, and the militant spirit manifested against the very basic things for which Christianity stands, call for Catholic lay leaders in great numbers. They must be informed, thoroughly Catholic-minded, fearless, and capable of stating simply and clearly the position of the Church on every vital question of today which has a moral aspect.

Given such leaders, Catholic Action cannot but profoundly influence public opinion. It must be clearly understood, however, that Catholic Action is not to be identified with political action. Each has its own domain.

The Catholic Church is not in politics. She is not allied with any political party. Catholic Action must neither become a political party nor an agency of any political party. Catholic Action moves in the sphere of the religious, the moral, and in the borderline zones where the interests of religion are directly or indirectly at stake, and where moral principles are to be defended.

Catholic Action, far from discouraging individuals from participa-

tion in civic and governmental affairs, rather impresses upon them
their duty to assume their full responsibility as citizens in the advancement of the commonweal. They must ever contribute what they alone
can contribute, the fearless declaration of the well-defined and unchangeable principles of morality which govern human conduct and
society. They must ever combat the false principle that morality is
something relative or conventional, and that public conscience, which
may change its judgment according to the circumstances of the times,
makes an act ethical or unethical.

The National Council of Catholic Men and the National Council of
Catholic Women, so often commended by the bishops at their annual
meetings, have, against great odds, done much for Church and country.
They deserve fuller recognition and the generous support of Catholics
of all classes. The field of Catholic Action invites them to a wider
participation in the work of the hierarchy, under the direction of the
Ordinary of each diocese.

Our Schools of Higher Learning. There is greater need of
Catholic education in our country than ever before. Heroic sacrifices
have been made during the past years, and are still being made, that
our children may receive religious training, that parental rights may
be guarded, and that freedom of education may be preserved. But our
schools are worth every sacrifice that has been made.

Dioceses conducting high schools and colleges, as well as religious
communities, have borne a crushing financial burden. All who have
the welfare of the Church at heart, and who are anxious to promote
Catholic leadership, should encourage and support Catholic institutions
of higher learning for both men and women. They should familiarize
themselves with the actual conditions of these institutions in their
locality. The Catholic University of America, under the patronage of
the bishops of the United States, was founded and has been maintained to teach the Sacred Sciences; to instill Catholic Philosophy,
and to give us that true philosophy of life which no secular institution
can possibly give; to turn out Catholic scholars whose mentality under
every test will be genuinely Christian; to conduct research work in its
various schools and departments, always under the inspiration of
Catholic teaching. Such a mission entrusted to the hierarchy, clergy,
and people of our country by the Holy See is a glorious one and should
be enthusiastically promoted by all.

There is much more that our colleges and universities could do if
they had greater resources. Because unbelief and skepticism are daily
becoming more widespread it becomes all the more necessary to

strengthen our courses in religion, and to have in every high school, college, and university well-trained priests who will make religion the most attractive of all the subjects taught. We need everywhere specially prepared apologists, not only among the clergy but among our laymen, who will become more and more articulate, and who because of their scholarship will be certain to secure a hearing. These scholarly spokesmen for the Church will carry on their apostolate governed entirely by supernatural motives, ever keeping in mind the eternal destiny of souls.

The Catholic Press. The Catholic press during the years of depression has given proof of its many virtues. Its editors have borne patiently and cheerfully financial anxiety and embarrassment. Out of love for the Church and in the hope of showing in this dark hour the sanity of the Catholic position and the value of Catholic principles, they have willingly made heroic sacrifices.

With the beginning of better economic conditions it is to be hoped that a Catholic paper will find its way to every Catholic home and be read by every member of the family. Catholic reading is necessary for Catholic life. The average Catholic is brought in daily contact with much that is calculated to pervert Catholic life and to weaken, or even destroy, Catholic principles. The Catholic press and Catholic publications will help to counteract the dangerous influences to which our people are exposed, owing to the atmosphere of worldliness, irreligion, and indifferentism by which they are surrounded.

Back to the Land. The unemployment and destitution of today are the consequence of a revolution in agriculture and industry, which commenced a century and a half ago, when machine power took the place of man power. The machine produced the factory and the factory the great industrial cities. These cities are now overcrowded, and, because of the increasing perfection in technological methods, they are becoming less and less capable of supporting their teeming populations. In addition, the city crushed men's souls as well as their bodies. It deprived them of the material comforts and the necessaries of life, and it made them an easy prey for radicals, who set before them the vision of a new order and a new world, replete with material happiness and advantages. This new order could be attained only through the adoption of a materialistic philosophy in which there was no place for God or religion.

One hope for relief in the universal misery of the present lies in the reversal of the policy which produced the factory and the factory system. This reversal without depriving men of the benefits of industrial progress, would reinstate them as independent home owners in rural communities. Such a change in the living conditions of millions of people would be a revolution, but some radical adjustment in restoring the balance between rural and urban population is imperative if our country is to survive and if our civilization is not to disappear.

A necessary preliminary or condition to such a comprehensive change in the living conditions of millions of people would be a revision of the ideas and standards which make country life appear less desirable than city life. This must be accomplished through religion. The Catholic Church has demonstrated, times without number, that it can place rural civilization on an attractive and permanent basis. In rural Catholic communities the people found the source and center of their activities in their parish church, and, under the guidance of their pastors, and through the tender ministrations of the religious orders of men and women, they were immune to the soul-destroying teachings of radicals, atheists, socialists, and communists. The Reconstruction of Rural Civilization is not merely a means to protect millions against the poverty, the excitement and the corruption of cities, not merely an escape from the grinding economic inequalities imposed by the machine age, it is an imperative duty to see that our people shall have homes if the moral and spiritual values of life are to be conserved and if the race is to be saved from extinction.

Already many millions of people have felt the logic of the situation and have returned to the land, not as refugees but as pioneers of a new and healthier civilization. This movement should be fostered and encouraged. Its possibilities are illimitable. If carried to a successful issue it would work a transformation in our entire civilization, but it is a movement that demands careful planning and sustained effort. It would require the best thought and the concerted labor of federal and state agencies, the good will of industrial leaders, and the co-operation of the Church. It is one scheme that will indubitably make a rich return for whatever outlay of effort or money it may entail in the happiness and security it will bestow on millions who are now homeless and destitute.

To speak of its benefits to religion is unnecessary. The very economic forces surrounding the farmer protect the unity of marriage and foster its permanence against birth control and divorce. Crowded industrial centers, on the contrary, especially in the congested districts of our large cities, promote the idea of restricted families and an unwholesome moral life in the divine institution of the home. As Pope Pius XI says, "the present economic régime, and above all the disgraceful housing conditions, prove obstacles to the family tie and family life."[24]

Spirit of the Gospel. Grave as are the problems of the present, and dark as the economic outlook may now appear, there is no reason why Catholics should not face the future with confidence and courage. We are the bearers of a great tradition, the tradition of religious, moral, and spiritual discipline, which commenced with the preaching of the Gospel and which gave to Europe and the world a new and more perfect culture and civilization. That culture did not develop as a result of legislative enactments or social and political upheavals, but because men and women took into their souls the spirit of the Gospel and because in their lives they gave a practical exemplification of the teachings of Christ. The greatest revolution in the institutional life of humanity was that which was wrought when those who professed to follow Christ lived the life of earnest and devout Christians. It was because those followers of Christ made faith the paramount influence in life and conduct, and Christian charity the source and goal of all effort that autocracy was dethroned and that mankind came to enjoy the benefits of freedom of conscience and of civil and political liberty, and it was because those who believed that all men without distinction of Jew or Greek, bond or free, are all one in Christ,[25] that the curse of chattel slavery vanished from the world.

The social implications of the teaching of Christ have made and are now making an irresistible appeal to the inarticulate but powerful masses of the disinherited. The institutions of society are no longer looked on as means to sustain the arrogance, the luxury and pride of a favored few. Change can be effected as it has been effected by the bomb, the rifle, and the torch, but such change means increased suffering and greater misery; or it can be brought about, without detriment to our heritage of Christianity and civilization, if those who believe in Christ enter with Christ on the road of humility and renunciation. The real authors of violent and bloody revolution in our times are not the radicals and communists, but the callous and autocratic possessors of wealth and power who use their position and their riches to oppress their fellows. It is the duty of Catholics to be mindful of their obligations, as bearers of the great Christian tradition, to be courageous in rebuking tyranny, luxury, and sordid egotism, and above all to be exemplary in their effort to make their deeds and lives reflect the faith they profess.

---

[24] *Ibid.*
[25] Gal. 3:28.

Prayer. We have insisted that Christ be given His rightful place in the nation and in the hearts of individuals. This must be done through prayer. Our hearts and minds must be lifted up to God to acknowledge His sovereignty over the universe, His divine plan for all His creatures, the eternal destiny of man and his dependence upon Divine Providence. The mystery of God's government of men and of nations must be proclaimed. We must pour forth our hearts in humble supplication for our personal needs, for the needs of the Church, and for the needs of our country, our state, and our community.

It was heartening to the people of our country, and an example to the world, that our President on the morning of his inauguration bowed down in humble prayer, begging God's blessing on his administration, asking Divine Providence to protect every individual of the nation, and to grant him guidance during the years of his tremendous responsibility. The first bishop of the United States, Archbishop Carroll of Baltimore, by writing his beautiful prayer for our civil rulers, has given us an example that should still inspire us. The virtue of patriotism should make us pray daily for our country and for all who govern it.

Jubilee Year. During the present Jubilee Year declared by our Holy Father we are observing the nineteen hundredth anniversary of the death of the divine Saviour of the world. It is a year of prayer and a year of penitential practices. The Lord Christ is anxious to save all. We need but to turn to Him in earnest, humble prayer, with the firm purpose of carrying out His injunctions. In the words of Pope Pius XI,[26] "Let us stimulate ourselves to prayer, to penitence for the sins committed by us, having in mind in our prayers and acts of expiation not only our eternal salvation, but also that of all mankind, led astray by so many errors, torn by so many discords and so much hostility, laboring under so many miseries, and fearful of so many dangers. Oh, may the Most Merciful Lord bring it about that the Holy Year . . . will bring peace to souls, to the Church that liberty everywhere due her, to all peoples concord and true prosperity."

During the Jubilee Year our Holy Father urges as many of his children as can throughout the world to go to Rome to gain the Jubilee indulgence. Under normal circumstances the number of pilgrims would have been extraordinary. Notwithstanding the present adverse conditions, many of the faithful will at the cost of real sacrifice visit the

---

[26] Promulgation of the Extraordinary Holy Year for the Nineteenth Century of the Redemption of Mankind.

Eternal City to kneel at the feet of the Common Father of Christendom. May the Jubilee year bring great blessings to America!

May we ever watch and pray that Christ abide in us and we in Him. May the Church ever prosper, and may our country in returning to prosperity realize that the Lord Christ is its greatest need!

Given at Washington, in conference, on the twenty-sixth day of April, 1933.

✝ Edward J. Hanna, *Chairman,*
Archbishop of San Francisco

✝ John T. McNicholas,
Archbishop of Cincinnati

✝ John G. Murray, *Treasurer,*
Archbishop of St. Paul

✝ Joseph Schrembs,
Bishop of Cleveland

✝ Hugh C. Boyle,
Bishop of Pittsburgh

✝ John F. Noll, *Secretary,*
Bishop of Fort Wayne

✝ Thomas F. Lillis, *Vice-Chairman,*
Bishop of Kansas City

61. STATEMENT OF THE ADMINISTRATIVE COMMITTEE, N.C.W.C., ON THE

DEGRADATION OF THE FAMILY DEMORALIZATION OF YOUTH AND THE CORRUPTION OF BUSINESS*

November 15, 1933

This statement was issued by the N.C.W.C. Administrative Committee on the occasion of the general meeting of the archbishops and bishops of the United States at the Catholic University of America, Washington, D. C., November 15 and 16, 1933. In this statement the bishops point out the root causes of the collapse of our financial and economic structure and attack those influences that have degraded the family, demoralized youth, and corrupted business.

---

* *Catholic Action,* December, 1933, pp. 3, 4, and 5; cf. also No. 67.

It would be folly to deny or to attempt to minimize the gravity of the situation with which the people of the United States are now confronted, and it would be craven to entertain for a moment the thought that this situation is beyond cure or that it calls for remedies so drastic as communism or a dictatorship. The responsibility for the situation, such as it is, lies at the door of the people at large and the cure is in their hands.

The collapse of the financial and economic structure a few years ago, which spread destruction and disaster everywhere, was not the result of a single, sudden catastrophe. It had its roots in forces which had been corroding and undermining the foundations of law, justice, and morality for years. When the crash came it spread universal havoc. Every institution of our civilization, every home, every individual was made to feel the effects of its destructive violence. All the moral activities of society were interrupted; business was paralyzed; transportation systems were crippled; agriculture was ruined; millions were thrown out of employment; and the deaths of thousands were averted only through the combined efforts of public and private relief agencies.

No good end can be served by enumerating again the long list of evils, social and political and economic, which are now pressing on the community at large, and which are making their presence felt by the increasing volume of demand, which goes up day by day, that they be removed. In their distress the people are turning to their governments, municipal, state, and federal, begging that an end be put to this period of horror, uncertainty, and suffering. Many of the present evils could, no doubt, have been averted by wise legislation or through prompt governmental intervention, but the people, themselves, are responsible for the kind of government they got. It was the fault of the voters that municipal government was so often synonymous with fraud, graft, corruption, misappropriation of public funds, and the unholy alliance between criminals and the police: that state governments, through extravagance, piled up impossible tax burdens: and that the federal congress squandered public money in such a fashion as to make a balanced budget an impossibility.

If government was lax, business was shot through with a spirit of greed that led to the perpetration of frauds on the public, the full heinousness of which is slowly coming to light through the investigations of the Senate Committee on Finance. The publication of the crooked and dishonest practices of stockbrokers and bankers to fleece the public as revealed in this investigation has done as much to destroy respect for the integrity of commercial institutions and to fan the flames of discontent as the preaching of radicals and communists.

The sacred character of the family has not escaped the general deterioration and corruption. The divorce courts have crowded calendars, and some communities have resorted to the degrading device of adding to their revenues by turning their halls of justice into divorce mills. Theaters and amusement places have been converted into centers for the exhibition of lewd and indecent performances, and for the presentation of plays and moving pictures that are constant stimulants to prodigality and vice. The printing presses have poured forth a never ending stream of obscene books and pictures that are a menace to the morals and the characters of the youth of the land.

Nothing can be gained by elaborating this catalogue of the vices that afflict our civilization. Their net result can be seen in the degradation and the poverty of masses of our people. Dishonesty in financial circles, crookedness in business, corruption in politics, perversion or maladministration of justice, murder, suicide, robbery, racketeering, kidnaping and violence are merely lurid manifestations of the general demoralization which has doomed millions to unemployment, famine, suffering, and despair. Black as the picture may be, it is not hopeless. The majority of our people have not yielded to the debasing tendencies of the age, and there are millions who believe in and practice the simple virtues which alone can offer a basis for any civilization that can hope to endure. The future of the country lies with those who still believe in the validity of the moral law, and who, if they desire to make their will felt, can save it from the morass of crime and corruption into which it has been thrown by a corrupt and irreligious minority.

Many measures have been undertaken by the federal government, under the leadership of the President, to bring this era of crime and lawlessness to an end. No person can live outside the scope and the activities of the various agencies that have been set in motion to restore to the people their inheritance of prosperity and morality. These agencies were created in obedience to a peremptory mandate by the people, they were planned and devised by the representatives of the people in Congress, and their execution was committed to the President as a constitutional and sacred duty. It is abundantly clear that the President has set himself to the performance of his task in the spirit and with the purpose his mandate from the people dictated. He has called to his assistance men who are experts in all the fields that demand his attention. They have given him of their best, but, before he or they could proceed with the work of reconstruction, it was necessary to remove the wrecks that blocked the way to any field of positive performance. The President, himself, has said he does not promise to work miracles, but already every section of industry, commercial, financial, and agricultural, every phase of economic life, all the departments of normal activity are commencing to feel, in greater or less degree, the influence of his activities and are being revitalized by his efforts. That he will, at times, make mistakes, and that those he has called to his assistance will sometimes be in error, is to be expected, but a good augury for the future is to be found in the fact that, so far, he has been so often right in the midst of so many possibilities for error.

The President stands in need of friendly co-operation and helpful advice, and he has not shut himself off in sullen isolation from his fellow citizens to work out his problems alone. The program he is seeking to carry out is the best he could devise, it is the best Congress could construct, and any attempt to make partisan profit out of the present misery and distress is a crime against fair dealing and humanity. Prudent suggestion and criticism are always helpful, but it is well to remember that the tooting of horns never turned on the green light.

The President and Congress planned the campaign and it is the part of good citizenship to help them fight it out on the lines they think best even though it should take all winter and all summer. The most effective way in which individuals can promote the cause of recovery is to enter into their own souls and to ask themselves how far they have been affected by the general demoralization that threatens not only our prosperity but the existence of our civilization. Such self-examination and self-analysis should have fruitful results. If public opinion can once more be made the expression of the moral law taught by Christ, no power on earth can prevent this nation from becoming what its founders hoped it would be, the home of liberty, of opportunity, and of plenty. The plague spots in our financial centers that destroyed business integrity and debased business methods must be made amenable to justice and decency; the pesthole that infects the entire country with its obscene and lascivious moving pictures must be cleansed and disinfected: the multitudinous agencies that are employed in disseminating pornographic literature must be suppressed, and all those forces and influences that bring starvation to the bodies of men and poison to their souls must be utterly destroyed. Before there can be any hope for a return to political liberty, social peace, or economic justice, the spiritual life of the nation must be renewed, there must be an awakening of faith in God and a renewal of trust in His providence.

Restoring the moral values and reawakening the life of the spirit through faith in God is the task of religion. The civilization we see crumbling before us, historically and fundamentally had its basis in the Gospel of Jesus Christ. Unless the Lord build the house they labor in vain that build it (Ps. 126:1). The house or the city or the state that the Lord builds rests on the humble and simple virtues of the people that live therein, and it is only such that can last. Any other foundation but that of the Gospel is a foundation of sand, and when the winds of adversity blow, and the floods of materialism rise the house that is built on sand shall fall and great shall be the fall thereof.

Every one of the evils with which the demoralization and infidelity of the present have afflicted our country is a crime against the Christian conception of society. The civil laws seem to be powerless to punish men for the destructive practices in finance, government, and business which have brought such deplorable consequences, or for the innumerable crimes against decency and good order which are destroying private as well as public morality, but such crimes cannot go unrequited in the face of an awakened public conscience.

Time after time the words of the Supreme Pontiffs have rung out over the world inculcating the truth about the Christian State, about the eternal principles that govern economic relations, and about the reconstruction of the social order. There is urgent need now that these words and these principles should be made familiar to all the faithful, and to all who suffer under the present collapse of our social order. We, ourselves, have not escaped the effects of the general calamity. Our schools are in many places crippled, the demands for relief have increased a hundredfold, but we must go on and rededicate ourselves to the cause of education, of preaching, and of religion, to every function of the sacred ministry that promotes the salvation of souls, and in this way we shall aid most effectively in the restoration and reconstruction of our country.

62. STATEMENT OF THE ADMINISTRATIVE COMMITTEE, N.C.W.C., DEFENSE OF THE

RIGHTS OF WORKERS TO ORGANIZE*

April 12, 1934

Following their regular spring meeting at N.C.W.C. headquarters in Washington, D. C., April 10–12, 1934, members of the Administrative Committee of the National Catholic Welfare Conference drafted a statement for presentation to the Committee on Education and Labor of the United States Senate in which a forceful defense of the rights of workers to organize freely into associations of their own choice was presented. The Administrative Committee asked that its statement be made a part of the committee's hearings on the Wagner Bill, which provides for the protection of the worker's right to self-organization and the establishment of a tribunal for the adjudication of industrial controversies. The bishops filed the statement in view of the fact that Pope Pius XI's encyclical on "Reconstructing the Social Order," or portions of it, were placed in evidence at the hearings on the bill. The statement signed in behalf of the Administrative Committee, N.C.W.C., by the Rt. Rev. John J. Burke, C.S.P., S.T.D., general secretary of the Conference, is directed to the Hon. David J. Walsh, chairman, with the request that it be filed for the record of the hearing on the bill in question.

In view of the fact that the text of the *Quadragesimo Anno* or portions thereof have been placed in evidence in the hearing on S. 2926 before the Senate Committee on Education and Labor, the Administrative Committee of Bishops, National Catholic Welfare Conference, judge it in order to send you the following statement and ask that it be filed with your committee in the hearings on this bill:

Congress is considering legislation providing for the protection of the worker's right to self-organization and the establishment of an indus-

---

* *Catholic Action,* May, 1934, pp. 3 and 4; cf. also Nos. 24, 25, 52, 60, 66, 68, 71.

trial tribunal for the adjudication of industrial controversies. Both purposes are in complete accord with and are required by the Catholic social program enunciated by Pope Leo XIII in 1891 and by the present Holy Father, Pope Pius XI, in 1931.

The statement issued in 1933 by the bishops of the Administrative Committee, National Catholic Welfare Conference, declares: "His (the workingman's) right to organize must not be interfered with. . . . Labor and trades unions offer one means of obtaining justice in wages and salaries. The normal working of such organizations, whether singly or as a federation of unions, should be to promote the general welfare and to insure for all workers, whether skilled or unskilled, maximum employment, adequate remuneration, the protection of their rights as men and citizens, and security against accident and indigence. . . . Capital and labor should work for the common welfare and for their mutual interest should encourage all workers to organize. Unions, embracing all groups of workers, should be governed by good sense. They should endeavor to distribute opportunity to the workers of every class. They should always seek competent and disinterested advisers, that their organizations may ever be characterized by sanity."*

The worker's right to form labor unions and to bargain collectively is as much his right as his right to participate through delegated representatives in the making of laws which regulate his civic conduct. Both are inherent rights.

The worker can exercise his God-given faculty of freedom and properly order his life in preparation for eternity only through a system which permits him freely to choose his representatives in industry. From a practical standpoint, the worker's free choice of representatives must be safeguarded in order to secure for him equality of contractual power in the wage contract. Undue interference with this choice is an unfair labor practice, unjust alike to worker and the general public.

To determine the rights of both worker and management and to resolve the conflicting claims of both parties, an industrial tribunal, with mediation and arbitration powers, is necessary. This procedure is dictated by the plainest requirements of reason and public order. The opposite is chaos and anarchy.

---

* Cf. Doc. 60. Quotes from pp. 290–291, this volume.

63. STATEMENT OF THE BISHOPS OF THE ADMINISTRATIVE COMMITTEE, N.C.W.C., DEPLORING

GOVERNMENT'S SILENCE ON MEXICO*

May 1, 1935

This statement of the Administrative Committee of the National Catholic Welfare Conference was written to condemn the "brutality seldom exceeded in human history" with which the government of Mexico was attempting to destroy liberty and religion in that country. The bishops also asked that the government of the United States be consistent "and live up to its own set policy to defend before its own people the principles upon which our Government is founded." The statement also notes that the Administrative Committee has asked of the President and other federal officials that the United States government make representations to the government of Mexico against not only its denial but its persecution of religion.

The bishops exressed their thanks to all who registered earnest protests against the persecution in Mexico and declared their determination to spread the knowledge of the facts with regard to the situation there and urged that the people of the United States petition the government to use its good offices with the Mexican government to restore liberty to its fifteen million citizens. This was the third statement dealing with Mexico.

We wish to extend our gratitude to our fellow bishops in the United States: to the vast number of Catholic citizens: to our non-Catholic citizens, for the public expression of their earnest protests against the persecution of religion in Mexico by the present Mexican government and its denial both to its own citizens and the citizens of other nations of the right of religious worship.

The Administrative Committee, National Catholic Welfare Confer-

* *Catholic Action,* June, 1935, pp. 3 and 4; cf. also Nos. 2, 22, 29, 31, 34, 58.

ence, in line with the charge given it at the general meeting of the bishops of the United States, has asked of our honored President and the official members of the present Federal Administration that in justice to our own country, and in support of the principle of freedom of religious worship, our government make representations to the government of Mexico against not only its denial but its persecution of religion.

The bishops of the United States in their pastoral letter of 1926, and again in their statement of last November, declared: "What we have written is no interposition of our influence either as bishops or as citizens to reach those who possess political power anywhere on earth, and least of all in our own country, to the end that they should intervene with armed force in the internal affairs of Mexico for the protection of the Church."

The government of Mexico is carrying out a vast propaganda in this country to the effect that there is no religious persecution in Mexico. Thousands of closed churches in which religious worship is prohibited are silent but convincing evidences to the contrary. In 14 out of 32 states of Mexico no minister of religion is permitted to function. The vast majority of the citizens of Mexico is deprived of the rights of liberty of education: forced to accept, under savage penalties, what an atheistic government imposes on them and their children. Government spies ferret out, torture, and even put to death those who in conscience resent such tyranny. The faithful of Mexico are giving to the world an example of heroic martyrdom, for conscience' sake. With a brutality seldom exceeded in all human history, the present Administration of Mexico is deliberately, ruthlessly, pursuing a policy whereby all religion, and consequently all true freedom, will be destroyed.

The Administration of Mexico realizes if the facts were known its conduct would be repudiated by the people of the United States. Therefore, through subtle propaganda it cloaks the facts. It radios here the natural beauties of the country: it invites tourists from the United States: it window-dresses its principal centers, allows a church or two to be open, and gives the tourist the impression there is no religious persecution in Mexico. All these in their measure deceive the people of the United States and intensify the force of communistic antireligious propaganda in our country at a critical period.

The present revolutionary government of Mexico was recognized by the United States — October 19, 1915 — on condition, and on Mexico's own given word, that freedom of religious worship would be guaranteed by Mexico to her own citizens.

We ask that our government be consistent and live up to its own set policy. We ask our government to defend before its own people the principles upon which our government is founded. The traditional policy of our government does not permit it to remain silent at the present moment and in the present crisis. We may not interfere with the internal affairs of another nation. But freedom of conscience, freedom of religious worship, freedom of education are principles on which, even for the sake of the least gifted of humanity, our government was never silent. Good will to neighboring nations means good will to the peoples and to the rights of those peoples, as well as to the particular Administration that is ruling them. Persecution does not cease to be persecution when invested with the dignity of constitutional or statute law.

We know, as all the world knows, that an entrenched minority can hold and control an enormous population. Such is the condition that rules today in Mexico. The great majority of its people is practically held in captivity by its government.

We, the Administrative Committee, National Catholic Welfare Conference, will further spread the knowledge of the facts with regard to Mexico at the present time. We will continue to urge our people to express individually and corporately their petition to our government that, in the role of the good neighbor, it use its good offices with the Mexican government to restore religious liberty to its fifteen million citizens.

Present at the meeting of the Administrative Committee were the following archbishops and bishops:

The Most Rev. John T. McNicholas, O.P., Archbishop of Cincinnati; the Most Rev. John Gregory Murray, Archbishop of St. Paul; the Most Rev. Archbishop Edward Mooney, Bishop of Rochester; the Most Rev. Thomas F. Lillis, Bishop of Kansas City; the Most Rev. Hugh C. Boyle, Bishop of Pittsburgh; the Most Rev. John F. Noll, Bishop of Fort Wayne; the Most Rev. John B. Peterson, Bishop of Manchester; the Most Rev. Edwin V. O'Hara, Bishop of Great Falls; the Most Rev. Emmet M. Walsh, Bishop of Charleston; the Most Rev. Francis P. Keough, Bishop of Providence; and the Most Rev. John A. Duffy, Bishop of Syracuse.

64. STATEMENT OF THE ARCHBISHOPS AND BISHOPS OF THE ADMINISTRATIVE BOARD, N.C.W.C., ON THE

LESSONS TAUGHT BY PAPAL ENCYCLICALS*

November 18, 19, 1936

In a statement issued by the archbishops and bishops of the Administrative Board, N.C.W.C., incident to their meeting at N.C.W.C. headquarters preliminary to the 1936 general meeting of the hierarchy, attention was called to the two diametrically opposed philosophies of life — the spiritual and the supernatural on the one side, and the materialistic and naturalistic on the other.

In the world-wide conflict of today between two diametrically opposed philosophies of life, the spiritual and the supernatural on the one side, and the materialistic on the other, there is no place for indifference or neutrality. The forces of atheism and neopaganism with their offspring Communism and despotism are attempting to rob life of all that is spiritual and supernatural. The fate of Western civilization which is rooted in Christian principles is bound up with the outcome of this struggle.

The dictatorships in the old world and in the new which have robbed men of the gift of faith, of spiritual and intellectual freedom, have subjected them to a regime of fear and force. In every quarter of the world where the Christian order has been destroyed, the process by which this was achieved was always the same. There were promises in one case of a larger share in the powers of government, in another of a restoration of national sovereignty and prestige, in still another of a juster distribution of property and wealth. Class antagonisms were aroused, the regime of law was set aside, men were encouraged to yield to the herd passion for murder and destruction and to the herd instinct for blind submission to a leader.

---

* *Catholic Action,* December, 1936, pp. 10 and 21.

Grim experience has given the lie to the promises and pretensions of all the founders of the modern despotisms. Those who are compelled to live under their tyranny have not the right to think, to read, or to pray, except by the grace and favor of their despotic masters. The people fear and are feared. The prying eyes and the strong hand of government follow them into every detail of their private lives. All the natural instincts, friendship, family affection, reverence for what is noble and true, must be subordinated to the overreaching claims of society. Fear of domestic enemies begets fear of outside foes until every communistic or totalitarian state becomes a mere agency for the maintenance of greater and more oppressive military establishments. Militarism flourishes as it never has flourished before and nobody can foretell when the spark may be set which will involve the world in a universal conflagration of death and destruction.

To remain indifferent to what is happening before our very eyes is not only blameworthy but criminal, and for Catholics such culpability is doubly grave because they have before them a clear and explicit program of action. For more than half a century the popes, in their encyclicals, have been calling on Catholics and all believers in religion to make common cause against a common enemy. If it is now necessary to attempt the arduous task of providing a new outlook in philosophy, politics, economics, science, and education, and of striving to restore the Christian ideal of marriage and the family, it is because the pleadings of the popes fell on deaf ears. Every word in these encyclicals brings into the clearest light the accuracy with which the popes diagnosed the ills of society and the sureness with which they prescribed the most effective remedies.

These encyclicals were issued to check the devastating course of the forces of error and disorder that were destroying spiritual values in life and uprooting all that was best in society and civilization. There is no evil of the present, whether it be exaggerated nationalism, Communism, state absolutism, social injustice, class warfare, or any of the multifarious evils arising from the inequitable distribution of wealth and property, which was not analyzed and evaluated in these authoritative utterances of the supreme pontiffs. These encyclicals contain a complete and systematic statement of Christian political and social philosophy, and a working program of action for all who are desirous of correcting the evils that are rampant in the world today.

Error can be checked only by truth. Catholics in common with millions of non-Catholics who are bewildered by the multitudinous theories of life and conduct presented for their acceptance need definite schemes of action and a clear and well-rounded philosophy of thought and conduct. The issues at stake are vital and call for concerted and unified action.

65. TO THE LATE RT. REV. MSGR. JOHN J. BURKE, C.S.P., GENERAL SECRETARY, N.C.W.C.

IN MEMORIAM*

November 19, 1936

American hierarchy's appreciation of the services to God and country of the Rt. Rev. Msgr. John J. Burke, C.S.P., late general secretary, National Catholic Welfare Conference.

Whereas, God in His Inscrutable Wisdom, before which we bow in humble submission, has deemed it fit suddenly and without warning to our great sorrow to call unto Himself in death the late Monsignor John J. Burke, Domestic Prelate of His Holiness and Religious of the Congregation of Missionary Priests of Saint Paul, the Apostle; and

Whereas, Monsignor Burke from its beginning with industry, prudence, and rare endowments, to the satisfaction and applause of the Hierarchy of the United States served as General Secretary of the National Catholic Welfare Conference; and

Whereas, This lamented Prelate in all things and under all circumstances showed forth his great priestliness and a simple yet extraordinary filial love for Holy Church, expressed in his unquestioning devotion to the Vicar of Christ and his almost scrupulous reverence for the word and the act of the Hierarchy; and

Whereas, By his sweet Christian gentility and rugged piety he, almost

---

* *Catholic Action,* Special Issue, December 15, 1936, p. 5.

unknowingly, made thousands debtors unto him, never giving a thought to self when another was to be served or a soul to be saved; and,

Whereas, Without violence to his utmost devotion to Holy Church, rather as a very consequence of it, with a constructive and intelligent and fearless patriotism he rendered distinguished services to his beloved Country:

Under the Authority given it by the Bishops of the United States assembled at Washington on the eighteenth day of November, 1936, the Administrative Board of the National Catholic Welfare Conference acknowledges with deep gratitude the outstanding contribution of Monsignor Burke to Church and Country and extends to his Religious Congregation and the members of his family sympathy in the sorrow which they share with the whole Church in the United States. May his soul rest in peace!

Archbishops and Bishops of the
Administrative Board,
National Catholic Welfare Conference

66. STATEMENT OF THE ADMINISTRATIVE BOARD, N.C.W.C., CONCERNING THE

CHRISTIAN ATTITUDE ON SOCIAL PROBLEMS*

November 28, 1937

This is the complete statement issued by the archbishops and bishops of the N.C.W.C. Administrative Board on November 28, 1937. The bishops, while defending the rights of labor, warn labor against coercion and injustice and urge the collaboration of employers and employees in seeking a just solution of social problems.

For generations the social purpose of property has been too much disregarded and self-interest has increasingly dominated social and economic life. Selfish interests or private profit rather than social well-being has succeeded in large measure in controlling the policies of governments, in directing finance and industry, and in subjecting labor policies to its own ends. Although an essentially disorganizing principle, it has unwarrantably claimed to be the sole organizing force in society, the guarantee of social order, and the cure for social ills. But the half-truths and half-solutions which this extreme individualism has begotten in the social order are now discredited in the minds of thoughtful men.

Nearly fifty years ago the voice of Pope Leo XIII pleaded with governments, with capital, and industry to abolish economic injustice and to establish in industry working conditions befitting the dignity of man, as well as sufficiency of income for family life and old age.

Since the close of the World War, economic evils have increased. Social injustice, oblivious to the need of providing self-respecting employment to millions, has embittered the jobless and the poor

---

* *Catholic Action,* December, 1937, pp. 7, 8, and 14; cf. also Nos. 24, 25, 52, 60, 62, 68, 71.

throughout the world. In many it has aroused the spirit of defiance and revolt.

It is to be deplored that the unrest caused by evils already grave and disturbing should be further increased by designing agitators or by cunning propagandists whose immediate interest is to create turmoil, bitterness, class conflict, and thus hasten a "revolutionary situation." Calmness, accuracy of statement, and prudent restraint are highly desirable qualities in every discussion of grievances and remedies.

Irresponsible doctrinaries have seized upon world-wide discontent and capitalized it. Adroitly, they have presented some fundamental truths of the Gospel of Christ as if they were the first to expound them. They condemn abuses which Christ condemned and which the Catholic Church has been condemning for nineteen hundred years. The false promises of Communism inspire a crusading spirit, a contagious hysteria. It appeals to personal sacrifice and captures the adventurous spirit of youth. It masquerades as the champion of the downtrodden, as the archenemy of capitalistic abuses, and as the redeemer of the poor and working classes.

In our country Communist leaders see three things in their favor: first, a sizable army of propagandists among left wing professors, teachers, and intellectuals; second, the very real dangers to our financial and economic structure; third, the growing articulate discontent among the masses of the people. Unhampered by any fixed moral principles, Communists would hasten the collapse of the structure of our government, calculating that they will be the beneficiaries as the leaders of the new order. If for the moment they are keeping their activities largely undercover, it is because they are biding their time, awaiting the hoped-for collapse. Meanwhile by arraying class against class, and by tactics of boring from within other organized groups they seek to further the destructive ends of Communism. Traditional and constitutional America means nothing to them. They use the liberty guaranteed by the Constitution to erect a new system of government which will deny that liberty which they now misuse. They are willing to use any means to attain their end. Their present restraint is expediency. Their delay is strategy.

Many of the promoters of organizations calling themselves peace and youth movements, sponsors of stage and screen entertainment, and so-called crusaders for "democracy," especially those upholding the Communism of Spain and refusing to condemn the Bolshevism of Russia are, consciously or unconsciously, propagandists and agents of Communism. They constitute part of the "United or Popular Front." The trickery of Communists, as Pius XI points out, knows no bounds. They try perfidiously "to worm their way even into professedly Catholic and religious organizations."

Pope Pius XI has challenged the attention of all groups who have had any part in this injustice and calls for a reconstruction of the social order. He advocates no dictatorship either of the right or of the left. He seeks no governmental bureaucracy. He desires to see the guild system re-established in a manner adapted to modern problems and conditions. Neither unrestrained competition nor monopoly nor class conflict nor ubiquitous governmental control provides a sound remedy. Social well-being can be attained best by vocational groups ordering their own economic life under the guidance and encouragement of government. An unjust economic system, he has demonstrated, has had much to do with the rapid spread of the world's social cancer — Atheistic Communism. His voice is for peace as against war between capital and labor. For labor, he has fearlessly demanded recognition of its right to organize, just wages, healthy and humane working conditions, and security for sickness and old age. The truest friend of the poor and the laboring man in the world today is Pope Pius XI.

Labor has the right and should be accorded recognition of the right to establish its own organizations, to bargain collectively, to choose freely its own representatives. It has its just claims to a reasonable living wage, to healthful working conditions, to security of employment without unfair discrimination. It may enforce its just demands by effective means, but these must always be consonant with the rights of others, the dictates of conscience, and God's laws.

Labor should not incur the charge of countenancing coercion and injustice. It is not only unwise but immoral and reprehensible to use physical violence either against fellow employees or against property. It is both dishonest and destructive of genuine progress for labor to violate contracts freely and honorably negotiated and accepted.

Not only should labor reject the philosophy as well as the political and economic system of Communism but it should energetically repudiate such tendencies amongst those who undertake to be organizers of labor, thus eliminating any danger of Communist leadership or domination.

There are many honorable employers whose motives and purposes are dictated by justice and charity. They should be commended. What is needed is a more widespread and profound study of the social problems, with mutual collaboration by both employers and employees in the solution thereof.

Pius XI calls attention to the tremendous economic power exercised by those who hold and control money and are able therefore to govern credit and determine its allotment. This control moreover is exercised by those who are not the real owners of wealth but merely the trustees and administrators of invested funds. Responsibility is thus divorced from ownership. Nevertheless, they hold in their hands the very soul of production since they supply its lifeblood and no one can breathe against their will.

The increasing ratio of debt to total wealth has also had its influence in lessening the responsibility and advantage which should attach to the ownership of property. It makes for insecurity. Its relationship moreover to the cost of living or a reasonable price level needs careful inquiry. Further study should be given, likewise, to the whole intricate problem of money and credit so that such evils as exist in the present system may be brought to light and suitable remedies introduced.

Another method of destroying the liberty of the people, although it begins by lauding democracy and proclaiming freedom, is to establish the dictatorship of an absolutist State. Referring to this totalitarian State, Pope Pius XI in *Quadragesimo Anno* asserts: "It is feared that the new syndical and corporative institution possesses an excessively bureaucratic and political character, and that, notwithstanding the general advantages referred to above, it risks serving particular political aims rather than contributing to the initiation of a better social order" (p. 30). This kind of State is contrary to the letter and spirit of the American Constitution.

It first gives to the people many services; and then it assumes a multiplicity of functions which no normal civil government should attempt to discharge. Gradually the totalitarian State assumes the responsibility and function of the capitalist, the industrialist, the agriculturist, the merchant, and the employer. All this inevitably leads, not to a free State, but to a slave State. The tendency of our time is to make more and more demands on government. Citizens and groups should not ask the government to do for them what they can do for themselves. Sound social policy requires government to encourage citizens to assume as much personal responsibility as possible.

The poor and the laboring classes should resist the tendency to set up the omnipotent State. Their chief economic defense is organization. The traditional and ideal Christian society is not an individualistic but an organic society in which the individual, through the instrumentality of his group, works for himself, his group, and the entire social body.

It is deplorable that in our country an internecine conflict has broken out between two large organized bodies of workers. Continuance of the struggle can only mean increased suffering and hardship for workers themselves. It is gratifying that conferences looking to conciliation have been initiated; and for the well-being of workers, employers, and the entire people it is earnestly to be desired that these conferences will continue in a spirit of give and take, thereby providing the basis for harmony and lasting peace.

It is essential that labor unions be governed by the principles of Christian brotherhood, justice, and fair play. They should embrace all groups of workers. While seeking to promote their own interests they should be guided by sound judgment, have regard for the common economic good, respect property rights, prove themselves worthy of the confidence of every community, and thus perform their rightful function in protecting the legitimate interests of their members and in giving strength and stability to the nation.

67. STATEMENT OF THE ADMINISTRATIVE BOARD, N.C.W.C., ON THE

SECOND WORLD YOUTH CONGRESS*

July 11, 1938

During the month of August, 1938, the Second World Youth Congress was held at Vassar College, Poughkeepsie, N. Y. In this statement the bishops pointed out that the Congress was "irreligious in character" from its inception and expressed the hope that Catholic youth groups would not participate in its meeting.

The grave concern which all feel for the special problems faced by young people today emphasizes the necessity of giving youth moral guidance and prudent direction. This is particularly true now because subversive influences are bringing unwarranted pressure on youth groups of every kind. The fact that Catholic youth associations are not immune from such pressure compels careful consideration of the so-called "Second World Youth Congress," which is scheduled for Vassar College, Poughkeepsie, N. Y., in August.

The "First World Youth Congress" was held in Geneva in 1936. Catholic youth groups did not take part in that congress because of its irreligious character. It is clear from statements made by the organizing committee for this year's meeting at Vassar that there has been no change in the attitude of those whose influence is dominant in the movement. We therefore voice the hope that American Catholic youth groups will refuse to participate in the Vassar Congress. In this they will stand with many other American youth associations which recognize the essential place of religion in the formation of character as well as in the conduct of personal and national life.

Peace and brotherhood are, indeed, worthy objectives, but we are convinced that this proposed "World Youth Congress" as now

---

* *Catholic Action,* July, 1938, p. 3; cf. No. 61.

directed will not promote such ideals in conformity with principles that are either Catholic or American. Instead, under the guise of furthering peace and brotherhood, it will provide an opportunity for the fostering of irreligion and the promotion of the class hatreds of Sovietism. Its spirit and method are contrary to Catholic principles; its leadership reflects a philosophy that is hostile to American ideals and traditions — and it is not, in fact, as its name would indicate, a gathering that is actually representative of the youth of the world.

68. STATEMENT OF THE ARCHBISHOPS AND BISHOPS OF THE ADMINISTRATIVE BOARD, N.C.W.C., ON

INDUSTRIAL AND SOCIAL PEACE*

October 14, 1938

The following statement was issued by the archbishops and bishops of the Administrative Board, N.C.W.C., immediately following the close of the three-day annual general meeting of the archbishops and bishops of the United States held at the Catholic University of America in Washington, D. C., October 12–14, 1938.

It is historically true that greed and selfishness, engendering hatreds among nations and individuals, have been the major, perhaps the basic, cause of the political, the social, and the economic evils that distress the world and that stand now as a baneful threat to world peace. And it is equally true that no lasting remedy can be found for this deplorable condition short of the universal application of the Perfect Law of Liberty prescribed by our divine Saviour: that we know and love God above all things and our neighbor as ourselves.

Each time that we, the bishops of the United States, have come

---

*Catholic Action, November, 1938, p. 14; cf. also Nos. 24, 25, 52, 60, 62, 66, 71.

together in annual conference, we have found ourselves obliged by certain exigencies of the times and in pursuance of our pastoral responsibility to speak out in clear and unequivocal fashion of the evils of the day, and to suggest, as far as in us lay, the true Christian remedy. We have known, we know now, of no effective remedy not founded on that sovereign remedy given to us all by Christ and taught through the centuries by the Church of His foundation. Hence with renewed and increased emphasis, as befits the perils of the times, we plead again for its acceptance.

While we rejoice that war between the nations of Europe seems, for a time at least, averted, we cannot close our eyes to the fact that greed, selfishness, suspicion, and hatred still smolder beneath the surface ready to break into world-wide conflagration at the touch of the tinder. And while we give thanks that, in our own beloved country, warfare between capital and labor seems to some measure to have abated, we grieve to see that it has but given way to warfare between labor and labor.

Once again, therefore, we turn to our people and beg of them to study anew the practical implications of the law of love, and to enthrone that law in their hearts. We earnestly beseech them to examine carefully, and to apply conscientiously, the saving principles enunciated in the providential encyclicals of His Holiness, Pope Pius XI. And turning to our separated brethren, in the spirit of Christian charity and brotherly love, we ask them, too, to seek in these encyclicals the common remedy for the harsh conditions of the day. To Catholic labor leaders and unionists, as well as to Catholic employers, we express the profound hope that they will bend their best energies to the realization of the Christian social order envisaged by the Holy Father, to the end that, achieving first a true industrial and social peace at home, we may thus contribute to a lasting peace among all nations.

69. STATEMENT OF THE ADMINISTRATIVE BOARD, N.C.W.C., REGARDING THE

AMERICAN GOVERNMENT'S EFFORTS FOR A PEACE CONFERENCE*

April 19, 1939

Prayerful hope that success might attend the American government's efforts to bring the world's nations to a peace conference table was expressed on behalf of the bishops of the United States by the members of the National Catholic Welfare Conference Administrative Board, meeting in the nation's capital, April 18–19, 1939.

In these days when good men everywhere are longing for peace, the words spoken by our Holy Father, Pope Pius XII, on Easter Sunday came to us like an echo of the greeting of the Prince of Peace to the world. Meaningfully, our Holy Father asks:

"How may peace be had if among nations there is lacking the mutual understanding which alone can encourage and impel people along luminous ways of civil progress, and if solemnly sanctioned pacts and the plighted word have lost that security and value which are the principal bases of reciprocal confidence and without which ardently desired disarmament, material and moral, becomes with each passing day less possible of realization?"

In the light of these words, we, the bishops, gathered for the meeting of the National Catholic Welfare Conference Administrative Board at Washington, prayerfully hope that the commendable efforts of our government to bring the nations of the world to a conference table will be successful and that in justice and charity their pressing problems will there be openly discussed, common sacrifices for the commonweal generously made, and lasting peace established.

Earnestly we hope that the nation in offering its friendly assistance to this end will not be thought to have yielded to those who would embroil us in alien conflicts and dissensions.

---

* *Catholic Action*, May, 1939, p. 5.

70. STATEMENT OF THE ADMINISTRATIVE BOARD, N.C.W.C.,

IN PRAISE OF
CHRISTIAN DEMOCRACY CRUSADE
AND CONDEMNATION OF BIGOTRY*

April 29, 1939

This statement was issued by the Administrative Board, N.C.W.C., in praise of the crusade being conducted by the Catholic University of America to promote "loyalties and civic virtues in a Christian democracy" and also to decry racial bigotry which is a "dangerous aberration" antagonistic to democracy and Christianity.

We wish to call attention to the laudable educational movement sponsored and directed by the Catholic University of America for a better understanding of loyalties and civic virtues in a Christian democracy.

We regret and deplore the widespread propaganda in the interest of systems and theories antagonistic to the principles of democracy and the teachings of Christianity. A Christian people will oppose these dangerous aberrations with all the might of Christian charity.

For that very reason our people will be on their guard against all forms of racial bigotry, of which Pope Pius XI, speaking of a pertinent instance, said: "It is not possible for Christians to take part in anti-Semitism."

---

* *Catholic Action,* May, 1939, p. 5.

71. STATEMENT OF THE ARCHBISHOPS AND BISHOPS OF THE ADMINISTRATIVE BOARD, N.C.W.C., ON THE

CHURCH AND SOCIAL ORDER*

February 7, 1940

INTRODUCTION

With sublime pathos Pope Pius XII in his first encyclical letter pleads with the peoples of the world to turn from the destructive ways of hatred and conflict to the healing ways of charity and peace. He reminds a forgetful world of the universality of divine love; he reconsecrates the whole human family to the Sacred Heart of the divine Redeemer; and, summoning men to return to Christ, he re-echoes the entreaty raised so often by his predecessors: "Behold your King" (John 19:14).

To re-enthrone Christ in the minds and hearts of men; to re-establish His kingship in human society; to impregnate the laws and institutions, the aspirations and final purposes of all nations with His spirit, is the supreme hope and purpose of our Holy Father.

> Perhaps — God grant it — one may hope [with Pope Pius XII], that this hour of direct need may bring a change of outlook and sentiment to those many who, till now, have walked with blind faith along the path of popular modern errors unconscious of the treacherous and insecure ground on which they trod. Perhaps the many who have not grasped the importance of the educational and pastoral mission of the Church will now understand better her warnings, scouted in the false security of the past. No defense of Christianity could be more effective than the present straits. From the immense vortex of error and anti-Christian movements there has come forth a crop of such poignant disasters as to constitute a condemnation surpassing in its conclusiveness any merely theoretical refutation.[1]

---

* Published by the N.C.W.C., Washington 5, D. C., 1940; cf. Nos. 24, 25, 52, 60, 62, 66, 68.

[1] *Summi Pontificatus*, pp. 11, 12, N.C.W.C. edition — 1939.

With all our hearts we thank him for his guidance and with such strength as we possess we emulate his example. We reaffirm the primacy of our Lord Jesus Christ, "Who is the image of the invisible God, the first-born of every creature: For in him were all things created in heaven and on earth, visible and invisible. . . . And he is before all, and by him all things consist. . . . Because in him it hath well pleased the Father, that all fullness should dwell" (Col. 1:15–19).

The peace which all right-minded men so earnestly desire, must be based upon a comprehensive program of restoring Christ to His true and proper place in human society. We must bring God back into government; we must bring God back into education; we must bring God back into economic life; we must bring God back indeed into all life, private and public, individual, and social. The truth of God, the law of God, the justice, mercy, and charity of God, must, by conscious effort and willing submission, be made to permeate all our social intercourse and all our public relations.

In the midst of human society, God has set His Church as "the pillar and ground of truth." To the Church Christ has given the divine mission to teach all things whatsoever He has commanded. The divine mandate permits no curtailment of the law no matter how diverse the circumstances and conditions under which man lives and works, nor any compromise with the full measure of its application to human conduct. The obligation comprehends the actions of man in his private and public life as an individual and as a member of human society.

Man is not an isolated individual living in a social vacuum, but a social being destined to live and work out his salvation in association with his fellow beings. He is a member of a community and he has, in consequence, duties of commutative justice and duties of social justice and duties of charity which emerge from this relationship. On no other foundation can man build a right social order or create that good society which is desired so ardently by the great mass of mankind.

Inasmuch as the right and duty of the Church to teach the fullness of the moral law and in particular "to deal authoritatively with social and economic problems" (p. 14),[2] are challenged in some quarters or are too frequently misunderstood in others, we judge it

---

[2] All citations unless otherwise mentioned are from the Encyclical "Forty Years After" (*Quadragesimo Anno*) of Pope Pius XI, N.C.W.C. edition, 1931.

wise and opportune to reaffirm the jurisdiction of the Church as the teacher of the entire moral law and more particularly as it applies to man's economic and social conduct in business, industry, and trade. To make our pronouncements authentic and to interpret truly the mind of the Church, we follow closely the teachings of our late lamented pontiff, Pope Pius XI.

First, let it be made clear that the Church is concerned only with the moral aspects of trade and industry and does not enter the field of business in matters that are purely material or technical. The Church is not concerned with the accuracy of economic surveys or the resultant data, nor with the problems of scientific organization, production, cost accounting, transportation, marketing, and a multitude of similar activities. To pass judgment on their aptitude and merits is a technical problem proper to economic science and business administration. For such the Church has neither the equipment nor the authorization. We frankly declare that it would be unwise on her part to discuss their operation except insofar as a moral interest might be involved (p. 14).

The Church does not prescribe any particular form of technical economic organization of society just as she does not prescribe any particular political organization of the state.[3] Pius XI makes this clear in his encyclical letter *Quadragesimo Anno* where he states: "It is hardly necessary to note that what Leo XIII taught concerning the form of political government can, in due measure, be applied also to vocational groups. Here, too, men may choose whatever form they please, providing that both justice and the common good be taken into account" (p. 28).

From the Sacred Scripture we learn that "the earth is the Lord's and the fullness thereof" (Ps. 23:1). No absolute or unlimited ownership therefore can be claimed by man as if he were free to follow his own selfish interests without regard to the necessity of others. The moral law teaches that he has indeed a right to private property but, as Pope Leo XIII points out, "the earth, even though divided among private owners, ceases not thereby to administer to the needs of all."[4]

Man is truly the steward of his possessions in the sight of God and has therefore definite responsibilities both of justice and charity toward his fellow man with respect to the use he makes of his property.

---

[3] Cf. *Divini Redemptoris*, N.C.W.C. edition, p. 24, par. 32.
[4] "On the Condition of Labor" (*Rerum Novarum*), Paulist Press, p. 7.

From divine revelation we learn that physical labor was decreed by God even after the Fall of man for the good of body and soul (p. 42). The laborer is worthy of his hire. If, however, human labor is treated as a mere commodity to be bought and sold in the open market at the lowest price, then it ceases to fulfill its proper function in society. What a sad perversion of the wholesome plan of Divine Providence that "dead matter leaves the factory ennobled and transformed, where men are corrupted and degraded" (p. 43).

From divine revelation we learn moreover that each human being has an infinitely precious personality. Pius XI in his encyclical *Divini Redemptoris* sets forth this truth with clarity, force, and beauty:

> Man has a spiritual and immortal soul. He is a person, marvelously endowed by his Creator with gifts of body and mind. He is a true "microcosm," as the ancients said, a world in miniature, with a value far surpassing that of the vast inanimate cosmos. God alone is his last end, in this life and the next. By sanctifying grace he is raised to the dignity of a son of God, and incorporated into the Kingdom of God in the Mystical Body of Christ. In consequence he has been endowed by God with many and varied prerogatives; the right to life, to bodily integrity, to the necessary means of existence; the right to tend towards his ultimate goal in the path marked out for him by God; the right of association and the right to possess and use property (p. 19).

Man cannot in consequence be treated as a mere chattel but rather with dignity and respect as a child of God. His labor is not a thing to be ashamed of, but an honorable calling, whereby he achieves a necessary livelihood and fulfills the divine plan of an earthly economy.

Because these are moral principles and spiritual truths, jurisdiction in expounding their full scope and obligation belongs to the Church which Christ established as the teacher of men in this world. We in our capacity as shepherds of the flock of Christ cannot be unmindful of our duties in these matters. "Take heed to yourselves," says the Apostle, "and to the whole flock, wherein the Holy Ghost hath placed you bishops, to rule the Church of God" (Acts 20:28).

It is an unfortunate fact that large numbers of workingmen have become alienated from religion. This is true even of Catholics in some of the older countries. In the words of the Supreme Pontiff it has become the great scandal of the modern world. No matter how we explain the defection, the fact remains that Christian truth and principles of conduct have become greatly obscured "so that we are confronted with a world which in large measure has almost fallen back into paganism" (p. 46).

To bring back those who have suffered loss of faith and with it the loss even of earthly hope and charity, it is necessary to re-establish the sound principles of Christian social teaching. To make our progress sure and effective we must recruit and train leaders from within the various ranks of society who know the mentality and aspirations of their respective classes and who with kindly fraternal charity will be able to win both their minds and their hearts. "Undoubtedly," as Pius XI says, "the first and immediate apostles of the working men must themselves be working men, while the apostles of the industrial and commercial world should themselves be employers and merchants. It is your chief duty, Venerable Brethren, and that of your clergy, to seek diligently, to select prudently and train fittingly these lay apostles, amongst working men and amongst employers" (p. 46).

In existing circumstances the obligation of the Church is manifest. Who can deny the close relationship between economic injustice and a long train of evils, physical, social, and moral? Unfair wages due to a greed for excessive profits and insecurity due to false and immoral economic principles lead directly to undernourishment, bad housing, inadequate clothing, and indirectly to irregular family re-lations, child delinquency, and crime. Excessively long hours of work in some industrial areas and in some industrial processes create dangers to life and limb, impair the health of workingmen, and impoverish whole families through infection, disease, and pre-mature death. Because human beings and not animated machines toil in industry, therefore the Church cannot abdicate her right and duty to speak out in defense of the rights of human personality nor fail to declare uncompromisingly the moral obligations of in-dustrial and economic life.

Today most controversy concerns itself with these questions: (1) ownership, (2) property and labor, (3) security, (4) wages, (5) establishment of social order. We shall here present the Catholic doctrine regulating these matters and in doing so we shall follow the exposition given by our late chief pastor of souls, Pope Pius XI, in his celebrated encyclicals.

I. OWNERSHIP

The Church has always defended the right to own private property and also to bequeath and to inherit it. We have vindicated this right even to the point of being falsely accused of favoring the rich against the poor. The Church teaches that the right to own property is based on the natural law of which God Himself is the author. By the law of nature man must provide for himself and his family and he can fully discharge this obligation only if there exists an established system of private ownership (p. 16).

It is essential to remember that ownership has a twofold aspect, the one affecting the individual, the other affecting society. To deny the individual character and aspect of ownership leads to some form of socialism or collective ownership; to deny the social character or aspect of ownership leads to selfish individualism or that form of exaggerated liberalism which repudiates duties and ends in complete irresponsibility to other persons and to the common good.

The two great dangers which society faces in the present state of economic organization are, first, the concentration of ownership and control of wealth and, second, its anonymous character which results from some of the existing business and corporation law, whereby responsibility toward society is greatly impaired if not completely ignored. The civil authority, in view of these dangers, must so regulate the responsibility of property that the burden of providing for the common good be equitably distributed. It must furthermore establish such conditions through legal enactment and administrative policy that wealth itself can be distributed so each individual member of society may surely and justly come into possession of the material goods necessary for his own livelihood. It is not however the government alone which has this responsibility, as will become clear from the further considerations to be noted.

Pius XI states:

> It follows from the two-fold character of ownership, which We have termed individual and social, that men must take into account in this matter not only their own advantage but also the common good. To define in detail these duties, when the need occurs and when the natural law does not do so, is the function of the government. Provided that the natural and divine law be observed, the public authority, in view of the common good, may specify more accurately what is licit and what is illicit for property owners in the use of their possession (p. 17).

In the application of the principles of social justice, an important instrument, therefore, is governmental authority. As Pius XI asserts, the civil authority has the obligation to adjust "ownership to meet the needs of the public good," and by so doing "it acts not as an enemy, but as the friend of private owners" (p. 17).

II. Property and Labor

Manifestly if every man worked either on his own land or with his own tools and in his own business, there would be no labor problem. Self-employment however is not the characteristic of our present economic organization. With the advent of machine industry and especially with the development of mass production there has developed an intensification of the individualistic spirit, creating new problems for labor.

It is freely admitted that modern industry requires considerable concentration of capital, but it is not admitted that concentration of ownership and control is consequently necessary or beneficial to the common good. The concentration of capital, however, with mass employment, does create a new and more impersonal relationship between capital and labor. The problem is one of providing equitably for the distribution of income between those who supply capital and those who supply labor.

In too many instances an undue portion of the income has been claimed by those who have ownership or control of capital, whilst those on the other hand who have only their labor to invest have been forced to accept working conditions which are unreasonable and wages which are unfair. This condition arises from the fact that labor policies have been dictated by false principles in the interests of the owners or capitalists. Second, it arises from the fact that labor frequently has had no voice in the regulation or the adjustment of these problems. Labor can have no effective voice as long as it is unorganized. To protect its rights it must be free to bargain collectively through its own chosen representatives. If labor when unorganized is dissatisfied, the only alternative is to cease work and thus undergo the great hardships which follow unemployment.

To remedy the situation, it is necessary to adopt right principles for the distribution of the income of industry. These principles must be both economically sound and morally just. The principle that labor should be compensated to such extent only that it remains physically efficient and capable of reproducing itself in new generations of workingmen, is a vicious principle, devoid of all respect for human dignity and opposed to all sense of social responsibility. It is true that this principle was never widely held in theory, but it has been frequently applied in practice. One such application is found in the policy that labor should be compensated solely according to the principle of supply and demand. This reduces labor to the position of a commodity and makes the workingman accept the fluctuating price in a labor market irrespective of the needs of himself and family. Neither present sufficiency of income nor security for the future play a part in determining his wage standard according to this immoral theory and practice. Such theory or practice is anti-social and anti-Christian, for it denies both social responsibility and the claims of Christian ethics and in their place substitutes the principles of selfishness and force.

New developments in the organization of labor under the great impetus which has been given by recent legislation and governmental policy, make it opportune to point out that the principle of force and domination is equally wrong if exercised by labor under certain conditions by means of a monopoly control. To defend in principle or to adopt in practice the theory that the net result belongs to labor and that capital shall receive only sufficient to replace itself is an invasion of the rights of property. This is only a more subtle form of the contention that all means of production should be socialized. Clearly all such proposals disregard the contribution which the owner of property makes in the process of production and are palpably unjust.

It is not however the excessive claims of labor on the income from industry which constitute the most immediate problem in labor relations today, but rather the abuse of power which not infrequently results in violence, riot, and disorder. Employers at times abuse their economic power by discriminating unfairly against unions, by establishing lockouts, by importing from outside the community strikebreakers who are furnished with arms, and by provoking in other ways ill feeling which precipitates violent disorder. Employees on their part allow themselves at times to be misled by men of evil principles so as to engage in the criminal use of violence both against persons and property. Leo XIII in his encyclical *Rerum Novarum* spares neither group in his denunciation of such immoral conduct. He calls upon the public authority to protect and defend vigorously the rights of all, forestalling preferably the rise of disorder by eliminating the economic abuse from which this disorder springs (pp. 12–24).

False principles generate false policies and as a consequence there grows and develops a false economic system which sins both against the true interests of human society and against the true principles of Christian morality. Pius XI insists that owners and employers may not hire working people exclusively for their own benefit and profit, nor divert all economic life to their own will, but must guard social justice, the human dignity of labor, the social nature of economic life, and the interests of the common good (p. 32).

The far-reaching need of social justice and its demands are seen from the following words of the Sovereign Pontiff Pope Pius XI:

> Now, not every kind of distribution of wealth and property amongst men is such that it can at all, and still less can adequately, attain the end intended by God. Wealth, therefore, which is constantly being augmented by social and economic progress, must be so distributed amongst the various individuals and classes of society that the common good of all, of which Leo XIII spoke, be thereby promoted. In other words, the good of the whole community must be safeguarded (p. 20).

III. SECURITY

Our present economic order rests upon the sanctity of private property. Private property, however, is not well distributed at present among the members of human society. While it is dangerous to exaggerate the disproportion between those who possess adequate property and those who constitute the proletariat or the propertyless, nevertheless, it is certainly within the bounds of truth to state that the existing situation constitutes a grave social evil. Private property in the judgment of many thoughtful men tends to become less and less the characteristic note of our present society. If the majority of our citizens possess insufficient private property to be independent of a wage income for even a short period of time, then there is grave danger to the entire social fabric. Social stability rests upon this basis of individual ownership of property. There should be more of it and not less of it, if our existing economic system is to remain secure.

The lack of sufficient private property leads to various forms of insecurity. This insecurity not only leads to the creation of a strong social tension expressing itself in social disorder, but is also contrary to the prescriptions of Christian morality. There can be no question but that in our country we possess adequate resources both in respect to raw materials, technical or scientific skill, and mechanical equipment sufficient to provide both a high standard of living and also comprehensive security for all classes of society. Workingmen should be made secure against unemployment, sickness, accident, old age, and death. The first line of defense against these hazards should be the possession of sufficient private property to provide reasonable security. Industry, therefore, should provide not merely a living wage for the moment but also a saving wage for the future against sickness, old age, death, and unemployment. Individual industries alone, however, cannot in each single case achieve this objective without invoking the principle of social insurance. Some form of government subsidy granted by the entire citizenship through legislative provision seems to be a necessary part of such a program.

We cannot overlook the fact that an important factor making for insecurity is the "immense power and despotic economic domination which is concentrated in the hands of a few and that those few are frequently not the owners, but only the trustees and directors of invested funds, who administer them at their good pleasure" (p. 32). Pope Pius XI then singles out one group in an especial manner as exercising this domination and despotic power.

This power [he states] becomes particularly irresistible when exercised by those who, because they hold and control money, are able also to govern credit and determine its allotment, for that reason supplying, so to speak, the life-blood to the entire economic body, and grasping as it were in their hands the very soul of production, so that no one dare breath against their will (pp. 32–33).

That there exists a serious problem from the standpoint of security for workingmen is clearly manifest from the present state of unemployment and the present huge demands on government for public relief against dire poverty. Very significantly our present Holy Father Pius XII writes in his letter addressed specifically to the American hierarchy:

May it also be brought about that each and every able-bodied man may receive an equal opportunity for work in order to earn the daily bread for himself and his own. We deeply lament the lot of those — and their number in the United States is large indeed — who, though robust, capable, and willing, cannot have the work for which they are anxiously searching. May the wisdom of the governing powers, a far-seeing generosity on the part of the employers, together with the speedy re-establishment of more favorable conditions, effect the realization of these reasonable hopes to the advantage of all.[5]

We do not wish to imply that individual employers as a class are willfully responsible for this present state of insecurity but we do claim that a system which tolerates such insecurity is both economically unsound and also inconsistent with the demands of

---

[5] "To the Church in the United States" (*Sertum Laetitiae*), N.C.W.C. edition, p. 18, 1939.

social justice and social charity. Security of the workingmen therefore, as against unemployment, old age, sickness, accident, and
death, must be frankly accepted as a social responsibility of industry
jointly with society. The distribution of the burden justly between
the various groups must be determined, first, through mutual council
and honest agreement between the employers and the employees, and
second, through the regulation of government acting in its sovereign
capacity as promoter of the common good.

Not all responsibility rests upon government. In truth a large
measure of responsibility rests upon the proper collaboration of
employers and employees or of property owners and wage earners.
The economic system itself and the principles which guide its
executives must help to achieve security by establishing a fair
distribution of income between capital and labor. It must strive
to establish an equilibrium between farm income and city income.
If the rate of wages (not the annual income) of the industrial
worker in the city is out of balance with the rate of returns of
the farmer in the country, then there is bound to be unemployment
and insecurity. Hence the duty of both groups is to work for a
just balance between themselves instead of encouraging selfishness
and greed which defeat the interest of both, and violate the principles
of morality.

The same can be said of the various classes of industrial labor.
Here also there must be a balance between various groups both
organized and unorganized. Unless this be true the economic system
cannot function smoothly and there will inevitably be unemployment,
because the one class of workingmen cannot buy the high-priced
products of the other class of workingmen with their limited income.
If skilled laborers, who, through rigid organization, have a monopoly
control of their craft, raise their rate of hourly wages too high,
they do not gain their advantage exclusively from the wealthy
but from the poor also, in terms of excessive prices. Higher wages
as a rule should come out of excessive profits and not out of increased prices.

Heartening indeed are the beginnings toward the greater security
of the people that have already been made through legislative enactment and public policy. The immediate benefits of these laws to
working people may be small and some modifications perhaps desirable, but it is highly gratifying that the principle upon which they
rest has become a part of our national policy.

IV. WAGES

In view of the fact that at present many industrial workers and also farm laborers do not possess sufficient private property to provide either a present livelihood or security for the future, the problem of wages assumes outstanding importance. At the outset it is necessary to state that the wage contract itself is not unjust nor in itself vicious as some theorists have falsely contended (p. 22). It is, of course, true that a contract between employers and employees would serve the purpose of individual and social welfare more effectively if it were modified by some form of partnership which would permit a graduated share in the ownership and profits of business and also some voice in its management. It is not intended that labor should assume responsibility for the direction of business, beyond its own competency or legitimate interest; nor has labor a right to demand dominating control over the distribution of profits. To set up such claims would amount to an infringement on the rights of property. Labor has, however, certain definite rights which have been frequently ignored or largely discounted.

The first claim of labor, which takes priority over any claim of the owners to profits, respects the right to a living wage. By the term *living wage* we understand a wage sufficient not merely for the decent support of the workingman himself but also of his family. A wage so low that it must be supplemented by the wage of wife and mother or by the children of the family before it can provide adequate food, clothing, and shelter together with essential spiritual and cultural needs cannot be regarded as a living wage.

Furthermore a living wage means sufficient income to meet not merely the present necessities of life but those of unemployment, sickness, death, and old age as well. In other words, a saving wage constitutes an essential part of the definition of a living wage.

In the effort to establish a criterion or standard of measurement of wages, it is necessary to consider not only the needs of the workingman but also the state of the business or industry in which he labors. Pope Pius XI states clearly that "it is unjust to demand wages so high that an employer cannot pay them without ruin, and without consequent distress amongst the working people themselves" (p. 24). Bad management, want of enterprise, or out-of-date methods do not constitute a just reason for reducing the wages of workingmen. It still remains true that a living wage constitutes the first charge on industry. If a business is prevented by unfair competition from paying a living wage, and if such competition reduces prices to such a level that decent and just wages cannot be paid, then those responsible are guilty of wrongdoing and sin grievously against moral principles as well as against the common good. The remedy lies, first, in the adequate organization of both employers and employees in their own proper associations and in their joint action; second, in adequate regulation and supervision by the state through proper legislative enactment.

No criterion or standard of wages, however, can be determined independently of price. A scale of wages too low, no less than a scale excessively high causes unemployment (p. 25). Likewise a scale of prices too low no less than a scale of prices too high leads to unemployment. Both create hardship and throw the economic system out of its proper equilibrium causing unemployment for the community and hardship even for the individual who is employed, for he must pay too high a price in view of his wages or he receives too low a wage in view of prices. What is needed is a reasonable relationship and a harmonious proportion. Pope Pius XI states:

> Where this harmonious proportion is kept, man's various economic activities combine and unite into one single organism and become members of a common body, lending each other mutual help and service. For then only will the economic and social organism be soundly established and attain its end, when it secures for all and each those goods which the wealth and resources of nature, technical achievement, and the social organization of economic affairs can give. These goods should be sufficient to supply all needs and an honest livelihood, and to uplift men to that high level of prosperity and culture which, provided it be used with prudence, is not only no hindrance but is of singular help to virtue (p. 25).

Wages are an essential element in the determination of prices. In the final analysis the cost of raw materials cannot be segregated from wage costs, for the production cost of raw materials presupposes a multiplicity of wage costs as a component element. If wages continuously change, then there must be a continuous change in prices, unless it is assumed that all wage changes will affect only the profits of owners. As a matter of fact they do not. The economic organization might function just as easily on one price level as another, but it cannot function well if the price level is frequently changing. Rapid or frequent fluctuations disturb the harmonious proportions between income and prices not only for owners and employers but also for the workingmen themselves.

This consideration is no argument against a necessary increase of wages whenever and wherever the wages are inadequate to provide a decent living. But it is an argument in favor of attaining a relative degree of stability in the price level as soon as commutative justice and social justice permit. A cogent reason for aspiring to such a condition of stability is the higher interest of the family as against the single or unmarried workingman or employee. The single man benefits more from a wage increase than does the family man if the end result is an increase in prices. The family man is penalized in multiple fashion with every increase in prices. Stability in the price level, therefore, and even a reduction in prices as a secular trend is desirable as one means of distributing our national income more widely and more effectively for the common good. Such a long-range policy will supplement the benefits of an increased family wage in view of increased family burdens as recommended by Pius XI.

We do not wish to imply that a universal increase of wages will automatically solve our problem of unemployment and idle factories. Some wage increases come not out of the profits of the wealthy but out of the increased prices for the poor. The first requirement, therefore, is that the lowest paid workingmen be the first to receive an increase of wages and simultaneously that prices be not raised but excessive profits be reduced. The ultimate aim, therefore, must be a reasonable relationship between different wages and a reasonable relationship between the prices obtained for the products of the various economic groups (p. 25).

Because economic society has not followed the moral laws of justice and charity, the principles of interdependence have been violated and we have precipitated unemployment with all its consequent hardships and misery. To withhold just and reasonable wages from the workingman has injured him directly and immediately, but it has also injured the common good and the interests of the very owners of property. Their factories, their commercial establishments, and their equipment have frequently stood idle as a result. Unless workingmen as a class have sufficient income to purchase their share of the goods which our economic system is capable of producing, the markets will automatically be closed to the sale of goods, and idle factories and unemployment are the disastrous result.

V. Establishment of Social Order

It would be unreasonable to expect that an economic system which has been predicated upon false principles and which has been operative over many decades could be reorganized suddenly or with the easy gesture of hasty legislation and new administrative policy. We face a problem which requires for its solution intellectual vision, moral integrity, and persevering effort. Many leaders both in the field of management and in the field of labor must first be convinced that economic laws and moral laws are in harmony and not in conflict with one another. No one section of human society can be grievously injured without that injury reacting harmfully in the final analysis upon all other sections of society.

The remedy for our problems is not so simple as some would have us think. The solution is to be found in clear thinking and in a right conscience. Relying upon God's providence we dare not be pessimistic but at the same time we frankly recognize that a full restoration to a Christian social order is a matter of steady growth and not a sudden transition.

There are two attitudes which represent extreme positions respecting our economic and social order. The one attitude is espoused by those who reject any and every kind of economic planning or organization. They constitute the group of extreme individualists or the so-called school of economic liberalism. They want no interference whatsoever with the individual either from the government or from the social pressure of group organizations. They will tolerate no restrictions upon individual initiative or personal enterprise. They are liberal only to the extent that they wish to be liberated from all social responsibility. They call it free enterprise but the freedom is for those who possess great resources and dominating strength rather than for the weak or those who depend simply on their own labor for their well-being.

They oppose all efforts to establish collective bargaining by organized labor and they resent the action of government in enacting laws which make such collective bargaining obligatory. If there is to be any social planning, they will do it themselves without the collaboration of labor, consumers, or the government. They want the government to be restricted to the function of a policeman or umpire in enforcing private contracts but not to be entrusted with the responsibility of promoting justice and the common good.

The second group reject totally this attitude of the individualists and rush to the opposite extreme. These latter desire to socialize all resources or establish a state collectivity. Either all property, as in pure Communism, or at least all productive property as in Socialism, should be owned in their theory by the community or by the State. The State or the community thereupon will engage through its bureaus and agencies in developing an elaborate system of national economic planning. The hope, impractical as that method may be, is to make provision for the needs of all citizens so that there will be no surplus and no deficiency. This system would ignore human nature and human rights as flagrantly as the afore-mentioned group of individualists. In fact, experience indicates that where this system has been tried human beings are victimized in a manner and to an extent even more disastrous. Persecution is the logical and inevitable result of such economic dictatorship.

Between these two extremes there is a "via media" completely consistent with Christian morality and with sound economic principles. It is manifestly impossible to expect good economic order if wages, prices, working conditions, and the public good are left to chance or to the haphazard methods of so-called free enterprise. "Free competition, however," says Pope Pius XI, "though within certain limits is just and productive of good results, but it cannot be the ruling principle of the economic world." Economic supremacy, he continues, can still less assume this function of a true and effective guiding principle, "for this is a headstrong and vehement power, which, if it is to prove beneficial to mankind, needs to be curbed strongly and ruled with prudence" (p. 29).

The true remedy will be found according to the mind of Pope Pius XI in accomplishing two reforms in our social order. In the first place, there must be re-established some form of guild or vocational groups which will bind men together in society according to their respective occupations, thus creating a moral unity. Second, there must be a reform of morals and a profound renewal of the Christian spirit which must precede the social reconstruction.

The social organism has been dismembered and broken up into fragments each seeking its own selfish interests instead of the common good of all. Until the organic nature of society is again recognized and re-established through vocational groups or guilds, either one of two things must happen. The State must assume all responsibility, that is, become an absolute economic dictatorship or else the individual remains helpless, defenseless, and completely overpowered by those who enjoy economic supremacy.

Not only must the moral principles of justice and charity be recognized and accepted by members of society, but the social and economic system itself must be so organized that these principles can freely function and become truly operative. Hence the need of a guild or corporative system which will establish sound prosperity and which respects the proper hierarchic structure of society.[6] Not only must employers and employees be organized singly and jointly but their organizations must be impregnated with Christian moral and social principles or else their work will be sterile or even productive of new disorders.

When we speak of the establishment of a right social order, we understand thereby a reform in the concept and organization of the State respecting its responsibility for public welfare; second, a reform in other fundamental social institutions; and third, and quite emphatically, a reform or correction of morals.

"When we speak of the reform of the social order," says Pius XI, "it is principally the State we have in mind." The State cannot do all things nor may we hope for salvation from its intervention alone. In fact, the State has been encumbered with all the burdens once borne by associations now extinct. The distinctive function of the State in consequence has become submerged and its authority overwhelmed by an infinity of affairs and duties (p. 26).

The State, however, cannot be relegated to the position of a mere policeman or umpire. It has the responsibility of providing for the common good. On the other hand it may not and should not become totalitarian in attempting to fulfill all social functions in the way of economic planning and direction. It should leave to the smaller vocational groups the settlement of business of lesser importance. It will then be free effectively to accomplish its real function of "directing, watching, stimulating, and restraining, as circumstances suggest or necessity demands" (p. 26).

The primary duty of the State and of all good citizens is to abolish conflict between classes with divergent interests. This may at first sight appear to be purely negative. There is, however, a positive responsibility to foster and promote harmony between the various ranks of society and that by specific means. "The aim of social legislation," says Pope Pius XI, "must therefore be the re-establishment of vocational groups" (p. 27).

The remedy for the class conflict which makes the labor market an

---

[6] *Divini Redemptoris*, p. 21, par. 32, N.C.W.C. edition.

arena where the two armies are engaged in combat, is to be found precisely in the reintegration of the social body by means of vocational groups, "which bind men together not according to the position they occupy in the labor market, but according to the diverse functions which they exercise in society" (p. 27). The chief qualifications of these vocational groups or guilds, as noted by Pius XI, are that they are autonomous, embrace whole industries and professions, are federated with other constituent groups, possess the right of free organization, assembly, and vote, and that they should dedicate themselves to the common good and with governmental protection and assistance function in the establishment of justice and the general welfare in economic life.

The State itself in the manner described above and the existing free organizations of economic life should prepare the way for the ideal type of vocational groups or that sane corporative economic system of which the Pope so frequently speaks, which he so ardently desired to see realized and toward which rightly conducted activities of these organizations can lead (p. 28).

The second reform is of equal importance; it is first in the logical order but simultaneous in the order of time. "Nowadays," states Pius XI, "the conditions of social and economic life are such that vast multitudes of men can only with great difficulty pay attention to that one thing necessary, namely, their eternal salvation" (p. 40). There grows in consequence a disorderly affection of the soul, having its source in original sin but aggravated by the present unhappy social conditions. This leads to an unquenchable thirst for riches and temporal possessions, and prompted by this greed for gain there develops a fever of speculation unrestrained by any scruple in committing the gravest injustices against others. The civil authority which might have mitigated the evil failed lamentably in the enforcement of the moral law and the spirit of Rationalism already in the ascendant accentuated the evil by giving free rein to an economic science devoid of moral principles (p. 42).

The remedy in the spiritual order is a frank and sincere return to the teaching of the Gospel. God must once more be recognized as the supreme end of all created activity; and all created goods as the instruments under God for the attainment of our final destiny. "Seek ye first the kingdom of God and his justice and all things else will be added unto you" (Matt. 6:33).

Unfortunately there has been a tendency among too many to dissociate the virtue of justice from the virtue of charity, with the result that life has been made even more selfish and heartless.

Charity is no substitute for justice, but it cannot be ignored or derided without failing utterly to comprehend its meaning and its potent influence in regulating and sublimating our social relations and responsibilities. We need justice without doubt or equivocation, but we also need charity if we are to put our lives in harmony with God's plan and promote that spirit of benevolence which will lift the burdens not only from the backs but also from the souls of men.

We understand well that a right social order with a lasting and comprehensive peace cannot be achieved solely through improvement in the economic sphere. The present Holy Father states this clearly in his first Encyclical letter:

> For true though it is that the evils from which mankind suffers today come in part from economic instability and from the struggle of interests regarding a more equal distribution of the goods which God has given man as a means of sustenance and progress, it is not less true that their root is deeper and more intrinsic, belonging to the sphere of religious belief and moral convictions which have been perverted by the progressive alienation of the people from that unity of doctrine, faith, customs, and morals which once was promoted by the tireless and beneficent work of the Church. If it is to have any effect, the re-education of mankind must be, above all things, spiritual and religious. Hence, it must proceed from Christ as from its indispensable foundation; must be actuated by justice and crowned by charity.[7]

Our economic life then must be reorganized not on the disintegrating principles of individualism but on the constructive principle of social and moral unity among the members of human society. In conformity with Christian principles, economic power must be subordinated to human welfare, both individual and social; social incoherence and class conflict must be replaced by corporate unity and organic function; ruthless competition must give way to just and reasonable State regulations; sordid selfishness must be superseded by social justice and charity. Then only can there be a true and rational social order; then only can we eliminate the twin evils of insufficiency and insecurity, and establish the divine plan of a brotherhood of man under the fatherhood of God.

"In the recognition of the royal prerogatives of Christ and in the return of individuals and of society to the law of His truth and of His love lies the only way to salvation."[8]

---

[7] *Summi Pontificatus*, pp. 33, 34, N.C.W.C. edition, 1939.
[8] *Ibid.*, p. 10.

Well-nigh fifty years have passed since the farsighted Pope Leo XIII stated the Catholic principles of social justice for the modern world. His successors have reaffirmed and elaborated upon them. On numerous occasions, individually and collectively, the bishops of the United States have not only stressed their importance but have formulated practical programs for their effective application to conditions in this country.

In giving renewed emphasis to these principles, we urge our people again to give them earnest study, so that they may come to know and love the way of justice; and to strengthen themselves spiritually, through prayer and the sacraments, that they may ever follow it. So doing, by God's grace they will, as a leaven in society, fulfill their appointed role in the establishment of the Kingdom of God among men.

Given at Washington, D. C., Ash Wednesday, February 7, 1940.

The Administrative Board
And Assistant Bishops of the
National Catholic Welfare Conference

✠ Samuel A. Stritch, *Chairman,*
Archbishop of Chicago

✠ John Gregory Murray,
Archbishop of St. Paul

✠ Joseph F. Rummel,
Archbishop of New Orleans

✠ John Mark Gannon,
Bishop of Erie

✠ Hugh C. Boyle,
Bishop of Pittsburgh

✠ Francis C. Kelley,
Bishop of Oklahoma City-Tulsa

✠ John B. Peterson,
Bishop of Manchester

✠ Edwin V. O'Hara,
Bishop of Kansas City

✠ John A. Duffy,
Bishop of Buffalo

✠ Edward F. Hoban,
Bishop of Rockford

✠ Emmet M. Walsh,
Bishop of Charleston

✠ Karl J. Alter,
Bishop of Toledo

✠ Charles Hubert LeBlond,
Bishop of St. Joseph

✠ Francis P. Keough,
Bishop of Providence

✠ Walter A. Foery,
Bishop of Syracuse

✠ Bartholomew J. Eustace,
Bishop of Camden

72. STATEMENT OF THE ADMINISTRATIVE BOARD, N.C.W.C., ON THE

CATHOLIC CHURCH AND NATIONAL DEFENSE*

July 4, 1940

The Catholic Church is committed by its very nature to the promulgation of the Gospel of Peace and to the elimination from human society of the causes of war. The ideal of the Church is the "Peace of Christ in the Kingdom of Christ." Again and again in these latter days the present Supreme Pontiff has reminded the world of this ideal and, even as his predecessors did before him, has striven with all the means at his disposal to preserve the world from the horrors of armed conflict. For this he has won the admiration of religious men and women of all creeds. Inspired by his leadership, Catholics in our own country have endeavored to promote international peace and have worked and prayed, and continue to work and pray, that God may avert from this favored land the disasters of war.

It seems that tragic circumstances of the present hour are demanding that we invoke the law of self-protection for our national security. Regretfully, Christians are obliged to realize that adequate national defense demands the training of large numbers of our citizens in the arts of warfare. It is imperative that the extent of the emergency and the consequent need for action should be generally realized. On the other hand, in the interests of sound procedure, it should not be overstated. Because of the character of the times, any program promoted by any group, be it militarist, isolationist, or interventionist, should be subjected to critical appraisal and cool, sound judgment.

The American way of life has developed certain definite democratic ideals. No emergency should be allowed to destroy the values that

---

* *Catholic Action*, August, 1940, p. 4.

are of the very essence of liberty as we know it in America. Consequently, no plan for the national defense should do unnecessary violence to the religious and educational traditions upon which our democracy is founded and apart from which it will not continue to flourish.

73. APPEAL OF THE ADMINISTRATIVE BOARD, N.C.W.C., FOR PEACE AND PUBLIC SUPPORT OF THE

GOVERNMENT'S DEFENSE PROGRAM*

April 26, 1940

Appealing for a peace "not based on the oppression or the destruction of peoples, but for a peace which will guarantee the rights and honor of all nations and satisfy their vital needs," the archbishops and bishops of the Administrative Board of the National Catholic Welfare Conference in a statement made April 26, 1941, called for fervent prayers for the guidance and strengthening of "our President, our Congress, and civil authorities in the overwhelming responsibilities of this tragic hour" as well as reaffirming the five points laid down by Pope Pius XII in his 1939 Christmas message as essential to enduring world peace.

The statement which was made public following a series of meetings held by the Administrative Board expressed concern for the spiritual welfare of the thousands of young men who have been inducted into the armed forces of the country, asked the fullest public support of the organizations (including the National Catholic Community Service) constituting the United Service Organizations for National Defense and expressed confidence that the forthcoming appeal for funds to carry on the work which

---

* Catholic Action, May, 1940, pp. 3–4.

these private agencies will be called upon to render will be accorded generous financial assistance by all classes of our citizens. The statement was signed by the following members of the Administrative Board, N.C.W.C.: Archbishop Edward Mooney, of Detroit, chairman; Bishop John B. Peterson, Manchester, N. H., vice-chairman; Archbishop Francis J. Spellman, New York; Archbishop John Gregory Murray, St. Paul, Minn.; Archbishop John T. McNicholas, O.P., Cincinnati; Bishop John Mark Gannon, Erie, Pa.; Bishop Edwin V. O'Hara, Kansas City; Bishop John A. Duffy, Buffalo, N. Y.; Bishop Hugh C. Boyle, Pittsburgh; and Bishop Francis C. Kelley, Oklahoma City and Tulsa. The complete text of the statement follows:

The American people has, through orderly democratic action, expressed its solemn judgment that to be safe in the world today our nation must be strong. That judgment is reflected in the greatest defense effort in the history of the United States. An adequate program of national defense, as we see it, embraces both strength in arms and strength in spirit. With armed strength, it is not for us as bishops to deal. We leave that to our civil and military authorities. Our particular part in any program of national defense must have to do with the things of the spirit.

We are deeply concerned, therefore, with seeing to it that the spiritual influences of their home communities shall follow our boys who answer their country's call to train themselves to be their country's defenders if the need arise. Our government has followed the best of American traditions in entrusting the task of maintaining morale for camp communities and defense areas to private agencies whose service is inspired and guided by faith in God and love for man. We deeply appreciate the confidence this invitation implies, the challenge it carries, and the co-operation it promotes.

The National Catholic Community Service is the agency which the bishops of the Catholic Church in the United States have commissioned to do their share in this providential work. In doing this work on a national scale, the National Catholic Community Service is associated with similar agencies, representing our fellow citizens and other faiths in the United Service Organizations for National Defense. A nationwide appeal for funds to carry on this work will be made during the month of June. We are confident that the soul of America will give a generous answer to this appeal for the means to throw the saving influences of home and church around the young manhood of America in whose hands the defense of all that we hold dear will finally rest. We are confident, too, that our Catholic people will co-operate wholeheartedly in making this answer an eloquent expression of their interest in the souls of their soldier-sons.

The will of America today is set on peace, not war, as the aim of our defense program. The strongest defense weapon with which we can equip the American soldier is a clear vision of the kind of peace that constitutes our ideal. An august voice has sounded again and again in an America still at peace, as well as in a Europe already at war, applying to the conditions of our day the Gospel message of peace on earth to men of good will. In his Christmas allocution of 1939, Pope Pius XII laid down these five essential points of world order, and therefore of enduring peace:

First — The assurance of all nations of their right to life and independence — the will of one nation to live never justifying the death sentence of another.

Second — Progressive disarmament, spiritual as well as material, and security for the effective implementing of agreements to this end.

Third — Juridicial institutions guaranteeing loyal fulfillment of peace terms and providing for revisions called for by changing conditions.

Fourth — Satisfaction of the fair demands of national and racial minorities.

Fifth — A deep sense of responsibility for the observance of the precepts of justice and charity among men and nations.

It is significant, indeed, that the authoritative spokesmen for widely divergent Christian groups in a great nation now at war have publicly accepted these five points as basic principles for a just peace and commended them to the consideration of their government. This action is an inspiration to all who have the cause of true Christian peace at heart. Those who so lightly dismiss high-minded statements of principle as hopelessly idealistic in what they would call a world of hard facts, can find no comfort in the pronouncements of the Pope. But those who long for a world in which men and nations can, if they will, open their hearts to Christian truth and mold their lives on Christian principle find heartening support in his grave words. What he and his predecessors have repeatedly said is a spiritual bulwark of national defense for every people that loves true peace and true freedom.

No armament for national defense for peace can be strong which lacks the spiritual armory of prayer for peace. Even though the news of the day seems to offer little prospect of an early peace which will be just according to Christian or even humanitarian standards, we know that "the hand of the Lord is not shortened that it cannot save, neither is his ear heavy that it cannot hear" (Isa. 59:1). In the spirit of Christian brotherhood, therefore, we shall pray, first of all, for the victims of cruel war in all lands. In the same spirit too, we shall pray for an early peace; we shall pray for a world-wide peace; we shall pray for a peace, not based on the oppression or the destruction of peoples, but for a peace which will guarantee the rights and the honor of all nations and satisfy their vital needs. And in our prayers we shall not forget fervently to beg God to guide and strengthen our President, our Congress, and all our civil authorities in the overwhelming responsibilities of this tragic hour.

74. LETTER OF RT. REV. MSGR. MICHAEL J. READY, GENERAL SECRETARY, ADMINISTRATIVE BOARD, N.C.W.C., TO HON. SENATOR WALTER F. GEORGE OPPOSING

TAX ON BENEFITS*

August 22, 1941

Honorable Walter F. George, Chairman
Senate Committee on Finance
United States Senate
Washington, D. C.

Dear Senator George:
I have been directed by the Administrative Board of Archbishops and Bishops of the National Catholic Welfare Conference to inform you and through you the Committee on Finance and the United States Senate of the attitude of the National Catholic Welfare Con-

---

* *Catholic Chronicle* (Toledo, Ohio), Vol. 7, No. 44 (September 19, 1941), p. 1; cf. *Catholic Action*, October, 1941, p. 18.

ference with respect to Section 541 (b) of the Internal Revenue Bill (H.R. 5417) now before the Committee on Finance of which you are the chairman.

It is proposed by Section 541 (b) to repeal Section 1701 of the Internal Revenue Code which has been law since February 26, 1926.

Section 1701 provides in effect that no tax shall be levied under the Admissions Tax Subchapter in respect to any admissions whose proceeds inure exclusively to the benefit of religious, charitable, or educational agencies.

The National Catholic Welfare Conference is deeply sympathetic with the task presently before the Congress in providing revenues with which to meet the heavy demands laid upon government by the National Defense program.

In revenue laws, state and federal, heretofore enacted, both before and during the present defense emergency, are embodied provisions which accept and safeguard the tax exempt status of religious, charitable, and educational agencies as inherent under the system of liberty prevailing in the relationship of these agencies to the state.

These agencies render a community service. The Congress understands the importance of this community service. Today that importance is enhanced because of the indispensable contributions these agencies make to the promotion and preservation of national morale.

To enact Section 541 (b), as it now stands, would impose a burden upon agencies rendering these important contributions to defense morale which we are convinced the Congress neither wishes nor intends to impose.

It may be argued that admission taxes are paid by the individual, and therefore place no burden upon the organization.

We respectfully submit that, while nominally and technically this is true, it nonetheless remains the fact that the morale-minded citizen who contributes to agencies rendering these services by purchasing admissions to programs and benefits given is forced to pay more than he would have had to pay had the tax not been imposed. The consequent handicapping of the work done by the agency is obvious.

The further fact is that the process results in a duplication of effort that is costly, at a time when the avowed purpose of the bill is to devote all possible effort to defense. The tax would be collected in order to realize revenue to be expended for public purposes. It follows that the tax should not be imposed upon agencies already rendering such services in order that government might realize monies to be expended through political agencies in rendering service already provided by voluntary agencies.

In addition, while the tax is on the admission, the responsibility and burden of collecting the tax and paying it to the government is placed upon the religious, charitable, and educational organization charging the admission. This is the first instance in federal legislation wherein these organizations would be placed in such a role.

The enactment of Section 541 (b) in its present form would constitute a departure by the Congress from a long and well-established policy of the United States Government.

We, therefore, respectfully submit that Section 541 (b) should be stricken from the Revenue Bill now being considered by your Committee.

Faithfully yours,
s/s MICHAEL J. READY,
General Secretary

75a. LETTER OF MOST REV. EDWARD MOONEY, CHAIRMAN, EXECUTIVE BOARD, N.C.W.C., TO HON. FRANKLIN D. ROOSEVELT, PRESIDENT, U.S.A., PLEDGING SUPPORT IN THE

NATIONAL CRISIS OF WORLD WAR II*

December 22, 1941

Dear Mr. President:

As Chief Executive of our nation you have called upon the American people for full service and sacrifice in a war of defense against wanton aggression. Congress in grave and inspiring unity has spoken the will of a great nation determined to be free. We, the Catholic bishops of the United States, spiritual leaders of more than

---

* *Catholic Action,* January, 1942, p. 4.

twenty million Americans, wish to assure you, Mr. President, that we are keenly conscious of our responsibilities in the hour of our nation's testing. With a patriotism that is guided and sustained by the Christian virtues of faith, hope, and charity, we will marshal the spiritual forces at our command to render secure our God-given blessings of freedom.

We will do our full part in the national effort to transmute the impressive material and spiritual resources of our country into effective strength, not for vengeance but for the common good, not for national aggrandizement but for common security in a world in which individual human rights shall be safeguarded, and the will to live on the part of all nations great or small shall be respected — a world in which the eternal principles of justice and charity shall prevail.

The ultimate strength of a people is in the things of the spirit. The historic position of the Catholic Church in the United States gives us a tradition of devoted attachment to the ideals and institutions of government we are now called upon to defend. Our predecessors, in the Third Plenary Council of Baltimore, solemnly declared: "We believe that our country's heroes were the instruments of the God of nations in establishing this home of freedom; to both the Almighty and to His instruments in the work, we look with grateful reverence; and to maintain the inheritance of freedom which they have left us, should it ever — which God forbid — be imperiled, our Catholic citizens will be found to stand forward, as one man, ready to pledge anew 'their lives, their fortunes, and their sacred honor.' "

Today, in the face of the peril they feared, we reaffirm their solemn words. We give you, Mr. President, the pledge of our wholehearted co-operation in the difficult days that lie ahead. We will zealously fulfill our spiritual ministry in the sacred cause of our country's service. We place at your disposal in that service our institutions and their consecrated personnel. We will lead our priests and people in constant prayer that God may bear you up under the heavy burdens that weigh upon you, that He may guide you and all who share with you responsibility for the nation's governance and security, that He may strengthen us all to win a victory that will be a blessing not for our nation alone, but for the whole world.

The undersigned, Chairman of the Administrative Board, National Catholic Welfare Conference, authorized to forward this letter in the name of the Bishops of the United States, has the honor, Mr. President, to be, with sentiments of high consideration,

Faithfully yours,

EDWARD MOONEY,

Archbishop of Detroit,

*Chairman, Administrative Board***

** The Administrative Board at this date had as members the Most Rev. Samuel A. Stritch, Archbishop of Chicago; the Most Rev. Francis J. Spellman, Archbishop of New York; the Most Rev. John T. McNicholas, O.P., Archbishop of Cincinnati; the Most Rev. John Gregory Murray, Archbishop of St. Paul; the Most Rev. John F. Noll, Bishop of Fort Wayne; the Most Rev. John Mark Gannon, Bishop of Erie; the Most Rev. Hugh C. Boyle, Bishop of Pittsburgh; the Most Rev. John A. Duffy, Bishop of Buffalo, and the Most Rev. Edwin V. O'Hara, Bishop of Kansas City.

75b.

THE PRESIDENT'S ACKNOWLEDGMENT
(of the foregoing letter) *

December 24, 1941

Dear Archbishop Mooney:

The letter which you forwarded under date of December 22 as chairman of the Administrative Board, National Catholic Welfare Conference, and in the name of the bishops of the United States, gives me strength and courage because it is a witness to that national unity so necessary in our all-out effort to win the war. Please convey to all of your brethren in the episcopate an assurance of my heartfelt appreciation of the pledge of wholehearted co-operation in the difficult days that lie ahead. In those days we shall be glad to remember your patriotic action in placing your institutions and their consecrated personnel at the disposal of the government.

We shall win this war and in victory we shall seek not vengeance but the establishment of an international order in which the spirit of Christ shall rule the hearts of men and of nations.

Very sincerely yours,

FRANKLIN D. ROOSEVELT

* *Catholic Action*, January, 1942, p. 4.

76. MESSAGE OF SYMPATHY BY THE MEMBERS OF THE EXECUTIVE BOARD, N.C.W.C., TO THE

BISHOPS OF FRANCE*

June 12, 1944

On June 12, 1944, the members of the Administrative Board, N.C.W.C., sent a message to His Eminence Luigi Cardinal Maglione, Papal Secretary of State, expressing their sympathy with the bishops of France and their "profound concern for the sufferings of their defenseless flocks" in air bombing raids. The message noted that the bishops of the United States have "repeatedly urged that every precaution be taken to avoid unjustifiable destruction of life and property" in the bombing raids.

Their message, which follows below, was signed by the ten members of the Administrative Board: the Most Revs. Edward Mooney, Archbishop of Detroit, chairman; Samuel A. Stritch, Archbishop of Chicago, vice-chairman; Francis J. Spellman, Archbishop of New York, secretary; John T. McNicholas, O.P., Archbishop of Cincinnati; John Gregory Murray, Archbishop of St. Paul; John J. Mitty, Archbishop of San Francisco; Joseph F. Rummel, Archbishop of New Orleans; John F. Noll, Bishop of Fort Wayne; Karl J. Alter, Bishop of Toledo, and James H. Ryan, Bishop of Omaha.

The text is as follows:

Your Eminence:

It is reported that the bishops of France have appealed to the bishops of the United States to intervene with responsible authorities in order that the civilian population and the monuments of religion and art of France and Europe be spared the horrors of bombing.

The bishops of the United States respectfully request Your Emi-

---

* *Catholic Action*, July, 1944, p. 5; cf. *Catholic Bulletin* (St. Paul, Minnesota), June 17, 1944.

nence to assure their brethren in France of their common and profound concern for the sufferings of their defenseless flocks. They concur in the attitude of their brother bishops of all countries in condemning indiscriminate bombing or similar methods of warfare which injure the innocent and helpless without the justification of military necessity. They ask, however, that all these be reminded that the bishops of this country since the outbreak of this frightful conflict have repeatedly urged that every precaution be taken to avoid unjustifiable destruction of life and property, and have expressed deepest sympathy for the innocent victims of such warfare, whether on the British Isles, the Continent of Europe, or Africa or Asia, or among the afflicted islanders of the South Pacific.

They have received assurances from their civil and military leaders that every precaution is being taken to confine the war within legitimate military objectives. The killing of innocent civilians and the destruction of property which is not being devoted to the war effort are indeed deplorable, and they hope that any such things which have occurred have been the result of accidents and miscalculations. It is gratifying that our authorities have shown their desire to save from damage and destruction monuments of culture and history in the war area by setting up the American Commission for the Protection and Salvage of Artistic and Historic Monuments in Europe, which co-operates closely with the military authorities.

The bishops of the United States beg Your Eminence to assure their distressed brethren in France that their tragic plight and that of their flocks does not cease to be the object of the concern, the sympathy, and the prayers of the bishops of the United States. In union with the Vicar of Christ, they beseech almighty God to lighten the burden of all suffering humanity and speedily to restore to all mankind the inestimable blessings of a peace of justice and of charity.

77. STATEMENT OF THE ADMINISTRATIVE BOARD, N.C.W.C., ON

WORLD PEACE*

April 15, 1945

The organization of the community of nations in an international institution to maintain world peace and achieve world co-operation will test the fullness of our victory. This conviction inspired the statement made by the Catholic bishops of the United States last November. The trend of events since then prompts us to reaffim and further interpret the principles of that statement.

A sound world organization is not a utopian dream. With honest good will in all the victors, it will be realized, and a new era in international relations will begin. If any one of them refuses it full support, or insists on introducing into its charter provisions which radically vitiate it, we shall witness the tragedy, so often recorded in history, of a glorious martial victory largely nullified by sheer political expediency. Experience warns us that unless strong, courageous leaders, with the full support of their peoples, put their hands to this task, there will be no genuine progress in international life. To yield to the fear that this thing cannot be done is defeatism. In nations, as well as in individuals, we must indeed face the fact of human weakness, but we must face it to conquer it; we must not accept it in a spirit of paralyzing fatalism. An opportunity is here, as in every world crisis, to begin a new era of genuine progress in the community of nations.

DISILLUSIONMENT BREEDS ISOLATIONISM

Isolationism, whether expressed in the refusal of a nation to assume its obligations in the international community, or masked in the setting up of a sphere of influence in which a great nation surrounds itself with weak puppet States, or disguised in a balance of power policy, is no answer to the world's problems, or indeed to the problems of any

---

* Published by the N.C.W.C., Washington 5, D. C., 1945.

nation. There is, however, the danger present at this time, that if in the name of realism an attempt is made to substitute for a juridical world institution what is in effect only an alliance of the Great Powers, many nations will take refuge in isolationism. Disillusionment in our country will express itself in the isolationism of the abstentionist.

The proposals for an international organization which will be presented to the coming San Francisco Conference have been studied by able and experienced men who, in a spirit of constructive criticism, have brought to light some of their outstanding defects. The admittedly tentative character of these proposals suggests that the delegates at San Francisco will be given the opportunity of free, open discussion and action. But the official information on agreements reached by the Three Great Powers — the United States, Russia, and Great Britain — on certain fundamental provisions in the Charter, gives rise to doubt and fear. We fail to see that the voting procedure in the Security Council agreed upon at Yalta is consistent with the sovereign equality of peace-loving nations recognized as basic in the Dumbarton Oaks Proposals. Whatever concessions may, under existing conditions, have to be made to certain nations in view of their power and corresponding responsibility, it seems inequitable and dangerous to give any nation in perpetuity a virtual veto on parity of treatment for all. It is a manifest denial of a prime attribute of a juridical institution to extend the veto to the execution of decisions of the World Court to which, by explicit provision, all justifiable disputes should be referred. And the concession in question is not even limited to cases directly involving the nation to which it is made. This makes the Charter give a preferred status not only to the powerful aggressor, but even to any aggressor with a powerful patron.

While there is reason in setting up a committee or council to act in emergencies, in the proposals the functions of the General Assembly are too restricted, and the functions of the Security Council are too broad. It is hoped, then, that the Security Council will be made more responsible to the General Assembly and, at least in time, will become merely its executive committee. It is imperative, too, that there be lodged in the international organization, and ultimately in the World Court, the authority to make changes in the peace settlements and other treaties which, in view of past mistakes or changed conditions, may be required. The proposals as they stand outline not the plan for an organization, under law, of the international community, but rather the draft of an alliance between the Great Victorious Powers for the maintenance of world peace and the promotion of international co-operation, in which these Powers definitely refuse to submit themselves in every eventuality to the world authority which they propose to invoke in compelling other nations to maintain world peace.

INTERNATION BILL OF RIGHTS

Sovereign equality among the nations demands that each nation be free in its internal government, and that its juridical personality be recognized in its international relations. It does not mean, however, that a nation is exempt from its obligations in the international community. Even in internal government, sovereignty does not include the authority to violate the inalienable rights of subjects. In all history, and particularly in modern history, dangers to world peace have come from the unjust treatment of minorities, the denial of civil and religious liberties, and other infringements on the inborn rights of men. To remove these dangers, the nations should adopt an Internation Bill of Rights, in which men and groups everywhere would be guaranteed the full enjoyment of their human rights. That this is definitely a matter of international concern is evident in the problem now confronting the Intergovernmental Committee in regard to displaced persons. If they are reluctant to return to their homelands, it is largely because they cannot look forward to the enjoyment of fundamental human rights under the new tyrannies in control. Active participation in the international organization ought to be conditioned on the acceptance of this Bill of Rights. Will a nation which does not make its own citizens secure in the enjoyment of their human rights work honestly and sincerely for the maintenance of world peace and mutual cooperation in the international community?

PROPOSALS ON POLAND DISAPPOINTING

The solution of the Polish question agreed upon by the representatives of the Three Great Victorious Powers in the Crimean Conference, was a disappointment to all who had built their hopes on the Atlantic Charter. Poland, which stood against the Nazi aggressor from the very beginning of the war; Poland, which has suffered more than any other nation in the war; Poland, which has fought and is fighting with our armies on every European Front, has been forced by her allies to surrender a very large part of her territory. In apparent exchange, it was guaranteed at Yalta that in the reconstructed world there will be a strong, independent Poland, with a government chosen in a free election by its own people. Pending the action of the people of Poland in a free election, agreements were made to set up a provisional regime which will be recognized by the Three Great Powers. This provisional government must not be the creation of a single foreign power but the choice of all parties to the Yalta engagements. Our President is pledged to see that in the choice of a permanent Polish government, the people of Poland be guaranteed in their right of free secret ballot. No foreign power must be permitted to influence this election in a way which will determine its results. The peace of the world demands a free, independent, democratic Poland. It must not be that Poland become a puppet State under the domination and control of any foreign power. If Poland is secured in its rights of freedom and independence, it will make great sacrifices and do its full part in the international community. If it is enslaved, and its leadership forced into exile or inhumanly liquidated, the love of freedom will not be crushed in Polish hearts, but the seeds of war will have been sown.

THE FATE OF THE BALTIC STATES

In reading official reports on current peace discussions, we are struck by the ominous silence of the Three Great Powers on Lithuania, Esthonia, and Latvia. Contrary to the protests of our government four years ago, and to the assurances of Soviet authorities even before that time, the indications are that they will be absorbed without their free and unfettered consent, in an alien system of government. The sympathy of all lovers of freedom goes out to them in their disaster. We hope that when the final peace treaty is framed and approved, it will not be recorded that our country condoned the enslavement of these freedom-loving nations.

We hope too that our government will discharge its full responsibility in re-establishing all the liberated nations of Europe under genuine democratic regimes which will accord to all their citizens the full enjoyment of their human rights and open to them an era of prosperity.

In the treatment of the enemy nations, justice must obtain. Justice, indeed, is stern. It is not, however, born of hatred or vengeance, and prevails only when the mind is clear and calm. Moreover, the common good of the whole world must be kept in mind in dealing with these peoples. They must be freed from tyranny and oppression, and they must be given the opportunity to reconstruct their institutions on the foundations of genuine democracy. There are things, too, which charity and a right sense of world co-operation urges us to do for them. Only in the unity of human brotherhood will it be possible for them to do their full part in the community of nations.

People living on the near-starvation level, without the means of even beginning the work of reconstruction for themselves, are not clear in their thinking and become easy victims of bad leadership. It is imperative indeed to keep before them the sound principles of genuine democracy, which is a product of our culture and at its base recognizes human rights of individuals and groups. It is equally imperative to keep them fit rightly to appraise sound principles. The work of relief before us is very great, and it must be done quickly and efficiently if there is to be a sound world peace.

Democracy and Marxism Incompatible

Every day makes more evident the fact that two strong essentially incompatible ways of life will divide the loyalties of men and nations in the political world of tomorrow. They are genuine democracy and Marxian totalitarianism. Democracy is built on respect for the dignity of the human person with its God-given inviolable rights. It achieves unity and strength in the intelligent co-operation of all citizens for the common good under governments chosen and supported by the people. It will advance, expand, and develop our culture. It will maintain continuity with our Christian past. It will give security for our Christian future. Fascism and Nazism, rampant in their might, sought its destruction. Fascism is gone, we hope, forever. And soon Nazism will be only a horrible historical memory.

However, we have to reckon with the active, cleverly organized and directed opposition of Marxian totalitarianism to genuine democracy. This system herds the masses under dictatorial leadership, insults their intelligence with its propaganda and controlled press, and tyrannically violates innate human rights. Against it, genuine democracy must constantly be on guard, quick to detect and penetrate its camouflage. Democracy's bulwark is religion, and justice is its watchword. We entered this war to defend our democracy. It is our solemn responsibility, in the reconstruction, to use our full influence in safeguarding the freedoms of all people. This, we are convinced, is the only way to an enduring peace.

✠ Samuel A. Stritch, *Vice-Chairman, Archbishop of Chicago*

✠ Edward Mooney, *Chairman,*   ✠ John T. McNicholas,
    Archbishop of Detroit   *Archbishop of Cincinnati*

✠ Francis J. Spellman, *Secretary,* ✠ John Gregory Murray,
    Archbishop of New York   *Archbishop of St. Paul*

✠ JOHN J. MITTY,
  Archbishop of San Francisco
✠ JOSEPH F. RUMMEL,
  Archbishop of New Orleans
   ✠ JAMES H. RYAN, *Bishop of Omaha*

✠ JOHN F. NOLL,
  Bishop of Fort Wayne
✠ KARL J. ALTER,
  Bishop of Toledo

78. APPEAL OF THE ADMINISTRATIVE BOARD, N.C.W.C., FOR

FOOD FOR THE CHILDREN OF EUROPE AND THE FAR EAST*

May 5, 1946

On April 30 and May 1, 1946, the annual spring meeting of the Administrative Board of the National Catholic Welfare Conference was held in Washington, D. C. Among other matters considered was that of famine relief, on which the following statement was given.

Famine is killing millions of people. Its victims, weakened in body and in spirit, increase in number each day. We who know not the pangs of hunger must hearken to the pitiful cries of our brothers in Christ. Self-discipline and self-denial on our part will save countless lives. From our overflowing granaries, yea, from what we wantonly waste, we can do much to relieve their utter destitution. Bread must become for us a holy thing; for it means life to a multitude of God's children.

Mindful of this dire need, the bishops of our country are appealing to the faithful to give unstintingly in the campaign for Food for the Children of Europe and the Far East during the week, beginning on Mother's Day, May 12. We are confident that the response will be a fitting testimony of Christlike love for our neighbors in need. Moreover, we earnestly urge our fellow Americans to heed the plea of our

---

* *Catholic Action,* June, 1946, p. 3; cf. N.C.W.C. "News Release," May 5, 1946.

government to release their reserve stores of wheat that the hungry may eat.

Relief of hunger is indeed the pressing need of the moment. We know that the shortage of food is due in large measure to the terrible devastation wrought by war. Yet, thinking men will not limit their vision to this fact. They will look beyond to find deeper causes for the chaos that now afflicts suffering humanity.

Europe's misery has been aggravated by moral and economic disorders that could have been prevented. Undue delay in reaching peace settlements has fostered instability and paralyzed reconstruction. Eastern or "Bread" Europe has been artificially walled off from western Europe. Multitudes of civilians and prisoners of war have been deported and degraded into forced labor unworthy of human beings. Occupying soldiery, living off the land, are consuming already depleted food stores. Great masses of unfortunate people have been stripped of their goods and then driven like cattle from their native soil into strange areas where they are homeless, helpless, and friendless. Inevitably, famine breeds fear and unrest; and unrest jeopardizes the hope of peace for which mankind is longing.

Justice cries out against these violations of the moral order. There can be no peace while they endure. Injustice is the helpmate of famine and their offspring is chaos. Order among men and nations can come only from the practice of justice and mercy in human relations. The moral order set down by the Maker of the Universe is the only charter given to men whereby they may find peace and security.

Signed by:

✝ SAMUEL CARDINAL STRITCH,
Archbishop of Chicago
✝ FRANCIS CARDINAL SPELLMAN,
Archbishop of New York
✝ JOHN GREGORY MURRAY,
Archbishop of St. Paul
✝ JOSEPH F. RUMMEL,
Archbishop of New Orleans
✝ JOHN J. MITTY,
Archbishop of San Francisco

✝ JAMES H. RYAN,
Archbishop of Omaha
✝ RICHARD J. CUSHING,
Archbishop of Boston
✝ JOHN MARK GANNON,
Bishop of Erie
✝ JOHN F. NOLL,
Bishop of Fort Wayne
✝ KARL J. ALTER,
Bishop of Toledo

79. STATEMENT OF SAMUEL CARDINAL STRITCH, CHAIRMAN, ADMINISTRATIVE BOARD, N.C.W.C., IN PROTEST OF THE

INJUSTICE OF THE TRIAL OF ARCHBISHOP ALOYSIUS STEPINAC, D.D., OF ZAGREB, JUGOSLAVIA*

September 30, 1946

The following statement on the trial of Archbishop Stepinac was issued by His Eminence Samuel Cardinal Stritch, Archbishop of Chicago and chairman of the Administrative Board of the National Catholic Welfare Conference.

To its sordid record of injustice, tyranny, and despotism, the Tito regime in Jugoslavia, in the arrest and trial of Archbishop Stepinac of Zagreb, his 74-year-old auxiliary bishop, and many priests, has now added another chapter which further shocks and horrifies the civilized world.

Few shepherds of souls in our troubled times have had such enormous responsibility in caring for their harassed flocks as the Archbishop of Zagreb.

Ravished, decimated, and crushed by five armies and armed terrorist groups during the war years, the people of Croatia had but one champion who stood fearlessly in defense of human rights against Nazi and Fascist oppression, as he has stood against the tyranny of those now in control. That champion was Archbishop Stepinac.

The civilized world knows from the story of his life, from his actions, and from his pronouncements how faithfully he discharged his mission as the protector of the people, how courageously he dealt with those who oppressed them and defrauded them of their human rights, and how appropriately they came to regard him as the symbol of justice, fairness, and decency.

---

* *Our Sunday Visitor* (Huntington, Indiana), October 6, 1946.

The protagonists of the rights of racial and religious minorities, Jew and Gentile alike, when they were bitterly persecuted by barbarous tyrants, found in him a friend and a valiant defender.

The record of those now in control in Jugoslavia leaves no room for doubt that they have little regard for justice. They have already murdered hundreds of priests, nuns, and helpless citizens. There is every reason to believe that their aim is to destroy the Church, the only remaining voice which can oppose their reign of terror. Apparently unable to intimidate the flock, they are determined to discredit or destroy the shepherd.

The civilized world has little reason to expect a trial that will be anything but a travesty on justice. For it is a travesty even to indict, as an enemy of the people, one whose life has been in constant peril for years because he has been the protector of the people. Patently false charges, contradicted by the life record of Archbishop Stepinac, will not hide the sinister purpose of the trial.

We fought against the monstrous tyrannies of Nazism and Fascism to liberate the people of Jugoslavia, and we promised them, as the fruit of our victory, the full opportunity to build for themselves institutions of genuine democracy. We have not refused to extend a helping hand toward the democratic reconstruction of Jugoslavia.

Our people stand for what is decent and right. They cannot stand by silent and witness the violation of inalienable rights.

Religious freedom is fundamental in our political creed. Often our government has used its influence to save, or try to save, from persecution outstanding champions of freedom. We hope sincerely that our government will voice its protest, and use its influence in behalf of Archbishop Stepinac and those who with him are victims of this persecution.

80a. APPEAL OF THE ADMINISTRATIVE BOARD, N.C.W.C., IN THE NAME OF THE HIERARCHY OF THE UNITED STATES FOR THE

INTERNATIONALIZATION OF JERUSALEM AND ITS ENVIRONS*

April 27, 1949, and November 21, 1949

The Administrative Board of the National Catholic Welfare Conference, assembled in Washington for its annual (1949) spring meeting, issued the following statement. The statement is signed by the Administrative Board.

Conscious of our sacred duty as leaders of the Catholics in the United States, we exhort our people to use their democratic privileges in this free nation to obtain from those in our government and in the United Nations continued assurances that the original commitments as to Christian rights in Palestine will be carried out. We feel it necessary at this time to insist that the internationalization of Jerusalem be implemented.

The General Assembly of the United Nations, in November, 1947, voted the partition plan for Palestine. The Christian world did not oppose this decision because it did safeguard our religious and humanitarian stake in the Holy Land. The international zone of all Jerusalem and its environs, free access to all sacred shrines, the freedom of religious organization, and the rights of ethnic and religious minorities, wherever located, were considered by all Christians as satisfactory guarantees.

These same guarantees were voted again by the General Assembly of the United Nations as late as December, 1948. Faced at this latter date with the problem of the vast hordes of refugees in the hundreds of thousands outside the confines of Palestine, the Assembly further

---

* Bureau of Information, N.C.W.C., April 27, 1949, and N.C.W.C. News Service, November 19, 1949. F.

Cf. *The Tablet* (Brooklyn, New York), April 30, 1949.

resolved that "the refugees wishing to return to their homes and live at peace with their neighbors should be permitted to do so at the earliest practicable date." The present sad plight of these harassed and hungry wanderers urges us to appeal once more to our brethren of America to continue what has already been an overflowingly bountiful campaign of mercy. We are further moved by a sense of elementary justice to point out, completely in accord with the United Nations' decision, that the end of all this misery can only come when the refugees will be permitted to return to their homes.

We know that millions of Americans share our sentiments, when we repeat that religious and humanitarian rights cannot be obscured or neglected in that land, for which every true Christian cherishes deepest devotion. We have the right to expect that these just sentiments, firmly rooted in the decisions of the United Nations, will now be respected by those to whom we should all appeal for their continuous affirmation.

Signed by :*

✝ Edward Cardinal Mooney,
    Archbishop of Detroit

✝ Samuel Cardinal Stritch,
    Archbishop of Chicago

✝ Francis Cardinal Spellman,
    Archbishop of New York

✝ Francis P. Keough,
    Archbishop of Baltimore

✝ John T. McNicholas,
    Archbishop of Cincinnati

✝ Robert E. Lucey,
    Archbishop of San Antonio

✝ Richard J. Cushing,
    Archbishop of Boston

✝ Patrick A. O'Boyle,
    Archbishop of Washington

✝ John Mark Gannon,
    Bishop of Erie

✝ John F. Noll,
    Bishop of Fort Wayne

✝ Karl J. Alter,
    Bishop of Toledo

✝ Michael J. Ready,
    Bishop of Columbus

---

*His Eminence Dennis Cardinal Dougherty, Archbishop of Philadelphia, and Archbishop Joseph E. Ritter of St. Louis, also members of the Administrative Board, were not present.

80b. STATEMENT OF THE ADMINISTRATIVE BOARD ON THE STATUS OF JERUSALEM AND THE HOLY PLACES

November 18, 1950

The question of the status of Jerusalem and the Holy Places, now before the United Nations, pre-eminently religious in character, is a matter of deep and intimate concern to Catholics in the United States. Through the centuries, Christians have held the Holy Places in Palestine as a sacred trust.

In the earliest years, they built there great sanctuaries and erected hospices for the care of the many pilgrims from all quarters of the civilized world. Since the thirteenth century, the Franciscan Fathers, supported by the offerings of the Catholic world, have been custodians of these Holy Shrines and hundreds of them have suffered martyrdom in defense of them. In the eighteenth century, an arrangement known as the *Status quo,* safeguarding the sacred character of the Holy Places and guaranteeing free access to them, proved to be workable in circumstances which were not wholly satisfactory.

Under the British mandate the provisions of the *Status quo* were enforced as law and the British acted for the Family of Nations. When the General Assembly of the United Nations on November 29, 1947, decreed the partition of Palestine into a Jewish State and an Arab State, it made the creation of an International Enclave of Jerusalem and its environs an essential element of the tripartite arrangement. Hence, with the surrender of the mandate by the British on May 14, 1948, the new provisions for protecting the Holy Places and for insuring free access to them became the responsibility of the Nations.

In spite of the regrettable war in Palestine during the intervening period when the United Nations was unable to set up an international regime, this responsibility was reaffirmed in the General Assembly of the United Nations on December 11, 1948, when it was resolved that the Jerusalem area should be accorded special and separate treatment from the rest of Palestine "and that it should be placed under effective United Nations' control."

To this end it established the Palestine Conciliation Commission which was instructed to present to the Fourth Regular Session of the General Assembly "detailed proposals for a permanent international regime for the Jerusalem area which will provide a maximum local autonomy for distinctive groups consistent with the special international status of the Jerusalem area."

The Commission has presented its proposal, and in the near future the General Assembly will act on it. This proposal, while pretending internationalization of the Jerusalem area, by no means achieves it.

Our Holy Father Pope Pius XII, time and time again, has made it clear that the only effective guarantee for the safety, and the sacred character of Jerusalem, for the protection of the Holy Places, for the free exercise of the indisputable rights of a Christian minority, and for free access of pilgrims to their shrines is a territorial internationalization of Jerusalem and its area under the sovereignty and the effective control of the Family of Nations.

There can be no question as to the meaning of internationalization in the papal letters. It is the concept originally expressed by the General Assembly itself in November, 1947. It is a truly international regime and not a mere control or curatorship. Therefore only such a real internationalization can establish peace in the area and effectively safeguard the Holy Places for future generations.

In our historic position as defenders of the sacredness of the Holy Places and of free access to them, we appeal to our civil authorities and to the nations for a real and effective internationalization of Jerusalem and its environs. For this truly Christian ideal Catholics the world over are united in prayer with Pope Pius XII.

We beg God to guide the delegates of the nations in their deliberations. May they see that the hope of true peace in this critical area lies only in the real and effective internationalization of Jerusalem and its environs.

Signed by the members of the Administrative Board.

81. STATEMENT OF THE BISHOPS ON

GOD'S LAW: THE MEASURE OF MAN'S CONDUCT*

November 18, 1951

The Catholic bishops of the United States, at the close of their annual meeting in Washington, D. C., November 14–16, 1951, issued the following statement. It was signed in their names by the Administrative Board of the National Catholic Welfare Conference.

An alarming parallel exists between the situation facing us today and that which faced the Roman Empire fifteen hundred years ago. The problems of the Empire closely resemble those which sorely test us now — barbarism on the outside, refined materialism and moral decay within. Confronted by those problems, what were men of that time concerned with? St. Augustine, who lived in that period, gives us the answer in a memorable passage:

> They do not trouble about the moral degradation of the Empire. All that they ask is that it should be prosperous and secure. "What concerns us," they say, "is that everyone should be able to increase his wealth so that he can afford a lavish expenditure and can keep the weak in subjection. Let the laws protect the rights of property and let them leave man's morals alone. . . . Let there be sumptuous banquets where anybody can play and drink and gorge himself and be dissipated by day or night as much as he pleases or is able. Let the noise of dancing be everywhere and let the theatres resound with lewd merriment. . . . Let the man who dislikes these pleasures be regarded as a public enemy." (*City of God*, Bk. II, 20)

Does not all this have a modern ring? Has not a great part of our society been doing and saying much the same thing? With the threat of the barbarian on the outside, does our conduct reflect the sobriety of citizens who are conscious that a bell may be tolling for them and for civilization?

We have sent our young men on military expeditions to far-off lands so that justice and freedom may be kept alive in the world; and yet at home we have become careless about the foundations of

---

* From N.C.W.C. "News Release," November 18, 1951

justice and the roots of freedom. It cannot go well with us if we continue on this course.

The lessons of history are evident to those with eyes that will see. The Roman Empire disintegrated from within; and moral corruption was the main cause of its decline and disappearance. The same fate will befall us if we do not awaken to the danger which threatens from within our own household. Mastery over material things will avail us nothing, if we lose mastery over ourselves.

Morality: The Need Today

Mastery over self is the primary concern of morality. The right ordering of our lives in relationship to all other beings so that we may attain our true destiny is the proper function of morality. The fundamental problem which faces us, then, is a moral one.

Morality involves the correct and careful regulation of three relationships: man to God, man to himself, and man to his fellow men. These relationships are so closely linked together that to disturb one is to disturb the whole moral order.

Morality, therefore, viewed in its entirety, has three dimensions: height, depth, and breadth. In its height, it soars up to God the Supreme Being, from whom it takes the definitive measure of what is true and good. In its depth, it penetrates the heart of man, laying hold of his entire personality so that even his innermost thoughts and motives are subject to its rule. In its breadth, it embraces men in every station and condition of life and establishes mutual rights and duties.

God's Will: Man's Measure in the Moral Order

By nature, man is a creature, subject to his Creator and responsible to Him for all his actions. By selfish inclination, at times, he chooses to be something else, assuming the prerogatives of a Creator, establishing his own standards of conduct, and making himself the measure of all things. This prideful folly on his part brings discord into his own life, and profoundly affects the whole moral order. Frustration rather than fulfillment becomes his characteristic mark because he does not possess wholly within himself the way to fulfillment. That he can discover only in God's plan.

God's will, therefore, is the measure of man. It is the standard by which all human actions must meet the test of their rightness or wrongness. What conforms to God's will is right; and what goes counter to His will is wrong. This is the great and controlling rule of the moral order. Unless man recognizes and lives by this rule, he cannot come to that abundance of life destined for him by God.

If man is to reach this abundance of life, which depends on the fullness of moral character, it must be through the way he lives his everyday life. He has no other course. It is idle and dangerous for him to dream otherwise. The thoughts, attitudes, motives, judgments, and deeds which make up his daily round will determine his growth in character. He must use all his powers to cultivate that growth as the condition for attaining the true purpose of his life. For this it is necessary that he should be guided by a knowledge of what is right and what is wrong in the particular situations of everyday existence.

THE MORAL ORDER AND HUMAN REASON

How does he come to such knowledge? How can man know what is his place in the divine plan, and what is God's will in the moral decisions he is called upon to make? God has endowed man with intelligence. When rightly used and directed, the human intellect can discover certain fundamental spiritual truths and moral principles which will give order and harmony to man's intellectual and moral life.

What are these truths which right reason can discover? First in importance is the existence of a personal God, all knowing and all powerful, the eternal Source from whom all things derive their being. Next comes the spiritual and immortal nature of man's soul, its freedom, its responsibility, and the duty of rendering to God reverence, obedience, and all that is embraced under the name of religion.

From man's position as God's rational, free, and responsible creature, destined for eternal life, spring the unique dignity of the human individual and his essential equality with his fellow men.

Out of the inherent demands of human nature arises the family as the fundamental unit of human society, based on a permanent and exclusive union of man and woman in marriage. From the essential character of marriage come not only the right of parents to beget children, but also their primary right and duty to rear and educate them properly.

Since neither the individual nor the family is completely independent and self-sustained, there arises the necessity of organized civil society, and, in turn, the mutual responsibilities of the individual and family on the one side and of the civil government on the other.

Man's social life becomes intolerable if not impossible unless justice and benevolence govern the operations of the state and relationships between individuals and groups. Without temperance, man can neither live in accordance with his human dignity nor fulfill his obligations to his fellow men. Without fortitude, he cannot bear the trials of life or overcome the difficulties with which he is surrounded.

Furthermore, it is clear that the inherent dignity of the individual and the needs of the family and of society demand a code of sexual morality within the grasp of every mature mind.

These are some of the basic elements of natural law, a law based on human nature; a law which can be discovered by human intelligence and which governs man's relationship with God, with himself, and with the other creatures of God. The principles of the natural law, absolute, stable, and unchangeable are applicable to all the changing conditions and circumstances in which man constantly finds himself.

NATURAL LAW AND REVELATION

These religious and moral truths of the natural order can be known by human reason; but God, in His goodness, through Divine Revelation has helped man to know better and to preserve the natural law. In the Old Testament this revelation was given to God's chosen people. Completed and perfected in the New, it has been communicated to mankind by Jesus Christ and His Apostles and it has been entrusted to the Church which Christ Himself established to teach all men.

While the natural law, taught and interpreted by the Church, gives us a guide in many areas of human life, the perfection of human nature is revealed to us in Christ Himself, God-become-Man, the Word-made-Flesh, "full of grace and truth," dwelling among us to be our Way, our Truth, and our Life. Prayer and the sacraments are the channels through which the grace of Christ comes to elevate human nature until it becomes like unto Him, Who is true God and true man. In the supernatural order of grace Christ, the God-man, is the measure of man.

Divine Revelation, then, not only includes the natural law, it complements it, and points the way to the supernatural order of grace. The natural moral law, however, remains the foundation of the supernatural order as it is the foundation of all man's relations to God, to himself, and to his fellow men. Upon that law, clarified by Divine Revelation, man, strengthened by grace, must build his life. He need never fear that it will give way under the weight of the trials and tests which life imposes; for he has the inspired words of the Psalmist to assure him: "The man whose heart is set on the law of the Lord stands firm."

When the human heart is governed by the law of the Lord, all human actions, no matter how commonplace or how removed from the eyes of men, are made pleasing to God and meritorious of eternal life. This means that God's will and God's plan for man are kept constantly in mind. When man has learned to direct his thoughts, his speech, and his actions in this way, it is a sign that he has mastered the great maxim of the moral order — "not my will but Thine be done." It is an indication that he realizes he must at all times be about his Father's business. The point of reference in his life is no longer his own selfish will, for such a man sees clearly that God holds the central place in his life. He also sees that he enjoys a unique status in that God has committed to him a work which no one else can do. His only reason for existence is to perform that work faithfully and diligently. This is the thought which Cardinal Newman so beautifully expressed:

> God has created me to do Him some definite service. He has committed some work to me which he has not committed to another, I have my mission . . . I have a part in a great work; I am a link in the chain, a bond of connection between persons. He has not created me for naught. I shall do good. I shall do His work. (*Meditations & Devotions*, pp. 400–401)

MORAL INTEGRITY

Doing God's work means doing God's will. This requires the services of the whole man at every moment of every day he exists. There is all too frequent today the spectacle of men who divide their lives to suit their own convenience. Only when it serves their selfish purpose do they conform to God's will. Their business life, their professional life, their life in the home, at school, and in the community occupy separate compartments unified by no central force. God's claims upon such men exist, but they are not honored. Expressions such as "my life is my own affair" or "I may do as I please," or "in politics, anything goes" are all too common today. They betray a gross misunderstanding of the moral order and the interlinking relationships which find their correct measure only in God's will.

We must be clear on this point. Man must either acknowledge that a personal God exists or he must deny His existence altogether. There is no middle course. Once he acknowledges that God exists, then the claims of God are coextensive with all the activities of His creatures.

To pretend that any part of his life can be a private affair is to violate the most basic claim which God has on man. Man is a creature. As a creature, he is subject to his Creator in all that he does. There is no time in his life when he is excused from obeying the moral law. The clergyman, the educator, the doctor, the lawyer, the politician, the employer, the employee, husbands, wives, and children are alike strictly bound. All human rights and obligations have their source in God's law; otherwise they are meaningless.

MORALITY AND EDUCATION

Morality, concerned with bringing human activity into conformity with God's will, has therefore, a bearing on everything that touches human rights and duties. It has a definite place in the educational life of a nation. The forming of character is part of the educational process; and character cannot be formed unless children are given a clear indication of what is right and what is wrong. This cannot be done without reference to the ultimate standard which determines right and wrong, namely God's law.

No state, no group of educators may reject a truth of the moral order to suit the claim of convenience. The process of determining moral values by the consent of the majority is false in principle and sanction. Morality has its source in God and it binds all men. It cannot be adequately taught without the motivation of religious truth. Although the training of children along moral lines is primarily the business of the parents and the Church, yet it is also the business of the school if education is to give formation to the whole human personality.

MORALITY AND ECONOMICS

Morality has its place in business and industry because the conditions under which men work, the wages they get, the kind of work they do, all are subject to the jurisdiction of the moral law. When economic conditions are such that the raising of a family by working people is made dishearteningly difficult and at times impossible, then, those responsible for this deplorable situation are guilty of breaking God's law and they are also accomplices in the sins resulting from their injustice.

MORALITY AND POLITICS

In politics, the principle that "anything goes" simply because people are thought not to expect any high degree of honor in politicians is grossly wrong. We have to recover that sense of personal obligation on the part of the voter and that sense of public trust on the part of the elected official which give meaning and dignity to political life. Those who are selected for office by their fellow men are entrusted with grave responsibilities. They have been selected not for self-enrichment but for conscientious public service. In their speech and in their actions they are bound by the same laws of justice and charity which bind private individuals in every other sphere of human activity. Dishonesty, slander, detraction, and defamation of character are as truly transgressions of God's commandments when resorted to by men in political life as they are for all other men.

Moral Standard Applies Universally

There are not two standards of morality. There is only one. It is God's standard. That single standard covers all man's relations to God, to himself, and to the world about him. It applies to every conceivable situation in life — in the home, in business, in the school, or in the field of entertainment. By its very nature, it precludes that double standard which not only tempts man to live his life on two levels, but beguiles him into thinking that this can be done without any compromise of moral principles. This two-faced way of living explains the scandalous anomaly, evident at times in our national life, of paying lip service to God while failing completely to honor his claims in daily life.

One and the same standard covers stealing from the cash register and dishonest gain derived from public office. It will not do to say, by way of extenuation, that the latter can be excused or condoned because it occurs in the political order. One and the same standard prohibits false statements about private individuals, and false statements about members of minority groups and races. It will not do, by way of excuse, to say that statements of the latter kind can be excused because of long-standing prejudice.

This single standard of morality sets a clear, positive, and complete pattern of right living. It gives an integrity of outlook and an integrity of action in daily life. By adhering to this standard, man's life becomes all of a piece, characterized by a sincere singleness of purpose. Such a life will not have its "Sunday side" in which God's claims are fully respected for a single day and its "weekday side" in which those claims are completely ignored for the remaining six. Rather, all aspects of life will be so integrated that the standard to which a man subscribes in his private life will be logically extended to his life in the community. Then, if faithful to moral principles as an individual he will be faithful to moral principles as a citizen, as a voter, and in all his actions as a member of society.

RELIGION AND MORALITY

To live by this single standard for morality man needs the motivations and sanctions which only religion can supply. He is not self-sufficient. He must have God's help. As a creature, he is obliged to adore his Creator, to thank Him for blessings conferred, to ask His pardon for wrongs committed and to pray daily for His help and guidance. Nothing less than the faithful discharge of these essential obligations of religion will enable him to attain integrity in his moral life.

We exhort Americans in every walk of life to rededicate themselves to the wisdom of our Founding Fathers — a wisdom which proclaimed God's rightful place in human affairs — a wisdom so memorably expressed by the Father of our Country in his Farewell Address:

> Of all the dispositions and habits which lead to political prosperity, Religion and Morality are indispensable supports . . . reason and experience both forbid us to expect that national morality can prevail in exclusion of religious principle.

✝ EDWARD CARDINAL MOONEY,
  Archbishop of Detroit

✝ SAMUEL CARDINAL STRITCH,
  Archbishop of Chicago

✝ FRANCIS CARDINAL SPELLMAN,
  Archbishop of New York

✝ FRANCIS P. KEOUGH,
  Archbishop of Baltimore

✝ ROBERT E. LUCEY,
  Archbishop of San Antonio

✝ KARL J. ALTER,
  Archbishop of Cincinnati

✝ JOSEPH E. RITTER,
  Archbishop of St. Louis

✝ PATRICK A. O'BOYLE,
  Archbishop of Washington

✝ JOHN J. MITTY,
  Archbishop of San Francisco

✝ JOHN F. NOLL,
  Bishop of Fort Wayne

✝ EMMETT M. WALSH,
  Coadjutor Bishop of Youngstown

✝ MICHAEL J. READY,
  Bishop of Columbus

✝ MATTHEW F. BRADY,
  Bishop of Manchester

Appendix

RELEVANT MATTERS
OF
N.C.W.C. DEPARTMENTS

82. DECREE OF THE SACRED CONGREGATION OF SEMINARIES AND UNIVERSITY STUDIES ON THE

ADMINISTRATION OF THE NORTH AMERICAN COLLEGE, ROME*

April 24, 1934

This decree sent by Cajetan Cardinal Bisleti, Prefect of the Sacred Congregation of Seminaries and University Studies, and Monsignor Ernest Ruffini, Secretary of the same Roman Congregation, to His Excellency, Most Reverend Amleto Cicognani, D.D., Apostolic Delegate to the United States, refers to the administration of the North American Pontifical College in Rome.

ENGLISH SUMMARY

a) To make proper provisions for the North American College in Rome pertains to me — says Cardinal Bisleti — in virtue of the double honor I enjoy (*a*) that of being Prefect of the Sacred Congregation of Seminaries and University Studies; and (*b*) that of being the Cardinal Protector of the said American college.

b) To provide better for the increase and welfare of the said college from which so many excellent preachers of the Gospel have gone forth, we have thought well on the occasion of the seventy-fifth anniversary of the existence of the said college, to amplify and augment the number of bishops to whom the administration of the college pertains.

c) When Leo XIII in virtue of his Apostolic Letters, *Ubi Primum*, October 25, 1884, canonically approved the American college and raised it to the rank of a *pontifical* college he entrusted anew the care and administration of the same to the archbishops and bishops of the United States of America, or to a committee legitimately appointed

---

* Excerpt from the "Analecta" of the *Ecclesiastical Review*, Vol. 91 (December, 1934), pp. 609–610. Cf. Nos. 48, 79. This decree is inserted by the personal wish of the late Archbishop John T. McNicholas, O.P., of Cincinnati, chairman of the Administrative Board.

by them — a charge the American bishops assembled at the Second Plenary Council of Baltimore (1866) had already gladly assumed.*

d) Wherefore in order that the afore-said wish of the Vicar of Christ and the decrees by the American bishops be properly executed, Cardinal Bisleti in his above-mentioned dual capacity of Prefect and Protector (cf. under *a*) ordered the administration of the North American Pontifical College in Rome be confided:

1. *Ex officio* to all the eminent Cardinals of the United States;
2. Likewise *ex officio* to the Archbishop of Baltimore;
3. To the four bishops elected by the North American bishops in their annual meetings in such a manner that each succeeding year one bishop drops out from the Administrative Board and correspondingly another be selected to fill the vacancy.

e) All of which His Holiness, Pope Pius XI, has deigned to approve and to confirm.

f) In conclusion we implore the Blessed Virgin Mary in the mystery of her Immaculate Conception to second our hopes that through the studious care and interest of the above-named Administrative Board great fruits accrue to the afore-said college.

g) With becoming cordial greetings, I beg to remain,

Your Excellency,

CAJETAN CARDINAL BISLETI, *Prefect*
ERNEST RUFFINI, *Secretary*
Sacred Congregation of Seminaries
and of
University Studies

The original Latin text follows:

---

* Cf. Peter Guilday, *A History of the Councils of Baltimore: 1791–1884* (New York: Macmillan, 1932), p. 212.

SACRA CONGREGATIO DE SEMINARIIS ET DE
STUDIORUM UNIVERSITATIBUS

PONTIFICII COLLEGII CIVITATUM FOEDERATARUM AMERICAE SEPTEMTRIONALIS ADMINISTRATIO

EXCELLENTISSIME DOMINE

a) Pontificii Collegii Civitatum Foederatorum Americae Septemtrionalis de Urbe res et fortunas tueri atque, pro temporibus rerumque adiunctis provehere, si proprium est Sacrae huius Congregationis, ad me pertinet etiam quia eiusdem Collegii tutelae iamdiu ut Patronus praesum.

b) Quem in finem, ut Institutum nempe tam praeclarum, ex quo plurimi Evangelii praecones ad pietatem et scientiam diligenti institutione informati prodierunt, nova incrementa accipiat, Nobis, occasionem LXXV anni ex quo Collegium conditum est nactis, visum est Episcoporum coetum, cui Collegium ipsum administrandi munus incumbit, ampliare et augere.

c) Leo XIII quidem, gloriosae recordationis, Litteris Apostolicis "Ubi primum" d. d. 25 Octobris 1884, quibus Collegium canonice erexit ac nomine et titulo Pontificio decoravit, inter leges ad quas idem Collegium moderandum esset praescribebat ut: "administratio universa Collegii ab Archiepiscopis et Episcopis Foederatorum Statuum Americae Septemtrionalis, vel a Praesulibus ab ipsis ad id muneris legitime deputatis gereretur". Quapropter laudatae Reipublicae Archiepiscopi voluntati plene obsequentes, omnes, uno animo, sibi proposuerunt memoratum Collegium *tueri, fovere, ornare et, quantum possent, collatis consiliis opibusque amplificare.*

d) Itaque, ut quod Christi Vicarius iam edixerat et locorum Ordinarii constituerant impleatur et plenum exitum sortiatur, haec decernimus quae sequuntur:

Collegii Administratio concredita sit:

1. Omnibus Foederatorum Statuum Americae Septemtrionalis Em.mis Cardinalibus, *ex officio;*

2. Archiepiscopo Baltimorensi item *ex officio;*

3. Quatuor aliis Praesulibus, in annuo Episcoporum conventu eligendis, quorum singulis annis unus e munere excidat et novus in eius locum succedat, ab eodem Episcoporum coetu similiter electus.

e) Quae SS.mo D. N. Pio Pp. XI cum subiecissemus, idem Summus Pontifex ea adprobare et confirmare dignatus est.

f) Spe autem certa suffulti, Administratorum impensis curis et studiosissima opera, salutares fructus Collegii multiplicatum iri, intimo ex animo caelestem gratiam, per Deiparam Immaculatam, illis imploramus.

g) Inter ea qua par est reverentia sensus obsequentis animi mei, Tibi, Excellentissime Domine, obtestor.

Romae, Aprilis 24, 1934
Excellentiae Tuae Reverendissimae
in domino addictissimus
CAIETANUS CARD. BISLETI, *Praefectus*
ERNESTUS RUFFINI, *Secretarius*

Excell.mo ac Rev.mo Domino
D. A. Ioanni Cicognani
Archiepiscopo Tit. Laodicen. in Phr.
Americae Sept. Statuum Foederatorum
Apostolico Delegato
Washington.

ADMINISTRATIVE BOARD MEMBERS 1918–1950

HISTORICAL NOTES – N.C.W.C.

1. PRELIMINARY COMMITTEE, founded August 11 and 12, 1917, at the Catholic University of America, from representatives of all dioceses and Catholic lay societies assembled by the authority and under the direction of Cardinals Gibbons, Farley, O'Connell —

NATIONAL CATHOLIC WAR COUNCIL

President: Rev. John J. Burke, C.S.P.
Secretary: Mr. Robert Biggs of Baltimore
Treasurer: Mr. John G. Agar of New York

COMMITTEE ON CHAPLAINS: Chairman, Rt. Rev. Msgr. M. J. Lavelle of New York

COMMITTEE ON LEGISLATION AND BY-LAWS: Chairman, Rt. Rev. Msgr. Edward Kelly of Chicago

COMMITTEE ON FINANCE: Chairman, Mr. John G. Agar of New York

COMMITTEE ON HISTORICAL RECORDS OF CATHOLIC WAR ACTIVITIES: Chairman, Rt. Rev. Msgr. H. T. Drumgoogle of Philadelphia

COMMITTEE ON RECREATION AND REST HALLS: Chairman, Mr. Charles I. Denechaud, New Orleans

COMMITTEE ON WOMEN'S ORGANIZATIONS: Chairman, Rt. Rev. Msgr. M. J. Splaine of Boston

2. CATHOLIC WAR COUNCIL

1918 First permanent episcopal committee of the Catholic War Council, proposed by Cardinal Gibbons by letter of November 21, 1917.*

Board of Archbishops becomes Catholic War Council utilizing services of clerical and lay gentlemen mentioned above who, as representatives of the bishops, had organized the National War Council.

---

* Cf. *American Catholics in the War* by Michael Williams (Macmillan Co., 1921), p. 144.

December 28, 1917, Cardinal Gibbons announced unanimous agreement on Board of Archbishops becoming the Catholic War Council. These thirteen archbishops were: Cardinals Gibbons (Baltimore), O'Connell (Boston), and Farley (New York) and Archbishops Mundelein (Chicago), Moeller (Cincinnati), Keane (Dubuque), Messmer (Milwaukee), Christie (Oregon), Prendergast (Philadelphia), Glennon (St. Louis), Ireland (St. Paul), Hanna (San Francisco), and Pitival (Santa Fe). The See of New Orleans was vacant at the time.

January 12, 1918, Cardinal Gibbons called the meeting of the newly formed Administrative Committee for January 16, 1918, at Catholic University. The Administrative Committee was made up of Bishops P. J. Muldoon (Rockford), Joseph Schrembs (Toledo), P. J. Hayes (Auxiliary of New York), and W. T. Russell (Charleston).

Two committees were appointed:
1. Committee on Special War Activities
2. Knights of Columbus Committee on War Activities.

1919 ADMINISTRATIVE COMMITTEE:
Archbishop Edward J. Hanna (San Francisco)
Archbishop Austin Dowling (St. Paul)
Archbishop Dennis J. Dougherty (Philadelphia)
Bishop J. F. Regis Canevin (Pittsburgh)
Bishop Joseph Schrembs (Toledo)
Bishop William T. Russell (Charleston)
Bishop Peter J. Muldoon (Rockford)

1920 Archbishop Hanna (San Francisco) — *Chairman*
Bishop Muldoon (Rockford) — *Vice-Chairman*
Bishop Russell (Charleston) — *Secretary*
Archbishop Dowling (St. Paul) — *Treasurer*
Archbishop Dougherty (Philadelphia)
Bishop Canevin (Pittsburgh)
Bishop Schrembs (Toledo)

1921 Archbishop Hanna (San Francisco) — *Chairman*
His Eminence Dennis Cardinal Dougherty (Philadelphia)
Archbishop Dowling (St. Paul)
Bishop Muldoon (Rockford)
Bishop Schrembs (Toledo)
Bishop Russell (Charleston)
Bishop Edmund F. Gibbons (Albany)

1922 Archbishop Hanna (San Francisco) — *Chairman*
Archbishop Dowling (St. Paul)

Bishop Muldoon (Rockford) — *Vice-Chairman*
Bishop Schrembs (Cleveland)
Bishop Louis S. Walsh (Portland)
Bishop Russell (Charleston)
Bishop Gibbons (Albany)

N.C.W. CONFERENCE

1923   Archbishop Hanna (San Francisco) — *Chairman*
Archbishop Dowling (St. Paul)
Bishop Muldoon (Rockford)
Bishop Schrembs (Cleveland)
Bishop Walsh (Portland)
Bishop Gibbons (Albany)
Bishop Thomas E. Molloy (Brooklyn)

1924   Archbishop Hanna (San Francisco) — *Chairman*
Bishop Muldoon (Rockford) — *Vice-Chairman*
Archbishop Dowling (St. Paul)
Bishop Schrembs (Cleveland)
Bishop Gibbons (Albany)
Bishop Walsh (Portland)
Bishop Philip R. McDevitt (Harrisburg)

1925   Archbishop Hanna (San Francisco) — *Chairman*
Archbishop Dowling (St. Paul) — *Treasurer*
Bishop Muldoon (Rockford) — *Vice-Chairman*
Bishop Thomas F. Lillis (Kansas City, Mo.)
Bishop Gibbons (Albany)
Bishop McDevitt (Harrisburg)
Bishop Schrembs (Cleveland)

1926   Archbishop Hanna (San Francisco) — *Chairman*
Archbishop Dowling (St. Paul)
Bishop Muldoon (Rockford)
Bishop Schrembs (Cleveland)
Bishop Gibbons (Albany)
Bishop McDevitt (Harrisburg)
Bishop Lillis (Kansas City)

1927   Archbishop Hanna (San Francisco) — *Chairman*
Archbishop Dowling (St. Paul)
Bishop Muldoon (Rockford)
Bishop Schrembs (Cleveland)
Bishop Gibbons (Albany)
Bishop McDevitt (Harrisburg)
Bishop Lillis (Kansas City)

1928   Archbishop Hanna (San Francisco) — *Chairman*
Archbishop Dowling (St. Paul) — *Treasurer, Education Dept.*
Bishop Schrembs (Cleveland) — *Lay Organizations*
Bishop Gibbons (Albany) — *Legal Dept.*
Bishop Lillis (Kansas City) — *Vice-Chairman, Social Action Dept.*
Bishop McDevitt (Harrisburg) — *Secretary, Press Dept.*
Bishop John G. Murray (Portland, Me.)

1929   Archbishop Hanna (San Francisco) — *Chairman*
Archbishop Dowling (St. Paul) — *Treasurer, Education Dept.*
Bishop Lillis (Kansas City) — *Social Action Dept.*
Bishop Schrembs (Cleveland) — *Lay Organizations*
Bishop McDevitt (Harrisburg) — *Secretary, Press Dept.*
Bishop Hugh C. Boyle (Pittsburgh)
Bishop Murray (Portland, Me.) — *Legal Dept.*

1930   Archbishop Hanna (San Francisco) — *Chairman*
Archbishop John T. McNicholas (Cincinnati)
Bishop Lillis (Kansas City) — *Vice-Chairman, Social Action Dept.*
Bishop Schrembs (Cleveland) — *Lay Organizations*
Bishop Boyle (Pittsburgh) — *Education Dept.*
Bishop Murray (Portland, Me.) — *Treasurer, Legal Dept.*
Bishop McDevitt (Harrisburg) — *Secretary, Press Dept.*
ASSISTANT BISHOPS:
Archbishop Samuel A. Stritch (Milwaukee)
Bishop Edward F. Hoban (Rockford)
Bishop John F. Noll (Fort Wayne)
Bishop Joseph F. Rummel (Omaha)
Bishop Emmet M. Walsh (Charleston)
Bishop John F. O'Hern (Rochester)
Bishop Edwin V. O'Hara (Great Falls)

1931   Archbishop Hanna (San Francisco) — *Chairman*
Bishop Lillis (Kansas City) — *Vice-Chairman, Social Action Dept.*
Bishop McDevitt (Harrisburg) — *Secretary*
Bishop Murray (Portland, Me.) — *Treasurer, Legal Dept.*
Archbishop McNicholas (Cincinnati) — *Education*
Bishop Schrembs (Cleveland) — *Lay Organizations*
Bishop Boyle (Pittsburgh) — *Press Dept.*

1931   ASSISTANT BISHOPS:

Archbishop Stritch (Milwaukee) — *Education Dept.*
Bishop O'Hern (Rochester) — *Executive Dept.*
Bishop Rummel (Omaha) — *Lay Organizations*
Bishop O'Hara (Great Falls) — *Social Action Dept.*

Bishop Walsh (Charleston) — *Legal Dept.*
Bishop Hoban (Rockford) — *Press Dept.*

1932 Archbishop Hanna (San Francisco) — *Chairman*
Bishop Lillis (Kansas City) — *Vice-Chairman, Social Action Dept.*
Archbishop John G. Murray (St. Paul) — *Treasurer, Legal Dept.*
Bishop Boyle (Pittsburgh) — *Secretary*
Archbishop McNicholas (Cincinnati) — *Education Dept.*
Bishop Schrembs (Cleveland) — *Lay Organizations*
Bishop Noll (Fort Wayne)
ASSISTANT BISHOPS:
Archbishop Stritch (Milwaukee)
Bishop Hoban (Rockford)
Bishop Walsh (Charleston)
Bishop Rummel (Omaha)
Bishop O'Hern (Rochester)
Bishop O'Hara (Great Falls)

1933 Archbishop Hanna (San Francisco) — *Chairman*
Bishop Lillis (Kansas City) — *Vice-Chairman, Social Action Dept.*
Archbishop Murray (St. Paul) — *Treasurer, Legal Dept.*
Bishop Noll (Fort Wayne) — *Secretary*
Archbishop McNicholas (Cincinnati) — *Education Dept.*
Bishop Schrembs (Cleveland) — *Lay Organizations*
Bishop Boyle (Pittsburgh) — *Press Dept.*

1934 Archbishop Hanna, (San Francisco) — *Chairman, Executive Dept.*
Bishop Lillis (Kansas City) — *Vice-Chairman, Social Action Dept.*
Archbishop Murray (St. Paul) — *Treasurer, Legal Dept.*
Bishop Noll (Fort Wayne) — *Secretary*
Archbishop McNicholas (Cincinnati) — *Education Dept.*
Bishop Schrembs (Cleveland) — *Lay Organizations*
Bishop Boyle (Pittsburgh) — *Press Dept.*
ASSISTANT BISHOPS:
Bishop John B. Peterson (Manchester) — *Education Dept.*
Bishop Walsh (Charleston) — *Legal Dept.*
Bishop Rummel (Omaha) — *Lay Organizations*
Bishop Hoban (Rockford) — *Press Dept.*

1935 Archbishop Hanna (San Francisco) — *Chairman, Executive Dept.*
Bishop Lillis (Kansas City) — *Vice-Chairman, Catholic Action
Study*
Archbishop Murray (St. Paul) — *Treasurer, Legal Dept.*
Bishop Noll (Fort Wayne) — *Secretary, Lay Organizations*
Archbishop McNicholas (Cincinnati) — *Education Dept.*
Archbishop Edward Mooney (Detroit) — *Social Action Dept.*
Bishop Boyle (Pittsburgh) — *Press Dept.*

1935 ASSISTANT BISHOPS:
Bishop Francis T. Keough (Providence) — *Executive Dept.*
Bishop Peterson (Manchester) — *Education Dept.*
Bishop Hoban (Rockford) — *Press Dept.*
Bishop Walsh (Charleston) — *Legal Dept.*
Bishop O'Hara (Great Falls) — *Social Action Dept.*
Bishop Rummel (Omaha) — *Lay Organizations*
Bishop John A. Duffy (Buffalo) — *Catholic Action Study*

1936 Archbishop Mooney (Detroit) — *Chairman*
Bishop Peterson (Manchester) — *Education Dept., Vice-Chairman*
Bishop O'Hara (Great Falls) — *Secretary, Social Action Dept.*
Bishop Francis C. Kelley (Oklahoma) — *Treasurer*
Archbishop Rummel (New Orleans) — *Legal Dept.*
Archbishop Stritch (Milwaukee) — *Catholic Action Study*
Bishop Boyle (Pittsburgh) — *Press Dept.*
Bishop Noll (Fort Wayne) — *Lay Organizations*
ASSISTANT BISHOPS:
Bishop Keough (Providence) — *Executive Dept.*
Bishop Hoban (Rockford) — *Press Dept.*
Bishop Walsh (Charleston) — *Legal Dept.*
Bishop Duffy (Buffalo) — *Catholic Action Study*
Bishop Karl Alter (Toledo) — *Social Action Dept.*

1937 Archbishop Mooney (Detroit) — *Chairman*
Bishop Peterson (Manchester) — *Vice-Chairman, Education Dept.*
Bishop Kelley (Oklahoma) — *Treasurer*
Bishop O'Hara (Great Falls) — *Secretary, Social Action Dept.*
Archbishop Stritch (Milwaukee) — *Catholic Action Study*
Archbishop Rummel (New Orleans) — *Legal Dept.*
Bishop Noll (Fort Wayne) — *Lay Organizations*
Bishop John Mark Gannon (Erie) — *Press Dept.*
Archbishop Murray (St. Paul)
Archbishop John J. Mitty (San Francisco)
ASSISTANT BISHOPS:
Bishop Duffy (Buffalo) — *Catholic Action Study*
Bishop Walsh (Charleston) — *Legal Dept.*
Bishop Bernard J. Sheil (Aux. of Chicago) — *Lay Organizations*
Bishop Keough (Providence) — *Education*
Bishop Hoban (Rockford) — *Press Dept.*
Bishop Alter (Toledo) — *Social Action Dept.*

1938 Archbishop Mooney (Detroit) — *Chairman*
Bishop Peterson (Manchester) — *Vice-Chairman, Education Dept.*
Bishop O'Hara (Great Falls) — *Social Action Dept., Secretary*
Archbishop Stritch (Milwaukee) — *Catholic Action Study*

Bishop Boyle (Pittsburgh) — *Legal Dept.*
Archbishop Rummel (New Orleans) — *Lay Organizations*
Bishop Gannon (Erie) — *Press Dept.*
Archbishop Mitty (San Francisco)
Archbishop Murray (St. Paul)
ASSISTANT BISHOPS:
Bishop Duffy (Buffalo) — *Catholic Action Study*
Bishop Walsh (Charleston) — *Lay Organizations*
Bishop Keough (Providence) — *Education Dept.*
Bishop Hoban (Rockford) — *Press Dept.*
Bishop Alter (Toledo) — *Social Action Dept.*

1939 Archbishop Mooney (Detroit) — *Chairman*
Bishop Peterson (Manchester) — *Vice-Chairman, Education Dept.*
Bishop Kelley (Oklahoma) — *Treasurer*
Bishop Duffy (Buffalo) — *Secretary*
Archbishop Rummel (New Orleans) — *Lay Organizations*
Archbishop Stritch (Milwaukee) — *Catholic Action Study*
Bishop Boyle (Pittsburgh) — *Legal Dept.*
Bishop Gannon (Erie) — *Press Dept.*
Bishop O'Hara (Great Falls) — *Social Action Dept.*
ASSISTANT BISHOPS:
Bishop Walsh (Charleston) — *Lay Organizations*
Bishop Bartholomew J. Eustace (Camden) — *Catholic Action Study*
Bishop Walter A. Foery (Syracuse) — *Legal Dept.*
Bishop Keough (Providence) — *Education Dept.*
Bishop Hoban (Rockford) — *Press Dept.*
Bishop Alter (Toledo) — *Social Action Dept.*

1940 Archbishop Stritch (Milwaukee) — *Chairman*
Bishop Peterson (Manchester) — *Education Dept., Vice-Chairman*
Bishop Kelley (Oklahoma) — *Treasurer*
Bishop Duffy (Buffalo) — *Secretary*
Archbishop Rummel (New Orleans) — *Lay Organizations*
Archbishop Murray (St. Paul) — *Catholic Action Study*
Bishop Gannon (Erie) — *Press Dept.*
Bishop Boyle (Pittsburgh) — *Legal Dept.*
Bishop O'Hara (Kansas City) — *Social Action Dept.*
ASSISTANT BISHOPS:
Bishop Walsh (Charleston) — *Lay Organizations*
Bishop Eustace (Camden) — *Catholic Action Study*
Bishop Hoban (Rockford) — *Press Dept.*
Bishop Alter (Toledo) — *Social Action Dept.*
Bishop Keough (Providence) — *Education*
Bishop Foery (Syracuse) — *Legal Dept.*

1941   Archbishop Mooney (Detroit) — *Chairman*
Bishop Peterson (Manchester) — *Vice-Chairman, Education Dept.*
Bishop Kelley (Oklahoma) — *Lay Organizations, Treasurer*
Archbishop Francis J. Spellman (New York) — *Secretary*
Archbishop Murray (St. Paul) — *Catholic Action Study*
Bishop Gannon (Erie)— *Press Dept.*
Bishop Boyle (Pittsburgh) — *Legal Dept.*
Bishop O'Hara (Kansas City) — *Social Action Dept.*
Bishop Duffy (Buffalo) — *Youth Dept.*
ASSISTANT BISHOPS:
Bishop Thomas K. Gorman (Reno) — *Press Dept.*
Bishop Keough (Providence) — *Education Dept.*
Bishop Foery (Syracuse) — *Legal Dept.*
Bishop Alter (Toledo) — *Social Action Dept.*
Bishop Charles H. LeBlond (St. Joseph) — *Social Charities*
Bishop Walsh (Charleston) — *Lay Organizations*
Bishop Eustace (Camden) —— *Catholic Action Study*

1942   Archbishop Mooney (Detroit) — *Chairman*
Archbishop Stritch (Chicago) — *Vice-Chairman, Treasurer*
Archbishop Spellman (New York) — *Secretary*
Archbishop McNicholas (Cincinnati) — *Education Dept.*
Bishop Boyle (Pittsburgh) — *Legal Dept.*
Bishop Noll (Fort Wayne) — *Lay Organizations*
Bishop Gannon (Erie) — *Press Dept.*
Archbishop Murray (St. Paul) — *Catholic Action Study*
Bishop Duffy (Buffalo) — *Youth Dept.*
ASSISTANT BISHOPS:
Bishop Foery (Syracuse) — *Legal Dept.*
Bishop Peterson (Manchester) — *Education Dept.*
Bishop Alter (Toledo) — *Social Action Dept.*
Bishop LeBlond (St. Joseph)— *Social Charities*
Bishop Aloisius J. Muench (Fargo) — *Rural Life*
Bishop Alter (Toledo) — *Health and Hospitals*
Bishop Gorman (Reno) — *Press Dept.*
Bishop John F. O'Hara (Military Delegate) — *Catholic Action Study*
Bishop Walsh (Charleston) — *Lay Organizations*
Bishop Richard O. Gerow (Natchez) — *Youth Dept.*
Bishop Wm. D. O'Brien (Aux., Chicago) — *Assistant Treasurer*

1943   Archbishop Mooney (Detroit) — *Chairman*
Archbishop Stritch (Chicago) — *Vice-Chairman, Treasurer*
Archbishop Spellman (New York) — *Secretary*
Archbishop McNicholas (Cincinnati) — *Education Dept.*

Archbishop Rummel (New Orleans) — *Legal Dept.*
Bishop Gannon (Erie) — *Press Dept.*
Bishop Noll (Fort Wayne) — *Lay Organizations*
Bishop Duffy (Buffalo) — *Youth Dept.*
Bishop Alter (Toledo) — *Social Action Dept.*
Archbishop Mitty (San Francisco) — *Catholic Action Study*
ASSISTANT BISHOPS:
Bishop O'Brien (Aux., Chicago) — *Treasurer*
Bishop Peterson (Manchester) — *Education Dept.*
Bishop Foery (Syracuse) — *Legal Dept.*
Bishop Gorman (Reno) — *Press Dept.*
Bishop Walsh (Charleston) — *Lay Organizations*
Bishop Gerow (Natchez) — *Youth Dept.*
Bishop LeBlond (St. Joseph) — *Social Action Dept.*
Bishop O'Hara (Military Delegate) — *Catholic Action Study*

1944   Archbishop Mooney (Detroit) — *Chairman*
Archbishop Stritch (Chicago) — *Vice-Chairman, Treasurer*
Archbishop Spellman (New York) — *Secretary*
Archbishop Rummel (New Orleans) — *Legal Dept.*
Archbishop McNicholas (Cincinnati) — *Education Dept.*
Archbishop Mitty (San Francisco) — *Catholic Action Study*
Bishop Noll (Fort Wayne) — *Lay Organizations*
Bishop Alter (Toledo) — *Social Action Dept.*
Archbishop Murray (St. Paul) — *Press Dept.*
Bishop James H. Ryan (Omaha) — *Youth Dept.*
ASSISTANT BISHOPS:
Bishop Gorman (Reno) — *Press Dept.*
Bishop Keough (Providence) — *Education*
Bishop Walsh (Charleston) — *Lay Organizations*
Bishop Bryan J. McEntegart (Ogdensburg) — *Legal Dept.*
Bishop O'Hara (Military Delegate) — *Catholic Action Study*
Bishop LeBlond (St. Joseph) — *Social Action Dept.*
Bishop Gerow (Natchez) — *Youth Dept.*
Bishop O'Brien (Aux., Chicago) — *Assistant Treasurer*

1945   Archbishop Mooney (Detroit) — *Chairman*
Archbishop Stritch (Chicago) — *Vice-Chairman, Treasurer*
Archbishop Spellman (New York) — *Secretary*
Archbishop Rummel (New Orleans) — *Legal Dept.*
Archbishop McNicholas (Cincinnati) — *Education Dept.*
Archbishop Mitty (San Francisco) — *Catholic Action Study*
Bishop Noll (Fort Wayne) — *Lay Organizations*
Bishop Alter (Toledo) — *Social Action Dept.*
Archbishop Murray (St. Paul) — *Press Dept.*

Bishop James H. Ryan (Omaha) — *Youth Dept.*
Assistant Bishops:
Bishop Gorman (Reno) — *Press Dept.*
Bishop Keough (Providence) — *Education Dept.*
Bishop Walsh (Charleston) — *Lay Organizations*
Bishop McEntegart (Ogdensburg) — *Legal Dept.*
Bishop John F. O'Hara (Buffalo)— *Catholic Action Study*
Bishop LeBlond (St. Joseph) — *Social Action Dept.*
Bishop Gerow (Natchez) — *Youth Dept.*
Bishop O'Brien (Aux., Chicago) — *Assistant Treasurer*
Bishop Michael J. Ready (Columbus) — *Assistant Secretary*

1946   Archbishop Stritch (Chicago) — *Chairman*
Archbishop Murray (St. Paul) — *Vice-Chairman, Press Dept.*
Archbishop Spellman (New York) — *Secretary*
Bishop Gannon (Erie) — *Treasurer*
Archbishop Ryan (Omaha) — *Education Dept.*
Archbishop Richard J. Cushing (Boston) — *Youth Dept.*
Archbishop Rummel (New Orleans) — *Legal Dept.*
Archbishop Mitty (San Francisco) — *Catholic Action Study*
Bishop Noll (Fort Wayne) — *Lay Organizations*
Bishop Alter (Toledo) — *Social Action Dept.*
Assistant Bishops:
Bishop O'Brien (Aux., Chicago) — *Treasurer*
Bishop Gorman (Reno) — *Press Dept.*
Bishop Walsh (Charleston) — *Lay Organizations*
Bishop Gerow (Natchez) — *Youth Dept.*
Bishop O'Hara (Buffalo) — *Catholic Action Study*
Bishop McEntegart (Ogdensburg) — *Legal Dept.*
Bishop LeBlond (St. Joseph) — *Social Action Dept.*
Bishop Ready (Columbus) — *Assistant Secretary*
Bishop Wm. A. Scully (Coadjutor, Albany) — *Education*

1947   Archbishop McNicholas (Cincinnati) — *Chairman*
Archbishop Murray (St. Paul) — *Vice-Chairman*
Bishop Ready (Columbus) — *Secretary*
Bishop Gannon (Erie) — *Treasurer*
Archbishop Ryan (Omaha) — *Education Dept.*
Archbishop Cushing (Boston) — *Youth Dept.*
Archbishop Rummel (New Orleans) — *Legal Dept.*
Archbishop Mitty (San Francisco) — *Catholic Action Study*
Archbishop Robert E. Lucey (San Antonio) — *Lay Organizations*
Bishop Alter (Toledo) — *Social Action Dept.*
Assistant Bishops:
Bishop O'Brien (Aux., Chicago) — *Assistant Treasurer*

Bishop Gorman (Reno)— *Press Dept.*
Bishop Walsh (Charleston) — *Lay Organizations*
Bishop Gerow (Natchez) — *Youth Dept.*
Bishop John O'Hara (Buffalo) — *Catholic Action Study*
Bishop McEntegart (Ogdensburg) — *Legal Dept.*
Bishop LeBlond (St. Joseph) — *Social Action Dept.*
Bishop Scully (Coadjutor, Albany) — *Education Dept.*

1948 Archbishop McNicholas (Cincinnati) — *Chairman*
Archbishop Murray (St. Paul) — *Vice-Chairman*
Bishop Noll (Fort Wayne) — *Secretary*
Bishop Gannon (Erie) — *Treasurer*
Archbishop Ryan (Omaha) — *Education Dept.*
Archbishop Lucey (San Antonio) — *Lay Organizations*
Bishop Alter (Toledo) — *Social Action Dept.*
Bishop Walsh (Charleston) — *Legal Dept.*
Archbishop Joseph Ritter (St. Louis) — *Catholic Action Study*
Bishop Ready (Columbus) — *Press Dept.*
ASSISTANT BISHOPS:
Bishop Keough (Providence) — *Assistant Chairman*
Bishop Scully (Coadjutor, Albany) — *Education Dept.*
Bishop O'Brien (Aux., Chicago) — *Assistant Treasurer*
Bishop McEntegart (Ogdensburg) — *Legal Dept.*
Bishop Gorman (Reno) — *Press Dept.*
Bishop O'Hara (Buffalo) — *Catholic Action Study*
Bishop Gerow (Natchez) — *Youth Dept.*
Bishop Matthew F. Brady (Manchester) — *Lay Organizations*
Bishop LeBlond (St. Joseph) — *Social Action Dept.*

1949 Archbishop McNicholas (Cincinnati) — *Chairman*
Archbishop Keough (Baltimore) — *Vice-Chairman*
Bishop Noll (Fort Wayne) — *Secretary*
Bishop Gannon (Erie) — *Treasurer*
Archbishop Cushing (Boston) — *Youth Dept.*
Archbishop Lucey (San Antonio) — *Lay Organizations*
Archbishop Patrick A. O'Boyle (Washington) — *Social Action Dept.*
Archbishop Ritter (St. Louis) — *Catholic Action Study*
Bishop Ready (Columbus) — *Press Dept.*
Bishop Emmet M. Walsh (Coadjutor, Youngstown) — *Legal Dept.*
ASSISTANT BISHOPS:
Bishop O'Brien (Aux., Chicago) — *Treasurer*
Bishop Brady (Manchester) — *Education Dept.*
Bishop McEntegart (Ogdensburg) — *Legal Dept.*
Bishop Allen Babcock (Aux., Detroit) — *Lay Organizations*
Bishop Gorman (Reno) — *Press Dept.*
Bishop Gerow (Natchez) — *Youth Dept.*

Bishop Alter (Toledo) — *Social Action, Hospitals*
Bishop LeBlond (St. Joseph) — *Social Action, Charities*
Bishop William T. Mulloy (Covington) — *Rural Life*
Bishop Peter W. Bartholome (Coadjutor, St. Cloud) — *Family Life*
Bishop O'Hara (Buffalo) — *Catholic Action Study*

1950 Archbishop McNicholas (Cincinnati) — *Chairman*
Archbishop Keough (Baltimore) — *Vice-Chairman, Education Dept.*
Bishop Noll (Fort Wayne) — *Secretary*
Bishop Gannon (Erie) — *Treasurer*
Archbishop Cushing (Boston) — *Youth Dept.*
Archbishop Lucey (San Antonio) — *Lay Organizations*
Archbishop O'Boyle (Washington) — *Social Action Dept.*
Archbishop Ritter (St. Louis) — *Catholic Action Study*
Bishop Ready (Columbus) — *Press Dept.*
Bishop Walsh (Youngstown) — *Legal Dept.*
Assistant Bishops:
Bishop Lawrence Shehan (Aux., Baltimore) — *Assistant to Chairman for Bureau of Information*
Bishop O'Brien (Aux., Chicago) — *Treasurer*
Bishop Brady (Manchester) — *Education Dept.*
Bishop McEntegart (Ogdensburg) — *Legal Dept.*
Bishop Babcock (Aux., Detroit) — *Lay Organizations*
Bishop Gorman (Reno) — *Press Dept.*
Bishop Gerow (Natchez) — *Youth Dept.*
Bishop O'Hara (Buffalo) — *Catholic Action Study*
Bishop Alter (Toledo) — *Social Action, Hospitals*
Bishop LeBlond (St. Joseph) — *Social Action, Charities*
Bishop Mulloy (Covington) — *Rural Life*
Bishop Bartholome (Coadjutor, St. Cloud) — *Family Life*

INDEX